Shakespeare Unbound

Shakespeare Unbound

Decoding a Hidden Life

René Weis

A John Macrae Book
Henry Holt and Company
New York

Henry Holt and Company, LLC
Publishers since 1866
175 Fifth Avenue
New York, New York 10010
www.henryholt.com

Distributed in Canada by H. B. Fenn and Company Ltd.

Library of Congress Cataloging-in-Publication Data

Weis, René, 1953–
  Shakespeare Unbound : decoding a hidden life / René Weis. — 1st ed.
    p. cm.
  "A John Macrae Book."
  ISBN-13: 978-0-8050-7501-4
  ISBN-10: 0-8050-7501-1
  1. Shakespeare, William, 1564–1616—Psychology. 2. Shakespeare, William, 1564–1616—Biography. 3. Dramatists, English—Early modern, 1500–1700—Psychology. 4. Dramatists, English—Early modern, 1500–1700—Biography. 5. Playwriting—Psychological aspects. 6. Drama—Psychological aspects. I. Title.

PR2909.W45 2007
822.3'3—dc22
[B]   2006047174

Published in the United Kingdom in 2007 in slightly different form under the title
Shakespeare Revealed.

First U.S. Edition 2007

Designed by Meryl Sussman Levavi

Printed in the United States of America

10 9 8 7 6 5 4 3 2 1

To my mother, Julie,
with grateful thanks

A Man's life of any worth is a continual allegory—and very few eyes can see the Mystery of his life—a life like the scriptures, figurative—which such people can no more make out than they can the hebrew Bible. Lord Byron cuts a figure—but he is not figurative—Shakespeare led a life of Allegory; his works are the comments on it.

—JOHN KEATS,
letter to George and Georgiana Keats,
February 14–May 3, 1819

Contents

Shakespeare Unbound

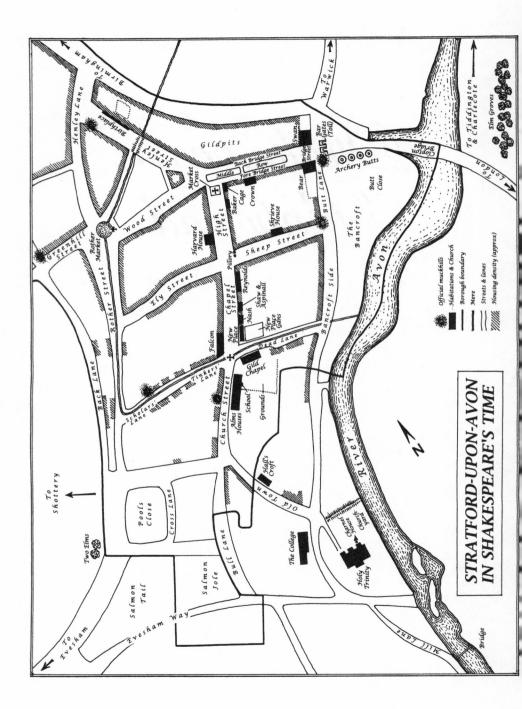

STRATFORD-UPON-AVON
IN SHAKESPEARE'S TIME

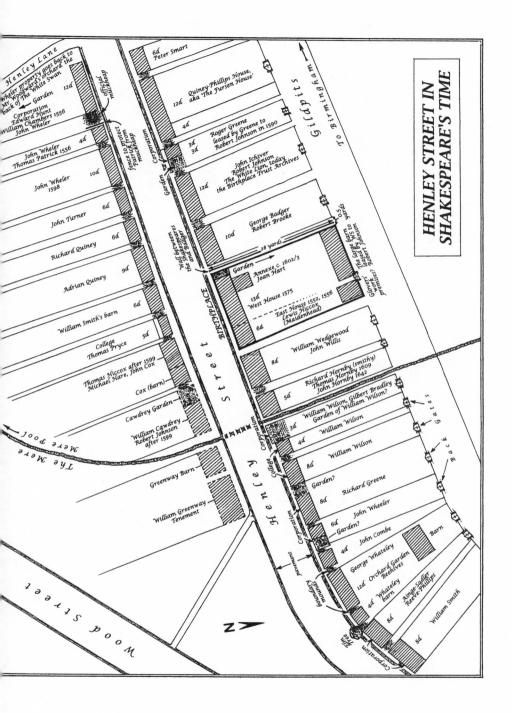

HENLEY STREET IN
SHAKESPEARE'S TIME

Henley Lane

Wheler property goes back to
Mr Woodward's orchard the
back of The White Swan

Corporation
Edward Hunt   12d
William Chambers 1556
John Wheler

official
muckheap

6d
Peter Smart

Gildpits

To Birmingham

John Wheler   4d
Thomas Patrick 1556

John Wheler   10d
1598

John Turner   6d

Richard Quiney   6d

Adrian Quiney   9d

William Smith's barn 6d

College   5d
Thomas Pryce

Thomas Hiccox after 1599
Michael Hare, John Cox

Cox (barn)

Cawdrey Garden

William Cawdrey
Robert Johnson
after 1599

Quiney-Phillips House,
aka 'The Fursen House'   12d

4d

Roger Greene   3d
leased by Greene to   3d
Robert Johnson in 1590

John Ichiver   12d
Robert Johnson
The White Lion, today
the Birthplace Trust Archives

fence to protect
from muckheap

Corporation

Garden

Wall between
the Shakespeares
and Badger

George Badger   10d
Robert Brooke

0.5

The large barn 150 yards
leased to
Robert Johnson

Glovers
premises? Robert Johnson

28 yards

Garden
Annexe c. 1602/3
Joan Hart

13d
West House 1575

East House 1552, 1556
Lewis Hiccox
(Maidenhead)

6d

William Wedgewood
John Willis   8d

Birthplace

Richard Hornby (smithy)
Thomas Hornby 1609
John Hornby 1642

5d

William Wilson, Gilbert Bradley
Garden of William Wilson?

3d   William Wilson

4d   William Wilson

8d   William Wilson

Garden?

8d   Richard Greene

Street

College

Corporation

Back Gates

The Mere   Mere Pool

Greenway Barn

William Greenway
Tenement

6d   John Wheler
Garden?

4d   John Combe

George Whateley   12d Orchard Garden
Beehives

4d   Whateley
barn

Ainge-Sadler
Reeve-Phillips

Barn

William Smith

8d

8d

Henley

Corporation

pavement

boundary
mounds

Tree
Gift

Corporation

N

Wood Street

Prologue

f there is one character in the later plays with whom Shakespeare is commonly identified, it is Prospero in *The Tempest*, his last solo play. Prospero sees himself as a magician whose art allows him to conjure up entire worlds of men and women, lord it over their lives, even resurrect them from death. Whatever else he may or may not have thought, Shakespeare did not take a modest view of his gifts and achievements, though Prospero is not Shakespeare and the Milan to which Prospero wishes to retire is not Stratford-upon-Avon.

The links between Shakespeare's life and his work are closer than is generally assumed. This book aims to show how deep these connections are. The plays and poems contain important clues to Shakespeare's inner life and to real, tangible, external events he experienced four hundred years ago.

There is a cumulative amount of circumstantial evidence that demonstrates beyond doubt that Shakespeare responded in his work to key events of his life. King Lear's rage reflects the bard's anger and frustrations and his need to vent them against the world at large. That does not mean that he tore off his clothes on a heath in Warwickshire, or that he had two daughters who were conspiring against him while a third, his youngest, was trying to save his life and sanity. Of course Shakespeare was neither king of England nor Prince of Denmark, not a middle-aged black man consumed by love and jealousy and rendered vulnerable to treachery because of his race, nor a Jewish financier seeking revenge on Christians for putting him out of business or spitting on him. The resonances in the work are much subtler, but the echoes across the boundary of life and art can clearly be heard if we only wish to listen for them. Shakespeare did not have three daughters, but we know he had two. If we were to discover that at the time of *King Lear* there were major tensions in the Shakespeare household and in his sexual life that might have helped influence the play's plot, why would we ignore them?

The most thought-provoking remark on the convergence of Shakespeare's life and works belongs to the English poet John Keats, one of Shakespeare's most assiduous and intelligent readers. In an 1819 letter, Keats wrote that "A man's life of any worth is a continual allegory—and very few eyes can see the mystery . . . Shakespeare led a life of Allegory; his works are the comments on it." For Keats Shakespeare's life and his plays and poems are inextricably linked in ways that are mutually reflective and illuminating. They merge to form a secret history, which this book sets out to decode. Keats's near contemporary William Wordsworth, the author of an important epic autobiographical poem, suggested that the Sonnets were the key with which Shakespeare had unlocked his heart. Far from distilling the essence of impersonality, Shakespeare's works tackle the human condition straight out of his own experiences. He poured his soul into his works, hence their intensity and imaginative power. He lived and breathed theater, composing countless iambic pentameters, memorizing lines, acting in his own plays and in those written by fellow dramatists, while at the same time reading widely in the classics and in English and Roman history. He wrote as the mood took him. The energy and intensity of his plays derive from Shakespeare's struggle to come to terms with the eternal issues of love, life, and death. Shakespeare went so far as to call one of his greatest works, perhaps the most famous tragedy in the world, *Hamlet* after his own dead son. To try to disembody the plays and poems from the life of their author is as counterintuitive as seeking to separate him from the national history of his era.

He lived emphatically in history, and few critics have doubted that this fascination left a deep imprint on his work. When he was born, the Protestant revolution had recently put the new English Bible at the core of the national culture. If it had not been for the

Reformation Shakespeare would not have read the scriptures, probably not have gone to school. He might never have lived beyond the
limits of a glover's life. On the other hand, neither would he have
lived in a country in which he watched the slaughter of innocent
people who served as bloody public spectacles because of their beliefs. Without the Reformation, he would have attended the same
mass as every other good Catholic of Stratford-upon-Avon; the England of his forebears would also have been his to inherit spiritually.
Their history and his would have been identical: Catholic, and European.

The Shakespeare story begins and ends in a Midlands market
town. He always thought of this place as home and returned to it finally at the age of thirty-three. It marked him more than any other
place, including the glitzy big city where he made his fortune. Knowing Shakespeare's Stratford intimately is a prerequisite for forming a
clear picture of the child who became the mature writer. If Shakespeare had never written anything at all, he would have remained a
witty and resourceful glover in Henley Street, probably would have
been featured in the annals of Stratford as a hardworking businessman who might have joined the council and become mayor, as his
father had—something that he conspicuously avoided in his real life
in Stratford. Though he would have attended the same local grammar school, his horizons would have been much more circum-
scribed. He would not have hobnobbed with the top people in
London; there would probably have been no extramarital affairs, and
above all there would have been no outlet for the pressure cooker
that was his imagination. Wordsworth called this fissile inner core
"the hiding places of man's power." Few passages in Shakespeare's
plays and poems better render his sense of the creative inner self
than Richard II's soliloquy in the dungeon of Pomfret Castle. The
King is alone and abandoned, without a realm, or a crown, or human
company. His boon companions, those parasites who poisoned his
mind, the infamous "caterpillars of the Commonwealth," are all gone.
His world has contracted to his prison cell and in despair he decides
to people it from within his own head: "My brain I'll prove the female
to my soul, / My soul the father"; between them, these two will engender a virtual parallel universe, a "little world" just like the larger

world itself. Inside his head, Richard is king of all he surveys and he freely weaves in and out of whichever role takes his fancy, whether king or beggar. So did Shakespeare. It may not be a coincidence that out of all his characters it should be a gay king to put in words the inner mechanisms of the imagination. Like Richard II, Shakespeare imagined worlds within worlds, and as with Richard so there are question marks hanging over Shakespeare's sexuality. Before his brain and soul could merge and multiply, Shakespeare needed to give them sustenance. This he did with an impressive amount of reading. He could never have done that if he had stayed in Stratford, even though his Stratford education provided him with the first key to the portals that led to Ovid, Virgil, Horace, Cicero, Plautus, and Terence. His years at the grammar school had equipped him with a superb command of rhetoric and an introduction to the classics.

Stories about Shakespeare started to circulate in his lifetime, and they continued in Stratford after his death and during the lives of his daughters and granddaughter. The material reality of sixteenth-century Stratford was Shakespeare's habitat. This was the physical space that the greatest writer of all time inhabited, and eventually he himself became his hometown's favorite subject of folklore. As it happens the lasting Stratford stories about Shakespeare have an uncanny habit of turning out to be true, or very nearly so.

1

Stratford 1564:
Birth of a Genius

fter William Shakespeare died, nearly four hundred years ago, a younger contemporary, Ben Jonson, wrote that he

> loved the man and do honour his memory, on this side idolatry, as much as any. He was indeed honest and of an open and free nature; had an excellent fancy; brave motions, and gentle expressions wherein he flowed with that facility that sometime it was necessary he should be stopped. . . . His wit was in his own power, would the rule of it had been so too.

Jonson is a great witness, trenchant, steeped in theater, and never fawning. This tribute provides a convenient starting point. He is talking about "the man," but almost at once conflates the man with the poet and playwright. Jonson did not distinguish categorically between the man and the work, and neither should we. The main reason for writing a biography of Shakespeare at all is those plays and poems, which have given untold pleasure to people the world over. If there is such a thing as a window into the soul of the subject, as in one of his sonnets Shakespeare suggested there was, his plays and poems are it.

Jonson has the immense advantage over us that he knew Shakespeare well. He anticipated that his friend would in the judgment of posterity outshine him and all his contemporaries, that he would be ranked above even Ovid, Virgil, Horace, and Homer. It was Jonson who best captured Shakespeare's legacy, in his elegy in the 1623

First Folio. He apostrophized his friend as the "soul of the age" and the "wonder of our stage" before, finally, claiming that Shakespeare "was not of an age, but for all time." In the course of this book, we will see how deep a trace his age and his own life left in these plays, which have proven every bit as timeless as Jonson predicted. We owe Jonson for authenticating the portrait of Shakespeare in the First Folio. His address "To the Reader" faces the famous egg-headed depiction of Shakespeare by Martin Droeshout. The Droeshout engraving has not pleased the many, but it is a true likeness and, in Jonson's judgment, not a bad one at that:

To the Reader

This figure that thou here seest put,
It was for gentle Shakespeare cut,
Wherein the graver had a strife
With nature to outdo the life.
O could he have but drawn his wit
As well in brass, as he has hit
His face, the print would then surpass
All that was ever writ in brass.
But since he cannot, reader, look
Not on his picture but his book.

B[en] J[onson]

It is comforting to be told by someone in a position to know that the artist hit Shakespeare's face to the life. Very few past lives of people from backgrounds like Shakespeare's afford this luxury. In Shakespeare's case we are lucky enough to have one other authenticated representation: the famous bust in the chancel of Holy Trinity in his hometown. It was erected in the church during the lifetime of Shakespeare's sister, Joan, his widow, and his daughters. It was in place by the time the First Folio was published.

Shakespeare spent much of his life in the Warwickshire town where he was born. Compared with London, Stratford-upon-Avon was a backwater, but it was not therefore backward, nor was it small. Since the 1490s, it had been linked to the south of the country by an

imposing stone bridge across the Avon. We know it as Clopton
Bridge, after its builder the Stratford benefactor Sir Hugh Clopton,
but in Shakespeare's day it was the "great bridge," "Stratford Bridge,"
or the "stone bridge." It was renowned throughout the region and it
was well looked after by the borough. Shakespeare's imagination
was steeped in the Warwickshire countryside as surely as William
Wordsworth's was in the lakes and mountains of Cumbria, and in his
imagery he frequently returns to it. This is as true of the painful, figurative English landscape of *King Lear* as it is of that so very
Warwickshire-like magic wood in *A Midsummer Night's Dream*.
Shakespeare never bought a property in London, choosing instead
to base himself in a huge and comfortable new house in Stratford-
upon-Avon after 1597. In London he was only ever a lodger, even
though the capital was the scene of his great triumphs and where he
kept company with the good, the true, and the reckless.

The outline of the Stratford that Shakespeare knew remains largely
intact, a parallelogram with two main arteries on a north–south axis
intersecting with a set of streets running from east to west. At the
southern edge of the town and in splendid isolation on the Avon sits
Holy Trinity, one of the most cherished silhouettes in all of rural England, as evocative as the paintings of Constable. Long ago, a medieval priory and township surrounded it: hence the name Old
Town by which the area was already known in Shakespeare's time.
A lane by that name still links Holy Trinity with the Bancroft, the
old common on the Avon.

The other place of worship in town was the Gild Chapel of the
Holy Cross. It sits right opposite the spot where the largest house in
town once stood. Shakespeare bought that house in the 1590s; he
and his family would have heard the din of the chapel bells every day
and every night. "And when the clock struck, that was the sound
that Shakespeare heard," wrote Virginia Woolf. The large bell in the
tower of the Gild Chapel dates from 1633. Since 1992, it has again
been sounding the curfew at eight o'clock each night. Shakespeare
never heard it, but his daughters did. On the outside, the chapel
looked the same in his lifetime as it does now. William was born just
too late to see the interior in its former Catholic glory. His father was
the borough chamberlain who in January 1564 paid for the mandatory

Protestant vandalism of its mural paintings: "Item paid for defacing images in the chapel 2 shillings, 10 January 1564." Another 240 years passed before the wonderful frescoes bled through the whitewash in the Gild Chapel. Then they started to fade for good and now, some two hundred years on, they have almost entirely disappeared. Mercifully, they were copied in good time, so we know what they looked like.

South of the Gild Chapel sits the King's New School, named after King Edward VI. Although the bulk of the modern school has mostly retreated east inside the old grounds, the core of Shakespeare's late medieval grammar school is extant. Its long classrooms on the first two floors were spaces that he must have known well, and one of its inside chambers to the left of the staircase, at the southeastern end of the building, served as the town council's meeting room. The town was led from this chamber. Adjacent to the school, another set of timbered fifteenth-century buildings have somehow survived and bulge out onto the pavement. These are the Stratford almshouses.

Shakespeare was baptised in Holy Trinity on Wednesday, April 26, 1564. (The date corresponds to modern May 6, because the Elizabethans computed the year by the antiquated Julian calendar and England did not adopt the Gregorian calendar until 1752.) The spring of 1564 was a bad time to be born, because the plague was about to hit the town. Less than three months after Shakespeare's birth, the register of Holy Trinity ominously records "Hic incepit pestis," "Here the plague began."* The statistics for Stratford baptisms tell their own story. In the year of Shakespeare's birth, the number of

---

*This was written into the register afterward. While the records of Holy Trinity are undoubtedly authentic, it is worth noting that what we have is a parchment copy made in 1600, when Richard Byfield was vicar, of a paper original. Byfield acted on the order of the ecclesiastical authorities. We do not know what happened to the original Holy Trinity register, nor can we prove that the transcripts are entirely accurate; there seem to be inexplicable gaps—for instance, there is no record of the marriage of Anne Hathaway's father to his second wife, Joan. For all these pre-1600 parish registers there were two copies, the original paper version and the parchment copy. It is therefore particularly unfortunate that both versions of other important registers, such as those at Billesley, Bishopton, Luddington, and Temple Grafton, have perished entirely or in part.

newborns dropped by half: whereas in each of 1562 and 1563 just over eighty children were born, in 1564 the total fell to thirty-nine. Among these twenty-five boys and fourteen girls was William Shakespeare. For 1565, the records show a rise again, to fifty-eight. The provinces were no more immune from visitations by the plague than London was, although there were no congested public places here for the infection to spread like wildfire, as it did in the big city.

This must have been an anxious time for Shakespeare's parents, John Shakespeare and Mary Arden. William was their third child and the first boy. Two sisters, Joan and Margaret, had preceded him, but neither had lived for more than a few months. Joan was baptised on September 15, 1558, and died, it seems, not long afterward. It took her parents four years to produce another daughter, Margaret, who died four short months later. The two girls were named after Mary Arden's sisters; as for "William," it was one of the most common first names in Elizabethan Stratford, although there were no Williams in the Shakespeare or Arden families. So the boy must have been named after a neighbor or friend or someone who was both. It is usually taken for granted that the haberdasher William Smith of Henley Street stood as Shakespeare's godfather. Smith and John Shakespeare had acted as the Corporation's "chamberlains" at the time of William's birth in April 1564. In this office they were charged with keeping the accounts of the borough that year, itemizing all its revenues and expenses. The two men seem to have got on well together, for William Smith called his son John, perhaps a reciprocal compliment. William Smith and John Shakespeare not only sat on the town council at the same time, they also lasted for fifty years in the same street in the same town.* But it is just as likely that William

---

*The Smiths of Henley Street should not be confused with a family of the same name who were mercers and owned shops in Middle Row, the central row of houses, shops, and taverns that divided Bridge Street into Fore Bridge Street (south) and Back Bridge Street (north). This William Smith lived on the western edge of High Street in a place called the New House and had a son by the name of William who proceeded from Stratford King's New School to Winchester because his mother, Alice Watson, had a brother, John Watson, who became bishop of Winchester. At Winchester the boy William Smith was registered as "William Smith of Stratford-upon-Avon." From here he went up to Exeter College in Oxford in 1583

Tyler rather than William Smith was Shakespeare's godfather. Tyler was a butcher with premises on the southeast side of Sheep Street near the Bancroft, roughly opposite the present "Cordelia" cottage. He was a few years older than John Shakespeare and he had a son called Richard who was born in the autumn of 1566. This Richard Tyler is famously remembered in the first draft of Shakespeare's will before being crossed out in the final version. He may also be linked to the naming of one of Shakespeare's daughters.

The fourth Shakespeare child to be born was another boy, Gilbert. He arrived in 1566 and was probably named after the glover Gilbert Bradley, who lived three doors east of John Shakespeare in Henley Street. For the next three years, Will and Gilbert were the only children in the family; they seem to have stayed friends and business partners throughout their lives. Gilbert was followed by a second Joan in 1569, and two years later another little girl arrived. She was called Anne after her mother's sister Agnes, the names Agnes and Anne being then interchangeable. Three years later, a further son arrived on the scene. He was baptised on March 11, 1574, and named Richard, after his grandfather Richard Shakespeare from the nearby village of Snitterfield. The next and last child was another boy, Edmund. He was baptised on May 3, 1580, when Will was sixteen, Gilbert fourteen, Joan eleven, and Richard six.

The name Edmund was rare in sixteenth-century Stratford and there were no Edmunds in the immediate Arden and Shakespeare families. The odds are that this child was named after Edmund Lambert from Barton-on-the-Heath, the husband of Mary Arden's sister Joan. There might be another reason for the choice of name: the connection to Edmund Campion. Campion became a saint of the Roman Catholic church in 1970; in 1580 his name was already revered in recusant circles, and the following year saw his martyrdom. Undoubtedly, some Edmunds were named for him. The Jesuit William Weston called himself William Edmunds to honor his friend Campion, with whom he had been at Oxford. His many years of incarceration at

---

while his likely schoolmate the glover Will Shakespeare was learning about fatherhood. The younger Smith has been dubbed "the aptest scholar of Shakespeare's class," which may or may not be true.

Wisbech in Cambridgeshire and in the Tower of London, followed by his eventual release into exile when he was on the verge of blindness, led to his saintly presence in Shakespeare's own lifetime. Shakespeare, Edmund Campion, William "Edmunds" Weston, Edmund Shakespeare, and Edmund (the bastard) Gloucester in *King Lear* all interleave in this story. The civil war between Catholics and Protestants was the deepest spiritual and political reality of the time.

Because of this, we may want to be aware of another man who was born in the same year as Shakespeare. The tall young aristocrat John Gerard joined the Society of Jesus at a time when to do so and return to England was virtual suicide. He did just that, and suffered dreadfully for his calling. There was a dash about this Jesuit Hotspur, who converted Penelope Rich (née Devereux) to the Catholic faith. She was the sister of the mercurial Earl of Essex and the object of the most famous sonnet cycle of the age, Sir Philip Sidney's *Astrophil and Stella*. Gerard, a master of disguises, a wonderful writer and autobiographer, was also the close friend of a priest who found his way into Shakespeare's *Macbeth*, Father Henry Garnett. Shakespeare's and Gerard's lives ran on parallel tracks in the England of the period: the one, Shakespeare, inside the tent even if perhaps only just, the other, Gerard, militantly outside and thus exposed fully to the vengeful savagery of the Elizabethan state. Gerard's autobiography offers the most intimate, immediate, and intensely lived account of the years and of the country that Shakespeare inhabited.

With the birth in 1580 of Edmund Shakespeare, the family was complete. Mary Arden was probably about forty then. On November 24, 1556, when her father, Robert Arden of Wilmcote, made his will, she was still a spinster. Little Joan was born in September 1558, so Mary and John probably wed in the summer or autumn of 1557. Assuming that she was around eighteen during that first pregnancy, this would place her birth in 1540. John may have been Mary's senior by some ten years, because he was renting property in Henley Street by 1552. After a full seven-year apprenticeship as a glover, and having clearly worked hard already to set up on his own in Henley Street, he must have been in his early twenties then; he was born probably in or near 1530. John had spent his youth in the village of

Snitterfield some three miles northeast of Stratford; his father, Richard, was a yeoman there. The name Snitterfield signifies "open land inhabited by snipe"; and the landscape is a bowl of rolling fields perfect for farming. When the Shakespeares pitched their tent here in the early sixteenth century, almost all the acreage around the village would have been held in common and cultivated. As a young man, John must have helped out his father in the family's fields down from their house and also in those that lay beyond the church on the right-hand side of the road to Luscombe and Norton Lindsey. These fields were known as Burman and Redhill; in the 1590s, Shakespeare's uncle Henry was fined for not maintaining a drainage ditch between them. Today a housing estate sits on fields that were once tilled by Shakespeares.

Thanks to sixteenth-century local records, we can identify Richard Shakespeare's farm, his messuage, with certainty. In 1504 the following property, which would become it, was sold to Mary Arden's grandfather Thomas Arden of Wilmcote: "one messuage and eighty acres of land at Snitterfield, the messuage being situated between the tenement of William Palmer and a lane called Maryes Lane, and extending in length from the King's highway to a small rivulet."* The rivulet is the Bell Brook, which meanders along today's School Road through the lower village toward the Green; "Maryes Lane" corresponds to Bell Lane, while the "King's highway" is Church Road. The property that now straddles the south corner of Bell Lane and Church Road occupies the site of Shakespeare's grandfather's house. Whenever William Shakespeare visited Snitterfield to see his aunt and uncle, he would have passed this very spot. His roots were right here. In due course, the Shakespeare farm and its substantial lands, which rolled down all the way to Bell Brook, reverted to the Ardens, who had owned the freehold all along and now bequeathed it to Mary Arden's brother-in-law Edmund Lambert, whose home village, Barton-on-the-Heath, Shakespeare would put in one of his plays.

How John Shakespeare of Snitterfield turned up in Stratford as a glover we do not know, but he was a restless spirit on the make, and make it big he did at first, doing more than gloving. Rather, he

---

*SBTRO BRU 15/2/4.

started to trade in wool on a lucrative scale, and not always legally. He may not have had a racket going, but he got close enough to attract his own personal surveillance agent, whose reports on him survive in the National Archives in Kew. In October 1556, John Shakespeare acquired the eastern wing of the Birthplace from Edward West, as well as a house of a similar size in Greenhill Street from George Turnor. It is likely that this Turnor was related to the John Turnor who lived across from the Shakespeares in Henley Street. John Shakespeare was becoming a man of substance and a serious property owner. He had proven himself to be an astute businessman and artisan. He was a rising man, he was ready to marry, and marry he did. Mary Arden was not quite the boss's daughter, but she was as good as, given the relationship between his father and hers, and she stood to inherit considerable property in Wilmcote. In 1557 John and Mary Shakespeare embarked on their married lives in the Henley Street house.

Twenty-two years separate the Shakespeares' firstborn daughter, Joan, and baby Edmund. What Will Shakespeare made of Edmund's arrival, we cannot know. As the eldest of the surviving children, he was the man of the house after his father, who was by now struggling badly with debts and potential insolvency. If young William helped out with baby Edmund, it would have been timely training, because before long he would himself be lumbered with children: his daughter Susanna was only three years younger than her uncle Edmund. One wonders how sixteen-year-old Will responded to the sight of his pregnant and aging mother. The rituals and the physicality of childbirth in the period were raw and unavoidable. Usually a group of women would gather in the home of the woman who was giving birth. There would be no escaping the pain and the screaming; everyone, men, women, and children, knew what was going on, outside in the street as well as within the house. These elemental facts of life would have helped shape Shakespeare's imagination as much as anything. Shakespeare knows a great deal about motherhood. A mother's "pains," as he puts it, are never far from his mind, although mothers are much less prominent in his plays than fathers are. This is partly because the statute that forbade women to act onstage made it harder to portray mothers than fathers, daughters than sons. The impressive number of daughters in Shakespeare's plays, in the teeth of this practical difficulty, underlines the emotional hold on him of this particular bond.

Mothers are nevertheless given a powerful voice. There is a tense moment toward the end of *Richard II* when young Aumerle is forced by his father, York, to reveal his disloyalty to the usurper king, Bolingbroke, Henry IV. Without a moment's hesitation, the aged father decides to report his son's treason to the king, in the full knowledge that this will mean certain death to the boy. Aumerle's mother protests vehemently:

> *Why, York, what wilt thou do?*
> *Wilt thou not hide the trespass of thine own?*
> *Have we more sons? Or are we like to have?*
> *Is not my teeming date drunk up with time?*
> *And wilt thou pluck my fair son from mine age,*
> *And rob me of a happy mother's name?*
> *Is he not like thee? Is he not thine own?*

When he refuses to heed her pleas, she retorts, "Hadst thou groaned for him / As I have done, thou wouldst be more pitiful." Here a mother's sufferings in childbirth are granted considerable moral authority. Knowing how hard it is to create life, the Duchess values it that much more intensely. Earlier in the same play, King Richard's Queen had called Green, the bearer of bad news, "midwife to my woe." Her soul, she claimed, had "brought forth her prodigy, / And I, a gasping new-delivered mother, / Have woe to woe, sorrow to sorrow joined." Shakespeare knew exactly what "a gasping new-delivered mother" was like.

The customs of childbirth in this period made it almost impossible to hide, and yet concealment is precisely what was happening in Stratford at the time. The only safe way to shield a birth from family, friends, or foes was to remove the pregnant woman to a neighboring village where she was not known. A woman generally had one of two reasons for not wanting a birth to be public knowledge: illegitimacy or a fervent desire to baptise her baby in a faith other than the prevailing one. In the 1550s, Stratford town council time and again fined local burghers for sheltering expectant mothers from outside the parish. On first perusing the borough records, the unsuspecting student may be moved by these repeated acts of kindness to strangers, by the readiness of Stratford's people to take into their homes big-bellied waifs and vagrants. Perhaps even the most hard-hearted of citizens melted at the thought of a heavily pregnant and vulnerable woman. In fact, the taking in of such women was mostly recusant in nature.

Eleven years before Shakespeare was born, the heads of four families were convicted in Stratford and fined by the manorial court, or "court leet," for receiving into their homes "women strangers" who were "brought to bed of children contrary to the order of the last leet court." The threatened fines ranged from twenty shillings to four pounds, although the actual levies were much lower. The term used by the borough's officers when they suspected their fellow citizens of harboring people illegally was "inmake" or "inmate." There was in place a raft of legislation about getting rid of inmates. Such illegal lodgers or transients, whether Catholic or not, were deemed undesirable because they might become a burden on the local public purse. Also, their presence meant that the Corporation was not entirely in control of its residents. In the autocratic state that was Elizabethan England, the free movement of people was restricted through stringent laws against so-called vagabonds. The immense hardships that this caused to some of the most unfortunate men and women in society are powerfully evoked by Shakespeare's poor Tom in *King Lear.*

In 1556 the shepherd John Cox was fined four pence for "receiving a woman great with child." Cox was a Henley Street fixture for forty-one years; Shakespeare knew him all his life because he lived opposite the Birthplace until 1594, when his house was destroyed by fire. His neighbor on the same south side of Henley Street was William Cawdrey, who headed a clan of diehard Catholics. That Cox sheltered a woman might suggest that he shared his neighbor Cawdrey's faith. Someone else from Henley Street was punished for shielding an inmate in 1557. This was Richard Reeve. He lived in what would eventually be the Ainges' house; that family also took in recusant mothers. Perhaps the Whateleys next door did so, too, since their Catholic credentials were impeccable. One wonders whether there was a Catholic caucus at the top of Henley Street, just as there seems to have been toward its middle, where the Catholic Cawdreys and Badgers lived near John Shakespeare. Reeve was a Clopton tenant, and the Cloptons were the godfathers of all things popish in Stratford. On these very premises in Henley Street, the Reeves preceded Roger Sadler, another suspected recusant, who in turn moved out to make room for the Ainges in the same house.

Given the spiritual ferment of the Midlands and the borough council's obsession with this issue, one can see how big this was. From the Catholic point of view, the need for Catholic women to fend for themselves in this way showed up the inhumanity of the Protestants. In a letter to his superiors in Rome, written at the height of the anti-Catholic hysteria in the Armada year of 1588, the Jesuit Henry Garnett complained:

> A certain woman with child, when her time of delivery drew near, travelled to another county where she might have her child. Catholics have to do this, for if they give birth in their own house the question always arises as to where the child is to be baptised. . . . It is a crime punishable at law for a mother to give birth to a child and not to have it baptised [by the minister], or for her to move about in public before she has been childed by him. So by chance it happened that this woman, after a short labour, gave birth in an open field by the road, without any other woman present; and then she carried her infant son at the breast to the house of a neighbouring [Catholic] lady.*

Garnett's note makes perfect sense in 1588, but in the period from 1554 to 1557, when the Stratford manorial courts were particularly exercised by the clandestine births in the town, the Queen of England was the militantly Catholic Mary. It seems that even then the borough had no intention of reinventing itself as a Catholic enclave.

On Sundays Mayor Shakespeare, wearing red robes, and his

---

*Caraman (1964), p. 90.

family were escorted to Holy Trinity from their home in Henley Street. At church, the Shakespeares would have been led to their pew, one at the very front. John Shakespeare would have worn his alderman's ring. These rituals must have left a strong impression on little William; he later recalled the alderman's ring on his father's finger. Henley Street was full of children and several of the "best" families of the town lived here. William would have played with them in a child's world, an idyll of gardens and orchards. A strong sense of family runs through Shakespeare's plays. It would hardly be so potent if his own family had not felt solid, sound, and secure. Mary and John Shakespeare must have run a mostly happy home.

Unlike others among his contemporaries, Shakespeare never left Stratford permanently; a yearning to be close to his family—his mother and father as much as his wife and children—must have played a clinching role in this. Stratford fostered his affinity for nature, and in Stratford were sown the seeds of his immense linguistic range. In this agrarian society, it would have been from his parents and grandparents that he learned the names of flowers, birds, and animals, as he helped his parents with chores around the house, lent a hand in the stables and out in the fields, and helped prune and harvest the fruit trees in the family's orchards in Stratford, Snitterfield, and Hampton Lucy. He listened and remembered, as a future actor and writer who would commit lines to memory at short notice while all the time writing them for others and himself too. The flora and fauna of Warwickshire as well as its folk memory find their way into the works at every juncture. It is one thing to read about the dive-dapper "peering through a wave" and ducking in when "being looked on"—and what an extraordinary image that is for the callow Adonis to use in *Venus and Adonis*—but to see a little grebe or dive-dapper on a pond or in a still corner of the Avon endows the image, and indeed the creature, with a particular kind of imaginative life. The only way Shakespeare could have learned to distinguish ducks from grebes, to know that one of the dive-dapper's characteristics is its extreme shyness, was through patient bird-watching on the river, through living close to nature in a way few do today.

2.

William Shakespeare's Schooldays: c.1570 – c.1578

s mayor, John Shakespeare could send his eldest son to the local school for free. The shrewd businessman and his wife can have been in little doubt about William's talents. His gift for language must have been present from the start, even if it had, as yet, no artistic outlet. The Stratford grammar school had existed since the fifteenth century. Its records have disappeared, but it is inconceivable that he went to a school farther afield. His plays demonstrate that he was familiar with the classic grammar school syllabus. Nicholas Rowe, who was born fifty-eight years after Shakespeare's death, wrote in 1709 that Shakespeare's father

> had bred him, 'tis true, for some time at a free-school where 'tis probable he acquired that little Latin he was master of; but the narrowness of his circumstances and the want of his assistance at home forced his father to withdraw him from thence and unhappily prevented his further proficiency in that language—upon his leaving school, he seems to have given entirely into that way of living which his father proposed to him.

According to Rowe, Shakespeare was forced to leave the King's New School before he reached fifteen, the normal school-leaving age for someone going full term. Quite when he left, we cannot know, but such is his knowledge of the classics and of rhetoric that it could not have been much before 1579, when, it seems, his father first hit rough waters. Free school education from the age of five or six was a privilege; John Shakespeare would have appreciated that knowledge meant power, that being able to read and write would be a huge asset to a glover. He himself signed with a cross sometimes, or else by drawing a pair of compasses. Given that he had kept the Corporation accounts for 1563 and 1564, it is nevertheless highly likely that he could read and that other members of his family could do so too. Whatever the wider national spread of literacy was, Shakespeare clearly assumed that craftsmen like weavers, carpenters, joiners, tinkers, tailors, and bellows menders, to mention only the so-called rude mechanicals in *A Midsummer Night's Dream,* could read and, in the case of at least one of them, Peter Quince the carpenter, write as well. As Bottom the weaver puts it on waking up from his wonderful dream about the Faerie Queene, "I will get Peter Quince to write a ballad of this dream." These are, in the words of the master of ceremonies of the Athenian court, "Hard-handed men that work in Athens here, / Which never laboured in their minds till now."

They may not stand on punctuation, and their misplacing of stops and commas is the reason why Quince's prologue turns into an egregious, supremely artful farce. It is, of course, Shakespeare's punctuation that delivers the brilliant double entendres of the speech, but then he was clearly never bottom of the class. There are true illiterates in the plays—for example, the Capulet servant in *Romeo and Juliet* who is dispatched to deliver invitations to a ball but cannot do so because he is unable to read the addresses on his piece of paper. He protests, comically, that "It is written that the shoemaker should meddle with his yard and the tailor with his last, the fisher with his pencil and the painter with his nets; but I am sent to find those persons whose names are here writ, and can never find what names the writing person hath here writ. I must to the learned." Enter to him Benvolio and Romeo. When the servant asks Romeo whether he can read "anything you see," Romeo replies, "Ay, if I know the letters and the language." The man who wrote these lines at the age of thirty-one not only knew more letters than anyone ever in the English language but would also master French and had some Italian too.

Like other such schools in the country, the Stratford grammar school subjected its charges to a tough regime. School started with prayers at six A.M. and continued until a lunch break from eleven to one. Little William undoubtedly went home for the meal. School resumed at one and went on for another five hours. In the winter these times contracted and school ran from seven A.M. to eleven A.M., then from one P.M. to four P.M. Elizabethan masters were quick to flog their charges, but the glover's son had, it seems, mostly fond memories of school, even if he was also intimidated by it. Shakespeare returned to those days repeatedly in his writings. The most famous reference of all occurs in Jaques's speech "All the world's a stage" in *As You Like It*:

> *At first the infant,*
> *Mewling and puking in the nurse's arms.*
> *Then the whining school-boy with his satchel*
> *And shining morning face, creeping like snail*
> *Unwillingly to school.*

The vignette shows that Shakespeare experienced school just like the rest of us. This is borne out further by Romeo's claiming outside Juliet's window that "Love goes toward love as schoolboys from their books, / But love from love toward school with heavy looks." That as a little boy William Shakespeare loved returning home from school implies that he was happy in Henley Street. Shakespeare wrote *As You Like It* when he was thirty-five years old, and the lines need not necessarily describe his own experience as a reluctant little boy at school in the early 1570s. By the time he embarked on the comedy, he would have seen his own brothers go to school. Like him, they were entitled to a free education there. Later, during his returns to Stratford, he would have watched Hamnet do the same. But of course one wants to think that Shakespeare is writing about himself here, wants to picture little Will with his satchel making his way to school while wishing himself home again with his parents. Childhood anxiety about school is all too recognizable in the cameo, as is the little boy's "shining morning face," spruced up by an affectionate mother sending him off perhaps just as unwillingly as he departs.

To walk from Henley Street to the school in Church Street takes barely ten minutes. For half the year, the streets would have been dark at six or seven A.M., although they would also have been far less deserted at that hour than they are in the twenty-first century. People rose with the sun, and often rather earlier, like the carriers in *Henry IV Part 1*. The lanes of an Elizabethan town would have been busy well before dawn. Other children would have joined Will Shakespeare on his daily calvary, including the son of his putative godfather, William Smith, Jr., whom he might have picked up just before turning into High Street. The Ainges, the bakers who were neighbors of the Smiths near the top end of Henley Street, probably had children at school too, provided they could afford it. And there were Whateley children, from that distinguished family of glovers, whittawers, and town councilors, who lived one door down from the Ainges toward the Shakespeares. These Elizabethan boys were the first generation to go to school the way children still do today.

Among the young scholars was probably one Robert Debdale, from a recusant family in Shottery. Many years later, Shakespeare would read a vicious diatribe against Debdale and his fellow Jesuits in a text that became an important source for *King Lear*. George Cawdrey, another Catholic boy at the school, was about a year and a half younger than Shakespeare. He was the son of Alderman Rafe Cawdrey, a major player in the town, who had family connections in Henley Street through his father, "old William Cawdrey." Eventually George joined the English seminary in Rheims and became a priest. Finally there was Richard Field, the son of a tanner. Field was two and a half years older than Shakespeare and would one day print his two long poems. Strong bonds were forged at school then as now, and in the case of Shakespeare and Field the friendship seems to have lasted throughout their lives. Both men fetched up in the metropolis, but Field, unlike Shakespeare, never returned permanently to Stratford. It is likely, though, that the two men teamed up occasionally for the journey back to Warwickshire. In these preindustrial times, men and women from the same areas or towns remained closely loyal to one another. There is, as we shall see in the course of this story, plenty of evidence to this effect as far as Stratfordians in London are concerned.

The Fields lived in Bridge Street; if Richard did join the boys coming from Henley Street on the school walk, it would have been at Market Cross, which they all passed on their way to Church Street. Its clock tower rang out the hour. On Thursdays the stall holders, and particularly those who, like Shakespeare's father, were among the privileged caste licensed to use Market Cross for their stalls, would have been setting out well before six when the schoolboys passed them on their way to learn Latin. Quite how precious those early ties were to Shakespeare can be gleaned from *Julius Caesar*, when the noblest of all his heroes, Brutus, evokes the memory of shared schooldays to prompt his friend to help him die:

> *Good Volumnius,*
> *Thou know'st that we two went to school together.*
> *Even for that, our love of old, I prithee,*
> *Hold thou my sword hilts whilst I run on it.*

Rosencrantz and Guildenstern were similarly Hamlet's "schoolfellows," and in a play full of huggermugger and duplicity this is seen as a natural source of strength and camaraderie. It should provide a bulwark against treachery, but it does not; this failure is yet another symptom of everything that is rotten in Denmark.

But it was not only the boys who were allowed to bond at school. Girls did too. The fact that girls were educated at all may come as a surprise, but that certainly was the case, although they did not as a rule proceed to grammar school. When, in *A Midsummer Night's Dream*, Hermia feels set upon from all sides, she appeals to her tall friend Helena for female solidarity in the name of "all the counsel" that they shared, their "sisters' vows," the happy hours they spent together when they "chid the hasty-footed time" for parting them, their "school-days' friendship, childhood innocence," when they sat together at needlework on a single cushion creating flowers between them on their samplers. At petty school (also known at the time as "ABC school" after the ABC or "absey" primer), girls acquired domestic skills and learned the alphabet from a hornbook, just like the boys, with whom they shared benches during class. That Helena and Hermia thought of themselves as having been "at school" together is clear from Helena's exclaiming "O, when she is angry, she is keen and shrewd. / She was a vixen when she went to school, / And though she be but little, she is fierce." There is a shared past here, just as there is for boys.

As the father of two daughters, who were twelve and ten years old respectively when he was writing *A Midsummer Night's Dream*, Shakespeare would have had parental experience of the schooling of girls in Stratford. We *think* we know that Anne Hathaway, his future wife, was several years older than the poet; otherwise, we might even wonder whether she attended a Stratford school, given that she came from a prosperous Shottery farm. Had that been so, he and she might have met at school.

As it happens, we have hard documentary evidence that there was a girls' school in Stratford, and it comes from the records of the dreaded Bridewell prison in London. It concerns two Stratford women, Elizabeth Evans and Joyce Cowden, who eked out a living in London as prostitutes in the early seventeenth century. Elizabeth Evans was the daughter of a Stratford cutler called William Evans. She, it is alleged, "went to a house of ill report in Moore lane" and to another such house in Islington. Joyce Cowden testified that she had been "to school together at Stratford-upon-Avon" with Elizabeth, and one George Pinder from Stratford correctly identified Elizabeth's father by hometown and profession.* The girls seemed to have plied their trade together in London for at least three or four years before their arrest. According to Pinder, Elizabeth and her friends were "very poor" and unable "to maintain" themselves. What he means is that they could not make an honest living and therefore resorted to soliciting. It is interesting that in the big city, Stratfordians

---

*Pinder was born in March 1566 and was the son of the John Pinder who was Stratford parish clerk in 1583. There is no record in the Stratford parish registers of the baptism of either Joyce Cowden or Elizabeth Evans, although several other daughters of William Evans are listed. If Elizabeth was entered under another name, she might, just possibly, be the Joan Evans who was baptised on September 20, 1579. It is possible that Pinder misremembered her first name or that she refused to give it. The reason for preferring Joan to the other sisters is that her date of birth fits with the only other woman who could be Joyce Cowden, and that is Joan Cowell, who was baptised March 4, 1579 (assuming that Cowden/Cowell is her maiden name, like Evans's). That makes the two of them contemporaries at school and around twenty-five at the time of their arrest.

could be found to identify the women, unless Pinder was their pimp, which is not impossible. Stratfordians stuck together in London, it seems, even those at the margins of society. When his friend Richard Quiney wrote to Shakespeare from a London inn he addressed him as "loving countryman," a phrase that probably carried more weight than we customarily assume.

The story of the two women is intriguing and pitiable, but its primary relevance for us here is that it proves there was an ABC school for girls in Stratford even though the Corporation records do not specifically refer to one. Boys and girls probably attended the same petty school in Church Street and were segregated only later, around the age of seven. If the premises of the girls' school were the same as the boys' it may have made both sexes' lives much more bearable, turning the school into a place that at least held out the prospect of childhood romances rather than just being a place of austere learning and all-male bonding. Brutus and Cassius are fine; Tom Sawyer and Becky Thatcher are better, at least when at the ages of seven or ten.

The size of the school is a matter of guesswork, for the written parchment register has vanished. It has been estimated that some forty pupils were taught at any one time by the master.* We can speculate about the school's likely population from the average number of children per family in the town and then multiply that figure by the number of all those who could have their children educated for free. At any given time there were twenty-eight aldermen and chief burgesses in the town. If these each had three children at the school, with perhaps four years between the eldest and youngest, they alone would add up to eighty-four children. The school may have had as many as eighty or ninety children enrolled in any one year.

The school had been set up in Stratford in around 1428 and now became a free grammar school. The founding principles of the King's New School reflect the moral earnestness of this Tudor project. Here are the words that established the school as the King's New School during the incorporation of Stratford. The charter (translated from its original Latin) states that the Crown was

---

*Wells, p. 11.

moved by the extraordinary love and affection to the end that we bring up the youths of our kingdom in the aforesaid county of Warwick so that the coming generations shall derive from a childhood more cultured and imbued of letters than was accustomed in our times, and that, when they will have come to a more advanced life, they shall go forth more learned, undoubtedly appreciating the English Church of Christ (whose changes in the land we are now carrying out), taught no less in literary affairs than in precedence for the benefit of all our kingdom, we do . . . establish a certain Free Grammar School with one Master . . .

This clarion call to education is an enlightened document by any sixteenth-century standard. As its everlasting reward, within less than twenty years this small school in a Midlands market town would be educating the greatest writer of all time.

Rarely can the restructuring of a town have had such far-reaching consequences. The wider overall organization of the borough now translated it from its medieval manorial and feudal status into an early modern, largely autonomous, self-governing, and semidemocratic oligarchy. From 1553 onward, the upper echelons of Stratford consisted of fourteen aldermen who chose the fourteen chief burgesses. Together these formed the Common Council. Each September, before the feast of St. Michael the Archangel, the aldermen and burgesses would choose the mayor, or "bailiff," for one year; the Earl of Warwick had to approve the candidate before he could be sworn in. The town also set up a charity in the form of "a certain alms House for twenty-four paupers." The poor would be paid four pence every seven days by the corporation, and poor relief now became an integral part of the newly incorporated borough. The almshouses, like the school, had stood in Church Street since the fifteenth century. Now they became the responsibility of the borough.

The schoolmaster's salary was fixed at twenty pounds, to be paid in four equal installments. Like the mayor, the master had to be approved by the Earl of Warwick. Similarly, the vicar of the church received twenty pounds a year in two equal installments, as well as forty shillings to be paid "at the court of First Fruits and Tithes at the festival of the Birth of our Lord." These were good salaries when compared with others in the kingdom, and signaled to all how highly the borough valued education. The schoolmaster lived in rooms at the back of the school's premises in an annex directly south of the Gild Chapel. The King's New School would at any given time have had a master and an usher, the latter doubling as janitor and teacher of the lower forms. Naturally, the masters of the King's New School have attracted a fair amount of interest. They needed to be well qualified, with the stamina to deliver a complex and demanding syllabus, and they were. Also, and above all, they taught William Shakespeare.

Of the seven masters who served here between 1554 and 1582, five were graduates of Brasenose and St. John's College Oxford, and one each of Corpus Christi Oxford and of Christ's College Cambridge. Whether any significance attaches to the preponderance among them of Oxford graduates, and of Brasenose and St. John's in particular, is hard to determine. One would expect Oxford to be a bigger provider of teachers simply because it is so much closer to Stratford than Cambridge. The link with Corpus Christi, though, may be important because the rumor that Shakespeare died a "papist" originates with two people, William Fulman (1632–88) and Richard Davies (d. 1708), who were both attached to this particular college in the seventeenth century. Davies was also at the root of another Stratford story about Shakespeare, which may be true after all in spite of having long been dismissed as almost self-evidently apocryphal, namely that he had poached deer on the property of a local lord.

The first of the teachers likely to have encountered Shakespeare was the Corpus Christi graduate Walter Roche. He taught at the King's New School from Christmas 1569 to Michaelmas 1571, and he may have just taught the infant Shakespeare in his ABC school if it was, as seems likely, on the same premises as the King's New School. The written records show him witnessing deeds by John Shakespeare in 1573 and again in 1575. Roche resigned from the mastership of the school after only two years, but the borough records for 1574 and 1582 show that he stayed put in Chapel Street. He became rector of nearby Clifford Chambers, a few miles south of

Stratford, and he served here from 1574 to 1578. Roche hailed from Lancashire. This would be of no particular importance except that Lancashire was the heartland of the Catholic resistance in England. Another master whose tenure at the King's New School was just as short retired to Lancashire after leaving his post, only to be succeeded by yet a third master from the same county. It is tempting to see some underground Catholic link among these several teachers with their Lancashire connections.

The question arises whether Roche formed part of a recusant network that reported back to its controllers through his old college or through the Lancashire connection. It is probably a coincidence that Roche, Fulman, and Davies all attended Corpus Christi, for they did so at different times over more than a century, but one cannot be sure. There are many apparent coincidences in this story, some of which are nothing of the kind. The fact that Roche settled into life in Stratford after retiring would seem to suggest that he was not tainted by recusancy, unless of course he was a sleeper, a long-term inactive spy patiently biding his time while embedded in the enemy's ranks. If Roche continues to be regarded with mistrust it may be partly because of the master who succeeded him. It is possible that Roche was induced to make way for him. After all, at twenty pounds a year, the job of the master was not to be given up lightly. The three-year gap between his departure from the King's New School and his beginning work at Clifford Chambers may further fuel questions about him.

Enter Simon Hunt as the new master. He almost certainly taught the young Shakespeare for four years, until he left in 1575. Hunt had been educated at St. John's College Oxford, which had been Campion's college from 1558 until 1570. Hunt went up in 1571. It may not be stretching credibility to detect a pattern here, or at least the possibility of one, since both Hunt and Jenkins, the next teacher at the Stratford school, had been at the same college. Although we cannot be absolutely certain, it is likely that Hunt was a Jesuit or "seminary priest" in the making. He was probably the same Hunt who enrolled at the University of Douai, one of the high citadels of northern European Catholicism, in around July 1575. In other words, he left the school to enroll in the Jesuit seminary. The dates certainly match up perfectly. The Jesuit Hunt died in 1585 in Rome, where he had succeeded Robert Parsons, the leader of the English Jesuits abroad, as English penitentiary at St. Peter's.*

If this priest and the teacher at the King's New School were indeed one and the same person, one would have to conclude that the school was probably being targeted by recusants with a view to indoctrinating its young charges, since religious education formed part of the syllabus. But there was another Simon Hunt, who died at Stratford in 1598. His estate was valued at one hundred pounds and the inventory of his goods was published recently.† We need at least to consider the possibility that he may have been the former Stratford schoolteacher. The waters are muddied by the existence of two Simon Hunts, three masters with Lancashire connections, and three masters from the same Oxford college.

It was in the year of Hunt's departure that the big world of London and the court descended upon Warwickshire, in the form of one of the grandest spectacles of Elizabethan England: the lavish entertainments laid on for the Queen by the Earl of Leicester at nearby Kenilworth in midsummer 1575. This pageant would have been the talk of the entire county; that John Shakespeare took little William to watch some of it with him has long been suspected. The Queen stayed for nineteen days; on the warm evening of Monday, July 18, she was treated to the "Lady in the Lake" pageant, which famously featured Arion riding on a dolphin's back. Is it this that lies behind the lines in *A Midsummer Night's Dream* when Oberon remarks to Puck that he once heard "a mermaid on a dolphin's back / Uttering such dulcet and harmonious breath / That the rude sea grew civil at her song"? Cupid that night takes aim at "a fair vestal thronèd by the west," but his shaft is

> *Quenched in the chaste beams of the wat'ry moon,*
> *And the imperial vot'ress passèd on,*
> *In maiden meditation, fancy-free.*

---

*Fripp (1928), p. 49.
†Jones (2002), vol. 1, pp. 176–77.

Shakespeare wrote his play twenty years after Kenilworth, by which time he could safely talk about Cupid's shaft missing its mark, for Leicester was dead and the maiden world of the Queen was a matter of historical record.

The impact of the Kenilworth spectacle on the local people was immense, and they flocked toward Leicester's country seat in droves. Among them may well have been John Shakespeare with eleven-year-old William in tow. For all we know, Stratford's aldermen and chief burgesses were invited guests at this most sumptuous of outdoor festivities. It may have been in Kenilworth that night that the seed of one of the greatest comedies in the English language was first planted. *A Midsummer Night's Dream* famously grafts Warwickshire onto its Athenian forest. There is every reason for thinking that its high plot with Puck, Oberon, and Titania carries at least the memory of the imprint of Leicester's Kenilworth extravaganza. A July night spent under a full moon in the rambling woodlands and clearings of Warwickshire, perhaps in "les busshes" of Snitterfield Bushes, a mile or so across the wold from Shakespeare's grandfather's home, might be most instructive about the magical forest behind the "wood near Athens."

During his schooldays, the young Shakespeare must have seen plays at Stratford Gildhall, where the various troupes played that passed through town from time to time. Many years later, Shakespeare's contemporary Robert Willis recalled a performance held at Gloucester town hall in the same year as the Kenilworth extravaganza. Such was the impact of the play that "when I came towards man's estate, it was as fresh in my memory as if I had seen it newly acted." Just in case one were to construe this as praise for drama, the Puritan Willis urges it as an example of how impressionable children are and warns against letting them see "spectacles of ill examples and hearing of lascivious or scurrilous words, for that their young memories are like fair writing-tables."

Luckily for us, Willis's memory was excellent. To him we owe a fleeting glimpse of what it must have been like to see the kind of play that would have been put on at Stratford's Gildhall. The eleven-year-old Willis saw what they called "the Mayor's play." Attendance was free, with the mayor of Gloucester paying the players according to their desert. It was at just "such a play my father took me with him, and made me stand between his legs, as he sat upon one of the benches, where we saw and heard very well." The dramatic fare that the good people of Gloucester enjoyed that night in 1575 was called *The Cradle of Security*. It reads like a cross between *The Magic Flute* and *A Midsummer Night's Dream*. Three ladies cause the King to desert "graver councillors" and

> joining in a sweet song, rocked him asleep that he snorted again, and in the meantime closely conveyed under the clothes wherewithal he was covered a vizard, like a swine's snout, upon his face with three wire chains fastened thereunto, the other end whereof being holden severally by those three ladies, who fall to singing again and then discovered his face that the spectators might see how they had transformed him, going on with their singing.

The sexy gargoyle scenes were probably rather more thrilling than the subsequent entry of the two armed Old Men who break the spell in the names of "the End of the World and the Last Judgement." It is quite possible that the (unnamed) players who staged this parable took it on tour to Stratford. Like Willis, young William Shakespeare would have been transfixed by such spectacles while being held by his father. He did not require *The Cradle of Security* to write his later masterpiece about animal metamorphosis, but that *A Midsummer Night's Dream* owes a debt to country pageantry and folklore is undeniable. One of the play's many wonders is its sheer relish in transporting Bottom all the way into the bower of the Faerie Queene. What in Spenser's epic poem *The Faerie Queene* was a stern and damned place, the Bower of Bliss, in Shakespeare metamorphoses into an innocent vision of sex and beauty granted to the irrepressible Bottom, who loves to play all parts at once. It is often said that *A Midsummer Night's Dream* lacks an obvious source, unlike most of Shakespeare's other plays. This is quite true. The play may be the purest fiction, made from memories of his salad days in the country.

It was also in 1575 that John Shakespeare purchased the western two-bay wing of the house in Henley Street. The Shakespeares' fortunes were in the ascendant and young William now walked home to one of the largest houses in the town. The fact that the deed had been witnessed by one of his former masters, Walter Roche, must have been a source of pride to the boy, who by now had probably been joined at school by his brother Gilbert.

By now, Thomas Jenkins was master at the King's New School. He taught Shakespeare from 1575 to 1579, the most impressionable period in his life, his pubescence and early teens, from eleven to fifteen. Jenkins taught his charges Latin poetry, drama, and rhetoric. He was probably Welsh even though he was born in London.* In Stratford, he found himself embedded in an indigenous Welsh enclave. There was John Welsh, whose real name was Edwards; the ironmonger and prominent town councilor Lewis-ap-Williams; a Fluellen (that is, Llewellyn); a butcher by the name of Griffin-ap-Roberts; one Morris Evans, and others. The Welsh were a distinctive feature of Stratford. They had probably migrated to the south Midlands and this particular market town because of the opportunities it afforded for work and trading.

Jenkins's Welshness may be echoed by a scene in *The Merry Wives of Windsor* that features an entertaining parody of Latin lessons with a Welsh parson, Sir Hugh Evans.† It is the first scene of Act IV, which, by pitting young William Page against the parson, turns into a wonderful parody of a Latin class played out before the uncomprehending Mistress Quickly and William's mother, Margaret Page. Mistress Quickly understands not a word of Latin, of course, but comically responds to what she thinks the phrases must mean judging by their sounds. And so "genitive case" becomes "Jinny's case" and *hic, haec,* and *hoc* are turned into unwittingly bawdy infinitives by her when she imagines that Sir Hugh is teaching the boy to "hic" and to "hac" and to lead him to *horum,* whoredom. Communication is further

---

*In a letter of December 12, 1566, Jenkins is described by Sir Thomas White of St. John's College Oxford as the son of one of his servants in London. This is not incompatible with his being Welsh.

†"Sir" here designates a parson or priest. For half a century one "Sir" William Gilbert was a Stratford relief teacher. He was also a curate (Sir Hugh Evans is a parson) and taught as under master in the 1560s and 1570s. He could well have taught the infant Shakespeare. He wrote out the will of Shakespeare's father-in-law, Richard Hathaway, in 1581, the year before Will and Anne married.

hampered when Sir Hugh comically Welshes the English language almost as much as Mistress Quickly does the Latin, making "fritters of English," according to Falstaff. Evans is given a number of phonetic idiosyncrasies that Shakespeare clearly associated with Welsh speech from his time in Stratford. These include unvoiced consonants, as in "prain" for "brain," "prabble" for "brabble," "focative" for "vocative," and "oman" for "woman"; later he uses "Got" for "God," "pinse" for "pinch," and the locution "I pray you." Some of these Shakespeare would deploy again in the affectionate parody of his most famous Welshman, Fluellen, in *Henry V.*

When William replies to Evans's "Well, what is your accusative" with "Accusativo, hinc," Sir Hugh reprimands him with "I pray you have your remembrance, child." The right answer, which is given in the standard textbook, Lily's *A Short Introduction of Grammar,* is of course *hunc,* with the feminine and neuter *hanc* and *hoc.* Evans's further "Accusativo hing, hang, hog" provokes from Mistress Quickly the comment " 'Hang-hog' is Latin for bacon, I warrant you." Evans's pronunciation of Latin and English and his quirky English syntax are as much a source of comedy as the Latin bouncing off Mistress Quickly, who thinks that Latin *pulcher* (meaning "fair") must mean "polecat," a prostitute. The entire scene closely follows Lily's grammar including the use of *lapis* (stone), which occurs at the top of the very page of *A Short Introduction* that Shakespeare is echoing. Under the heading "Articles" Lily writes, "Articles are borrowed of the pronoun and be thus declined," which corresponds verbatim to two of William's lines in the scene.

In this benign and affectionate scene, Sir Hugh is portrayed with considerable indulgence. He calls the boy William throughout, rather than use his surname, Page. Shakespeare elsewhere enjoys playing on his name, so he may here be signaling that this is really *him* and no one else; or perhaps in Shakespeare's time the boys at the King's New School were called by their first names. Perhaps our idea that Elizabethan schools were redoubts of enthusiastic "breeching"— flogging—has been too generic, does not apply to the King's New School. William is threatened with flogging, but the threat is immediately countermanded with "Go your ways and play; go."

Shakespeare's wordplay on the collision of Latin and English phonetics is sophisticated. The rhetorical demands made by the Elizabethan theater never cease to surprise one, even if in this particular case the cross-linguistic jokes may have been written in especially for the Queen, whose command of Latin was legendary. Much more of Shakespeare's education is reflected in his work than appears from this. His school syllabus included a deep grounding in classical rhetoric; the pupils were trained in Latin versification and plays, particularly Terence. That Virgil, Ovid, and Horace featured prominently constitutes a huge tribute to the forward thinking of Elizabethan educators. In Ovid, and particularly in the *Metamorphoses,* Shakespeare discovered an imaginative world that would profoundly affect him. The great Roman poet became his favorite classical author, above even Virgil. It has been said that when Shakespeare left the King's New School, his command of Latin would have matched that of a classical scholar today. Perhaps he would have been an even stronger Latinist, for at school the older boys were expected to communicate in Latin rather than in English. A letter written in fluent Latin to his father by the eleven-year-old Richard Quiney, Jr., the future brother-in-law of Judith Shakespeare, is usually cited in this connection. But it is true, too, that we now sometimes tend to overplay the achievement of those who mastered what is ultimately "just" another language. It is worth remembering that throughout the Middle Ages and early Renaissance all educated people used Latin; it was the European language of international and diplomatic communication.

Shakespeare also learned English grammar at his school, and he drew on the experience in *Love's Labour's Lost.* This time he fields two pedants, a curate called Sir Nathaniel and a schoolmaster by the name of Holofernes. They enter together from a dinner of "sharp and sententious" conversation only to discover that they are no match for the page Moth and the clown Costard who outwit them even at plain punning and language games. Particularly illuminating is Holofernes's obsession with the mismatch between English spelling and pronunciation:

> I abhor such fanatical phantasims, such insociable and point-
> device companions, such rackers of orthography, as to speak

"dout," *sine* "b," when he should say "doubt"; "det" when he should pronounce "debt"–d, e, b, t, not d, e, t. He clepeth a calf "cauf," half "hauf"; neighbour *vocatur* "nebour"–neigh abbreviated "ne." This is abhominable–which he would call "abominable" ...

Holofernes is on the losing side. The modernizers have it, as his use of the archaic form "clepeth" for "call" further suggests. Shakespeare, like Jonson, was forever excited by language and loved experimenting with it. Not that he did not avail himself of the great retro-chic poem of the period, Spenser's *The Faerie Queene,* when it suited him to do so. Like Jonson, though, he may have harbored doubts about the wisdom of Spenser's reverting to Malory in the fifteenth century in search of a language for an English epic. Shakespeare's deep and dynamic love affair with English was fostered by the study of grammar and rhetoric at school. The sheer pleasures afforded by syntax and by translating from Latin into English and back again into Latin, from *lapis* to "stone" and from "stone" back to *lapis* (and not to "pebble," as William does in *The Merry Wives of Windsor*), these were among the nourishments he assimilated at school. By then, the Bible had been available in English for at least forty years, and the English people heard God speaking in their own language. Now everyone could talk to the Almighty without intermediary, and could listen to God's word in church and understand it.

It is clear from the gusto of the adult Shakespeare's recollections of his schooldays how much he enjoyed his time in Church Street. Those many anxious early-morning walks to school had their compensations in Latin tuition and classical literature, in declining and conjugating as well as in role playing. Not only did Shakespeare forge friendships and absorb the kind of learning that had hitherto been reserved for a small elite, but also, and above all, he acquired a set of intellectual perspectives that far transcended Stratford. It was here, among his teachers, that young William first met people who had been educated in places called Oxford and Cambridge. He may himself have wanted to go on to university, but events caught up with him and he probably left school not long before Jenkins did. The reason was almost certainly the collapse of his father's business career. The teenage Shakespeare may have been alone among all the chief burgesses and aldermen's sons at school in having his father headed for some kind of bankruptcy. If so, he would have been deeply humiliated. For better or worse, the children at the King's New School were the new self-making bourgeois elite of Elizabethan England; to be the son of a failure may have marked the young Shakespeare for good. Hence, perhaps, the striving and endless investing that would become such a characteristic feature of his life.

Throughout his schooldays, the young Shakespeare would have assisted his father in the gloving business. It had been a successful business, but now he found himself catapulted into the harsh Elizabethan realities of debt and creditors. And then his sister Anne died. Her death is recorded in the parish register dated April 5, 1579, where we read of the burial of "Anne daughter to Mr. John Shakespeare." Her grief-stricken parents laid out eight pence for tolling the bell for her, one penny for each year that she had lived. It must have been a tremendous shock for William to lose his little sister. She was the only one of his siblings to die during his youth, so, unlike many of his contemporaries, he was at least spared multiple ordeals. There is no way of knowing how Anne died and whether her death contributed to her father's erratic career on the Stratford council.

A few months later, on December 17, 1579, another event happened that left its mark on the fifteen-year-old Shakespeare: the drowning of Katherine Hamlet. The Avon's treacherous currents claimed victims every year; Katherine died at Tiddington, a mile or so upriver toward Charlecote. The town conducted an inquest to establish whether she drowned by accident or suicide. The inquest was held at Warwick on February 11, 1580, and may lie behind Shakespeare's portrayal of the death of Ophelia in *Hamlet*. The body of poor Katherine Hamlet was exhumed from the cemetery of Alveston; the town clerk, Henry Rogers, who was steward to Sir Thomas Lucy (Shakespeare's future nemesis) as well as the town's coroner, presided. The inquest report found that Katherine had gone to draw water from the river at Tiddington and that, "standing on the bank of the same river," she suddenly slipped and fell in. The death was an accident; why suicide had been suspected we will never know, but unwanted pregnancy would have been a common reason for young women to drown themselves. Before drowning, the mad Ophelia wanders about singing of young men who will insist on having sex when given the chance, so that maids are maids no more when they depart from their bedrooms.

The name of Stratford-upon-Avon is written in water for the very good reason that the Avon forms an integral and defining part of the town. Quite how rough it could become is evident from the detailed account of the flash flood that struck in the Armada year. Such was the river's ferocity that no one alive, or dead, had ever witnessed anything quite like it, not even "old father Porter," the local Methuselah, of legendary longevity and the living chronicle of the area, who died at the age of 109 in 1584. Father Porter had seen every flood since the reign of the Queen's grandfather, who had defeated Richard III at Bosworth Field.

It was around eight in the morning on Thursday, July 18, 1588, when the Avon unleashed its power and

> brake up sundry houses in Warwick town and carried away their bread, beef, cheese, butter, pots, pans, and provisions; it took away ten carts out of one town and three wains with the furniture of Sir Thomas Lucy's; it broke both ends of Stratford bridge. . . . It did take away suddenly one Sale's daughter of Grafton out of Hilborow meadow removing of a haycock that she had no shift but get up upon the top of the haycock and was carried thereupon by the water a quarter of a mile wellnigh, and till she came to the very last bank of the stream, and there was taken into a boat and so was saved, but both she and the two that rowed, boat and all, was like to be drowned but that another boat came and rescued them soon. Three men going over Stratford Bridge when they came to the middle of the Bridge they could not go forwards and then returned presently but they could not go back for the water was so risen it rose a yard every hour from eight to four.

The Avon has as many faces as Stevie Smith's lecherous old foul river—sly, treacherous, and triumphalist. But it has a benign and gentle side, too. One languid summer's evening in July 2004, the author of this book stood outside the Royal Shakespeare Theatre before a performance of one of Shakespeare's plays. Several urchins mingled incongruously with stray members of the audience before plunging into the Avon, again and again, Huck Finns in Stratford's Mississippi. Earlier that Saturday afternoon, the Avon up toward Tiddington and Charlecote had been as busy as Henley during the Regatta. The river taxis, those shallow-draft *African Queen*s that shuttle between the camping sites of Tiddington and Oxstalls, were plying their way through flotillas of small rowing boats and motor-ized launches. Had Ratty and Moley joined in no one would have turned a hair—or a hare, for that matter—in the meadows that hug the border of the Avon here.

As a child during the dog days of summer, Shakespeare must have gone swimming in the river with his siblings. Many years later, in a play written during his retirement together with his successor at the King's Men, Shakespeare has Cardinal Wolsey reflect on his own hubris:

> *I have ventured,*
> *Like little wanton boys that swim on bladders,*
> *This many summers in a sea of glory,*
> *But far beyond my depth; my high-blown pride*
> *At length broke under me, and now has left me,*
> *Weary, and old with service, to the mercy*
> *Of a rude stream that must for ever hide me.* *

Among those little boys using pigs' bladders to support them in the water may well have been young William. And later, perhaps, Hamnet Shakespeare. The playwright took a compulsive interest in water and drowning, from the brilliant nightmare vision of Clarence sinking down to the "slimy bottom of the deep" and its scattered "dead bones" in *Richard III* to the drownings and resurrections in *Twelfth Night* and *The Tempest*. Writers on Shakespeare have long wondered about the plotting of *The Tempest*, which has no obvious source. In light of Katherine Hamlet's death, the river's sporadic unleashing of elemental powers, and its manifest danger to local children, one may well wonder whether this brilliant parable of

---

*Henry VIII, III, 2, 358–64.

redemption and the wishful triumph over death by water may not after all have a source in the darkest imaginable, real deaths by drowning.

The ten years after 1579 would have been among the hardest in Shakespeare's life, and they were among the most difficult and uncertain for the entire nation. In Stratford, the decade was marked by the arrival of yet another new master at the King's New School. John Cottom, from Lancashire, served two years only. He had graduated from Oxford the same year as his predecessor Jenkins, so they must have known each other. No accusation of recusancy has ever been pointed at Jenkins, but we cannot be sure that he and Cottom were not in league with each other any more than we can be certain about Roche and Hunt. Strangely, Jenkins was paid six pounds by the Stratford chamberlains for surrendering his mastership to Cottom in July 1579, but the records do not tell us why.

Cottom's move to Shakespeare's school in 1579 coincides with the mission to England that was being planned at that very moment by the Jesuit William Allen, who ran the English College at Douai, and by Robert Parsons. Not long afterward, Parsons secured for the mission the blessing of Claudio Acquaviva, the General of the Society of Jesus. Campion landed in England on June 24, 1580, and was put up at Sir William Catesby's house, Bushwood, in Lapworth, ten miles or so from Stratford, at a time when Robert Parsons, who obviously knew his successor Simon Hunt in Rome, also sojourned in the Midlands. The younger brother of the newly appointed Stratford schoolmaster, Thomas Cottom, was a Jesuit and a companion of Campion. On May 30, 1582, a few months after his master, Thomas Cottom (today the Blessed Thomas Cottom) was in turn tortured and put to death at Tyburn.

The Jesuits were in England to stay and to die. When he was arrested, Thomas Cottom was carrying a secret letter addressed to John Debdale of Shottery. It is inconceivable that during this trip Cottom should not have wanted to meet his brother John at the King's New School, since his mission to Shottery took him within a mile of Church Street. John Cottom brought the King's New School close to the heart of the Catholic resistance. Although the record does not say so specifically, he was probably forced out of his job in

1581 by the national events then unfolding. He returned to his father's home in Lancashire and became a prominent local recusant. Perhaps he felt he needed to honor his brother's supreme sacrifice. He was determined not to surrender his religion. Neither was the family whom his brother had intended to visit, the Debdales of Shottery.

3

Meeting the Neighbors
in 1582

y the late 1570s, Shakespeare's father was plunging ever more deeply into insolvency. That much is clear from his attempts to raise money by selling off property in Wilmcote and Snitterfield, the ancestral villages of the Ardens and Shakespeares, and from his failure to attend council meetings between January 1577 and September 6, 1586, for fear, probably, of arrest for debt. He was treated with considerable forbearance by his fellow aldermen during this period when it came to fines and levies. Thus, for example, on November 19, 1578, when the council instructed all aldermen to pay four pence weekly toward poor relief, John Shakespeare was one of only two (out of fourteen) "who shall not be taxed to pay anything."* The idea that he shunned the town as a recusant and that the family fortunes collapsed through a string of (unrecorded) fines levied on the Shakespeares as obdurate Catholics seems untenable. There is simply no evidence for it.

The evidence is that Shakespeare's father was hugely committed financially in wool dealing, not all of it legal. Large sums of money changed hands in these unregulated transactions. When the going was good, fortunes could be made, and were, by the man from Henley Street. When Nicholas Rowe wrote that Shakespeare's father "was a considerable dealer in wool" he scored a notable first by asserting long before anyone else did that John Shakespeare had

---

MA, vol. 3, p. 24.

been trading in wool on a grand scale.* In the local economy wool was second only to malting, so it is no surprise that John Shakespeare was at it, like almost everyone else. He probably turned part of his premises in Henley Street into a wool shop. Indeed, he may have purchased the western wing of the property with his wool-dealing operations in mind, hoping to expand the business. New legislation regulating and restricting the wool trade may have cost him dearly.

By the time he joined his father's business in, probably, 1578 or 1579, William knew how his hometown worked economically and politically. Stratford, bustling, busy, and competitive, was a microcosm of Elizabethan England. The townspeople represented just about every profession, art, craft, and trade that one could imagine in a rural preindustrial economy, this at a time when almost everybody also farmed, owned orchards, and kept livestock ranging from hens and cocks to pigs and sheep.† On Thursdays the town doubled or trebled in size as traders and farmers from the surrounding villages converged on the market. The place must have resembled a frenzied beehive as stalls radiated out from Market Cross into the adjacent streets. Every inch of space was tightly controlled by the council; the glovers, an elite fraternity among stallholders, occupied pride of place at the Market Cross. Stratford in the late sixteenth century must have felt like the center of its own universe. Small fortunes could be made here, even if the town had its poor and was afflicted at least three times during Shakespeare's lifetime by severe fires as well as plague.

---

*The full extent of John Shakespeare's financial troubles is charted in a study by Robert Bearman, "John Shakespeare: A Papist or Just Penniless?" in *Shakespeare Quarterly* 2006.

†Shakespeare's Stratford had apothecaries, bakers, blacksmiths, brewers, bricklayers, butchers, button makers, carpenters, chandlers, clock makers, coopers, corvisors or shoemakers, curates, cutlers, drapers, dyers, fishmongers, glovers and whittawers, glaziers, goldsmiths, haberdashers, hatters, husbandmen, ironmongers, linen drapers, masons, maltsters, mercers, midwives, millers, painters, plumbers, publicans, rough masons, saddlers, shearmen, solicitors, street cleaners, surgeons, tailors, tanners, teachers, tinkers, vintners, weavers, wheelwrights, wool drivers, woolen drapers. It would be easy to pair almost every one of these trades with multiple names from the extensive Stratford Corporation records. What this miniature survey of arts, crafts, trades, and professions demonstrates is quite how buoyant the town was.

Stratford was full of orchards with apple, quince, pear, and cherry trees. Parts of the town were still deeply rural, boasting ashes, chestnuts, crabs, limes, maples, oaks, and planes. The ravages of Dutch elm disease were 350 years in the future, and Stratford claimed several kinds of elm. These were grown for timber on plantations toward Tiddington on the east bank of the Avon; others, perhaps the large classic English elms, served as borough boundary markers. In one particular minute, for October 8, 1617, we read that "At this hall it is agreed that 2 elms shall be set up at the place where the other two elms were cut down by Evesham way." The reason for the instant replanting was that these two felled elms marked the outer southwestern boundary point of the borough, which was known at the time as Two Elms.

Elms visually defined Elizabethan Stratford. It is not clear why they were so much more important than oaks; the latter abounded in the Forest of Arden, which had provided medieval Stratford with most of its building timber. Even the Birthplace includes considerable oak. As a rule, elms grew out from earth mounds or boundary ridges between the houses, or else in the groves and orchards in the town and around it. We know exactly where a number of them stood in the year of Shakespeare's marriage, 1582, because just then the Stratford Corporation published a survey of all its property, including an inventory of its trees. Freeholders like John Shakespeare, George Whateley, the Quineys, and many others in Henley Street were covered by a separate manorial survey of 1590; Corporation tenants and freeholders lived side by side. A case in point is the 1557 boundary quarrel between the freeholder George Whateley of Henley Street and his neighbor to the east, the Richard Reeve of the "in-make" fine, who was a Corporation tenant. Whateley and Reeve were in dispute over ownership of the border elm that stood between them at Whateley's barn. The council found in favor of Whateley and furthermore instructed Reeve that he had to "set and pitch his mounds between him and William Smith."* It seems that Reeve posed problems for his neighbors on either side. For us, this kind of minor local skirmish provides valuable information about

---

MA, vol. 1, p. 61.

where residents lived at any given time—and, of course, about how they got along.

The 1582 survey listed around a thousand elms, to which we would have to add probably another two hundred to three hundred to take account of the holdings of the rich and powerful freeholders. The counting of elms strengthens the view that the town's streets were not terraced, as has been argued from time to time; rather, almost all the houses were separated by passages between them, which were marked off by boundary ridges and elm trees.

Elms were taxed heftily, or at least borough tenants paid for them as part of their rent. Thus Humphrey Bracer assured the council that of the twenty-eight elms on his property his "predecessor" had already paid for four of them. He was eager to be remitted at least those four, and we can readily see why when we consider quite how much elms cost their owners. The wealthy John Gibbes had to disburse the impressive sum of forty shillings to the corporation in 1594 "for elms in his orchard in Henley Lane," today's Windsor Street. Twenty-six elms and twelve ashes grew in his orchard; he also owned a grove of elms in front of his house in Rother Street. Of all trees, only elms, it seems, were taxed; the levy on Gibbes's orchard suggests a rate of roughly one and a half shillings per elm. This was serious money and raises but does not answer the question of why anyone would bother growing elms if they were that expensive.

The country end of Henley Street and the entire stretch west of Henley Lane (or Hell Lane) consisted of orchards, elm groves, and fields; similarly with the backs of the houses on the south side of Henley Street, in the triangle formed by Mere Pool Lane, Henley Lane, and Henley Street. Four elms grew behind William Greenway's barn, which stretched back south toward Wood Street.* Greenway lived as a freeholder in Bridge Street but rented premises and a barn opposite and east of the Shakespeares, not far from his in-laws the Cawdreys. The Shakespeares knew Greenway well. He operated a mail shuttle service between Stratford and London and had interesting and dangerous family connections.

---

*"Greeneway" in the originals, which Wells and I read as "Greenway." Shapiro (2005) and Jones have "Greenaway."

In the sixteenth century, Henley Street was a busy thorough-fare for traffic heading toward Coventry and Birmingham. It was paved, or metalled, and had been so since before 1557, when the town council referred to "the repairing of the paving of the streets in Stratford." It seems that the town's streets had proper pavements; house owners and tenants were responsible for maintaining and mending them.* At the time, almost everyone in Henley Street was in business and would have been keen to pick up the travelers' trade. Indeed, such was their zeal for business that the good burghers of Stratford even tried to trade when they were not supposed to. Thus the majority of all the summonses to the so-called Bawdy or Consistory Court were for trading outside licensed hours, usually after the bell that summoned the citizens to church had stopped ringing. Stratfordians preferred business to prayer, and who can blame them?

When Shakespeare turned in to Henley Street he would have seen a busy and competitive crowd of people selling their wares quite literally from out of their windows, which were improvised stalls. The scene would have resembled a daguerreotype of a bustling 1880s east London street such as Brick Lane, and would have been similarly congested with carts and horses. Almost everyone would have been talking to everyone else. Shakespeare's culture was much more oral than ours. There were no newspapers or other mass media. Instead, talk kept everyone in the know. Shakespeare called it "Rumour painted full of tongues" in the second part of *Henry IV.* This world is echoed in a fine moment in *King John* when Hubert of Angiers relates the rumor about young Arthur's death. In these lines, the great Stratford antiquarian and life trustee of the Birthplace, Edgar Innes Fripp, detected a specific memory of Henley Street:

> *Old men and beldams in the streets*
> *Do prophesy upon it dangerously.*
> *Young Arthur's death is common in their mouths,*
> *And when they talk of him they shake their heads,*

---

*MA, vol. 1, p. 103.

And whisper one another in the ear;
And he that speaks doth grip the hearer's wrist,
Whilst he that hears makes fearful action,
With wrinkled brows, with nods, with rolling eyes.
I saw a smith stand with his hammer, thus,
The whilst his iron did on the anvil cool,
With open mouth swallowing a tailor's news,
Who, with his shears and measure in his hand,
Standing on slippers, which his nimble haste
Had falsely thrust upon contrary feet,
Told of a many thousand warlike French
That were embattailèd and ranked in Kent.
Another lean unwashed artificer
*Cuts off his tale, and talks of Arthur's death.**

This animated scene, and particularly the telling detail of the tailor who in his haste has put his slippers on the wrong feet, may well have been one that Shakespeare witnessed in Henley Street. The Shakespeares' neighbors to the east were indeed a tailor and a blacksmith. The tailor was a bigamist by the name of William Wedgewood and the blacksmith was Richard Hornby. The Hornbys stayed on for centuries in this house; it still stands today and is now linked umbilically to the Birthplace as its shop and official exit. Shakespeare could have chosen any of the many professions of his hometown for the scene in *King John,* but instead he opted for a tailor and a smith simply because a tailor and a smith were his family's neighbors.

One of the distinctive features of this cameo is its lifelike comic detail. The young Shakespeare was not only a fast and avid learner but also a keen observer. The gestures, the gripping by the wrist, the rolling eyes, the hurriedly put-on slippers—these argue not only that he watched carefully how people behaved but also that he instinctively knew how to render it on the page. Instead of getting a lengthy description, we are invited to see, to think visually. This is what Shakespeare does time and again, and he does so from the start. The

---

*Fripp (1928), p. 16.

little boy who watched the tailor and blacksmith in Henley Street is present in the adult writer who conjures up a street scene from memory. "Always assimilate" seems to be the motto of the young Shakespeare. It makes perfect sense that the first, and very public, attack on him should charge him with overassimilation: plagiarism.

Let us accompany Will Shakespeare returning home from an imaginary evening out with some of his friends at one of the two grand local inns. The year is 1582, the year when Shakespeare courted Anne Hathaway, made her pregnant, and married her. On this imagined evening he may have run into some of his former schoolmates, those same young men who would eventually land him in trouble. Perhaps they were just like the young men in *Romeo and Juliet,* always spoiling for a fight and always talking about girls. Just then, Shakespeare was heading home from the Swan or the Bear down at the bottom of Bridge Street, those real-life versions of the Boar's Head in the *Henry IV* plays. Perhaps the Bear rather than the Swan, because the Shakespeares were friendly with the Bear's owners, the Sadlers, and with its publican, who was known as Barber of the Bear. He managed the hostelry for a generation and Shakespeare knew him all his life.

Just before entering Henley Street, Shakespeare would have walked past the Newalls's Angel tavern and then the home of his possible godfather, William Smith, the current number 1 on the righthand side. In 1582, a large pile of logs belonging to Smith was leaning precariously against the Angel, damaging it. The town council ordered him to remove the logs. Newall's landlord was the Catholic Arthur Cawdrey, whose brother was a priest. Smith, in turn, was not a freeholder but rented his property as a tenant of the Corporation. Its taxable ground rent of eight pence means that it was substantial, although in 1590 it was less than half the size of the Shakespeares' house. Smith also owned a sizable barn on the south side of Henley Street, which stood nearly opposite the Shakespeares.

Next on his way toward the Birthplace stood the relatively modest abode of the Ainges, with a frontage of some thirty feet or so. John Ainge was a licensed baker. The Shakespeares must have known the house well; the freehold property of the rich and powerful John

Clopton, it had formerly been the home of Roger Sadler, a friend of John Shakespeare's who was appointed constable with him. Roger Sadler had also been a baker. Clearly the Sadler-Ainge house possessed a special bread oven, which is why it passed from baker to baker. At some point Sadler toyed with the idea of diversifying by keeping an alehouse as well. The council sternly reprimanded him and forced him to choose between baking and running a tavern. If he preferred the latter, he would be expected to put up a proper alehouse sign. Sadler opted for baking. Eventually, and long before young Shakespeare's hypothetical 1582 walk, Sadler moved out to a house on the corner of High Street and Sheep Street, the same place where his nephew Hamnet Sadler, William Shakespeare's friend, would one day live. On his death in 1578, the baker left his estate to his wife, Margaret, and to Hamnet Sadler. His debtors included Richard Hathaway of Shottery, Anne Hathaway's father, and there is mention in his will of "sureties for John Shakespeare." He may have wanted to help his old friend out even in death, since the Shakespeare fortunes were then in decline and would continue so for the next twelve years or more.

The next house that Shakespeare would have passed was a grand one and, just possibly, the one in which he met his future bride. It belonged to one of Stratford's most distinguished citizens and public servants, a glover by the name of George Whateley. It is not impossible that Shakespeare was apprenticed to him rather than to his own father. The main reason for preferring his father is that we know that things had become very bad for John Shakespeare, so the family might not have been able to pay to apprentice Will to someone else. Also it may have been the custom locally for sons to be apprenticed to their fathers: in the household of Shakespeare's neighbors the Badgers, George Badger, Jr., was apprenticed to his father as a glover in 1596. Whateley lived at what are today numbers 4 and 5 Henley Street. He was mayor in the year Shakespeare was born and his house, like John Shakespeare's, doubled as home and woolen draper's shop. In a sign of prosperity, it boasted glass in the hall, the parlor, and the upstairs chamber. Beehives ("stalls of bees") stood in the garden, and "wax, honey, and other things" were found in its "apple chamber," which may have formed part of the buttery.* This large house also included a cellar, a granary "next to the garden," a "stable," a gatehouse, and, at the back, a barn and yard. The frontage of the property was just under eighty feet, which made it the second largest in Henley Street, second only to John Shakespeare's. George Whateley was rich, and in his will in 1593 he endowed a school in his native Henley-in-Arden.

From the Whateleys' to his home was a two-minute walk for Shakespeare, past another seven or eight houses and barns. One of these had formerly belonged to Gilbert Bradley, his brother Gilbert's likely godfather.† Now it belonged to the whittawer William Wilson, who in 1579 had married an Anne Hathaway from Shottery, the daughter of one George Hathaway.‡ He was probably the uncle of the future Mrs. Shakespeare's father, Richard Hathaway (who was also known as Gardner), so that the two Anne Hathaways were second cousins. As whittawers and glovers from the same street, the Wilsons and Shakespeares would have known each other well. After the 1595 fire, the Wilsons had to rebuild their house; the more fortunate Shakespeares were spared. The Wilsons' dwelling sat on the site of the present public library, directly east of a gutter that cut right across Henley Street on a north–south axis. Through this conduit, which at the time was called "the cross gutter before Bradley's door," flowed the Mere. It was hardly a deep stream, but it was enough to be a striking feature of the town's landscape as it then was. The Mere was not much wider, perhaps, than the large flagstones that must have covered it to allow carts to cross, but it was wide enough to prevent the fire that devastated the eastern part of Henley Street from spreading farther west. Just to the southwest of Henley Street, at Rother Market, the Mere formed a pool, known until recently as Mere Pool; hence the name Meer Pool Lane for Mere Street. It has been alleged that this innocent burn one day wiped out England's greatest writer. But the people of sixteenth-century Stratford would

---

*Jones (2002), p. 126.

†Since at least 1574, if not since 1563 when Bradley's lease expired, the Bradley house had been occupied by William Wilson (SBTRO BRU 8/8/4).

‡A whittawer was a processor of hides.

no more have dreamed of drinking from the Mere or any other brook than Londoners would from the Fleet River. The borough by-laws of Stratford endlessly threatened and enforced sanctions connected to hygiene.

The town was rightly concerned with regulating its sanitation. Thanks to its punctiliousness, we know that some twelve years before William Shakespeare's birth his father was fined for keeping an unlicensed muck heap outside the house in Henley Street. How bad this behavior was becomes apparent when we realize that at the time the official rubbish tip for this area of the town sat less than eighty yards away from the Birthplace, at the so-called country end of Henley Street, across the road from Peter Smart, himself a former Corporation chamberlain. Smart's house was the last one on the same (north) side of the street as John Shakespeare's. His neighbors opposite were William Chambers (a wheelwright) and Thomas Patrick; the rubbish tip sat between their houses. Years earlier, at a time when the muck heap on Henley Street was still privately owned by Chambers, the council had forced him to screen his neighbor Patrick from it. Patrick must have protested about the filth, hence the instruction to fence it off. The threatened fine to Chambers was a severe one, underlining how seriously the town took hygiene and the nuisance caused by untended garbage.

Originally these designated muck hills were contracted out to private individuals but eventually the town council took them back under its direct control and made a handsome profit from them. Around the time of Shakespeare's birth there were six municipal garbage dumps altogether, at the bottom or nether end of Sheep and Bridge Streets, in the gravel pits in Tinker Street (Scholars' Lane), in Greenhill Street "by Nicholas Lane's hedge," in Church Street by John Sadler's barn, and "in Henley Street one other dunghill in the old place accustomed," that is, near the house of Chambers at the far end of the street toward Henley Lane.* These garbage heaps were cleared away twice a year, at Whitsun and Michaelmas. Only certain kinds of refuse could be disposed of on the common muckhill, and fly-tipping was illegal. Thus butchers were required to deposit their

---

*MA, vol. 1, p. 124.

waste from slaughter at certain designated points on the outside of town after nine P.M. The bylaws stipulated that offal had to be taken away from the municipal dumps to be deposited into the country, on a daily basis probably, by borough subcontractors like Chambers and his waste disposal colleagues, who levied a small fee for their services. Some, like Rafe Cawdrey, chose to ignore this rule; their selfish disregard for basic hygiene incurred the wrath of the town fathers, as did butchers' pouring the blood from slaughter into the common gutters.

The borough insisted that the gutters be kept free from offal and human waste. Phrases like "for not scouring their gutters they are amerced" and "for not keeping clean his gutter" are commonly used in the record of fines. On April 14, 1559, John Shakespeare is found again among offenders who failed to keep their gutters clean. It is a tribute to the town's vigilance about hygiene that there were not more outbreaks of serious diseases and food poisonings. We often assume that the Elizabethans' sense of smell must have been more blunted than ours, but the strewing of rushes in houses and the obsession with sweet breath suggests otherwise. In *The Tempest,* Caliban's fishy smell offends Trinculo's nostrils; so does his own odor later, when he protests, "Monster, I do smell all horse-piss, at which my nose is in great indignation." Perhaps we've had it all wrong: perhaps they were intensely aware of the requirements of hygiene precisely because they had so few opportunities to wash and keep clean. There were strict injunctions against dogs fouling the streets, pavements, and gutters, and bylaws forbade dogs to roam free in the streets or go unmuzzled. Bitches in heat were a recurrent source of concern, and ducks and geese were prevented from going unattended, as were pigs without nose rings.

The first house beyond the Mere was the smithy of Richard Hornby. With the stream running past his house, Hornby was well placed, for a blacksmith's business required a plentiful supply of water. This is probably one of the reasons for the longevity of the Hornby family on this very spot. The next building was two joined-up houses that had been merged into a large home by the 1580s and were owned by a cantankerous tailor from Warwick, William Wedgewood. A contemporary document describes him as "contentious, proud and slanderous, oft busying himself with naughty matters and quarrelling with his honest neighbours," and the Earl of Warwick noted that he never wanted to see him again.* Richard Hornby was just the kind of "honest" neighbor that Wedgewood routinely annoyed, and sure enough the two of them became embroiled in a boundary dispute before too long. Hornby's house and the tailor's were separated by another earth mound. No customary elm stood here, but where it would have been there rose a post on Wedgewood's side to mark off the boundary of his property. Both neighbors were firmly ordered by the council to maintain their half of the boundary mound, which ran the whole distance between Henley Street and Gild Pits. Wedgewood had left Stratford by 1575. There is no record of him falling out with his neighbors to the west, the Shakespeares.

On this journey of 1582, William Shakespeare has now reached his own home. Things were not so good these days, but his parents' house was still the biggest in Henley Street and, although John Shakespeare was starting to shift assets, the family had not so far needed to sell up. John had probably already sold off the house in Greenhill Street that he had acquired in 1556, since no trace of the sale appears among later Shakespeare transactions. It may be, of course, that John had sold Greenhill Street to finance the purchase in 1575 of the western two bays of the Birthplace, which must have been costly owing to Henley Street's cachet among the Stratford elite. Even though the family now numbered seven and the house doubled as a working glover's premises and a wool shop, there seems to have been plenty of room by the standards of most people. By 1582, the death of the Shakespeares' youngest daughter may no longer have dominated their lives, and now that their economic fortunes were declining they had to harness all their energies to weather the storm and hope that at some point things would look up again.

It may be hard to imagine the young Shakespeare as a glover in light of the extraordinary achievements that came later, but there is no reason why he should have been anything other than good at

---

*Kemp, p. 208.

what he did. Gloving was one of the most respected crafts of the period, and he would hardly have turned up his nose at his own father's profession, which had, after all, secured the family's prosperity in the first place. In Rowe's words, Shakespeare appeared "to have given entirely into that way of living which his father proposed to him." Someone needed to take the Shakespeare gloves and other produce to Market Cross on Thursdays, and if his father could not do it then someone else from the house must.

Although the Shakespeares were the biggest single owners of frontage in Henley Street, the Whateleys were wealthier now and at least one other family living here was also richer and more influential: the Quineys. The Quineys were the first family of Stratford after the Cloptons and Combes. The phrase "social mobility" may not have existed at the time, but the concept certainly did. Shakespeare himself and his entire family bear witness to that, as do others who made good. The Quineys were yeoman merchants who had turned themselves into a local dynasty through a propitious marriage alliance with another family of Henley Street grandees, that of Thomas Phillips. Phillips had served alongside Adrian Quiney, in the first ever group of aldermen of the newly incorporated Stratford. The Phillips residence stood some way up west from the Birthplace, between the Ichiver-Johnson house, which later became the White Lion Inn and eventually the site of today's Birthplace archives, and the house of Peter Smart. It was a substantial property, consisting of a large barn and a three-bay house, the "fursen" house.*

Directly west of the Birthplace lived a family called Badger, which enjoyed close links with the Quineys. The George Badger who occupied this house during Will Shakespeare's time in Henley Street may have been Richard Quiney's godfather.† The Badger house boasted an impressive frontage of fifty feet or so. It was separated from the Shakespeares' by, probably, a narrow garden rather

---

*This would seem to be the same as calling it the "gorse" house. The Phillipses' was a substantial dwelling and there is no record of gorse being traded in Stratford. They may of course have grown broom ornamentally around the house, but this seems an implausible source for the name.

†*MA*, vol. 4, p. 40, n. 3.

than just the customary earth mound. Eventually Badger bought a strip of land between John Shakespeare and himself for fifty shillings, a not inconsiderable sum. According to the deed of sale this strip, or "toft," which ran the entire length between Henley Street and Gild Pits, measured half a yard wide and twenty-eight yards long.

Why Badger wanted to purchase such a narrow strip of land has never been satisfactorily explained, for a boundary, which was the shared responsibility of both owners, probably separated the Shakespeares and him already. It is just possible that Badger desired to erect a wall or fence for some reason connected to the fact that he was, in the parlance of the Protestants, an "obstinate" Catholic. Badger may have been preparing to set up a safe house for local Catholics and that is how his house may have been used in the end during the Gunpowder Plot. We do know that Badger never reneged on the faith of his forebears. We do not know whether it was he who slipped his neighbor John Shakespeare a copy of a Catholic testament that would be found one day, as we shall see, hidden in the house in which Shakespeare was born. The Jesuit mission of 1580 used the Midlands as a center and Badger would have known about it as surely as the Catholics over in Shottery. There is no evidence that Campion and Parsons passed through the Badger house during this period, but neither can we be certain that they did not. Stratford was, after all, wide open, with only toll gates down at the bridge. Furthermore, the Catholic Cloptons sat in their large mansion not far away, in the Welcombe Hills. From the Cloptons to the Badgers in Henley Street would have taken all of forty minutes cross-field in the sixteenth century. The hamlet of Shottery, traditionally a crucible of organized Catholic resistance, is almost equidistant in the other direction. Not only did the teenage Shakespeare marry into a Shottery family, but years earlier his father had already had business dealings with the Hathaways. The young Shakespeare would have known pretty well everyone's allegiances locally. It is a tribute to the prevailing climate of tolerance in Stratford even in the troubled 1580s that most of its citizens just got on with their lives and kept religion at arm's length when it came to business and much else.

There was another Catholic connection in Henley Street, and that was through the Stratford carrier and quasi postman William

Greenway, who ensured that Shakespeare, Field, and Badger's son Richard, who joined a firm of London stationers, would have had regular news of their loved ones while in London. We do not know how often Greenway undertook the round-trip to London, whether it was once a month or twice. It took an experienced, well-horsed traveler less than three days each way. As well as himself shuttling between London and Stratford, Greenway also seems to have provided the means for others to do so. No one really knows why Greenway operated this service or why he heaved himself off to London with a certain regularity, but as so often in Stratford, in case of doubt, one may want to think Catholic.

Greenway lived in Middle Row, where he ran a draper's business. But he also rented a house and a barn on the south side of Henley Street.* From their house, the Shakespeares looked out directly across at the ancestral house of the Quineys, whose head then was Adrian Quiney, with the Cawdreys to the east (left) of them and Greenway even farther over to the left, probably opposite Hornby. There is no clear indication of why Greenway required these additional and rather costly premises, which were Corporation property and featured four elm trees. An informed guess would be that he used them for stabling horses, that these were the premises from which he ran a kind of rental business, perhaps in partnership with the blacksmith Hornby who would shoe his horses. Greenway's property holdings were substantial. Eventually he allied himself through marriage with his Henley Street neighbor William Cawdrey, the brother probably of the butcher Rafe Cawdrey from Bridge Street among whose children were the future Jesuit George Cawdrey and a daughter called Ursula. It is this Ursula Cawdrey whom Greenway married in 1569. He was henceforth the brother-in-law of a zealous young Catholic who may well have met Jesuits during their stay in the Midlands. Within three years of Campion's death on December 1, 1581, George Cawdrey was ordained.

Not long before the ordination, Greenway had called on Robert

---

*Some Stratford historians, notably Fripp and Jones, place his house on the site of the present 46–49, in which case his property would have sat opposite the Shakespeares'.

Debdale of Shottery in London. By then the young man, who had come over with Campion, was interned in the Gatehouse prison at Westminster, usually the first port of call for Catholic internees before they were carted off to the Tower or any of the other major prisons of London. It was on November 3, 1581, that Greenway, acting on behalf of the Debdale family, conveyed to their son two cheeses, a loaf of bread, and some money. It is unthinkable that the carrier would not have talked about this to his family and to his friends and neighbors in Henley Street, or that the fate of young Debdale would not have been a major talking point in Shottery and Stratford, the more so since these were the weeks immediately preceding Campion's execution.

Debdale was released unharmed from the Tower, but the reprieve was temporary. Five years later, he was executed in London, at the age of twenty-six. He had been received into the Society of Jesus in Rheims only two years earlier; his time there had overlapped with young George Cawdrey's. These two Catholic Stratford boys obviously knew each other well, and both must have known Will Shakespeare. The young Shakespeare did not need to follow John Cottom to Lancashire to pursue a personal Catholic agenda, assuming that he harbored such yearnings at all. The Catholics were on his doorstep in Stratford, and he needed to look no farther than Shottery to meet the diehards. The role in the Catholic insurgency of this small hamlet on a brook in a gentle dip a mile or so west of Stratford awaits a full investigation. Here, after all, was a community locked into recusancy, a place in which a few closely knit families lived cheek-by-jowl in mutual support.

By 1582, the year of his imaginary stroll home from a tavern, the teenage apprentice Will Shakespeare must have been touched by the deep divisions in the nation. They were starkly reflected in his own town. But he also clearly learned to live with them, as most of his contemporaries did. Whether he felt attracted to one faith rather than another is impossible to determine. His works provide little guidance. Unlike Spenser in *The Faerie Queene* or Milton in *Paradise Lost,* Shakespeare never shows his colors. The glorious muddle over religion in *Hamlet,* whether that of the Catholic purgatory or the Wittenberg theses, echoes the divided allegiances of the nation, and perhaps of the Shakespeare family. When religion finally does emerge as an imaginative force in the last plays, and particularly in *The Tempest*, it is blandly ecumenical, a general spiritual source of comfort.

It was during these early days, probably, that the young Shakespeare learned discretion. His school may well have been infiltrated by a Catholic fifth column tasked to influence the hearts and minds of their young charges. The cumulative evidence about the staff there certainly points that way, and the masters in question would have found Stratford a fertile breeding ground. Not only were Simon Hunt, Robert Debdale, and George Cawdrey Catholics, but also two of them were of Will's generation. We can readily imagine the teenage Shakespeare catching up on Debdale through Greenway, as others in Henley Street must have done. Of course, he would talk to the "messenger" from across the street just as the tailor and smith do to each other in *King John*. Of course, he would have known that the Badgers were recusant. Whether he knew the full extent of their involvement with the Catholic cause is a different matter, but undoubtedly his parents would have. One of the greatest riches of Shakespeare's imaginative works is their dialectical duality, his extraordinary ability to see everything from different points of view. This is as deeply true of the plays as a whole as it is of his soliloquies, whether in *Hamlet* or in *Macbeth*. It is commonly understood as an intrinsic part of his enormous talent and range, and so it is. But it is also a response specifically to life as he encountered it at just this moment in time, in a provincial town split along sectarian lines but not radically divided against itself. The good people of Stratford were too engrossed in business, materially too competitive even, to be swayed totally by politics. The big world of national politics was best left to the local lords of the manor. They ran the show, anyway, or so people assumed.

For that matter, Shakespeare throughout his life deeply distrusted demagogues and particularly, perhaps, the so-called tribunes of the people. This theme runs through the plays, from the very early second part of *Henry VI* and the rebellion spearheaded by Jack Cade to the rabble-rousers in the late tragedy *Coriolanus*. The businessman in him ever erred on the side of conservatism and skepticism, but as the child of a culture balanced on a knife edge between two faiths he could be both everything and nothing. Above all, he was circumspect. The fate of Debdale, the threat to Cawdrey, and the stirrings of sedition at his school may all have contributed to forging an identity that was always hard to pin down. It is not because of the generic conventions of drama that Shakespeare became elusive; it is because being elusive could be a matter of life and death in the country in which he grew up. We cannot possibly know what John Shakespeare told his sons as, one after the other, they attended the King's New School. But we can be reasonably sure that he instructed them to keep their noses clean where politics and religion were concerned, whether or not his own views leaned toward either creed.

By the time he had reached the age of eighteen, Shakespeare had probably been working for his father for three or four years. That it was a struggle we can hardly doubt, for the Shakespeares' straitened circumstances continued to be treated sympathetically by the council. Will had grown up rich and now was struggling to keep the family afloat, or at least to save them from having to sell their house in Henley Street. It may have been worth anything upward of £500, to judge by other properties in the same street. This period of his family's humiliation must have rankled deeply. It may be the reason why he could never really leave Stratford behind.

4.

Enter Wife and Daughter: 1582–83

oward the end of the summer of 1582, Will Shakespeare made Anne Hathaway pregnant. He was eighteen years and four months old; she may have been twenty-six. The only reason for thinking that she was his senior by eight years is that the inscription on her tombstone declares that she was sixty-seven when she died in 1623. But the figures 1 and 7 are easily confused; if she was sixty-one rather than sixty-seven when she died, she would have been Will's contemporary at the King's New School. The parish records for Holy Trinity begin only in 1558, which is unfortunate, since a sixty-seven-year-old Anne would have been baptised in 1556. Of course, she may not have been recorded in Holy Trinity at all but rather in one of the adjacent parishes; nothing, however, has yet come to light.

The Hathaways of Shottery and the Shakespeares of Henley Street knew one another before their children got together. They knew one another quite well, in fact: John Shakespeare twice stood as surety for Anne Hathaway's father, Richard Hathaway or Gardner, as he was known, in 1566 and paid off substantial debts for him. The Hathaways were major players in Shottery. Hewlands Farm had been in their possession from at least 1543. The main building there today is largely the mid-fifteenth-century farm that Anne and Will knew, whereas the higher house toward the gardens was probably added by Anne's brother Richard in the early seventeenth century. The hall, the buttery, and the imposing old bake oven would all have been archi-familiar sights to Anne Hathaway and perhaps also to young Will Shakespeare; "perhaps," because he may not have done much of his courting here and his relationship with the other Hathaways may have been a fraught one. The location of the farm just beyond Shottery burn is a rural idyll. It fits perfectly with Celia's directions in *As You Like It* to the "sheep-cote" in a dell "down in the neighbour bottom," where a "rank of osiers" stretches past a "murmuring stream." In the eighteenth century, the Stratford antiquarian John Jordan (1746–1809) called the prospect south from Anne Hathaway's ancestral home "one of the finest meadows in England." It still is.

We do not know how Will and Anne met, or how they found the opportunity for what in *Measure for Measure* Shakespeare called the "stealth of our most mutual entertainment." What we do know is that they had sex during the summer of 1582, before they were married. "Young men will do't if they come to't, / By Cock, they are to blame," the mad Ophelia intones, and she continues with "Quoth she 'Before you tumbled me, You promised me to wed,'" to which she imagines the young man replying, "'So would I 'a' done, by yonder sun, / An thou hadst not come to my bed.'" Shakespeare is here without a doubt recalling his own proverbial roll in the hay, the difference being that as a young man he did honor his commitment to Anne and married her. No wonder Shakespeare is so sympathetic to young Claudio and Juliet in *Measure for Measure,* who were already lawfully married before sexual congress took place, even though their union had yet to be sanctioned by the church. Will and Anne consummated their relationship in the teeth of church and religion. When Anne told him that she was missing her "courses," the term commonly in use at the time, he must have known exactly what it meant.

On Tuesday, November 27, 1582, the Worcester diocesan consistory court granted William Shakespeare and Anne Hathaway a special license allowing them to marry without the full three proclamations of the banns. They were in a hurry, since she was three months pregnant. Canon law forbade the reading of banns between Advent Sunday, which fell on December 2, 1582, and the Octave of Epiphany, on January 13, 1583. This left only November 30 for a single reading of the banns, as stipulated by the bond lodged the day after the grant of the license. As a minor, Shakespeare was not required to be present on that Tuesday in Worcester Cathedral's south aisle, where the consistory court convened.

The grant of the special license in the Bishop's Register at Worcester reads, tersely, "Item eodem die similis emanavit licencia inter Willelmum Shaxpere et Annam Whateley de Temple Grafton," which translates as "On that same day was issued a similar license between William Shakespeare and Anne Whateley of Temple Grafton." On the following day, Wednesday, November 28, a bond of sureties was posted by two farmers from Shottery, Fulke Sandells and John Richardson, who were friends of the bride and her family. The purpose of this bond, which at £40 was huge, was to indemnify the Bishop and the consistory court in case of legal action arising out of impediments to a marriage that had not gone through the usual procedures. It seems to have been a formality, but the conditions were certainly rigorous:

> The condition of this obligation is such that if hereafter there shall not appear any lawful let or impediment by reason of any precontract, consanguinity, affinity or by any other lawful means whatsoever but that William Shakespeare on the one party and Anne Hathaway of Stratford in the diocese of Worcester, maiden, may lawfully solemnize matrimony together and in the same afterwards remain and continue like man and wife according unto the laws in that behalf provided, and moreover if there be not at this present time any action, suit, or quarrel or demand moved or depending before any judge ecclesiastical or temporal for and concerning any such lawful let or impediment, and moreover if the said William Shakespeare do not proceed to solemnisation of marriage with the said Anne Hathaway without the consent of her friends, and also if the said William do upon his own proper costs and expenses defend and save harmless the right Reverend father in God Lord John [Whitgift] Bishop of Worcester and his officers for licensing them the said William and Anne to be married together with once asking of the banns of matrimony between them and for all other causes which may ensure by reason or occasion thereof, that then

the said obligation to be void and of none effect or else to stand and abide in full force and virtue.*

According to the *grant of the license,* Shakespeare married Anne Whateley of Temple Grafton, a hamlet four miles southwest of Stratford, while the *bond* identifies the bride as Anne Hathaway of Stratford. This is an unusual case of disagreement between the bonds and the entries granting licenses in the Worcester register. The entry for the license in the Bishop's register was almost certainly copied from the application (or "allegation"), which would have contained all the relevant details for the various parties involved.† It follows that the woman whom William Shakespeare married was called Anne Whateley of Temple Grafton on the allegation that we no longer have, and that Anne Whateley from Temple Grafton, of the register and allegation, and Anne Hathaway from Stratford, of the bond, are both Anne Hathaway from Shottery. For reasons that we do not fully understand, the church authorities in Worcester accepted a bond for a bride who had two different names and two different addresses.

How Anne Hathaway from Shottery turned up on November 27, 1582, as Anne Whateley from Temple Grafton is one of the enduring mysteries of the Shakespeare story. Since the 1582 bond was discovered only in 1836, by the brilliant Stratford antiquarian Robert B. Wheler (1785–1857), it follows that until the publication of Rowe's life in 1709 no one in the wider world knew that Shakespeare had married Anne Hathaway. Rowe knew neither the register nor the bond, but he knew the bride's true identity. Shakespeare, he wrote, "thought fit to marry while he was yet very young" (Rowe says nothing of Anne's seniority to her husband), and "his wife was

---

*Chambers (1930), vol. 2, pp. 41–42.

†The entry is a clean transcript, and was not made on the day but written up later (Brinkworth, p. 88), but Schoenbaum disagrees. Following J. W. Gray's classic study (1905) of the Shakespeare marriage, Schoenbaum writes that "the clerk, one suspects, was copying from a hastily written temporary memorandum, or from an unfamiliar hand in an allegation; he had just been dealing with Whateley [William Whateley], and by a process of unconscious association made the substitution" (Schoenbaum [1975], p. 71).

the daughter of one Hathaway, said to have been a substantial yeoman in the neighbourhood of Stratford." One wonders how in 1709 Rowe knew about Hathaway: the only written records from the period that were available to him were the registers of Holy Trinity, which are silent about Shakespeare's marriage. Nor does Anne's maiden name appear on her gravestone, which merely tells us that she was "Anne wife of William Shakespeare." Rowe does not engage with Anne's pregnancy because he knew nothing about the Worcester license and bond, and the proof they afford of Shakespeare's impetuous sexual behavior. But he did know, and without access to any of the sources available to us, who Anne was. For the first time, and in a widely available text, the surname of Shakespeare's bride was revealed in 1709.

Rowe's authority was the oral tradition of Stratford and ultimately the poet and playwright William Davenant. Davenant lived long enough to know the famous Restoration actor Thomas Betterton, who was Rowe's main source for his life of Shakespeare. In Rowe's words, Betterton's love of Shakespeare "engaged him to make a journey into Warwickshire, on purpose to gather up what remains he could of a name for which he had so great a value." Betterton was born in 1635 and may have traveled up to Stratford after becoming a major Shakespearian actor in the Restoration theater, sometime between the 1660s and 1680s.* The earlier Betterton went up to Stratford, the more reliable may be the information he imparted to Rowe, since Shakespeare's daughter lived until 1662 and his granddaughter until 1670, and his sister's family lived in Henley Street until 180 years after his death.

Richard Hathaway had died in September 1581, and shortly afterward her brother left home for Tysoe near Stratford. Anne may also have left Shottery after her father's death. Perhaps neither she

---

*Some biographers have implied that Betterton journeyed to Warwickshire on Rowe's behest. While there is nothing contentious about that, it would make the date of Betterton's journey later, as does the *Oxford Dictionary of National Biography* entry ("Late in his life Betterton journeyed to Stratford-upon-Avon to do research on Shakespeare..."). Betterton died in 1710; Halliwell-Phillipps argues that he is not likely to have undertaken his trip to Stratford toward the end of his life but rather earlier.

nor her brother got on with their stepmother, Joan, and their various younger stepsiblings. But who was the mother of Anne Hathaway, her four brothers (Bartholomew and three Richards), and her sister Catherine? This remains a mystery. Nothing is known about Anne Hathaway's mother or where she came from. She and Richard Hathaway must have married at some point in the 1550s. If she was a Whateley of Temple Grafton, then Anne may have returned to Temple Grafton after her father's death because it was her mother's home village. It seems then that the people who drafted the application for the Worcester license may have been Anne's mother's family from Temple Grafton, while the huge bond was posted on behalf of the Hathaways, who owed John Shakespeare for past favors.

In our search for the church where Will and Anne married, it would assist us greatly to know where Anne's father wed his second wife, Joan. The obvious place would have been Holy Trinity, but there is no record of such a union in the church's register even though, in his will, the same Richard Hathaway asked to be buried in Holy Trinity's churchyard. Nor do we know where Anne's brother Bartholomew married. Since later Hathaways are quite happily affiliated to Holy Trinity, it is hard to argue that they might have had some principled objection to using the Stratford parish church. But just such ideological objections have been adduced as the possible reason for Will's and Anne's choice of a church other than Holy Trinity, a church just like that at Temple Grafton. The reason suggested is that the minister at Temple Grafton was a notoriously stubborn Catholic.

On November 2, 1586, at the height of the trouble with Mary Queen of Scots and during the buildup toward the confrontation with Catholic Spain and the Armada, the church commissioners published a document entitled "A Survey of the State of the Ministry in Warwickshire." In it they scrutinized the ministers of the various parishes at that time in an attempt to stamp out or roll back recusancy. Stratford-upon-Avon is given the all clear, but John Frith, the vicar of Temple Grafton, did not find favor. He was "an old priest and unsound in religion." He could, it seems, "neither preach nor read well," and his main interest was the curing of "hawks that are hurt or diseased, for which purpose many do usually repair to him."

He was clearly recusant but to all appearances a harmless eccentric.

Or maybe he only seemed so: that interest in hawks may not have been quite as innocuous as the Protestant inquisitors thought, for the role of hawker was one of the preferred disguises adopted by fugitive Jesuits in England. We know this from John Gerard's account of how he went to ground after landing near Mundesley in Norfolk in November 1588. He needed to make a plausible excuse if he were challenged for wandering about and chose to pretend that he was looking for his stray falcon. This same excuse was used by other priests, it seems. According to Gerard, he had no sooner split from his companion Oldcorne when he saw people heading toward him. He went up to them and asked whether they had seen his hawk: "perhaps they had heard its bell tinkling as it was flying around." He intended to convey the impression that he was wandering about aimlessly searching for it, since that was how falconers behaved. This would make it seem less strange that he found himself in unfamiliar lanes; instead, "they would merely think that I had wandered here in my search." He was credible enough on that occasion, and the good people of Norfolk commiserated with him over his lost hawk. In this light one may well muse whether old John Frith's passion for hawks was not a cover for Catholic activities, to enable Jesuits and ordinary recusants to repair to him under the pretext of consulting him about their hawks. If so, Frith was not found out, even though the authorities clearly knew of his Catholic sympathies. He was vicar of Temple Grafton for many years and probably knew Anne Hathaway's mother and the Whateleys of Temple Grafton well. That John Frith married William Shakespeare and Anne Whateley/Hathaway cannot be ruled out; it might even be likely, if we could somehow show that the couple wanted to marry in the old faith. But the records for Worcester suggest otherwise. In those cases where we have both the entry in the Worcester register and documentary proof of where the couple subsequently wed, the two places are rarely the same. The records do demonstrate that the parish cited in the Worcester grant of a license is usually the parish of the bride's residence rather than the parish of the groom or the parish of the marriage; this strengthens the idea that Anne was a Whateley from Temple Grafton.

We should consider two further matters relating to the marriage. The first one concerns the church at Billesley, and the second the odd business of Shakespeare's father dragging himself out of retirement from the town council to vote at just the time when his son was having sex with Anne Hathaway. For a long time now the chapel at Billesley has been high on the list of potential settings for the Shakespeare wedding. The reason is that Shakespeare's granddaughter Elizabeth chose it for her marriage in 1649 to John Barnard of Abington Hall. No one has ever established why she would pick Billesley of all places. Billesley is today little more than a clump of farms less than a mile or so across the wold from Shakespeare's mother's home over in Wilmcote. Perhaps something as prosaic as that suggested it to Will and Anne as a venue. Who is to say that Shakespeare had not played or roamed around here—he who loved the countryside as deeply as Wordsworth did. The same recusancy survey that damned Temple Grafton and Baddesley Clinton sounds a mellow note about Billesley. The parish was serviced by one "Robert Spenser, no preacher nor learned, a companion and goodfellow in all companies well liked and commended of his parishioners for an honest quiet fellow as ever came among them." Instead of being married by dissolute recusants, Anne and Will may have tied the knot through the good offices of an approved servant of the Anglican church.

To recapitulate, then, there is a distinct possibility that toward the end of November, or perhaps on Saturday, December 1, 1582, William Shakespeare married Anne Whateley of Temple Grafton, who was the daughter of the deceased Richard Hathaway of Shottery and his first wife. If the wedding did indeed take place on December 1, immediately after the reading of the banns on the previous day, then the Shakespeares were married on the first anniversary of Campion's martyrdom in London. If the marriage took place in a recusant church such as Temple Grafton it would be nearly impossible not to think of this timing as a deliberate act of commemoration. Over and against that, though, are the biological imperatives that expedited this marriage. Anne's mother probably having been a Whateley from Temple Grafton, it was likely this side of the family that gave her away; at least, it was they who completed the application for the license to marry that lies behind the entry in the Bishops' register in Worcester. A separate bond for *both* parties was posted by friends of Anne Hathaway and her family, and this document refers to Anne as a Hathaway. That bond remained undiscovered until the nineteenth century. Temple Grafton may have been the place of the wedding, but the wider evidence from Worcester regarding licenses and weddings generally suggests otherwise. Hence the possibility that the chapel at Billesley may have served.

There was no particular reason for young Will Shakespeare to find his way to Shottery, where his family had no relatives; the only Shottery family that the Shakespeares of Henley Street are on record as knowing were the Hathaways. If Anne lived in Temple Grafton, as she seems to have done in 1581–82, it is most unlikely that Will would have met her there. As so often in this story, the answer may lie rather closer to home. We should not rule out the possibility that Anne Whateley may have been related to the Whateleys of Henley Street, that she may have been a cousin or second cousin of that family, and that in the months between her father's death in September 1581 and November 1582 she may have been in the habit of visiting her relatives in Henley Street. None of this can be proven, of course. The Henley Street Whateleys had strong Catholic connections, with George Whateley's brothers John and Robert being recusant priests. Robert was reported by the recusancy commission of 1592 for Henley-in-Arden to be "an old priest called Sir Robert Whateley, who used to come to his friends, he being a man of four score year old." If this means anything it is that he visited his friends' home to say mass in secret, the way Campion, Parsons, Garnett, Gerard, Oldcorne, Southwell, and all the others did. Of course, in 1592 any eighty-year-old priest would almost inevitably be a Catholic. A second certificate by the recusancy commissioners, of September 25, 1592, also about Henley-in-Arden, refers to "one Sir Robert Whateley presented there for a recusant, an old massing priest, resorting often thither, but hardly to be found." One wonders whether either Robert or John Whateley married Will Shakespeare and Anne Hathaway (or Anne Whateley) in their parish church over at Henley-in-Arden. It is an intriguing thought, which has never yet been explored. It is true that none of the Shakespeare wills or wills related to them seem to include any reference to the Whateleys. Then again, there is no reference in

Shakespeare's will to the Hathaways, either. Perhaps they had been opposed to the marriage in 1582, or perhaps it was Anne who desired to break off all contact with her father's new family.

The Whateleys were grand and remained so throughout this period of the Shakespeares' misfortunes. If they underwrote Anne's marriage out of loyalty to her mother, then the Shakespeares could be thought to have done well with this union. If only there were some documented connection between George Whateley and the Shakespeares other than the fact that they were both glovers and whittawers in the same street.

As it happens, there may be, and it involves one of the minor mysteries of the Shakespeare story. It takes the shape of the town council meeting of Wednesday, September 2, 1582, just around the time when Will and Anne's daughter Susanna was conceived. The Michaelmas meeting was the most important of the year: its remit was to elect the new mayor for the following year. What renders this meeting more special even than usual is that John Shakespeare emerged from his house in Henley Street and walked to the Gildhall to vote. He had not done so since January 1577, nor would he do so again before he was dismissed from the council in September 1586. There is no doubt that on this day John participated in the meeting: he is "pricked"—that is, checked in by a dot against his name—and the clerk indicated how he voted. The question is why now.

On that Wednesday in September 1582 the council of fourteen aldermen and eleven burgesses chose a new mayor from three alderman candidates: Adrian Quiney, John Sadler, and George Whateley. Sadler won with eleven votes to Quiney's eight and Whateley's two. The only people to vote for Whateley were Quiney's own son (who therefore voted against his father) and William Smith. John Shakespeare voted for his old friend John Sadler, one of the wealthiest property owners in town, who held real estate in Church Street, the Bear inn, and the mill on the Avon. He was almost certainly closely related to Hamnet and Judith Sadler. We will never know why so many votes were cast for him. He never served as mayor but excused himself, probably on the grounds of ill health, since he died within six months of this meeting. The office of mayor was expensive as well as prestigious, but Sadler was rich and unlikely to balk at that.

Adrian Quiney, whose grandson would one day marry John Shake-speare's granddaughter, was runner-up and duly served as mayor of Stratford for the 1582–83 year in lieu of Sadler. However opaque the politics of this meeting may be, it is fairly clear that something was up. There would otherwise be no reason to vote for a man too old to serve and whose election was bound to cross Whateley.

The presence of John Shakespeare is surely significant. It can hardly be that Sadler needed his vote. There must have been personal reasons for John to appear, when he seems to have lived under virtual house arrest. The only possibility that accords with the facts we have is that there was some link to the romance between Will and Anne. We know that these two were now lovers. We know very little else about the Shakespeare family during this month and so the temptation is to connect the vote and the liaison. If they are linked, then John Shakespeare's voting against Whateley was a hostile act. It would confirm that Anne was, as her surname suggests, related by blood ties to this family and that the two Henley Street clans had come to grief over the love affair between their children. If there was such a fight, it was unlikely to have been over Will's impregnating Anne, which was probably not yet known. For all we know, John Shakespeare rejoined the council briefly to assert his status to Whateley before all his assembled peers. His fellow councilors must have been stunned to see him there after so many absences.

After they were married, the young couple would have lived together, as was the custom, in his parents' house in Henley Street. By 1582 the house was pretty full, and with Edmund Shakespeare barely two years old it must have been noisy, too. Will and Anne would soon add to the noise with their baby. Anne Shakespeare and her in-laws needed to get along; all sorts of complex negotiations will have been going on. We can only speculate, but the grinding routines of domestic life will have taken up much of the young couple's energies. During the day Will was probably working as a glover on the premises while his mother and Anne shared the rearing of little Edmund. John, Will, and Gilbert must have worked as glovers downstairs in the eastern part of the building and in the barn at the back of the garden, while the women would have displayed their wares from the windows facing out into Henley Street. They would undoubtedly have helped with preparing the skins and leather to be molded and cut into gloves, and they might have taken it in turn to deal with customers or passing trade on its way up to Coventry and Birmingham or down to Oxford and Banbury.

That the newlywed couple needed a bedroom and some privacy is self-evident and we should not shy away from imagining the place on the basis of available clues. Their bed, rather like ours today and just like Kate's in *The Taming of the Shrew*, would have had pillows, bolsters, coverlets, and sheets. The room undoubtedly had a chamber pot. Eventually, a cradle was added, and then a trucklebed for the children. If Shakespeare's parents occupied the room that was called "the best chamber" or "the great chamber" in two contemporary inventories of the Birthplace, then he and Anne probably lodged across the stairs in the so-called stairhead chamber or "the chamber of the hall," the second-best bedroom in the house.* At

---

*These terms derive from the inventories of Lewis Hiccox (1627) and John Rutter (1648), who occupied the Birthplace at different times. During Hiccox's period of residency, Shakespeare's sister and her family still lived in a wing of the house, and when the Rutter 1648 inventory was drafted, Joan Shakespeare-Hart had been dead for only two years. Both her nieces were alive; Judith would be so for another fourteen years.

The Hiccox and Rutter inventories mirror each other quite closely, which is to be expected, as they show the same house a mere twenty years apart. What differences there are arise from the different terminology employed by different inventory takers. Since Hiccox acquired his lease on the property from Shakespeare himself, this was the house that Shakespeare had himself lived in, although the cottage at the back was not there when the playwright moved house in 1597. Hiccox turned the house into an inn; his inventory lists no fewer than thirteen discrete spaces, whose contents are itemized. These include the kitchen and the brewhouse as well as the cellar (similarly in Rutter), which leaves something like ten rooms. It is not surprising to find these stuffed with beds in the inventory of an inn, whose purpose would have been to accommodate as many people as possible overnight.

The inventories are tantalizing documents. They tease us with the amount of detail they provide about the Shakespeare house(s) (the plural is used in Hiccox, which makes it clear that the entire house minus the back cottage is meant), but without, of course, telling us how John Shakespeare and his family lived here. Nor do we know whether the terms used to describe the rooms date from the Shakespeares or were invented by the two publicans. Rooms in inns *did* have names, and for this we need look no further than Shakespeare's *Henry IV* plays or, indeed, the huge inventory for the Swan inn down near the Stratford bridge.

night in winter they were kept warm thanks to the open-plan design of the house, which would have diffused the heat from the fire in the main chimney. Later, during her father's long months away in London, Susanna probably slept in her mother's bed while the twins shared the trucklebed.

At the back of their house, the Shakespeares obviously had a privy or jakes, or, as polite Londoners called it at the time, a place of easement. It has been alleged that their house must have smelled from the vats of urine needed for gloving, but such vats probably sat outside in a barn at the bottom of the garden. Acidy deposits have been discovered in the soil toward the bottom of the former Shakespeare garden, pointing perhaps to glovers' activities in this area. Bearing in mind that the Birthplace garden must have contained a well, neither the Shakespeares' privy nor any of the glovers' vats could have stood anywhere near it or been decanting into the soil close to it. We know that the Shakespeares owned a big barn on Gild Pits, at the far end of the bottom of the garden. This must have been partly glovers' work premises and a storage space for wool, which may be why John Shakespeare built it in the first instance.

The Birthplace was as good a house as any and better than most, since it was the single largest three-bay house in Henley Street. From the way the ground rent was pegged to a proportion of burgage we can tell that John Shakespeare's original purchase of the Henley Street property in 1556 was the eastern bay of the house, which to this day conveys the impression from the outside of a self-contained dwelling. The famous 1590 list of manorial tenants (effectively freeholders) of Henley Street rates the eastern wing at sixpence ground rent, exactly half a burgage, and the western part of the house, the two smaller bays, at thirteen pence, that is, just over a complete burgage. Its entire frontage runs to an impressive ninety feet.* According to the best-informed current opinion on the house, the whole three-bay structure is really one rectangle. The western two bays must have been partitioned off from the eastern one until John bought the

---

*Burgages were calculated at 3.5 perches by 12 perches, with a perch measuring 16.5 feet. In other words, a full burgage would have a frontage of 57.75 feet and a depth of 198 feet and yield an annual rate of 12 pence.

rest of the house in 1575, for his purchase records "two messuages" with two gardens and two orchards. In other words, until 1575 the Birthplace may have been divided into three discrete units consisting of the Shakespeares' eastern bay and a middle and western bay. It is just possible that some of the inner partitioning of the house was retained or restored by John Shakespeare as his family expanded after 1575. This would explain why the Hiccox inventory of the house (he acquired the lease from William Shakespeare) uses the plural "houses." Conversions were fashionable at the time and the young couple may have been grateful for space to themselves.

On Sunday, May 26, 1583, Anne and William Shakespeare took their firstborn, a baby daughter, to be baptised. The name Susanna was neither in their families nor common in Stratford. When names in this period fall outside the family, our first instinct should be to look for likely godparents, as with the next two Shakespeare children, the twins Hamnet and Judith: we are almost certain that the Shakespeares' friends Hamnet and Judith Sadler stood as godparents.

The name Susanna appears for the first time in Stratford in 1574; Susanna Shakespeare was only the sixth person to be so named in the town. It was a name favored by Puritans and derives from the Apocrypha, where Susanna is the virtuous wife of Joachim.* If Susanna was named after anyone locally it is likely that she was Susanna Woodward, the wife of the same Richard Tyler who was taken out of William Shakespeare's will. The fact that Susanna Woodward had a sister called Judith and two daughters called Susanna and Judith is hardly a coincidence. John Shakespeare and Richard Tyler's father, William, had served together on the town council in the 1560s; William Tyler may have been Shakespeare's godfather. There would be a family logic to William and Anne Shakespeare asking young Tyler's wife in turn to stand as godmother to Susanna, a second-generation godparenting by the Tylers of the Shakespeares: William Tyler of William Shakespeare, followed by

---

*Even his daughter's name confuses the issue with regard to Shakespeare's religious beliefs (assuming that the choice of name has a bearing on them at all), since the book in which Susanna occurs, the Book of Daniel, is canonical for Roman Catholics and is considered apocryphal by Protestants.

Susanna Tyler (née Woodward) of Susanna Shakespeare, and perhaps even Judith Woodward of Judith Shakespeare. The choice of a Puritan name further muddies the waters around Shakespeare's religious inclinations. No one has ever pursued the ramifications of this scenario, but if Anne and Will Shakespeare chose Susanna Woodward as their firstborn's godmother, we ought to try and find out why they might have done so. The Woodwards lived in Shottery Manor alongside the Burmans and Paces, neighbors of Anne Hathaway's family and of the devoutly Catholic Debdales.

Susanna Shakespeare's likely godmother was the granddaughter of Robert Perrott, the Puritan owner of Luscombe Manor in Snitterfield, a wealthy brewer and the lessee of a building that survives intact today in Rother Market as the White Swan. In the sixteenth century this was a tavern called the King's Hall or the King's House. Its striking sixteenth-century mural of Tobias and Raphael was rediscovered in 1927 and can again be enjoyed in the same spot where it has been for centuries. The tavern is so close to Henley Street that Shakespeare must have seen it; he probably drank an occasional ale or sack in that very room. His daughter's godmother was the daughter of Master Richard Woodward and was the only child to inherit nothing from her wealthy Puritan grandfather. It seems that Susanna Woodward married the twenty-two-year-old Richard Tyler without her parents' consent, because Perrott's will stipulates that her siblings stood to inherit from him the "residue of my stock and goods" provided that they "be dutiful and obedient and match themselves in marriage with the consent of their parents." Even Susanna Woodward's father cut her out, though he left some money for her son's schooling. To be doubly disinherited must have been a bitter blow for the newlywed Susanna and Richard. One wonders whether old Perrott acted out of mere pique, or whether there may be a Catholic angle here: perhaps the Tylers were too Catholic for the Puritan Perrott. By marrying a Tyler, Susanna Woodward may have crossed a sectarian divide that the rest of her family could not bridge. However, the names she and her husband chose for their children suggest otherwise. The odds are that the Tyler-Woodwards were Protestants. If so, and if the Shakespeares were indeed close to them, as the first draft of the 1616 will also indicates, then Will and Anne Shakespeare may have chosen in 1583 to ally themselves with one of the few committed Protestant families of Shottery.

If there is a Shottery connection here, then perhaps Anne Shakespeare had the final say over her daughters' names, and perhaps she chose as godparents the only Protestant friends she had in Shottery. Perhaps she left Shottery for this reason. How that would play with the recusant Whateleys or, for that matter, with Shakespeare's mother, Mary Arden, and her Catholic Arden links is anyone's guess. If Anne Hathaway was a committed Protestant at heart, that would dispose of any idea that she and Will sought out a Catholic priest to marry them. Billesley with its conformist vicar becomes ever more likely as the site of the wedding.

There is more to suggest that there may be a distinctly Protestant aspect to the name of the Shakespeares' firstborn. Of the six Stratford Susannas from this period, three were so named in the space of six weeks: Susanna, daughter of William Perrott (Robert Perrott's cousin), on April 9, 1583; Susanna, daughter of Richard Baker, on April 29, 1583; and Susanna Shakespeare, on May 26, 1583. Three Susannas with the surnames Perrott, Baker, Shakespeare, the first two being arch-Protestants. This is, to say the least, strange company for the future chief dramatist of England to keep, and particularly when other evidence about his faith seems to point in a diametrically opposite direction.

The Sunday before Susanna's baptism in Holy Trinity was Whit Sunday, May 19, 1583. For this Whitsun, Stratford Corporation had commissioned a pageant, laying out thirteen shillings fourpence toward the expenses of "Davy Jones and his company for his pastime at Whitsuntide's."* This is the first such entry for homegrown talent in Stratford. In 1569, when John Shakespeare was mayor or high bailiff of Stratford, the Queen's Players were paid nine shillings and the Earl of Worcester's Players twelve. Davy's must have been an impressive show to warrant such lavishness. If he cajoled the council into hiring him as impresario along with a supporting company, some of the credit would presumably have to go to his connections to the powerful Quineys, whose writ ran in Stratford. In June 1577,

---

*MA, vol. 3, pp. 129, 137.

Jones had married Elizabeth Quiney, the sister of the same Richard Quiney who fifteen years on from these Whitsun revels would write a famous letter in London addressed to Shakespeare. The name Davy occurs repeatedly in Shakespeare's *2 Henry IV*, a play with a number of autobiographical resonances that hark back to the Midlands if not directly to Stratford. Perhaps Davy was a model for Bottom in *A Midsummer Night's Dream*. His company may have included several callus-handed men who "toiled their unbreathed memories" to entertain the good burghers of Stratford. Conversely, the company may have consisted of the schoolchildren of the King's New School, perhaps counting among them Gilbert Shakespeare and, who knows, Will's fourteen-year-old sister, Joan, if the statutes against cross-dressing did not apply to amateur theatricals such as these.

That children from the grammar school may have played in this pageant is suggested by a telling reference to Whitsun festivities in an early play, *The Two Gentlemen of Verona*. When Julia, disguised as Sebastian, is quizzed by Silvia about her height, she replies that Julia is just as tall as she, as evidenced by the fact that s/he played in Julia's gown in the Whitsun play:

> . . . *for at Pentecost,*
> *When all our pageants of delight were played,*
> *Our youth got me to play the woman's part,*
> *And I was trimmed in Madam Julia's gown,*
> *Which servèd me as fit, by all men's judgements,*
> *As if the garment had been made for me;*
> *Therefore I know she is about my height.*
> *And at that time I made her weep agood,*
> *For I did play a lamentable part.*
> *Madam, 'twas Ariadne, passioning*
> *For Theseus' perjury and unjust flight;*
> *Which I so lively acted with my tears*
> *That my poor mistress, movèd therewithal,*
> *Wept bitterly; and would I might be dead*
> *If I in thought felt not her very sorrow.*

The young Shakespeare may have taken time out from looking after his wife on May 19, or she may have accompanied him to the show, which would have played in the large ground-floor room in the Gild Hall, or more probably in the school's gardens. The thought of homegrown adaptations of Ovid or plays about Robin Hood and merry old England suggests a carnivalesque atmosphere in Stratford that Sunday. The town had not yet been afflicted by the pusillanimous Puritanism that would one day pay the most famous company in the country *not* to play. There is no reason why the Pentecost pageants put on by Davy Jones should have been any different from the ones recalled by Julia. Shakespeare is clearly expecting his audience to recognize their own experience of these "pageants of delight." We may be fairly certain that Davy & Co. would not always "stand upon points," any more than Peter Quince does when speaking the prologue to the burlesque of Pyramus and Thisbe in *A Midsummer Night's Dream*. In a much later play, one deeply rooted in rural Warwickshire, *The Winter's Tale*, Shakespeare has a young princess dressed as a shepherdess recall Pentecost fun and games: "Methinks I play as I have seen them do / In Whitsun pastorals." Davy Jones's may have been the first ever Maying pageant in Stratford; although the Corporation accounts do not record further disbursements to Jones in the years that followed, Shakespeare never forgot these boisterous attempts at drama. He returned to them time and again in his plays.

What the young Will made of parenthood we cannot know; his poems and plays do not really help here, although he became the most wonderful imaginer of children, as in, for example, little Macduff; or, more darkly, in Juliet as a teenage daughter or in little Mamillius and Perdita in *The Winter's Tale*. These early days of Susanna's life must have been exciting ones as well as tiring for the new parents. How households of the period coped with infants and how the Shakespeares coexisted in Henley Street as an extended family, this we can only imagine. But imagine it we should, if only to ground our sense of the future poet and dramatist in a world that will have been recognizably domestic, mutually supportive, and demanding, and on premises that are extant to this day. Mary Arden and John

Shakespeare would have expected more grandchildren to arrive soon. They may well have been apprehensive about this, particularly since John's fortunes were at a low ebb; but the probability had to be faced, for there was no reliable contraception then.

In the late summer of 1584, Anne Shakespeare was pregnant again; on February 2, 1585, she and Will took their twins, Hamnet and Judith, to be baptised. Anne was still only twenty-nine when the twins arrived, and there was no reason why she should not have had several more children; her mother-in-law was around forty when she had her youngest, Edmund. One would like to think that these were comparatively happy times for the young couple, even if business was no longer what it had been in those halcyon days before John's great crash. There is no reason to think that Shakespeare did not love Anne Hathaway at this time, that he and she did not have many long conversations about everything in their lives, and not only about the rearing of their children. He clearly enjoyed domestic scenes such as, for example, a mother chasing a runaway chicken while her baffled infant tries to keep up with her, thinking that this must be Mama's new game. And he was clearly bewitched by his twins. One of the many blessings of his incomparable talent was that it would allow him to articulate that fascination in two of the greatest twin plays ever written, *The Comedy of Errors* and *Twelfth Night,* the latter containing boy-girl twins like his own. Furthermore, as we will see later, there is a direct and tangible link between this play and the Shakespeare twins. For Will Shakespeare, the early 1580s in Henley Street may have been happier than has sometimes been assumed.

Just as well, perhaps, because in the larger world things were very bad, and the world was not far from Henley Street. Within a few months of Susanna's christening in May 1583, something happened that affected everyone's life locally in one way or another. This was the arrest of Edward Arden of Park Hall, the head of the grand and ancient Catholic family of the Ardens. It must have come as a terrible shock to many in Stratford when Edward Arden and his wife, Mary, were hauled down to London and indicted and on what were then, and are now, thought to have been trumped-up charges. The family was destroyed, although in the end charges were dropped against Mary Arden, and her son Robert eventually recovered most of his parents' estate. Their fate must have brought home to the Shakespeares how dangerous a place their country really was. Moreover, as well as the Ardens, the charges involved Sir Thomas Lucy from Charlecote, of the rival Warwickshire family and next to the Earl of Warwick one of the most powerful men in the region.

In brief, the fall of the house of Arden was triggered when Arden's son-in-law John Somervile boasted in an inn near Banbury that he was heading down to London to kill the Queen. Somervile must have been seriously unbalanced to make such threats in a public place. He was arrested and put through the usual horrors inflicted on anyone who dared defy the Cecilian establishment. The fiction that torture was illegal under English law was believed by no one. Almost as grotesque as the torture itself is the fact that this fiction went unchallenged in the courts. When the Jesuit poet Robert Southwell protested at his trial in 1595 that he had been tortured ten times, the Queen's tormenter-in-chief, Richard Topcliffe, interjected, "If he were racked, let me die for it." Southwell replied, "No, but it was as evil a torture, of late device." Topcliffe's scoffing retort was "I did but set him against a wall," a cynical euphemism for a torture that is described in detail by John Gerard, who suffered and survived it.

Somervile implicated the Ardens, and the Queen's inquisitors arrived in Warwickshire shortly afterward to make their headquarters at the Lucys' of Charlecote. Relations between the Ardens and Lucys had long been strained; now the time for settling old scores had come. It was Sir Thomas Lucy who arranged for the escorting of the Ardens under armed guard down to London. Lucy had been a justice of the peace since 1559; Shakespeare's father would have met him during his tours of duty as chamberlain and mayor in the 1560s. He was repeatedly entertained at the Corporation's expense at the Bear and Swan inns. The grim and bloody story of Somervile and the Ardens, both Edward and Mary, left its mark indelibly on Warwickshire. While it may be wrong to judge the sixteenth-century judicial system by modern standards, or to underestimate the danger that the nation felt itself to be in from foreign Catholic powers, it is impossible and, perhaps, immoral to ignore the cruelty and ruthlessness with which the state wielded its power.

Everyone in Stratford knew about the nemesis visited on the

Ardens. Many years later, the seventeenth-century historian of War-wickshire, Sir William Dugdale, recorded the fact that people locally blamed the Earl of Leicester, the son of a traitor and yet the darling of the Queen. Arden had publicly insulted Leicester, who, with his brother the Earl of Warwick, may have bided his time in their neigh-boring fees of Kenilworth and Warwick. The Lucys of Charlecote eagerly toed the Leicester line. It must have earned them consider-able hatred among the recusant community and from other right-minded people in the county. Be that as it may, they were big and powerful by the standards of the ordinary people of the borough. Even so, someone would dare to cross them before the end of the decade. That person was William Shakespeare.

How and why he found himself doing battle with powerful mem-bers of the local gentry remains shrouded in mystery, which is why people have searched sedulously elsewhere for the elusive so-called lost years after 1585. The argument goes that, rather than clashing with the Lucys, Shakespeare instead returned to the alleged Catholic roots of his family and followed John Cottom to Lancashire. Here he would have joined the household of Sir Thomas Hesketh at Houghton Towers and gone under the name of Shakeshaft. A carefully docu-mented literature has grown up around this hypothesis of a resolutely Catholic Shakespeare's escape to Houghton Towers.

There can be no question about the devastating impact that the fallout from the Reformation had on the country, and it must have affected everyone, even in Stratford and surrounding villages like Shottery. To argue, though, that young Will Shakespeare followed in the footsteps of contemporaries like Debdale and Cawdrey, albeit in a less radical fashion, raises many questions. It also involves a se-ries of assumptions about the Shakespeare family's allegiances and the still hotly contested issue of John Shakespeare's will.

An important late-seventeenth-century witness in this story, Richard Davies, who is also one of three independent witnesses to the story of Shakespeare's poaching from the Lucys, states laconi-cally toward the end of a reference to Shakespeare that "he died a papist." It is not impossible that he did, and that his father did so, too: some of the very persecutors of the Catholics died in the old faith, if John Gerard can be believed. In the end, though, there is no hard evidence to connect Shakespeare to Lancashire. Had he wanted to join the Catholics, he could have done so locally—very locally, as it were, since his neighbors next door in Henley Street, the Badgers, were Catholic. And the Whateleys, Cawdreys, Cloptons, Greenways, Ainges, Reeves, and indeed others would gladly have helped out, one imagines, with spiriting away an eager and intelligent young man if they had so desired. The so-called lost years, between the birth of the twins in 1585 and a verbal attack on Shakespeare in London by a rival playwright in 1592, have assumed a mystique of their own. Surely the life of this brilliant man must have left a trace somewhere besides the single official reference in 1587, which casually mentions him in the context of a land dispute between his parents and Edmund Lambert. That life did leave traces, but not in a form much favored in recent years.

℘oaching from the Lucys: 1587?

here has long been an explanation for Shakespeare's vanishing from view after the birth of his twins in 1585, and that is the reason given in 1709 by Nicholas Rowe. After telling us that Shakespeare married (he calls marriage "settlement") Rowe goes on:

> In this kind of settlement he continued for some time, till an extravagance that he was guilty of, forced him both out of his country and that way of living which he had taken up; and though it seemed at first to be a blemish upon his good manners, and a misfortune to him, yet it afterwards happily proved the occasion of exerting one of the greatest geniuses that ever was known in dramatic poetry.... He had, by a misfortune common enough to young fellows, fallen into ill company, and amongst them some that made a frequent practice of deer-stealing engaged him with them more than once in robbing a park that belonged to Sir Thomas Lucy of Charlecote near Stratford. For this he was prosecuted by that gentleman, as he thought, somewhat too severely; and in order to revenge that ill usage, he made a ballad upon him. And though this, probably the first essay of his poetry, be lost, yet it is said to have been so very bitter that it redoubled the prosecution against him to that degree that he was obliged to leave his business and family in Warwickshire, for some time, and shelter himself in London.

This is the only account with roots reaching back into the seventeenth century to offer any explanation for Shakespeare's leaving his wife and his entire family behind. Many reasons have been sought for the strange metamorphosis from provincial glover into metropolitan playwright, and yet the only one to stand up may be this one whose credibility has repeatedly been impugned. At the very least, it has the authority of a written source close to Shakespeare with links as far back as Shakespeare's lifetime. Unless we assume that Rowe and with him Betterton and, possibly, Davenant set out to mislead posterity, we have no good reason to distrust Rowe; furthermore, the poaching story can be cross-referenced to other late-seventeenth-century accounts, which Rowe could not possibly have known.

There is no reason why someone as scrupulous and intelligent as Rowe should seek to peddle a lie, one that is moreover damaging to the moral character of his subject, and more so in the early eighteenth century than it seems to us today. Rowe wrote his account before gullible tourists on the Shakespeare trail started to descend on Stratford; he had nothing to gain from making up scabrous gossip. If anything, the opposite applies. And although information is mangled in transmission, the distortion is not usually complete.

One point commonly cited against Rowe is that Charlecote did not possess a deer park at the time. However, this first great Elizabethan mansion in Warwickshire, built in the year of the Queen's coronation, stood in woodlands rich in chestnuts, elms, oaks, and sycamores and inhabited by plenty of game, including hare, pheasants, and roe deer. (The fallow deer that live there now arrived only in the eighteenth century, we are told.) For all we know, the roes of Charlecote may be the reason why Shakespeare used "fleeter than the roe" and "the fleet-foot roe" in *The Taming of the Shrew* and *Venus and Adonis*. Other nearby landowners, including the Grevilles of Alcester, owned fallow deer, and Shakespeare refers to different kinds of deer in his plays. The Lucys' game reserve was patrolled by several keepers, one of whom may have arrested the young Shakespeare. A character in *Titus Andronicus* asks, "What, hast not thou full often struck a doe, / And borne her cleanly by the keeper's nose?" Perhaps young Will Shakespeare tried just that once too often.

Henry James rhapsodized that the "venerable verdure" of the Lucys' park seemed "a survival from an earlier England ... whose innumerable acres, stretching away, in the early evening, to vaguely seen Tudor halls, lie there like the backward years receding to the age of Elizabeth." Quite so. According to Rowe, Shakespeare teamed up with others who "made a frequent practice of deer-stealing" and with them he robbed "a park that belonged to Sir Thomas Lucy of Charlecote near Stratford." It is hardly hairsplitting pedantry to point out that the reference to Charlecote serves primarily to locate Lucy's residence for the benefit of a London audience. It does not situate the park, although the natural assumption is that the park is the one surrounding the house and thus close to Stratford. The great Shakespeare scholar and antiquarian J. O. Halliwell-Phillipps, and Sidney Lee, who wrote a classic essay on Shakespeare for the original *Dictionary of National Biography* (1897), both admired and trusted Rowe while acknowledging his mistakes over how many children John Shakespeare had. We would do well to heed Halliwell-Phillipps's warning about shortchanging Rowe. Writing in 1887, he stressed "Rowe's general accuracy": a few minor errors notwithstanding, Rowe's wider biographical sketch was drawn up "mainly from reliable sources . . . every word of his essay deserving of respectful attention."*

Even if the park at Charlecote was a rabbit warren rather than a deer park, the odds are that if Shakespeare poached from the Lucys it would have been at Charlecote simply because the grounds lie fairly close to Stratford—but only fairly close. If the young glover and some other tearaways from Stratford did indeed catch deer at the Lucys, one may well ask how they would have hauled them down to Stratford, a project that would require a well-organized group. The obvious way to get carcasses from Charlecote to Stratford would be to use the current of the Avon, which skirts the western

---

*Halliwell-Phillipps (1887), vol. 1, pp. xii–xiii. The chorus of voices approving of Rowe was joined by J. W. Gray in his groundbreaking study of the Shakespeare marriage in 1905. Rowe's sources and his researcher in Stratford did not realize that another John Shakespeare with children had lived there at the time. He was a shoemaker or "corvisor" from Bridge Street and does not seem to have been related to the poet. Rowe's most striking omission was Shakespeare's son Hamnet. We will never know for certain now, but the absence of Hamnet from Rowe may be deliberate on the part of one of his main sources, Davenant. Perhaps it suited him to forget about Shakespeare's son. Why this might be so we will see later.

edge of the park on its way down to Clopton bridge. The alternative would be to transport the illegal cargo toward Ingon by cart and from there to Stratford. The Warwick road, which then as now led into Stratford, would have been off limits to poachers; they would have had to cut through the Welcombe Hills, carrying their prey on horseback. There was no other practical way of doing it.

That much seems to be clear from an entry in the chamberlains' accounts of January 1595, which notes that at the swearing-in of the new bailiff and town council on October 4, 1594, "Master Greville's buck" was eaten for which gift the council incurred a "keeper's fee and horse hire"—that is, the buck was brought by Greville's keeper "on the back of a horse."* The fee for the keeper and the hire of the horse came to thirty shillings and sixpence. That a gang of youths from Stratford would poach farther afield than Charlecote or the near environs of town seems unlikely, if only for logistical reasons.

Shakespeare may be recalling his nights as a poacher in the hunt in *3 Henry VI*:

> *Under this thick-grown brake we'll shroud ourselves,*
> *For through this laund anon the deer will come,*
> *And in this covert will we make our stand,*
> *Culling the principal of all the deer.*

The word "laund," meaning glade, occurs only once more in Shakespeare's works, in *Venus and Adonis*: "and homeward through the dark laund runs apace." This matters because the poem was carefully proofread by, probably, Shakespeare himself, so the usage is undoubtedly his and so is the hunting passage in *3 Henry VI*. There is a great deal here, and in *Love's Labour's Lost, The Merry Wives of Windsor,* and elsewhere, about hunting, far more than in any other playwright of the period.

Deer skins were needed for gloving. It is not impossible, given John Shakespeare's economic misfortunes, that young Will decided to take a few shortcuts. In the late sixteenth century, poaching was punishable only by a fine. The fact that Lucy agitated in Parliament in

---

*MA, vol. 5, p. 31.

the late 1580s for tougher laws against poachers may be connected to nocturnal raids in his grounds; it is hard to think why else he would be so exercised over this issue and at this time. According to Rowe, Shakespeare was caught by Lucy's men and punished rather "too severely" in his own estimation. Perhaps Lucy, the chief local justice of the peace, acted as prosecutor, judge, and jury in this case.

What happened next makes perfect sense if one takes the view, as I believe one must, that the glover Will Shakespeare was always a writer first: according to Rowe, he retaliated against the Lucys with his pen. He wrote a ballad, just as Bottom hoped Peter Quince might do about his night with the fairy queen, the difference being that both sets of verses put forth as the Lucy ballad are savage satires.

The ballads surfaced in the eighteenth century; successive commentators on Shakespeare have tried to discredit both without producing any hard evidence against their authenticity. The argument is that they must be forgeries by local people increasingly conscious of the value of Shakespeare as a marketable commodity. In this view, the poems were intended to plug a gap hinted at by Rowe in his reference to the lost ballad.

One set of verses appeared in the late 1680s, when Joshua Barnes, professor of Greek at Cambridge, seems to have presented his hostess in a Stratford inn with a gown as thanks for the following two stanzas:

> *Sir Thomas was too covetous.*
> *To covet so much deer,*
> *When horns enough upon his head*
> *Most plainly did appear.*
>
> *Had not his worship one deer left?*
> *What then? He had a wife*
> *Took pains enough to find him horns*
> *Should last him during life.*

The word "covetous" occurs frequently in Shakespeare, and the reference here is particularly to Sir Thomas's surplus of deer and horns, notably those bestowed on him by his dear/deer/doe, his wife. In the eighteenth century the literary scholar and Shakespeare editor Edmond Malone warned that its source was "full of forgeries and falsehoods of various kinds." On the other hand, the writer knew about Lucy's marital problems in the 1580s, and Shakespeare was fond of horn jokes.

The other ballad is a rather different matter, because it may connect directly with passages in one of Shakespeare's plays. The text, a single stanza from a larger whole, was preserved by one of Shakespeare's first great editors, Edward Capell (1713–81). Capell remarked that it "has the appearance of genuine." Its pedigree is traced back through a Thomas Wilkes, the grandfather of the person who gave the ballad to Capell, to one Master Thomas Jones of the village of Tardebigge near Stratford-upon-Avon. Thomas Jones, who died in the year 1703

> aged upwards of ninety, remembered to have heard from several old people at Stratford the story of Shakespeare's robbing Sir Thomas Lucy's park; and their account of it agreed with Master Rowe's, with this addition—that the ballad written against Sir Thomas by Shakespeare was stuck upon his park gate, which exasperated the knight to apply to a lawyer at Warwick to proceed against him. Master Jones had put down in writing the first stanza of this ballad, which was all he remembered of it, and Master Thomas Wilkes (my grandfather) transmitted it to my father by memory, who also took it in writing, and his copy is this:

> > *A parliament member, a justice of peace,*
> > *At home a poor scare-crow, at London an ass,*
> > *If lousy is Lucy, as some volke miscall it,*
> > *Then Lucy is lousy whatever befall it:*
> > > *He thinks himself great,*
> > > *Yet an ass in his state,*
> > *We allow by his ears but with asses to mate.*
> > > *If Lucy is lousy, as some volke miscall it,*
> > > *Sing lousy Lucy, whatever befall it.**

---

*Chambers (1930), vol. 2, pp. 289–90.

Jones was a Welsh Stratford surname; the Jones who preserved the ballad may or may not be related to the Davy Jones of the Stratford Whitsun revels. The possibility cannot be ruled out. Since Davy Jones was married to a Quiney, he would have known the Shakespeares' business rather well, as these two families were evidently close. Also, there were Joneses at Stratford who married Hathaways in Shakespeare's lifetime. According to Jones, his sources were the old people of Stratford-upon-Avon. As for the ballad, in case we miss the pun in lousy/Lucy, Capell helpfully explains that people in Warwickshire pronounce "lousy" like "Lucy." He then adds, intriguingly, that the Jones who handed down the ballad is also the source for the story connecting Shakespeare to the part of Old Adam in *As You Like It.* This suggests that old Thomas Jones was at some point a neighbor, in Stratford or elsewhere, of one of Shakespeare's relatives who once saw him act. No deceased Thomas Jones is found in the relevant Tardebigge parish registers, so maybe he lived, and indeed died, elsewhere: Stratford, perhaps, though no Thomas Jones is recorded there, either, for the right period. Establishing the identity of this Master Jones would be quite important, because if he turned out to belong to the wider Quiney-Jones family he would de facto become a significant witness to the Shakespeare story. It may not be a coincidence that Mary Hart, who was born in 1641 and was the granddaughter of Shakespeare's nephew Thomas Hart from Henley Street, lived herself in Tardebigge at the same time as Thomas Jones.

If only we knew whether Sir Thomas Lucy had large ears that stuck out! But it is more likely that the ears are there chiefly to underpin the ass metaphor. Whatever the case, this is an offensive piece of writing, and if Shakespeare did pen it he must have known that serious consequences would follow if it were traced back to him. To call Lucy a louse-ridden ass was reckless. Through his father, Will Shakespeare would have known about the long arm of the Lucys and their accommodation with Protestant power. No lesser person than the Queen had spent two nights at Charlecote in Shakespeare's lifetime. It was hardly the prerogative of a yeoman glover to lampoon such a man. If Shakespeare took on the Lucys because they had helped destroy the Ardens, or because the Lucys' gamekeepers had arrested him and given him a good hiding, he took a tremendous risk. It is sometimes alleged that Shakespeare, unlike many of his fellow dramatists, never fell foul of the establishment. Perhaps that is because in his youth he had learned a bitter lesson.

Shakespeare's authorship of the ballad may be supported by its use of "volke" for "folk," a usage that also occurs in *King Lear* when Gloucester and Edgar are challenged by Oswald. Edgar is disguised as a poor peasant and his language sounds rural and uncouth. I quote from the quarto of 1608, because behind this text lies Shakespeare's own manuscript, so the phonetics are definitely his. This is his version of rural speech:

> EDGAR Good gentleman, go your gate. Let poor volk pass. An
> 'chud have been swaggered out of my life, it would not have
> been so long by a vortnight. Nay, come not near the old man.
> Keep out, 'che vor' ye, or I'll try whether your costard or my
> baton be the harder; I'll be plain with you.

Notice the substitution of voiced for unvoiced fricatives in the two words "volk" and "vortnight." As for "lousy" and "Lucy," the convenient confusion of the two in some people's pronunciation, as "some volke miscall," gives the writer an opening. If the ballad is authentic, then the young man who wrote it was both angry and fearless.

The poaching story is independently corroborated by witnesses from the seventeenth and eighteenth centuries such as Thomas Jones and, most intriguingly, Richard Davies. Davies was the chaplain of Corpus Christi College in the 1670s; he not only linked the poaching story to *The Merry Wives of Windsor* but also alleged that Shakespeare died a Catholic. Davies's remarks interleave with some bland notes by William Fulman, whose papers he somehow inherited. (Among those papers was Fulman's correspondence with Anthony Wood, who in turn knew John Aubrey and the Davenants. Wood and Davies also knew each other: the latter famously referred to Davies's "red and jolly" complexion, of the kind induced, as Wood noted, by fish dinners at Corpus Christi.) Fulman's notes merely cite the year and place of Shakespeare's birth; Davies added in the margin that Shakespeare was much given to all unluckiness in stealing venison and rabbits particularly from Sr–Lucy who had him oft whipped and sometimes imprisoned and at last made him fly his native country to his great advancement. But his revenge was so great that he is his Justice Clodpate and calls him a great man and that in allusion to his name bore three louses rampant for his arms.

This is the first written reference ever to Shakespeare's alleged poaching. Clearly "Justice Clodpate" is a mistake or a joke, a bit like calling Shallow Justice Nitwit, but there is no mistaking Davies's corroboration of Rowe or failing to notice, just as Rowe noticed, the possibility of a link between the poaching at Charlecote and *The Merry Wives of Windsor.*

Finally, a striking statement in a late play by Shakespeare chimes remarkably with what I have argued here. The play's idiom is rural, pastoral, and Warwickshire, and its world consists of sheep-shearing fairs, traveling peddlers, shepherdesses, and maying queens. It is *The Winter's Tale,* and it was probably written in Stratford during the spring of 1611. We are in the third act of the play, immediately after the famous stage direction that sees off Antigonus with "Exit pursued by a bear." A full-blown storm is raging when there enters a shepherd. He is searching for two lost sheep by the seaside and is in a reflective mood:

> SHEPHERD: I would there were no age between ten and three-and-twenty, or that youth would sleep out the rest; for there is nothing in the between but getting wenches with child, wronging the ancientry, stealing, fighting–hark you now, would any but these boiled-brains of nineteen and two-and-twenty hunt this weather . . .

The shepherd is Shakespeare talking about his own turbulent teens and early twenties. He was twenty-three years old in 1587, which happens to be the last time that we hear of him in Stratford: he is cited alongside his parents in a lawsuit against Edmund Lambert over his mother Mary Arden's estate in her native village of Wilmcote. Like the generic young man in the shepherd's speech,

Shakespeare got a woman with child in his teens, and the question as to whether he also committed the other misdeeds, "wronging the ancientry, stealing, fighting," is here emphatically answered in the affirmative. "Ancientry" meant one's elders but also nobility and stately traditions, as in "full of state and ancientry" in *Much Ado About Nothing.*

A picture emerges of Will Shakespeare as a rebellious youth, who may have been closer in temperament to Marlowe than is commonly assumed. In the mellow glow of *The Winter's Tale,* a play that has its share of suffering but somehow manages to end on a note of peace and stasis, he seems to look back at his own early years with some regret. There is no mention here of park lodges, stolen deer, or petty and corrupt country justices. Sir Thomas Lucy had been dead since 1600 and here, in a play written over a decade afterward, Shakespeare seems to be blaming testosterone for his actions of the 1580s. Perhaps he never quite forgot how fortunate he had been to come through after such tough beginnings; if the Lucys did persecute him unjustly they also unwittingly launched him on a brilliant career in London. The join between the play and Shakespeare's memory of his own past life is very intimate. The shepherd's reflection is placed right at the very point in the play when a sound of hunting youths ("boiled-brains of nineteen and two-and-twenty") is heard offstage. Just then the shepherd finds little Perdita, a princess who will reconcile the houses of Sicily and Bohemia after growing up in the shepherd's own household. This is the turning point in the play: the old shepherd tells his son, who has seen Antigonus eaten by a bear, "thou met'st with things dying, I with things new-born." "Perdita" means "the lost one," but it is she who brings peace and plenitude to the feuding families in the play. Looking back in 1611 at the events of a quarter of a century earlier, Shakespeare also perhaps saw the hunt at Charlecote as his crossroads. He, too, was lost; only in retrospect would he see that his loss was destined to turn into his greatest gain.

That William Shakespeare poached at Charlecote and was caught by Sir Thomas Lucy's gamekeepers seems highly likely. He would have fallen in with a crowd of local lads who together raided Lucy's estates. How they got their deer home, if their prey was deer, is hard to say, but the river is a distinct and obvious possibility. Shakespeare may have poached deer for the sake of his father's gloving business and for food. A deer could have sustained the whole Henley Street household for a week or more, while also providing a hide for leather. Shakespeare knew all there was to know about hunting, because he had hunted himself in Warwickshire, probably poaching as well as legally helping out as a beater, provoking the animals to dart out of their shelter for the hunters.

Until 1586–87, Shakespeare had managed to stay out of trouble. After all, he had three small children to look after and was probably the acting head of the family. John Shakespeare's situation had become more precarious than ever in September 1586, when he finally lost his seat on the council, because "he doth not come to the halls when . . . warned nor hath not done of long time."* Perhaps the family was even more vulnerable now to debt collectors. It took them ten years to recover their prestige in the town. Whatever his domestic circumstances, in around 1587 Shakespeare seems to have slipped up. Earlier we imagined him returning home from drinking with some of his friends in one of the great local inns. Perhaps they plotted their poaching trips over drinks, the way Falstaff and his crew do the Gadshill robbery in the opening scenes of *Henry IV Part 1*. Rowe blamed Shakespeare's companions for being habitual deer poachers and said that he fell in with them "more than once." If the riotous behavior of London apprentices is anything to go by, then Stratford will have had its share of aggressive and restless young men. Knives were everywhere, and not just in butchers' shops. There were relatively few violent crimes in the Stratford of the time, except for brawls, one of which would cost Shakespeare's friend Richard Quiney his life. Another ended with a butcher stabbing the owner of the Swan to death.

Elizabethan Stratford boasted a small prison. It replaced the medieval one, the "Cage" on the corner of High and Bridge Streets, which had become a coveted private residence and business premises. The new jail stood a few doors south of the Cage. Although the borough's accountants from time to time itemized expenses incurred

---

*MA, vol. 3, p. 170 (Sept. 6, 1586).

in running it, there are no references to anyone actually being kept prisoner there except, it seems, Shakespeare's uncle Harry. As with the jail so also with the overt local symbols of punishment, like the stocks. These were located outside the home of Shakespeare's friend Hamlet Sadler, at the corner of High and Sheep Streets. As a little boy at school in Church Street, Shakespeare walked past the stocks at least four times a day during the week. They furnished one of the images in his mental landscape that we may find hardest to visualize. Given the likely events in Charlecote, one wonders whether he and some of his mates had been stocked on that corner of Sheep Street, whether the conversation between Kent in the stocks and the Fool in *King Lear* may not reflect a painful memory. The Corporation is remarkably silent about the stocks' use, though the records refer freely to their upkeep; the same is true of the cucking-stool, called the gumstool locally. This was a seat into which scolds were strapped and then ducked in water. The town fathers showed due care for its good function and yet there is no mention anywhere in the extensive borough documentation of its actual use. Anna (also Agnes) Spurton might have been a prime candidate since the borough court declared her to be "a common scold and an un-quiet woman"; or Elizabeth Wheeler, who appeared before the so-called Stratford Bawdy Court "for continually brawling and abusing and not attending church." On one occasion, she notoriously railed against the court with the words "God's wounds, a plague a God on you all, a fart of one's arse for you," for which she was excommuni-cated. But then again that was probably a rather severer punishment than ducking in the Avon or the Mere Pool, the bracken pond at Rother Market.

Most infringements of the law were small local affairs, almost in-variably to do with the borough bylaws. Offenses such as fly-tipping were duly recorded. No court papers about Shakespeare and the Lucys have so far been found, but the Lucy ballad or ballads were, and unless we can *prove* that they are bogus we should reserve judg-ment. What is baffling is the sheer defiance and recklessness shown by young Shakespeare in compounding his theft with a provocative ballad. In the late 1580s, his life must have seemed to be unraveling, particularly if he had made enemies of the Lucys. It is unthinkable that they would have tolerated open flaunting of their authority by a young glover in their own fee.

Shakespeare had a long memory; he never forgave the Lucys, and ten years after the events in Charlecote he would once more return to this fray, again through the written word and in the wake of his second major clash with the authorities. If life in the early and mid-1580s had been hard for the two households in Henley Street, it would become much tougher still now that their main breadwinner had become a felon. His anger and frustration we can only imagine. As a mere yeoman, he could not possibly hope to win against the Lucys, but he tried anyway. He showed courage and daring and a kind of wisdom in directing his attack at Lucy's private life rather than his politics, but he also let down his loved ones badly, and not for the first time. There had clearly been problems over his marriage to Anne Hathaway, and to have inflicted the Lucys' wrath on his family when their fortunes were already at a low ebb showed scant regard for them. If he turned poacher to put food on the table in Henley Street, that is one thing, but if he was moved by sheer lawless camaraderie, that is a different matter altogether. And it is the latter that seems more likely, since the Shakespeare family never quite hit rock bottom. They did not sell the Birthplace, nor did they part with the barn or garden at the back. Had they done so, we would know that things were as bad as they could be. So if Will poached, it was probably because he enjoyed hunting, because he and his friends felt as little bound by the law as Falstaff and his cronies in the *Henry IV* plays. If Shakespeare seems to be having it both ways in those plays it is because he was both himself: earnest, farsighted, even puritanical, yet simultaneously a reveler and adventurer, Hal and Falstaff in one. He was surely caught in Charlecote, but to follow up that episode with ballads, if he did, would have sealed his fate. It would not do, not even for a joke.

$ound for London: 1587

nd so, in around 1587, William Shakespeare set out for London, perhaps to escape the threat of prison and persecution. There was no better place to seek refuge: the metropolis had swollen to 170,000 people and was becoming one of the biggest and fastest-growing cities in Europe. Of course there were Stratfordians here, but his school friends were hardly likely to betray him and the Lucys' writ did not run here. Leaving behind his parents, his siblings, his wife, and particularly his children, with Susanna barely five and the twins only two years old, must have been heartbreaking. So will have been the parting from everything that he had known up to that day, the memories of his childhood, those early years in the golden Stratford of the broad streets and the thousand elms, as Homer might have put it. How culpable he must have felt, if it was all his fault, and how fervently he must have hoped that the future would bring salvation. Now his father would need to look after Will and Anne's children as well. At least Gilbert was now twenty-one, and he could call on the other grown-up children for assistance as well. If Will was not family-minded before, he would become so now that he needed his family to bring up his children and care for his wife. If we want to know why this highly successful businessman never invested in property in London during the twenty years that he worked there, the answer may be right here. Perhaps he had vowed to himself that if he were ever granted a second chance at home he would never leave again, or perhaps the reason was the death of his son; more probably, it was both.

The moment came when the twenty-three-year-old William Shakespeare stepped out of the house in Henley Street, turned left, and, perhaps for the first time in his life, walked toward Back Bridge Street knowing that he would not return that evening. His future destiny will not have been apparent to the young glover as he made his way out of Stratford toward Clopton Bridge and then headed south toward Banbury or Oxford. As he turned the corner of Henley Street, he must have wondered when he would again see the faces of his loved ones. A memory of this parting may be captured in a masterly piece of light banter in *The Two Gentlemen of Verona,* one of Shakespeare's first plays ever, dating from the early 1590s. Lance reflects on how his entire household was moved to tears by his leaving except his dog, Crab:

> Nay, 'twill be this hour ere I have done weeping. All the kind of the Lances have this very fault. I have received my proportion, like the prodigious son, and am going with Sir Proteus to the Imperial's court. I think Crab, my dog, be the sourest-natured dog that lives. My mother weeping, my father wailing, my sister crying, our maid howling, our cat wringing her hands, and all our house in a great perplexity, yet did not this cruel-hearted cur shed one tear. He is a stone, a very pebble stone, and has no more pity in him than a dog. A Jew would have wept to have seen our parting. Why, my grandam, having no eyes, look you, wept herself blind at my parting. Nay, I'll show you the manner of it. This shoe is my father. No, this left shoe is my father. No, no, this left shoe is my mother. Nay, that cannot be so, neither. Yes, it is so, it is so, it hath the worser sole. This shoe with the hole in it is my mother, and this my father. A vengeance on't, there 'tis. Now, sir, this staff is my sister, for, look you, she is as white as a lily and as small as a wand. This hat is Nan, our maid. I am the dog. No, the dog is himself, and I am the dog. O, the dog is me, and I am myself. Ay, so, so. Now come I to my father: "Father, your blessing." Now should not the shoe speak a word for weeping. Now should I kiss my father. Well, he weeps on. Now come I to my mother. O that she could speak now, like a moved woman! Well, I kiss her. Why, there 'tis. Here's my mother's breath up and down. Now come I to my sister. Mark the

moan she makes—now the dog all this while sheds not a tear
nor speaks a word. But see how I lay the dust with my tears.

Perhaps just being able to write like this—and, deep within himself, always knowing that he possessed this incomparable gift—
helped Shakespeare to put some of his life in perspective. By the
time of *Two Gentlemen,* he had repeatedly been back and forth between London and Stratford. The darkest night of his early life was
over and he was heading for stardom. Hence the impeccably comic
idiom of what is, after all, a scene of sorrow and parting.

The people in Lance's lines are suggestive: a mother and father,
a blind grandmother, one willowy sister, and a maid called Nan. No
brother appears in this tearful scene, a version of which would have
been enacted every time Shakespeare left for London, although
nothing, one imagines, could have matched the depth of sadness of
that first parting with his parents, his three brothers, his one surviving sister, Joan, his wife, and of course his children. And then there
were the pets, a cat and a Crab. We tend to assume that people of
the time could not afford the luxury of pets as such, and that is probably right; but most households of the period had cats, for they
needed to protect themselves from being infested by mice. Dogs
were kept by farmers as guardians, though against foxes and ferrets
rather than thieves.

There can be no doubt that Shakespeare wrote home to his
loved ones. His father could read and, probably, write, and Mary Arden may have been literate. As for Will's siblings, they must have
gone to school, at least before their father's fortunes crashed. Even if
they were removed around 1577–78, Gilbert and the second Joan
would have acquired enough learning to read and write; if John and
Mary could not write, the children could have taken dictation. The
bearer of letters between the Shakespeares was probably William
Greenway.

Right now, in 1587, Shakespeare was heading for London. The
question is whether he had it in mind even then, on that long journey south, to join a theatrical company there. The year of his departure had been a vintage year for drama in Stratford, with no fewer than
five troupes performing in the ground floor of his old school, including

the Queen's, Sussex's, Essex's, and Leicester's Men. It is inconceivable that Shakespeare would not have sensed his own gift for rhetoric and theater. Above all, around the time that he left Stratford and disappeared from the records for five years, something potentially relevant happened in the village of Thame, in a close called the White Hound. It was the evening of June 13, 1587. Two actors from the Queen's Men started fighting and in the brawl that ensued one of them, John Town, killed William Knell. The Queen's Men was then the premier company in the land, with Richard Tarlton as its star until his death in 1588. It had been founded in 1583 as a propaganda tool by Sir Francis Walsingham, the secretary of the Privy Council and also the spymaster-general, along with the Earl of Leicester.

Actors were always fighting, but two facts may make this particular altercation significant for Shakespeare. First, there was now a vacancy in this company; some writers have thought that Shakespeare filled it. If he was still in Stratford at this point he would have found out about Knell's death there and then, because the company, one man short, proceeded from Thame to play in Stratford. Here they were paid the impressive fee of twenty shillings, twice as much as the Earl of Leicester's Men and four times as much as Essex's Men, who also played Stratford in 1587. But that a young glover would have replaced Knell is most unlikely, not least since the Queen's Men were soon joined by John Symons, probably filling the gap left by Knell. This is not to say, though, that Shakespeare may not have fallen into conversation with them and have decided there and then that the theater was where he really longed to be.

The second reason why this particular manslaughter matters to a biography of Shakespeare is more tangible. In 1588, nine months after Knell's death, his sixteen-year-old widow, Rebecca, married a John Heminges from Droitwich in Worcestershire. One day this same Heminges would become famous throughout the world for heading up, with Henry Condell, the syndicate that gave posterity the First Folio of Shakespeare's works. The union between Heminges and Rebecca Knell turned out to be happy and fruitful; they produced fourteen children and stayed devoted to each other until her death in 1619. If only we knew how Heminges came to join the Queen's Men and whether he encountered Shakespeare in Stratford. Droitwich is less than twenty miles from Stratford, and Heminges is a Stratford name. The beadle of the town in 1601 was called John Heminges. One cannot rule out links between the actor John Heminges and the Heminges of Stratford, Shottery, Snitterfield, and indeed Temple Grafton, where Anne Hathaway probably lived at the time of her marriage. The Shakespeares undoubtedly knew families called Heminges, but we have no way of knowing whether these were related to the player from Droitwich. Even if they were, it is more likely that Shakespeare and Heminges met in London in the late 1580s, as Heminges had lived and worked in the city since 1578. He was admitted to the Grocers' Company in April 1587 but playing and the theater must have been in his blood. How else could he have met the teenage widow of a player from the Queen's Men in time to marry her in London in March 1588? We know that he and Shakespeare became partners when the Lord Chamberlain's Men were created in 1594, but they knew each other before then, perhaps meeting after Shakespeare started to make a name for himself as a playwright.

The journey from Stratford to London involved a well-trodden road from Stratford to Banbury through Pillerton Priors, Edgehill, and Drayton on what is now the A422 highway. From Banbury, the road took the traveler into west London by way of Aylesbury, Amersham, and Uxbridge, and from here through Hayes and Hanwell to Shepherd's Bush, Paddington, and Tyburn (Marble Arch); then down Tyburn Road, today's Oxford Street, and hence into the walled City of London proper. The Stratford–Banbury–Uxbridge road seems to have been the preferred route at the time, but another route, a slightly longer one, ran from Stratford to Oxford and then bore down on London through Wycombe or High Wycombe and Beaconsfield to Uxbridge. While the roads and tracks that linked the Midlands to London were negotiated by privately rented carriages, no regular coach service as such yet operated. Men and women walked or, if they could afford it, rode. The hundred-mile distance from Stratford to London may seem to us rather daunting to walk, but it would have appeared less so at a time when people as a rule walked far more. We know from the medieval French transhumance that Occitan shepherds thought nothing of striding two hundred and fifty miles across the Pyrenees from the south of France into Catalonia, all while guarding huge flocks of sheep. Similarly, the unsvelte Ben Jonson did not balk at the prospect of walking from London all the way up to Scotland and back. By then he was already forty-six years old with a huge gut.

So the twenty-four-year-old Will Shakespeare probably set out on foot. He would have carried with him money for staying at various inns on the road, a pouch with water, and perhaps some memorabilia of his loved ones. The roads at the time were busy and reasonably safe. Later, when he became a commuter, Shakespeare would make the journey on horseback and stay in the kinds of inns evoked by William Harrison in his section "Of Our Inns and Thoroughfares" in Holinshed's *The Chronicles of England*. Harrison noted proudly that English inns were then "very well furnished with napery, bedding, and tapestry," that the table linen was "commonly washed daily," and that each lodger lay in "clean sheets, wherein no man hath been lodged since they came from the laundress or out of the water wherein they were last washed." Guests received the keys to their rooms and "if his chamber be once appointed he may carry the key with him, as of his own house, so long as he lodgeth there." Travelers who arrived on horseback did not pay for their rooms, only for the horses, but if they journeyed on foot they were charged a penny for the bed. Harrison's inns were huge, able to lodge "two hundred or three hundred persons and their horses at ease."* These were the five-star hotels of the period, with large numbers of staff and vast areas of accommodation. The horses needed to be stabled and groomed and would have taken up at least as much space as the human residents.

The young Shakespeare's roadside accommodation on that first trip must have been a rather different affair, much more like the below-stairs world of the two carriers in *1 Henry IV*. There are no clean sheets; the men are up long before dawn, and they are already running late. It is dark and they need lanterns to see. Their

---

*Harrison, pp. 397–406.

first concern is for the horses, which suffer from poor riding and shoddy saddling as well as "bots," intestinal worm from dank provender. The "house," the carriers claim, is not what it used to be, and to prove it they have been badly bitten by fleas. They were not even given jordans—chamber pots—and therefore relieved themselves into the fireplaces, thus, they ruefully concede, further lowering the hostelry's standard of hygiene. This fleapit is a far cry from some of the sophisticated London inns that flanked Bishopsgate, Aldersgate, and particularly the Borough High Street or Long Southwark as it was known at the time; for that matter, it is worlds away from the Bear and Swan in Stratford. In the case of the Swan we know that not only did it have huge supplies of linen as well as all kinds of drinks, but also it boasted outside lavatories and an ample supply of chamber pots.

In the same scene in *1 Henry IV*, a rascal called Gadshill appears and asks Tom, the second carrier, when he means to be in London. Tom, who is heading for Charing Cross, replies, "Time enough to go to bed with a candle"—meaning, perhaps, that he intends to be in London by nightfall or at least before the night is over. From this it appears that the distance from Rochester to central London, at least thirty-five miles as the crow flies and therefore considerably more on the road, could be covered in a long day's ride with a reasonably fit horse.

We can form a fairly accurate idea of the journey from Stratford to London and back in the late sixteenth century thanks to a delegation from Stratford that descended on the capital in 1590 to petition the Privy Council and particularly William Cecil, Lord Burghley, who was Lord Treasurer of England. Since they were traveling on Corporation business, they kept a "bill of charge," an itemized record of their expenses, for which they would be reimbursed by the borough. The delegates were the Stratford town steward, Master John Jeffereyes, and the famous Barber of the Bear, a man of substance and an ally, probably, of the Shakespeares. Master Thomas Barber enjoyed a lifelong let of the Bear courtesy of the Shakespeares' close friends the Sadlers. Shakespeare knew Barber almost all his life. At the time of the London visit Barber was alderman of the chamber and its treasurer, hence his presence on this journey.

Barber and Jeffereyes set out on May 15, 1590, and spent the first night in Oxford, where they laid out three shillings on their supper and "horse-meate." Their lodging is not itemized separately, presumably because it was included in the feed for the horses. The following day they proceeded to Wycombe, where they lunched and fed their horses before pushing on to Uxbridge. Here they stayed Saturday night, spending twenty-two pence on their own supper and the same sum on provender for the horses. Lodging was again included in the fee, rather more than they had paid in Oxford: even then, it seems, the closer one drew to the capital the higher the price tag. The next day, Sunday, May 17, they were in London for both lunch and dinner at a cost of only two shillings. They had probably stabled their horses somewhere in the Elizabethan equivalent of a rental-car dropoff. The total cost of keeping their horses in London over a fortnight came to a princely thirteen shillings and eight pence. Although we cannot be sure where they stayed, the Bell in Carter Lane south of St. Paul's is a safe guess: it was the preferred inn of Stratfordians.

Among the expenses reclaimed by the two councilors was the hiring of a boat to Greenwich, where the Court sat at the time, and seeing "counsel" as well as one Master Cowper, for whose services they disbursed twenty and five shillings respectively, impressive honoraria. Barber and Jeffereyes did something else. In their bill of charge one entry reads "Friday for Master Greene's dinner [lunch] and ours xxd [twenty pence] supper iis [two shillings, or twenty-four pence]." Lunch, on this occasion at least, was cheap and dinner or supper expensive. The delegates' visit to Greene may be significant for us because this may be a relative of the same Thomas Greene, Shakespeare's cousin, who would eventually turn up in Shakespeare's grand house in Stratford. One wonders whether Barber and Jeffereyes called on this Master Greene for legal advice before meeting with counsel and Cowper the following day, unless Greene was the Queen's counsel whom they had visited earlier. Thomas Greene, Sr., the father of Shakespeare's cousins Thomas and John, was buried at Stratford only two months before this meeting, on March 6, 1590. He was called Thomas Greene *alias* Shakespeare, which may suggest that he was the brother of Master John Greene of Warwick and that these Greenes and John Shakespeare were kinsmen.* Certainly the younger Thomas Greene called Shakespeare "my cousin Shakespeare." Thomas Greene would one day become town clerk of Stratford; his brother John would later act for Susanna Shakespeare in the matter of the Blackfriars gatehouse. This same John was training at Clement's Inn in the mid-1590s, just when Shakespeare lived in London and wrote a play with a lecherous old country justice of the peace called Shallow who loves to reminisce about his salacious past at Clement's Inn. Shakespeare knows a vast amount about the law, knowledge he may have picked up from the two Greene boys; John, as has been mentioned, was at Clement's Inn (an inn of chancery) and Thomas at Middle Temple (an inn of court).† Both places are associated with Shakespeare through *2 Henry IV* and *Twelfth Night*.

Although we may never know the specific nature of the link, there is no real doubt about the closeness of the Greene family to Shakespeare. One would like to ask, of course, whether this lunch and dinner party of the two Warwickshire delegates also touched on Will Shakespeare, whether he was the ghost at the feast. By the time Barber and Jeffereyes arrived in London, Shakespeare had been there for more than two years. Within a few short months of their visit, he would write seventeen poems to one of the rising stars of the London

---

*Fripp (*MA*, vol. 3, p. 55). See also Chambers ([1930] volume 2, pp. 149 ff) on Thomas Greene, a full and intelligent discussion of his possible links with the Shakespeare family. Fripp (*MA*, vol. 1, p. xxxii) also writes that a sister or a daughter of Shakespeare's grandfather Richard may provide the link with the Greenes: "A sister of Richard Shakespeare may have been the mother, or his daughter may have been the wife of Thomas Greene of Warwick . . . who died in July 1590, and whose son, afterwards Town Clerk of Stratford, and a friend of William Shakespeare, called himself Thomas Greene *alias* Shakespeare."

†Inns of chancery and court were comparable institutions at the time of the play although chancery inns were subordinate to the "four principal inns" of court, Inner Temple, Gray's Inn, Lincoln's Inn, Middle Temple. The inns of chancery prepared students for admission to the inns of court, which alone could admit its residents to practice at the bar. Clement's Inn, founded in the fifteenth century, was affiliated with the Inner Temple.

aristocracy and command the attention of just the kind of people whose help they were seeking to enlist.

The Stratford councilors stayed on until Saturday, May 30, 1590. They took a slightly different route home, bypassing Oxford and traveling up, separately, by way of Uxbridge, Aylesbury, and Banbury. A few months later, Jeffereyes was down in London again, this time to petition the Privy Council and specifically Lord Burghley to allow the Corporation to nominate its own vicar and schoolmaster. These posts had hitherto been in the gift of the Earl of Warwick, although he usually rubberstamped the town fathers' choices. Another item on Jeffereyes's wish list was permission "for one fair and market more," to perk up the stagnant local economy. Jeffereyes traveled by way of Banbury and got as far on the first day as Stratton Audley, a hamlet well south of Banbury and near Bicester. The following morning he pushed on to Aylesbury, where he lunched before making his way to lodgings in the small village of Chenies on the Amersham Road.

It is worth pausing for a moment over Stratton Audley. This tiny place sits midway between Stratford and London and not far from an ancient village called Grendon Underwood. In 1681, John Aubrey claimed that not only did Shakespeare pass through Grendon at the end of the sixteenth century but that the idea for Dogberry came to him in this very spot. Shakespeare, Aubrey wrote,

> began early to make essays at dramatic poetry, which at that time was very low, and his plays took well. He was a handsome, well-shaped man, very good company, and of a very ready and pleasant smooth wit. The humour of . . . the constable in *A Midsummer Night's Dream* he happened to take at Grendon in Bucks. which is the road from London to Stratford, and there was living that constable about 1642 when I first came to Oxon [Oxford]. Master Jos.[eph] Howe is of that parish and knew him. Ben Jonson and he [Shakespeare] did gather humours of men daily wherever they came.

In the marginal note to "Grendon" Aubrey added, "I think it was midsummer night that he happened to lie there." Aubrey gets it wrong, of course, about Dogberry, who is a character in *Much Ado*

About Nothing, not *A Midsummer Night's Dream*, but that is less significant than his claim that Shakespeare and Jonson used real people
for their characters and that the model for Dogberry was not only
alive in 1642 but that one Master Howe had known him. The idea
that the real Dogberry lived in Grendon sounds too good to be true
until we discover in the parish records that a Master Howe did indeed live there in 1642. The Reverend Mr. Thomas Howe, moreover, heads a list of Grendon Underwood's contributions to the Irish
campaign in 1642.* The collector received the sum of four pounds,
three shillings, and sixpence "for Grendon Underwood by the hands
of one Mr Howe the minister but whether the acquittance was given
to him or the high constable I do not remember."

Master Howe was called Thomas rather than Joseph, but Jos. is
the undoubted reading of Aubrey's manuscript. It is worth noting
that of the forty-three people on the Ireland list no fewer than fifteen
are called Thomas, not one Joseph. "Thomas" was one of the most
common first names in Grendon. A search of the parish records reveals that there were no Joseph Howes in the parish at all. There
was, however, a Josias Howe, son of Thomas Howe, who was christened on March 29, 1612. I believe that in 1642 Aubrey somehow
got wind of a Shakespeare connection with the small village of Grendon and did the logical thing, consult the local minister. This was
Thomas Howe; some forty years later, Aubrey misremembered the
man's first name. Unfortunately no Dogberry is listed among the Ireland contributors, not that one would expect to find such an obviously made-up comic name. In the Grendon records there is,
however, one family name that might, just possibly, lie behind "Dogberry": a William Soulberry is listed in 1642. He may have been
the William, son of Humphrey Soulberry, who was christened on
December 7, 1599. Soulberrys lived in Grendon in the late 1590s
when Shakespeare was writing *Much Ado About Nothing*, which is

---

*Further details are in the *Buckinghamshire Record Society Publications,* ed. John
Wilson, no. 21 (1983). This was the so-called Confederate Wars, which started with
Irish Catholics in October 1641 rising against English and Scots Protestant settlers.
The conflict spread rapidly and by the spring of 1642 it had engulfed large parts of
Ireland.

commonly dated to 1598–99. It is not impossible that a Soulberry of Grendon Underwood became Dogberry of Messina in the crucible of Shakespeare's imagination. Unfortunately, there is no way of establishing who the constables of the parish were, let alone whether they were given to egregious malapropisms. Nevertheless, there may be more than a grain of truth in Aubrey's account. Moreover, the words "dog" and "soul" may be more archly interchangeable than might at first appear. It was commonly rumored at the time among Catholics that one of the coteries frequented by Marlowe enjoyed vulgate word games that included spelling "God" backward. As Catholics saw it, this highlighted the incompatibility of the language of revealed religion—the word of God—and that spoken by ordinary people in the street. If "God" becomes "dog," then "soul" might do so too. It is only a thought, but with this master punner, a writer who freely ranges within the zodiac of his own wit and rhetorical inventiveness, in whose culture language itself had become a major bone of contention, we should not rule out some such pun or allusion.

7

Early Days in Shoreditch: 1587–90

hen Shakespeare finally arrived in London, perhaps by way of Stratton Audley and Grendon, the obvious way to earn a living would have been to offer his expertise as a glover. Instead, as Rowe reports, he seems to have made more or less straight for the theaters. Here is the Stratford tearaway in London now in 1587, on his own, lonely, frustrated, angry, and at loose ends. He encountered its authoritarian and repressive face long before seeing any of its glories. As he strode up from Shepherd's Bush through what are now Holland Park Avenue, Notting Hill, and Bayswater Road, he would have glimpsed from afar off the massive triangular cross-beamed gallows at Tyburn, which towered over the middle of today's Edgware Road at Marble Arch. The high gallows' triangularity is remarked on in *Love's Labour's Lost*, when Berowne refers to its shape: "Thou makest the triumviry, the corner-cap of society, / The shape of love's Tyburn that hangs up simplicity." The spot is marked by a memorial stone today.

The multiple gallows had been erected here comparatively recently (1571), although the site had been the main place of executions in London since Chaucer's time, that is, from the late fourteenth century on. If Shakespeare had indeed fallen foul of the law back home, the sight of Tyburn may have given him grim pause. He had almost certainly never seen an execution before. Stratford was clear of such horrors, although Warwick was not and the English countryside was dotted with gibbets. This facet of life in Shakespeare's

England is too often ignored, partly out of a wish to avoid prurience, but particularly because public hanging seems so unreal. But to ignore the intense and literal reality of Elizabethan state terror is in the end to shortchange Shakespeare and his entire culture. Only if one realizes the sheer horror of the penalties exacted by the state does one also begin to grasp how deep must have been the conviction that led hundreds of young Englishmen to embrace an unimaginable death for the sake of their faith and salvation as they saw it.

Shakespeare was not able to escape such sights in London because the government put people to death in whichever part of the city seemed symbolically most fitting. Thus, for example, in 1586 Anthony Babington and his fellow conspirators were executed in Holborn outside the church of St. Giles-in-the-Fields, close to where they had plotted their alleged coup to supplant Queen Elizabeth with Mary Queen of Scots, in a spot near today's Centrepoint. Five years after Babington, the priest Edmond Gennings was fully conscious when he was slaughtered outside Gray's Inn Fields. His suffering horrified onlookers except, it seems, the sadistic Richard Topcliffe who relished such spectacles and preferred to enjoy them hanging on the scaffold. At Gennings's execution something happened that Catholic martyrologists would eagerly record: when the hangman carelessly flung one of his upper quarters into the basket, his attached arm dangled over the edge and a recusant woman eagerly clutched his dead hand. The fingers, so the memoir reads, came off miraculously in her grip, a precious relic.

John Rigby died a similar death on the Old Kent Road in June 1600. He had been found guilty of recusant recidivism. His fate would haunt the Jesuit John Gerard, who had converted him. In his autobiography, Gerard recalled how, as Rigby was dragged on a hurdle to the scaffold, he passed the Earl of Rutland who, when seeing "what a well-built and handsome man he was," exclaimed, "You were made for a wife and children, not to die for your faith." Rigby replied, "As for a wife, I ask God to bear me out that never in my life have I had intercourse with a woman."* Rigby's death is the stuff of nightmares:

---

*Caraman (1965), p. 81.

After he had been cut down by the hangman he stood up-
right on his feet like a man a little amazed, till the butchers
threw him down. Then coming perfectly to himself he said
aloud and distinctly "God forgive you. Jesus, receive my soul."
And immediately another cruel fellow standing by, who was
no officer, but a common porter, set his foot upon Mr. Rigby's
throat, and so held him that he could speak no more. Others
held his arms and legs while the executioner dismembered
and bowelled him, and when he felt them pulling out his
heart, he was yet so strong that he thrust the men from him
who held his arms. At last they cut off his head and quartered
him. . . . The people going away complained very much of the
barbarity of the execution; and generally all sorts bewailed his
death.*

There is no point trying to sanitize Elizabethan culture, though it
is a troubling thought to most people now that the same crowd who
watched this atrocity might the following day attend a spectacle called
As You Like It or *Twelfth Night,* both almost exactly contemporary with
the death of John Rigby. The theater of violence in the capital was
state-sponsored terror. It was meant to deter, but while it succeeded in
intimidating some—Ben Jonson, for one—nearly all Catholic priests
remained steadfast when confronted with such deaths.

Shakespeare displays a robust sense of humour about the gallows in his plays. It is an everyday fact of life for him, as one imagines
it was for most of his contemporaries. Yet his only major dramatic
meditation on capital punishment, *Measure for Measure,* pulls away
from this moral brink at the last minute. It is also in this play that
Shakespeare recalls the penalty of pressing to death, which had been
passed on a prominent Catholic noblewoman a few years earlier.
Shakespeare's humanity did not let him exploit his culture's cruelty
to the full. The author of the greatest emotional roller coaster in the
language, *King Lear,* could not condone such acts inflicted upon fellow human beings. With regard to capital punishment, which is
sanctioned by the Bible, Shakespeare's own private and imaginative
morality is not that of his time.

---

*Challoner, pp. 244–45.

When Shakespeare arrived in London, drama was no longer the sleeping beauty of English literature. It had just recently burst into life, just as Sir Philip Sidney had predicted in his famous *Defence of Poesy* (c.1582–83; published posthumously in 1595). According to Rowe, Shakespeare "was received into the company then in being, at first in a very mean rank; but his admirable wit, and the natural turn of it to the stage, soon distinguished him, if not as an extraordinary actor, yet as an excellent writer." However the theater and Shakespeare met, there must have been a *coup de foudre* and that was that. Quite what is meant by "a very mean rank" is not clear, although common sense suggests that Shakespeare started out as the proverbial dogsbody. A story reported by Samuel Johnson in the preface to his 1765 edition of Shakespeare's works may cast light on this. He had got it from Alexander Pope, who in turn claimed to have heard it from Rowe. In Johnson, these lines are therefore appended to his reprint of Rowe's *Life*:

> *To the foregoing accounts of Shakespeare's life I have only one passage to add, which Master Pope related, as communicated to him by Master Rowe.* In the time of *Elizabeth,* coaches being yet uncommon, and hired coaches not at all in use, those who were too proud, too tender, or too idle to walk, went on horseback to any distant business or diversion. Many came on horseback to the play, and when *Shakespeare* fled to *London* from the terror of a criminal prosecution, his first expedient was to wait at the door of the playhouse and hold the horses of those that had no servants that they might be ready again after the performance. In this office he became so conspicuous for his care and readiness that in a short time every man as he alighted called for *Will. Shakespeare,* and scarcely any other waiter was trusted with a horse while *Will. Shakespeare* could be had. This was the first dawn of better fortune. *Shakespeare* finding more horses put into his hand than he could hold hired boys under his inspection who when *Will. Shakespeare* was summoned were immediately to present themselves, *I am Shakespeare's boy, Sir.* In time *Shakespeare* found higher employment, but as long as the practice of riding to the playhouse continued the waiters that held the horses retained the appellation of *Shakespeare's Boys.*

There is no reason for Pope to have fabricated this story. It has the ring of authenticity, not least because it shows a competitive and entrepreneurial Shakespeare rapidly expanding his horse-guarding business: the record suggests that he was always competitive and an astute businessman. The passage is made the more credible by the reference to "the practice of riding to the play-house." It is not clear how familiar with the early history of the Elizabethan professional theater Rowe, Pope, and Johnson were, but indeed riding to the theater belongs to the days of the Theatre (1576) and the Curtain (1577), which were set in open fields in Shoreditch and Moorfields some distance north of the city gates and particularly Bishopsgate. There could be no question of crossing London Bridge on horseback to see a play at the Globe in 1599, or even at the Rose before that. Only squires from Kent would have used horses to go to the Bankside theaters (if they did); most London audiences either walked across the bridge or took wherries, as the river taxis were known. Pope's and Johnson's chronology and topography fit: riding to the theaters belongs to the two north London venues.

That Shakespeare fetched up in Shoreditch is confirmed by John Aubrey, who remarked that "he was not a company keeper, lived in Shoreditch." Here, in this north London "liberty"—that is, a parish outside the jurisdiction of the City of London—stood the first two theaters. The one with which Shakespeare became associated was the Theatre. It had been built by the Burbage family and opened its doors in 1576 to be followed a year later by another playhouse not far down the road, the Curtain, near the site of today's Hewett Street. The Burbages were in all likelihood Kentish, but Stratford also had its Burbages, including one who was mayor in 1558. That Will Shakespeare knew the Burbages of his hometown is not in doubt, for one of his father's most protracted lawsuits involved a William Burbage of Stratford.* The Kent Burbages had pitched their headquarters right

---

*This is *John Shakespeare versus William Burbage.* In 1589, the two litigants had sought judgment before the notoriously conservative Sir Edmund Anderson "and his fellow justices" of the Queen's bench (*MA,* vol. 4, p. 151). Anderson had become chief justice of the Court of Common Pleas in 1582, coincidentally the same year that this lawsuit was first thought to have been settled in Stratford with an injunction

above the shop, since they lived inside the old inner cloister yard of what had been, before the Reformation, the priory of St. John the Baptist Holywell. In the 1580s the old priory was still surrounded by fields on all sides, although most afternoons, before and after performances, large crowds of people trampled across these green spaces.

When Shakespeare first laid eyes on the Theatre it sat within an eight-acre square. Curtain Road and Shoreditch High Street marked its western and eastern borders, while Bateman's Row and Holywell Lane hemmed it in from the north and south respectively. These streets survive today and by those same names, but additional ones have since been driven into the plot. Of these, the one that cuts through its middle on an east–west axis, New Inn Yard, is the most important for our purposes, because the Theatre sat almost exactly north of it. Since 1920 a plaque on numbers 86 and 88 Curtain Road has commemorated the building. Not only would this playhouse be the first professional English theater, but there is a direct line of descent to both the first and second Globes. The reign of the Theatre therefore could be said to stretch from 1576 to the closure of all London playing spaces by the Puritans in 1642. The Theatre did not quite verge on New Inn Yard but a crumbling barn, known at the time as Great Barn, did. This barn the Burbages had converted into tenements or flats to generate additional income from rents. It is possible that Shakespeare lived in one of them in the early years of his career.

The playing spaces were never entirely respectable, neither in Shoreditch nor on Bankside. In Elizabethan London, theaters and "stews"—brothels—stood cheek-by-jowl. The area around Holywell and the two playhouses remained relatively free of brothels and

---

to John Shakespeare to repay Burbage "at the sign of the Maidenhead in Stratford aforesaid between the hours of one and four o'clock in the afternoon" (*MA,* vol. 4, p. 59). Anderson had prosecuted Campion in November 1581 and during the trial had used a term to Campion that Shakespeare later made famous in *Hamlet*: "Had you come hither for love of your country, you would never have wrought a huggermugger, had your intent been to have done well, you would never have hated the light; and therefore this budging deciphereth your treason." If John Shakespeare harbored even the smallest Catholic sympathies, here was an old judge with Catholic blood on his hands from his recent clash with the saintly Campion. Anderson ruled against John Shakespeare, but the glover was back in court in 1592.

pimps, probably because too many wealthy Londoners were investing in Finsbury and Moorfields around the time when the playhouses sprang into being. The entire area to the north and west of
Bishopsgate and Bedlam, which straddled the site of what is now
Liverpool Street railway station, underwent an economic boom by
being developed into formal parklands and a suburban second-home
area for wealthy Londoners, a kind of *rus in urbe*. By the time the so-
called Copperplate map of London was drafted in about 1557, there
were at least three houses in the Elizabethan garden patchwork that
became Finsbury Fields.* As London's population swelled toward
200,000 in around 1600, the northern green belt of the Tudor city
rapidly eroded. The district west of Bedlam became a patchwork of
gardens verging on the common sewer and the land used for stretching cloth in Moorfield. Farther up were the archery butts and the
windmills in what was then called Finsbury Fields. Today the same
area is bordered by London Wall to the south, Bunhill Row to the
west, Old Street to the north, and, of course, Bishopsgate and
Shoreditch High Street to the east. By the end of the sixteenth century, it had become a haven of isolated residential holiday homes. In
his famous *Survey of London* (1603), John Stow disapprovingly noted
that it had become an *enclosed* garden district for the rich and foolish,
who, he lamented, were building "many fair summer houses . . . some
of them like midsummer pageants, with towers, turrets, and chimney
tops, not so much for use or profit as for shew and pleasure." These
second-home owners were a far cry, he writes, from the "ancient citizens" of London, who used their wealth to provide hospitals and
almshouses for the less fortunate.†

Not all the houses were grand. Some were just cottages, discreetly
screened off from the two lanes, today's Appold Street and Primrose
Street, that at the time cut through the area directly east of what is
now Finsbury Square. It was here, and within less than a hundred

---

*Copperplate is the first full map of London and of considerable topographical
interest for understanding the Tudor city. Only three plates out of fifteen survive, two
of them in the Museum of London and one in the Anhaltische Gemäldegalerie in
Dessau. One of the extant sections of the map shows Bishopsgate and Shoreditch
and the road leading north toward the Curtain and Theatre playhouses.

†Stow (1603/1908), vol. 2, p. 78.

yards or so of the Curtain and the Theatre, that the Jesuits made their headquarters. Henry Garnett, their leader in the late 1580s, chose a summer house in just this area from where to conduct a spiritual insurgency. In a letter dated March 17, 1593, to his superior in Rome, Cardinal Claudio Acquaviva, he remarked that many London citizens "own small gardens beyond the city walls, and a number of them have built in these gardens cottages to which they resort from time to time to enjoy the cleaner air."* Such cottages would be a perfect cover: being outside the City walls, they were not only isolated from nosy neighbors and therefore safer, but also had the advantage of being more accessible to recusants than any location inside the City gates. In addition, many of these small properties lay empty much of the time and were therefore of no obvious interest to the government agents, who were busy patrolling suspect districts and even individual houses.

For several years, Garnett ran the Jesuits from here and provided shelter for visiting priests. The cottage he rented was permanently shuttered and the lane or path that gave access to it seemed secure enough. All the cooking was done at night, and no fires were lit except after dark, even in deepest winter, so that smoke would not be seen billowing from chimneys. The cottage was a safe if spartan place: a few years later, in 1591, it was finally raided, but almost nothing was found and no one was arrested. The items confiscated did not suffice to incriminate the Jesuit sympathizer who was present. The reason for the raid's failure was that in its cellar this cottage contained a substantial priesthole built by the master mason of the Catholics, that fervent supporter of the Jesuits' cause Nicholas Owen. Owen was an aspiring Jesuit, known as Little John, as distinct from his friend and companion Long John of the Little Beard, John Gerard. Cecil's henchmen searched everywhere for Garnett's hideout but ultimately found it only by chance. Their fumbling attempt to seize the premises and its occupants was pure Dogberry, undistinguished by the dreaded astuteness that generally characterized Cecil's and Walsingham's intelligence network. Or perhaps it was the sheer presence of mind shown by the cottage's caretaker that saved Garnett's papers and many other things from being discovered.

---

*Caraman (1964), pp. 68–69.

The events that triggered the raid on Garnett's cottage were haphazard: a youth mistakenly claimed to have spotted a Jesuit whom he had allegedly seen in Spain! One is tempted to see all this as a diversion, perhaps to protect an agent from being exposed, but the particulars of the search, which involved Richard Young, the chief justice of Middlesex and a close collaborator of Topcliffe, makes that unlikely. Young would have been sure to pounce at the right moment, just as the intelligence services had done in the summer of 1586 when they destroyed the Babington plot. There can hardly have been anyone alive in England who would not have known about Anthony Babington and his associates; rumors that they were framed were probably rife then as now, at least among the Catholic community. That sorry tale culminated in the execution of Mary Queen of Scots and was widely seen as a prelude to the showdown with the Spanish Armada in 1588.

It also intersects, indirectly, with the story of Shakespeare, Marlowe, and the wider Catholic community's relationship with this area and the theaters. It was in Hog Lane (Worship Street) that Father William Weston was captured on August 3, 1586. He had just returned to London and was knocking at the door of one of the few houses here when he was arrested by someone who seemed to be a private individual but was in fact the keeper of the Clink prison in Southwark. Weston tried to resist arrest but a passing butcher threatened to knock him out. It had been Weston's extreme bad fortune to walk into a surveillance operation involving Babington, who was at that moment holed up in Robert Poley's house in Hog Lane, unaware to the end that Poley was working for the government. Just before his capture Babington sent a short note to the treacherous Poley, which reads, "My beloved Robin, as I hope you are, otherwise of all two-footed beings the most wicked." This is the most poignant and ingenuous document from the entire Babington tragedy; it is an eerie thought that "the most wicked" Poley was one of the three men who were present at Christopher Marlowe's death in Greenwich.

Weston had been recognized and the team watching Babington may have assumed that he was part of the conspiracy. The government clearly suspected that the area was a hotbed of Catholics and acted accordingly. This may well be why, the good burghers' investments in summer cottages notwithstanding, the authorities erected gallows on Curtain road. On August 28 1588, the priest William Gunter was executed at "the new pair of gallows set up at the Theatre," and on October 5, 1588, William Hartley suffered the same fate here, "his mother looking on."* Shakespeare was by then probably employed in Burbage's playhouse, so these two deaths may have been his first sight of man's inhumanity to man. Not that capital punishment either deterred the Catholics or instilled in the likes of Marlowe a respect for the law. It was not far from the new gallows, in the very same Hog Lane where Weston was arrested, that Marlowe and the poet and translator Thomas Watson killed William Bradley in a brawl in 1589. The killing marked the end of a feud between Watson and Bradley, but for Marlowe it seems to have been just the kind of thing that happened around him or that he caused to happen. This area was evidently his backyard, as the court records indicate that at the time of the killing he lodged in Norton Folgate, obviously to be close to the theaters where his plays were being performed.

The actors probably stayed put here quite a bit. There were, it seems, several taverns or inns for them to gather and drink in, and of course to meet women. When the Swiss traveler Thomas Platter visited London he stayed in an inn outside Bishopsgate, perhaps at the Dolphin near St. Botolph's or else at a hostelry farther up toward Spitalfields and Hog Lane. In his diary he conjures up a vivid picture of the Shoreditch tavern culture and the fact that men and women mingled freely, just as they did in the audiences of plays. Women dropped in at these taverns both alone and in small groups to drink and laugh together and, perhaps, even to socialize with the players. One wonders whether among these rumbustious pub-crawling players was Will Shakespeare. The raucous scenes in the Boar's Head from the two *Henry IV* plays come to mind. They take us to the heart of this culture of inns and taverns.

---

*Challoner, pp. 135, 150.

8.

Likely Lads: Kit Marlowe and Will Shakespeare

he young provincial Will Shakespeare probably lodged in one of Burbage's "rents" while tending to customers' horses; established actors and writers also lived close to the Theatre, the rakehell Marlowe, the poet Thomas Watson, and the playwright Robert Greene among them. Marlowe and Greene had overlapped at Cambridge for three years. Greene had been at St. John's, the former college of Elizabeth's chief minister, Burghley, and eventually the college of the young Earl of Southampton. At just the time when Shakespeare pitched his tent in Holywell Lane, the legendary comedian and actor Richard Tarlton died. The year was 1588. Intriguingly Tarlton was "lying at that time in the house of one Em Ball in Shoreditch in the county of Middlesex" who was allegedly "a woman of very bad reputation." This Em Ball was closely related to Robert Greene's mistress, "in all likelihood her daughter."*

To live near the theaters was the obvious thing for theater professionals to do. That Marlowe lived either in Holywell Lane or a stone's throw away to the south in Norton Folgate (the area included the current Norton Folgate and Folgate Streets, as well as the area that later became Spitalfields Market) makes perfect sense. Like all the others he needed to be close to the playhouses. For Marlowe, the actor who came first and foremost was Edward Alleyn, one of the great stars of the age alongside Richard Tarlton,

---

*Eccles (1934), p. 126.

Richard Burbage, Will Kemp, Robert Armin, and several others. Alleyn, unlike Tarlton, excelled in the rolling epic and tragic scripts that Marlowe wrote for him. Through acting and marriage alliances, he became wealthy and in the end a benefactor to the nation. Eventually he bought the manor of Dulwich, where in 1619 he founded the College of God's Gift, now known as Dulwich College.

Kit Marlowe's symbiotic relationship with Alleyn may have proved a mixed blessing. His plays, for all their poetic verve, suffer from a sense of having been written primarily as brilliant declamatory rhetoric: the speeches are a vehicle for a single voice rather than dialogue that dramatically communicates with other characters. Shakespeare seems always to write instinctively for an ensemble cast, even when, in the Lord Chamberlain's, he could avail himself of stars like Kemp and the brilliant young Burbage. That Marlowe wrote one, if not two, of his plays when he was still at Cambridge suggests that he was less bound to theater as a group activity and profession than Shakespeare. Marlowe's plays never quite sound the note of "total theater" so characteristic of Shakespeare's; he was always more a great dramatic poet than a poetic dramatist. Edward Rudyerd, one of Shakespeare's Puritan contemporaries, pilloried Marlowe as "a Cambridge scholar, who was a poet and a filthy play-maker." Marlowe's plays may have been filthy enough—that is, atheistical and Machiavellian—but even this hostile writer acknowledges that he was a poet.

Marlowe's habits, too, reflect that he was a poet first and a dramatist second: from the records, we know that he was simply not present enough in London to be immersed in the theater as actor and writer, even though he and the playwright Thomas Kyd shared lodgings and wrote in the same chamber at some point in 1591, perhaps even inside the Rose. Marlowe never seems to have acted or been a shareholder in the various companies to which he belonged at different times. The extant documentation indicates that, if anything, he was busy above all on behalf of Her Majesty's government. Or perhaps he was just behaving badly for his own selfish purposes, as he did in Flushing.

The Shoreditch theaters had been operating for ten years when

Shakespeare arrived; in 1587–88, they struck gold with Marlowe's brilliant and revolutionary play *Tamburlaine*.* (The likely venue was the Theatre, where *Dr. Faustus* played the following year.)† *Tamburlaine* was blasphemous and atheistical as well as dangerously subversive in celebrating the fourteenth-century Tartar warrior king, who proudly proclaims, "I am a lord, for so my deeds shall prove,/ And yet a shepherd by my parentage." Nothing could have been more antagonistic to the Great Chain of Being, that Tudor fiction of an organic society in which everyone occupies an allotted place with the King or Queen at the top of the heap by divine right. Tamburlaine's maverick and self-created royalty, if not divinity, seems moreover to enjoy the full blessing of its youthful creator. The very first words spoken onstage are not even Tamburlaine's but Marlowe's, in the Prologue, warning off the political and moral faint-hearts:

> *From jigging veins of rhyming mother wits,*
> *And such conceits as clownage keeps in pay,*
> *We'll lead you to the stately tent of War,*
> *Where you shall hear the Scythian Tamburlaine,*
> *Threat'ning the world with high astounding terms*
> *And scourging kingdoms with his conquering sword;*
> *View but his picture in this tragic glass,*
> *And then applaud his fortunes as you please.*

This is a self-advertising, defiant, and fearless new voice. That it was passed by the censor of plays is a major tribute to the state's relative tolerance toward the new art form of theater. Shakespeare could hardly have timed his arrival more propitiously. It was the year of Marlowe and the play to see was *Tamburlaine*—or the two

---

*We know that the play was in existence by the summer of 1587, because in a letter dated November 16 of that year one Philip Gawdy, a law student, reported home to his father how during a performance of a scene from the sequel to *Tamburlaine* a child and a pregnant woman in the audience were killed when a live musket used on stage was accidentally discharged into the crowd.

†Our source is Thomas Middleton's *Black Book,* where Lucifer refers to one of his "devils in *Dr Faustus* when the old Theatre cracked and frightened the audience."

*Tamburlaine*s, since Marlowe may have written the sequel almost immediately to capitalize on the first play's commercial success. The two works mark a turning point in English drama, and if they were the first plays that Shakespeare ever saw, as they may have been, the meeting of minds was nothing short of providential.

In 1587, Marlowe became the unchallenged king of the theater. His contemporary dramatists knew it instantly. No one else could write like that. Here was the most finely tuned poetic ear in the country. The magic of Marlowe's blank verse stems from its sonorous grandiloquence and epic reach, his ability effortlessly to sound the right notes and to conjure entrancing vistas and thus explore, in his audience's imagination, foreign lands of the mind. He was a highly accomplished classicist, who had translated Ovid's *Amores* while still at Cambridge—where, too, probably in partnership with his friend Thomas Nashe, he had written *Dido Queen of Carthage,* a play based on the *Aeneid.* Marlowe's time in Cambridge is of enormous importance to an understanding of who he was and, perhaps, to how he became so strangely freethinking. And, of course, it bears famously on his allegiances, since it is chiefly through his run-in with the authorities in Cambridge and the subsequent intervention of the Privy Council in London that we know he was involved in the murky world of intelligence.

This is not the place to discuss at length Marlowe's record in espionage. Suffice it to note that the Privy Council instructed Cambridge in 1587 to award Marlowe its master of arts. The minutes of the meeting make it clear that, far from being a papist, he was doing sterling work on the Crown's behalf.

According to the council minutes, the University of Cambridge had misunderstood the true nature of Marlowe's visits to France, which constituted "faithful dealing," that is, loyal service:

> Whereas it was reported that Christopher Morley was determined to have gone beyond the seas to Rheims and there to remain, their Lordships thought good to certify that he had no such intent, but that in all his actions he had behaved himself orderly and discreetly, whereby he had done her Majesty good service and deserved to be rewarded for his faithful

dealing. Their Lordships request was that the rumor thereof should be allayed by all possible means and that he should be furthered in the degree he was to take at this next Commencement, because it was not Her Majesty's pleasure that any employed as he had been in matters touching the benefit of his country should be defamed by those who are ignorant in the affairs he went about.*

In other words, if he was sniffing around Rheims, where Jeanne d'Arc had famously crowned Charles VII in 1429 and which now harbored a notorious Jesuit college run by Cardinal William Allen, it was on Her Majesty's behalf. It was probably this school, more than any other place in Europe, that trained young Englishmen for martyrdom. Officially, therefore, and as far as the Privy Council knew, Marlowe was a loyal servant—though their view may not have been borne out by the evidence that leaked out shortly before his death and in its wake.

Marlowe's seven Cambridge years, from 1580 to 1587, matter for a number of other reasons, notably for the people that he met while he was there. These included the same Robert Greene who attacked him repeatedly and, in the end, famously alongside Shakespeare and Thomas Nashe. Both Greene and Nashe were Marlowe's contemporaries at Cambridge. Also overlapping with Marlowe, if for no more than two years, was Henry Wriothesley, the young third Earl of Southampton and protégé of the most powerful man in the land, Elizabeth's chief minister, Burghley.

There is little doubt of Marlowe's homosexuality. After his death, this was proclaimed in a string of scandalous allegations by a government agent, Richard Baines. Baines had himself several years earlier infiltrated the same Rheims seminary that Marlowe may have targeted and that had aroused Cambridge's suspicions. Baines, getting much further than Marlowe, had enrolled in the College. When his cover was blown, he was arrested and tortured by Allan before being released. It seems that he did not crack or, if he did, that he might have agreed to become a double agent. In any case, he did have direct connections to Marlowe: they had teamed up as counterfeiters and

---

*Quoted in DNB entry on Marlowe.

were both hauled before Sir Robert Sidney (the governor of the English-held town of Flushing, in Holland), which tends to strengthen the charges in his "Note containing the opinion of one Christopher Marly concerning his damnable judgement of religion of scorn of God's word."

The statements attributed to Marlowe in this document, outrageous in his time, chime strangely with modern freethinking and Marxist views about power and the abuses of religion, particularly the way religion is used by its acolytes to repress the people. The note implies that notwithstanding his scorn for religion Marlowe leaned toward Catholicism, but the most explosive allegations link Marlowe's contempt for religion with a taste for sex with men. According to Baines, Marlowe claimed that "the woman of Samaria and her sister were whores and that Christ knew them dishonestly," that "St John the Evangelist was bedfellow to Christ and leaned always in his bosom, then he used him as the sinners of Sodoma, that all they that love not tobacco and boys were fools." The note goes on to cite Marlowe's interest in counterfeiting, something he had already done while in Flushing although he was apprehended before he and his confederate, a goldsmith by the name of Gifford Gilbert, could do any damage. Marlowe and Gilbert were betrayed by this same Richard Baines, who had been their "chamber-fellow." So when Baines wrote that Marlowe asserted that "he had as good a right to coin as the Queen of England and that he was acquainted with one Poole a prisoner in Newgate who hath great skill in mixing of metals," he knew exactly what he was talking about.

However malicious the note may be in its specific phrasing, which seems calculated to inflict maximum damage on Marlowe, most of the allegations are probably true: they are corroborated independently by other witnesses, such as Marlowe's onetime roommate Thomas Kyd. They are also consonant with the man who emerges from both the plays and the historical record—a tearaway, always up to mischief and repeatedly involved in fights. At least three of these, two in London and one in Canterbury, ended in court. The first one, in which Bradley was killed, landed Marlowe in Newgate in 1591, although both he and Watson were acquitted of murder on the ground of self-defense.

It is this same homosexual, brilliant, dangerous Kit Marlowe whom Shakespeare, his junior by two months, came to admire and perhaps even love, if the glowing tribute he wrote seven years after Marlowe's death can be trusted. The considerable circumstantial evidence makes it almost unthinkable that they were not close, as friends and as rivals. They were of similar backgrounds (Marlowe's father was a cobbler). Both were born in 1564, one in Stratford, the other in Canterbury. Marlowe went on to a great cathedral school in Canterbury, called King's School, while Shakespeare attended a modest local grammar school, although it was modest only by comparison with Eton, Westminster, and other great schools. (That the headmaster of Eton earned only half what Shakespeare's schoolmaster took home as pay provides food for thought. The Stratford Corporation took the master's salary seriously because they valued his job.) Marlowe proceeded on a scholarship endowed by Archbishop Matthew Parker, a former master of Corpus, to Cambridge where he was a sizar, that is, a student supported financially by his college; Shakespeare may not even have finished out grammar school. Now their paths diverge, but not just for reasons of education. Rather, the two men responded very differently to their environment.

Marlowe and Shakespeare must have been aware of each other, for they both wrote for Strange's Men and then Pembroke's Men, they lived in the same part of town, and one of them was probably gay (Marlowe), the other bisexual (Shakespeare). They shared a passion for Ovid. That the rivalry between Marlowe and Shakespeare expressed itself in specific works is argued by Stephen Greenblatt, who writes that the contest progressed "from the momentous early works, *Tamburlaine* and *Henry VI,* to a brilliant pair of strikingly similar history plays, Shakespeare's *Richard II* and Marlowe's *Edward II,* and an equally brilliant pair of long erotic poems, Shakespeare's *Venus and Adonis* and Marlowe's *Hero and Leander.*"* There is little to gainsay in this. It makes and reinforces the important point that there are just too many parallels between the two men's literary endeavors to account for by coincidence. A Marlowe and Shakespeare

---

*Greenblatt (2004), pp. 256–57.

double act may have emerged at the Theatre in the late 1580s, when both men were in their mid-twenties.

The way Marlowe conducted his short life may seem incompatible with his being the friend of the kind of person one imagines Shakespeare to have been. But although the two men clearly differed in temperament, Shakespeare, as we have seen, probably had a delinquent past. And we have a glimpse of another Marlowe, on an occasion in Canterbury in November 1585, at the house of Katherine Benchkin, the mother of one of his Cambridge friends. Marlowe and various relatives, including his father, witnessed the Benchkin will, and Marlowe read it out "plainly and distinctly" before signing it. The image of the future author of *Tamburlaine* mundanely discharging his duty to read aloud a will as the most literate person present should, perhaps, make one reconsider one's sense of incompatibility between him and Shakespeare. Human beings are infinitely complex and self-divided; the author of *Tamburlaine* could brawl, spy, translate Ovid, be friends with the gentler, brilliant young Shakespeare, and yet be himself. Shakespeare knew all this, none better.

But there was a side to Marlowe's life that, as far as we know, Shakespeare never touched. His links to the intelligence services would have set alarm bells ringing with anyone who, like Shakespeare, was eager to grasp the opportunity theater offered to earn money for a family at home. After all, unlike the maverick from Canterbury, Will was a parent, and the cost of dissidence was horrendous as Shakespeare knew well from the human heads that decorated several of London's gates and notably London Bridge.

If Shakespeare lived a double life, as a secret Catholic and outwardly conformist Anglican, the provocatively skeptical Marlowe would undoubtedly have been irresistible. But Shakespeare does not seem to take his gods too seriously. His is not a drama of faith any more than Marlowe's, although when Machiavelli, in the Prologue to *The Jew of Malta*, proclaims that religion is cant, "but a childish toy," and that "there is no sin but ignorance," we are in a febrile political world that Shakespeare never touches. Neither Iago in *Othello* nor Edmund in *King Lear*, both characters divorced from conventional Christian morality, would ever say something like this, even if their imagined characters secretly agreed. An even stronger contrast is provided by Shakespeare's Richard III from the first cycle of histories. When the character first propels himself to prominence, in the third part of *Henry VI*, he taunts us with "I can add colours to the chameleon, / Change shapes with Proteus for advantages, / And set the murderous Machevil to school." And he does, but never in the way Marlowe would. For Richard III, to be Machiavellian is to be devious, ruthless, and practical; to kill; and to have fun on the way. Marlowe's Barabas also enjoys his wickedness to the full, but the Prologue articulates a position quite different from the play's; Machiavelli's views on religion are remarkably similar to those attributed, rightly or wrongly, to Marlowe himself. The fact that in *The Jew of Malta* they are spoken by the political bogeyman of Elizabethan culture—Niccolò Machiavelli was sometimes known as McEvil or Old Nick—makes no difference. Such distancing fooled no one, particularly not when the villain of the piece is for good measure also its endlessly resourceful comic Machiavellian protagonist.

There can be little doubt that both Marlowe and Shakespeare were fascinated by politics and political philosophy. Marlowe engaged with politics directly, while for Shakespeare it was a much more internalized affair, a deep and relentless search for a national identity through the English history plays, from *King John* through the Plantagenets and finally all the way to *Henry VIII* and the prophecy of peace and prosperity under Elizabeth I. The ten plays dealing with the nation's destiny probe and question loyalty, moral being, even the divine right of kings when that finds itself divorced from moral foundations or legitimacy. It may have been Marlowe who inspired or fostered Shakespeare's lively interest in history. He has in the past been credited with writing parts of the *Henry VI* plays. Certainly there is proof of his borrowing from the third part of *Henry VI*, which suggests that he may have been as relaxed about borrowing from Shakespeare as the latter was about echoing others when it suited him to do so.

As it happens, there exists an anonymous play that may have

started life as a collaboration between Shakespeare and Marlowe in around 1589, *The Taming of a* [not "the"] *Shrew.** Its distinct Marlovian strain points either at Marlowe as collaborator or at Shakespeare trying to write like Marlowe—that is, the rookie modeling himself on the star. The phrasing and metaphor are Shakespearian, and some striking broader similarities exist between *A Shrew* and *A Midsummer Night's Dream,* particularly the characters called Sly and Bottom. In *A Shrew,* Sly wakes up from a vision of himself transformed into a lord watching a play and tells the tapster who wakes him, "I have had / The bravest dream tonight that ever thou / Heardest in all thy life." This seems to anticipate Bottom's awakening from sharing the bower of Titania: "I have had a most rare vision. I have had a dream past the wit of man to say what dream it was. Man is but an ass, if he go about t'expound this dream."

On their own these two comparable passages might just coincidentally share an interest in fantasy and reality, but this is unlikely in the broader context here. The verse sounds a Marlovian Shakespearian note, as when women's eyes are said to be "fairer than rocks of pearl and precious stone" and lovelier ultimately than "the morning sun, / When first she opes her oriental gates." This reads like a dry run for some of the key metaphors of *Romeo and Juliet,* and there is yet another analogous passage in *A Midsummer Night's Dream.* When Oberon tells Puck that they are privileged spirits, he notes that he "like a forester the groves may tread / Even till the eastern gate, all fiery red, / Opening on Neptune with fair blessed beams, / Turns into yellow gold his salt green streams." The lines from *A Shrew* carry a Marlovian charge in their luminosity and in the hard-edged precious stones that adorn their texture; yet, though the play strains throughout toward Marlovian sublimity, it

---

*E. K. Chambers long ago suggested this date, because lines from the play seem to be parodied by Robert Greene in his 1589 romance *Menaphon* and in its prefatory epistle by Nashe. Chambers noted further that the play imitated passages from *Tamburlaine* (c. 1587) and *Dr. Faustus* (c. 1588) and then wrote that Shakespeare was often credited with a hand in *The Taming of a Shrew* (Chambers [1923], vol. 2, pp. 48–49).

always just misses.* No one, with the possible exception of Shakespeare or Jonson at the limit of their rhetorical powers, could pull off Marlowe's sweeping and resonant classical style. By the time Shakespeare wrote *A Midsummer Night's Dream* six years later he had assimilated his Marlovian lessons. From the memory of a metaphor of suits "spotted with liquid gold, thick set with pearle" (*A Shrew*) Shakespeare had moved on to the full moon "decking with liquid pearl the bladed grass" (*Dream*). The one is static, the other dynamic, painting in words the magic of a midsummer night under a full moon in a Warwickshire wood near Athens, and during a daylight performance at that (as was customary in the London theater of the time). As for the melting pearls, they are like a Shakespearian signature tune. Shakespeare must have loved pearls. They figure throughout his works, from Silvia's "sea of melting pearl which some call tears" (*The Two Gentlemen of Verona*) to Cordelia's famous tears in *King Lear,* which are "as pearls from diamonds dropped," and finally to the "pearls that were his eyes" in the marine metamorphosis in *The Tempest.*

If *A Shrew* was written in 1589, it would have started life as an Admiral's or a Strange's property before migrating to Pembroke's Company. The head of the latter sat on the Privy Council. Through Pembroke's Company, Shakespeare and Marlowe sailed into the orbit of Sir Philip Sidney's family: the Earl of Pembroke was the husband of Sidney's sister Mary Herbert. When Marlowe evoked Lord Strange to Sir Robert Sidney in January 1592, did he also tell Sidney

---

*In connection with those precious stones: a character by the name of Polidor quests for "those lovely dames" who to him seem "Richer in beauty than the orient pearl / Whiter than is the Alpine crystal mould, / And far more lovely than the Tyrian plant, / That blushing in the air turns to a stone." Again, phrases like "heaven cristalline," "liquid gold," "pretious fiery pointed stones of Indy," the "azure down, / That circles Citherea's silver doves," the "crystal Hellespont," which yields rich coffers of "wealthy mines" in which "millions of labouring Moors" seek rare stones, the "topless Alps," all unmistakably evoke the famous topless towers of Ilium from *Dr. Faustus. Faustus* is echoed again in "Grecian Helena / For whose sweet sake so many princes died, / That came with thousand ships to Tenedos," and when Philema proposes to freight ships "with Arabian silkes, / Rich affrick spices Arras counterpoines ... sweet smelling Ambergreece," we are in a world of language that yearns toward Marlowe.

that he was at that very moment working for his brother-in-law?* *A Shrew* features a young woman so thoroughly "tamed" by a young man that, at the end, she casts herself as a penitent daughter of Eve who urges all women to obey, love, keep, and nourish their husbands. The stage direction reads *"She lays her hands under her husband's feet."* The Petruchio character in *A Shrew*, Ferando, has won his wager in causing this self-abasing of a woman, who is called Kate just as she is in the more famous play *The Taming of the Shrew*.

A Shrew also has an induction featuring one Sly, but this induction truly frames the play: at the end, Sly wakes as if from a dream. He moreover wakes in the course of the play itself. During one such intervention, he protests that he is, after all, none other than *"Don Christo Vary."* He isn't Don Anything—the play's opening line calls him a "whoreson drunken slave," and he has sunk into an intoxicated stupor by line 19. His *"Don Christo Vary"* is a joke on the name Christopher, which means "carrier of Christ," from the Latin *Christus* and *ferre*. This may be Shakespeare's "sly" feeding into the play clues in the form of the real names of his acquaintances. Marlowe never does this, and indeed the taking of liberties with Marlowe's name further points to Shakespeare's authorship. *A Shrew* may be his breaking-away work, the one in which he worked free from the influence and idiom of his friend and mentor, taking what Bullough called his "first shot at the theme."† Rare words appear, such as "chud," which Shakespeare would use in *King Lear* and may have used earlier against Sir Thomas Lucy; other usages, too, point to Shakespeare. Among them are "lief" and "liefest," meaning "dear" and "dearest." Shakespeare uses "liefest" once elsewhere, in *2 Henry VI,* a play from the early 1590s that would be closer in composition to *A Shrew* than most.

In May 1591, Marlowe, the Admiral's Edward Alleyn and Alleyn's brother John, as well as Augustine Phillips, George Bryan, Thomas

---

*Gurr ([1996], p. 271): "I am almost convinced that Shakespeare was with his plays in Pembroke's Company at the Theatre in 1592 and 1593." The fate of the company may well have been sealed by the onset of the plague in midsummer 1592.

†Bullough, vol. 1, p. 58.

Pope, and perhaps John Heminges defected from the Theatre in the aftermath of a fierce row the previous November between the Alleyns and the Burbages. They headed south and teamed up with the tycoon Philip Henslowe, a Southwark entrepreneur, brothel keeper, and owner of the Rose. They now joined Lord Strange's Men, which is why Marlowe could boast to the governor of Flushing in January 1592 that he knew Ferdinando Strange. The split must have been a traumatic event for the Theatre and the Burbages, for at one stroke they lost their star writer, their chief actor, and several other important players. However, the playhouses were not, it seems, as a rule linked to permanent companies, so the loss of players did not entail the closure of the house. One company/one house is a model that came in later, with the creation in 1594 of the London-based Lord Chamberlain's Company, which, after 1599, played at the Globe and eventually at both the Globe and the Blackfriars. The first records of an Elizabethan company associated with a single house for an extended period of time come from Henslowe's account book (the so-called Diary) for 1592, which records a five-month-long association between the Rose theater and Lord Strange's Men.

Marlowe probably moved to live south of the river, in Southwark near the Old Kent Road. He was, after all, Kentish and a visitor at Thomas Walsingham's house at Scadbury in Chislehurst in Kent, where he would one day find himself under house arrest. His absence from the Theatre and probably from Shoreditch, too, must have been keenly felt by Shakespeare, but it also provided him with an opportunity. The remnants of the Lord Admiral's Men at the Theatre now needed someone to fill Marlowe's shoes, and that someone was Shakespeare. There were just two, possibly three, other dramatists in the frame: Kyd, Greene, and perhaps George Peele. Kyd must have teamed up with Marlowe, since they are listed as sharing a workroom in 1591. This leaves only Greene and possibly Peele as senior dramatists, if the latter was indeed around at the Theatre and with the Admiral's at the time of the split.

Shakespeare probably started working for the Burbages as a jack-of-all-trades—a jobbing actor, reviser of plays, junior collaborator, prompter, bookkeeper, and generally useful person about the house. His exceptional facility with language will have been evident at once and the company, whether Lord Strange's or Pembroke's, seems to have had the good sense to recognize this. Perhaps he did to old plays what in Peter Shaffer's play *Amadeus* Mozart does to a promising but as yet wooden piece of music by Salieri: Mozart sits down at the keyboard and, improvising on Salieri's basic musical line, sends the piece soaring on angels' wings. If so, it might account for some of the jealousy and frustration that Shakespeare provoked in one of his fellow dramatists, and for why he was accused of plagiarism and arrogance. Obviously he did not have this effect on Marlowe, whose voice is at least as distinctive as his own, even, perhaps, in ways that also distill its limitations, for its grand poetic register may in the end be too univocal. Marlowe hit the ground running and wrote for the theater before he worked in it professionally. Only with the three *Henry VI* plays, in around 1590–91, did Shakespeare make the headlines, drawing fulsome tributes from Marlowe's friend and fellow Cambridge man Thomas Nashe, and enjoying a run of performances unprecedented in that day. No wonder Marlowe has been suspected of taking a hand in this first cycle of history plays.*

---

*Henry VI was played fourteen times, with "large takings," at the Rose, between March 3 and June 20, 1592, according to Henslowe's Diary. Michael Wood calculates that the audience figures were around thirty-two thousand (Wood, p. 142).

9

ℒiving the Sonnets: 1590—

arlowe's departure from Shoreditch set Shake-
speare free. In the two and a half years between
1590 and the closure of the London theaters in
1592, he wrote the second and third parts of *Henry VI*, a blood-
curdling tragedy with much brilliant writing in it, *Titus Andronicus*,
and *The Two Gentlemen of Verona* and *The Comedy of Errors*. This latter
is one of the greatest farces ever written and revolves, not entirely
unexpectedly perhaps for this father of twins, around two sets of
same-sex twins.* Shakespeare moved fast, always, as the sure-
footedness of *The Comedy of Errors* amply testifies. No one in the period comes anywhere near it. If *The Comedy of Errors* were the only
Shakespeare play to survive, we would still think that he possessed
the most instinctive dramatic flair for the timing of comic scenes of
anyone writing at the time.

We do not know whether the friendship between Shakespeare
and Marlowe now turned into friendly rivalry, although it is hard to
see that it could have become anything else since their plays in
Shoreditch and Bankside were competing for the same pool of audiences. If Shakespeare missed the company of the excitingly lawless
Kit Marlowe, fate, good fortune, or a mutual friend had put the
young Earl of Southampton in his way the year before. Young

---

*The so-called first part of *Henry VI* is probably a collaborative work. Vickers
(pp. 148–243) makes the strongest case yet for George Peele as Shakespeare's collaborator in *Titus Andronicus*.

Henry Wriothesley, third Earl of Southampton, had grown up in the London household of the powerful Cecils. The master of the house was the most adroit politician in the land, William Cecil Lord Burghley, a relic from the age of Henry VIII and Queen Mary and the present Queen's chief minister and most trusted adviser. Cecil occupied a grand brick-and-timber mansion in the Strand, opposite the Savoy. It backed up toward Covent Garden and was wedged between what are now the Lyceum and the London Transport Museum. The name of Burghley Street still recalls the Cecils' presence here. From their palace in the Strand, the Cecils ruled a fractious realm; here Southampton lived as Burghley's ward. Burghley's son Robert Cecil, who was Southampton's senior by over ten years, overlapped there with him. In this powerhouse of intelligentsia, where the provost of St. John's College was among the private tutors (Burghley was chancellor of Cambridge and an alumnus of St. John's College), Robert Cecil was being groomed by his father for the succession. He would brilliantly deliver on his early promise in spite of severe physical disabilities, which included splayed legs and a deformed spine.

At a time when a person's physical appearance was commonly thought to reflect the inner self, when physical blemishes were all too often attributed to the judgment of the Supreme Being, Robert Cecil, the most successful man in the land, the heir to his father's gifts, deviousness and addiction to hard work, was a hunchback. This in a period when Londoners apparently took their children to see the lunatics at Bedlam in Bishopsgate rather as we might take them to the zoo. Cecil was a year older than Shakespeare. The two men must have come to know each other, because from 1591 Cecil sat on the Privy Council alongside the Hunsdons, who were patrons of the arts and closely connected with Shakespeare's company. The country's executive intimately involved itself in monitoring the new and burgeoning theatrical culture. This may seem odd at a time when, according to its own lights, England was constantly struggling to survive in the face of a Catholic threat. It is perfectly understandable that Edmund Campion and Henry Garnett, the head of the Jesuit mission in England, should be interviewed by members of the Privy Council; it would seem to be quite another matter for the council to see Ben Jonson over suspected papist matter in *Sejanus*. Yet see him they did.

The deformed Robert Cecil and the impetuous young Southampton seem to have enjoyed a close relationship. One day the younger Cecil's intervention would save Southampton from certain death after he was found guilty of treason. Southampton's mother was a diehard Catholic, and although there is no evidence to suggest that her son was disloyal, it may have a bearing on his relationship with Shakespeare. Both the poet and the earl may have had Catholic skeletons in their cupboards, while the Cecils' Protestant credentials were unimpeachable. Moreover, in 1589 Robert Cecil married Elizabeth Brooke, the daughter of Sir William Brooke, Lord Cobham. It was Cobham who during his brief tenure as Lord Chamberlain would subject Shakespeare and his company to the most notorious act of Protestant censorship of the age.

That Shakespeare knew Southampton well is a matter of record. They seem to have met in the summer of 1590. The play-loving young aristocrat had returned to London from Cambridge the previous year and enrolled at Gray's Inn. At the university, he had been a younger contemporary of Marlowe, Nashe, and Greene, the last two of whom were at St. John's with him (he had matriculated at the tender age of twelve). It may well have been one of them who introduced Shakespeare to Wriothesley. Shakespeare's two famous narrative poems, *Venus and Adonis* and *The Rape of Lucrece,* which were published in 1593 and 1594 respectively, are both dedicated to Wriothesley. The two homages are cast in the formal language of Elizabethan court literature, but even so there is little doubting the intimacy of tone, particularly in the second dedication, to *The Rape of Lucrece.* Here it is:

> To the Right Honourable Henry Wriothesley, Earl of Southampton, and Baron of Titchfield.
>
> The love I dedicate to your lordship is without end: whereof this pamphlet without beginning is but a superfluous moiety. The warrant I have of your honourable disposition, not the worth of my untutored lines, makes it assured of acceptance. What I have done is yours, what I have to do is

yours, being part in all I have, devoted yours. Were my worth greater, my duty would show greater, meantime, as it is, it is bound to your Lordship; to whom I wish long life still lengthened with all happiness.

Your Lordship's in all duty, William Shakespeare.

Whereas in *Venus and Adonis* Shakespeare had been somewhat reticent about the propriety of choosing a prominent member of the aristocracy as a patron—"so strong a prop to support so weak a burden" and only "the first heir" of the poet's invention—in dedicating *The Rape of Lucrece* he is firing on all cylinders without the slightest inhibition.* Shakespeare freely expresses his "love" and enjoys, he states, the youth's reciprocal affection. Even more remarkable than a professed love affair between a glover from Stratford and a leading young aristocrat is the fact that the love is openly advertised in both publications. *Venus and Adonis* went through nine editions in Shakespeare's lifetime and was more frequently alluded to in the period than any other among his works. *The Rape of Lucrece* had gone through no fewer than nine editions by 1655, some five or six of

---

*The full text of the dedication of *Venus and Adonis* reads:

To the Right Honourable Henry Wriothesley, Earl of Southampton, and Baron of Titchfield

Right Honourable, I know not how I shall offend in dedicating my unpolished lines to your lordship, nor how the world will censure me for choosing so strong a prop to support so weak a burden. Only, if your honour seem but pleased, I account myself highly praised, and vow to take advantage of all idle hours till I have honoured you with some grave labour. But if the first heir of my invention prove deformed, I shall be sorry it had so noble a godfather, and never after ear so barren a land for fear it yield me still so bad a harvest. I leave it to your honourable survey, and your honour to your heart's content, which I wish may always answer your own wish and the world's hopeful expectation.

Your honour's in all duty,
William Shakespeare

As will be seen later, Shakespeare's use here of the word "deformed" to describe his first long poem for the young earl may be open to a more literal interpretation than has been customary hitherto.

which came in Shakespeare's lifetime, with one of them appearing in the year of his death. Everyone knew about the relationship. In the seventeenth century it was rumored, too, that Southampton had been munificent toward Shakespeare to the tune of a thousand pounds. According to Rowe, Shakespeare

> had the honour to meet with many great and uncommon marks of favour and friendship from the Earl of Southampton.... There is one instance so singular in the magnificence of this patron of Shakespeare's that *if I had not been assured that the story was handed down by Sir William Davenant, who was probably very well acquainted with his affairs,* I should not have ventured to have inserted that my lord Southampton at one time gave him a thousand pounds, to enable him to go through with a purchase which he heard he had a mind to. A bounty very great, and very rare at any time ... [my emphasis].

This gift may have helped Shakespeare not only to buy property but also to redeem both his father's debts and his own fines. The sum seems immense, but that very figure was nevertheless being floated in Stratford-upon-Avon in the middle of the seventeenth century. Thus the Reverend John Ward noted in his diary in 1662 that "Shakespeare supplied the stage with two plays every year, and for it had an allowance so large that he spent at the rate of £1,000 a year, as I have heard."* Ward carefully, and twice, stresses the fact that he has "heard" this reported in Stratford. The thousand-pound figure seems to conflate rumors about Shakespeare's large earnings with the gift to him from Southampton. We cannot simply dismiss it, any more than we can ignore a further testimony about it by the Reverend Joseph Greene (1712–90), scholar, master of Shakespeare's school, antiquary, and almost casual discoverer of Shakespeare's last will. According to Greene, writing in *The Gentleman's Magazine* in 1759, the "unanimous tradition of the neighbourhood where he lived is that by the uncommon bounty of the then Earl of Southampton he was enabled to purchase houses and land at Stratford, the place of his nativity." Greene's reference to a "unanimous tradition" in the

---

*Ward, pp. 183–84.

"neighbourhood" is important. It is unlikely that Rowe, Ward, and Greene were all wrong. A thousand pounds was the equivalent of two thirds of the building costs of the magnificent second Globe theater of 1614. It could have bought Shakespeare some ten houses in Stratford and still left him with cash in hand.

Perhaps this lavish gift was Southampton's thank-you present for *Venus and Adonis* and *The Rape of Lucrece*. Both poems were printed by Shakespeare's Stratford friend Richard Field; it may have been through him, if not through Shakespeare himself, that the story of Southampton's spectacular gift found its way back to Stratford. Field was one of Shakespeare's closest friends throughout his life and Shakespeare paid him a most mystifying tribute in a very late play, *Cymbeline*. When its heroine, Innogen, is asked her master's name, she replies: "Richard du Champ. If I do lie and do / No harm by it, though the gods hear, I hope / They'll pardon it." "Du Champ," of course, means "of the field." Only those in the know—that is, those who, like the playwright, were aware of Richard Field's marriage to a French Huguenot, the widow of his former employer—would have appreciated the archness of the Gallic allusion. It helps to know that in his Spanish-language publications Field usually signed himself "Ricardo del Campo."*

And there is more. When Innogen dons male attire to survive in a play in which she is persecuted by almost everyone, including a tricked husband, she assumes the name Fidele. Meaning "the loyal one" (French *fidèle*), it serves to underline her faithful, selfless character as an innocent wronged wife. "Fidele" is a near anagram of "Field." Together with her reference to Richard du Champ, it leaves little doubt that Shakespeare is conducting some kind of private dialogue with Field beyond the fiction of the play. By doubling as Field's fictional alter ego in the guise of Fidele, the unshakably loyal Innogen pays a stirring tribute to the printer from Bridge Street in Stratford-upon-Avon, Richard Field as Richard the Faithful. At the height of Shakespeare's friendship with Southampton, Field may have been there for Shakespeare. It seems that he always *was* there for Shakespeare, which is probably why Shakespeare put him in *Cymbeline* in the first place.

---

*Shapiro (2005), p. 150.

Perhaps no relationship in his life left as deep a mark on Shakespeare as the one with Southampton. At its most innocuous, their friendship was one of homage and patronage, at its most daring a full-blown homoerotic affair, which stopped just short of physical consummation. The question is whether the authorities, and particularly the Cecils and the Earl of Essex, would have tolerated a scenario in which Southampton was drawn into the ambit of gay players and theater entrepreneurs. The young man's dazzling androgynous beauty must have opened him to countless advances from both sexes. His looks are evident from the various portraits of him that have reached us, particularly a striking miniature by Nicholas Hilliard from 1594, which shows the twenty-one-year-old Wriothesley as a sultry and effeminate-looking young man with long flowing hair. This was almost certainly the face that launched the one hundred and fifty-four most famous sonnets in the English language. No wonder that the poet warns his friend of the dangers of narcissism and self-destruction. In Sonnet 93, a strikingly intimate and erotic poem about the young man's beauty, this same face is said to have been decreed by Heaven to be the place where "sweet love should ever dwell." But, the poet warns, this outward beauty must be a true mirror of the soul, or else the young man's looks will one day catch him out: "How like Eve's apple doth thy beauty grow, / If thy sweet virtue answer not thy show." The youth's appearance might turn out to be a brittle and cruel sham waiting to be exposed, a hostage to time like the bloom of Dorian Gray. In respect of his mane, the young man was the antithesis of his thirty-year-old poet friend, whose baldness is all too evident in the only two authenticated representations of him that survive. No wonder Shakespeare remarks wistfully in *The Comedy of Errors* that "There's no time for a man to recover his hair that grows bald by nature." When asked why time "is such a niggard of hair, being as it is so plentiful an excrement" the reply comes, "Because it is a blessing that he bestows on beasts, and what he hath scanted men in hair he hath given them in wit."*

---

*Southampton still had long hair during his two-year spell in the Tower, from where he was released on April 10, 1603. A few years earlier, some of these locks had been pulled out by one Ambrose Willoughby, a gentleman of the Queen's Chamber,

There is no consensus on the status of the Sonnets as either pure fiction or an imaginative documentary record. Some of their best readers and editors have always believed that they reflect real episodes and that they can legitimately be seen as, in part, a subjective record of a particular time in Shakespeare's life. The poems offer an exhilarating rhetorical spectacle and deeply reflect on the human condition in general, to some extent conventionally and generically. Their topics include the promise of youth and the ravages of age; the inevitable passage of time; man's natural desire to evade death and to reproduce himself through procreation; the poet's ability to confer a superior kind of immortality by commemorating the object of his affection in verse; sexual betrayal and the conflicting loyalties of friendship and romantic love. But there are also quite clearly moments that convey the impression of a poetic diary, of a real-life record of a turbulent relationship involving a number of different people, both male and female.

Literary criticism has been reluctant to commit itself to a firm dating of the cycle. The poems' history, from the initial verses in 1590 to the publication of the entire cycle in 1609, encompasses almost twenty years. Stretching the dates of writing from beginning to end is bound therefore to hit the mark with some poems somewhere. But a time span of 1590 to 1609 is not satisfactory. It broadens the scope of the search for real-life parallels to the poems so widely as to render it almost meaningless. And there is no hard evidence for dating the writing of the poems to any time after 1599, when Sonnets 138 and 144—the latter only ten poems off the conclusion of the entire cycle—appeared in a collection called *The Passionate Pilgrim*. All the poems had almost certainly been written by then, since some general chronological diary-style principles clearly underlie the story revealed by the cycle. Some of the few poems that

---

during an altercation. The source for this information is Rowland Whyte, who relates how Southampton, Ralegh, and one Parker were at primero in the presence chamber. When they were asked by Willoughby to give over and retire since the Queen had gone to bed, they at first refused. Willoughby threatened to call the guard, at which point they relented: "But my lord Southampton took exceptions at him between the tennis court wall and the garden, struck him and Willoughby pulled off some of his lock" (Akrigg, p. 68).

have traditionally been dated late and that scholars have matched with some confidence to outside events after 1599 may need to be reassessed.

One such poem with an apparently identifiable reference to the outside world is Sonnet 107. It starts with "Not mine own fears nor the prophetic soul / Of the wide world, dreaming on things to come" and includes the lines "The mortal moon hath her eclipse endured, / And the sad augurs mock their own presage." "Mortal moon" and "her eclipse" have been widely read as referring to the death of the virgin (and hence lunar) Queen on March 24, 1603. The smooth transition to the Stuarts that followed could be thought to have given the lie to the prophets of doom, who themselves now join in rejoicing at this political triumph and, relieved, laugh at their own false "presage." Such interpretations may be valid in the abstract, but there are in fact good reasons for dating 107 back to the mid-1590s when Shakespeare wrote *A Midsummer Night's Dream*, in which he does indeed compare the Queen with the moon and plays with lunar images. The idea for his moonlit play and poem may well have come to him after one or both of the full lunar eclipses of April 24 and October 18, 1595.

One might argue that Shakespeare inserted Sonnet 107 as a freshly composed poem into Thomas Thorpe's 1609 collection. But there is no reason for him to write a poem about the death of the queen regnant in 1609. Moreover there are further documentary records that favor dating all the poems to before the autumn of 1598. In that year Francis Meres wrote in *Palladis Tamia, Wit's Treasury* that "the sweet witty soul of Ovid lives in mellifluous and honey-tongued Shakespeare, witness his *Venus and Adonis*, his *Lucrece*, his sugared sonnets among his private friends." Meres's hugely long tome was entered in the Stationers' Register on September 7, 1598. For him to refer to the sonnets as circulating among Shakespeare's "private friends" implies that there were several copies around and that Meres and others outside the inner court loop had read them or at least heard of them for a while before *Palladis Tamia*. And there may even be a particular reason for setting the latest likely date of composition as August 1596, for it was then that Shakespeare's son, Hamnet, died in Stratford. It is hard to imagine a grieving father writing deeply involved love poems to a youth who, whatever spell he cast, was self-absorbed, shiftless, and untrustworthy.

That the story dramatized in the Sonnets took place in the early to mid-1590s may be borne out by Sonnet 94, one of the most famous and most frequently anthologized of all the poems. It opens with "They that have power to hurt, and will do none," and its final couplet concludes, "For sweetest things turn sourest by their deeds, / Lilies that fester smell far worse than weeds." This mature and complex poem comes two thirds of the way into the cycle and must be earlier than 1595. The "festering lilies" line appears verbatim in an anonymous play called *Edward III,* and the line that follows it in the play, "And every glory that inclines to sin / The shame is treble by the opposite," paraphrases the thirteenth line of the same Sonnet 94. The thought process is the same; demonstrably, the play and the sonnet are closely related. There is now almost universal agreement that Shakespeare had a major hand in *Edward III,* a play that dramatizes events from the English king's wars against Scotland and France and his adulterous wooing of the virtuous Countess of Salisbury. The hypnotizing rhetoric and lyricism of the scenes of seduction have commonly been attributed to Shakespeare. If the play did not find its way into the First Folio of Shakespeare's works it may have been because its subject matter included the defeat of the Scots, and this could not easily pass muster at a time when a Stuart occupied the throne; also the editors of the First Folio probably knew that the play was not all by Shakespeare. Some scholars now think that his main collaborator was Marlowe. If this is correct, then the play has to date from before May 1593, and Sonnet 94 likewise. The commonly held assumption that some of the Sonnets lie beyond the expressive power of the younger Shakespeare seems misplaced, since even his early solo works are strikingly mature. *Titus Andronicus* may be a violent orgy, but it is also a brilliant piece of theater; its linguistic texture is rich and complex, as are the early comedies, the second and third parts of *Henry VI,* and *Richard III.* Shakespeare hit the ground running and he learned fast. His muscular dramatic syntax and exceptional gift for perceptive and illuminating metaphor were there from the start.

All the Sonnets were, I believe, written between 1590 and 1596.

The first seventeen poems encourage the young man they address to marry in order to replicate himself. The poet seems to want to trick the youth into marriage by appealing to his pride and vanity. At the time, Burghley was urging Southampton to marry Elizabeth Vere, the daughter of the same Edward de Vere, Earl of Oxford, who would one day be championed by some as the author of Shakespeare's plays. In the mid-1590s, Shakespeare would have walked past Oxford's former home, the grand and mad "Fisher's Folly," every day as he shuttled between the playhouses in Shoreditch and his lodgings in St. Helen's Bishopsgate. As well as being the only Elizabethan nobleman ever charged with sodomy, the irascible Oxford—pederast, patron of boy actors, and enemy of Sidney—was Burghley's son-in-law. For the young earl to defy and thus humiliate Burghley took some courage. As Master of the Wards, Burghley may not have been quite as determined and ruthless with his charges as he was reputedly in politics.* Here he was thwarted, probably fairly publicly, by a young man who had spent nearly five years in his house, but he did not, it seems, exact punishment—at least, not yet.

Shakespeare's seventeen poems, perhaps presented as a gift for the Earl's seventeenth birthday (on October 6, 1590), were hardly going to change Southampton's mind and the poet soon gave up. However, the first seventeen sonnets demonstrate that chronology is indeed one of the cycle's structuring principles. The first seventeen poems were also written first.

Sonnet 18 famously starts with "Shall I compare thee to a summer's day" and confidently ends with a promise of eternal life conferred by the poet's art. This sounds a very different note from what

---

*The Master of the Wards was a lucrative sinecure, which, in this case, was granted to Lord Burghley. He acted in loco parentis for orphaned (or semi-orphaned as in the case of Southampton) wealthy young noblemen. These were in fact royal wards, but the Queen farmed them out to favorites like Burghley. The wards were educated and brought up in his household and he used this office and position of trust to forge powerful political alliances, primarily by arranging their marriages. The disreputable Earl of Oxford, Edward de Vere (descended from a famous English family, unlike the Burghleys), had been one of Burghley's wards and was married off to his daughter Anne in 1573. Later Burghley would hope to marry off Southampton to the daughter of de Vere and Anne Cecil, but he refused.

has gone before. It signals a shift in the relationship between the poet and the young man, between Will Shakespeare and Henry Wriothesley. Shakespeare may in the first instance have been commissioned to write his poems to the young earl. If so, one can only assume that the instruction came from Cecil House, if not from Burghley or Robert Cecil himself. How the Cecils might have discovered Shakespeare's existence, however, is a mystery; it is hardly likely that the two most driven politicians in the realm would have been wending their way to Shoreditch to see the actors, besides which, Shakespeare's star had not yet ascended high enough in the late 1580s to attract attention. Still, he was undeniably making an impact in London and *The Taming of a Shrew* may just possibly have given him the kind of exposure that led to their noticing him. It is, after all, a play about persuasion to marriage.

Strange, even bizarre as it may seem, Cecil House is known to have procured the help of a resident writer to hold a mirror up to Wriothesley's recalcitrant nature. John Clapham, one of Burghley's secretaries, wrote a Latin poem called "Narcissus," which he dedicated to the young Southampton. It was the young Earl's first such gift. Clapham translates the Narcissus story into an English setting, but retains Ovid's basic moral that self-love is ultimately futile and destructive. If Clapham was co-opted to coax the young man into seeing the error of his ways, Shakespeare might have been brought in for the same reason. He had the necessary confidence, as the promise of eternity in Sonnet 18 demonstrates, and he most certainly had the talent to make anyone think again. But, to judge by the sonnets from 18 onward, if the Cecils did initially bring Shakespeare into the fray they got more than they bargained for.

Almost immediately after Sonnet 18 came Sonnet 20, in which the youth is called "the master-mistress of my passion," a phrase that fully faces up to the nature of the developing relationship. What follows from now until the last poem in the sequence is nothing less than a highly wrought imaginative diary of the poet's relationships with his friend and lover. In 20, the youth is said to be possessed of all aspects of womanhood, such as gentleness and physical beauty, while being superior to the so-called fair sex by virtue of his constancy and truthfulness. But just in case, and as a strategic caveat,

Shakespeare notes that nature has equipped the young man with a penis and thereby rendered him off limits:

> *A woman's face with nature's own hand painted*
> *Hast thou, the master mistress of my passion,*
> *A woman's gentle heart, but not acquainted*
> *With shifting change as is false women's fashion;*
> *An eye more bright than theirs, less false in rolling,*
> *Gilding the object whereupon it gazeth;*
> *A man in hue, all hues in his controlling,*
> *Which steals men's eyes and women's souls amazeth.*
> *And for a woman wert thou first created,*
> *Till nature, as she wrought thee fell a-doting,*
> *And by addition me of thee defeated*
> *By adding one thing to my purpose nothing.*
> > *But since she pricked thee out for women's pleasure,*
> > *Mine be thy love and thy love's use their treasure.*

As yet the poet is careful and diplomatic, but this *is* a love poem from one man to another, from a married yeoman father of three to one of the great nobles of the land. It gets worse. Far from persuading the Earl to marry, the poet now turns into his adoring lover. Quite how intense this relationship really had become can be gleaned from Sonnet 27: "Weary with toil I haste me to my bed," the poet writes, but he is too lovesick to sleep. As he lies gazing on the dark the way blind people do, his "soul's imaginary sight" shows up the youth's "shadow to my sightless view,/Which like a jewel hung in ghastly night,/Makes black night beauteous and her old face new." Shakespeare would use this very conceit again, in one of the most celebrated love scenes ever written. When Romeo first catches a glimpse of Juliet, he exclaims that she "doth teach the torches to burn bright!/It seems she hangs upon the cheek of night/As a rich jewel in an Ethiop's ear/Beauty too rich for use, for earth too dear."

That Shakespeare should evoke his own desperate love for Southampton in the rhetoric of Romeo and Juliet need be neither surprising nor shocking. This is clearly how he imagined ideal love, even if his love for Southampton has no chance of the consummation that he so readily grants to his teenage lovers. His relationship with Southampton, albeit probably not of a physical nature, was a kind of infidelity. It hardly accorded with his trothplight to Anne Hathaway ten years earlier. Even so, the absence of sex from this relationship may explain why, in addressing the youth, he never once refers to his own status as a married man.

If the poet and youth are indeed Shakespeare (born around April 22, 1564) and Southampton (October 6, 1573), then nine years separate them. In Sonnet 22 the poet rues this fact but defiantly asserts:

> *My glass shall not persuade me I am old*
> *So long as youth and thou are of one date.*
> *But when in thee time's furrows I behold,*
> *Then look I death my days should expiate.*

The passage of time and the transience of beauty, particularly the fading bloom of young women, is of course a traditional poetic motif. Nowhere is it more famously articulated than in Pierre de Ronsard's sonnet to his unobtainable beloved, "Quand vous serez bien vieille, au soir, à la chandelle, /Assise auprès du feu, dévidant et filant" (When in the future you are old, at night, sitting by the fire and spinning by the light of a taper). Ronsard (1524–85) had been Mary Stuart's poetry teacher and a founding member of the Pléiade, an influential school of lyric poetry that left its mark on Shakespeare's sonnets. Here Ronsard, not without a barb, reminds the young woman that one day in the future all that will be left of her beauty will be the collective memory that once, long ago, it inspired Ronsard's poetry.

This conflict between eternity and human physical decay is there from the start in the Sonnets, particularly in the first seventeen. But in the later poems the poet promises his friend eternity through art instead. At the same time his own mortality and age start to become an obsession: if only he and the youth were more perfectly matched, rather than with nine years between them! He speaks of being old, though that does not necessarily mean what we would commonly think it does. Sonnet 138, more than any other, throws interesting light on this: "And wherefore say not I that

I am old?" Shakespeare asks. At that moment—the sonnet was published in 1599—he is thirty-five at most, and probably younger. That he saw himself as old in his thirties may not have been quite so odd in Elizabethan England, where male life expectancy averaged around forty-five. In the Sonnets, age is moreover a dialectical concept, defined with reference to a relationship of a younger man with an older one.

Sonnet 73 offers the cycle's most powerful statement about the poet's age and readiness for death. One of the most accomplished lyrics in the cycle, it conjures up a sunset view of the poet, of someone who is close to the end of his life and at peace with it. The rhetorical texture and felicitous density of the poem show Shakespeare at his most assured. The poem's portrayal of the writer's age needs to be seen in the context of a local quartet of poems that all suggest they were written in the wake of a serious illness (71, 72, 73, 74). Here is the calm, seductive, if not death-embracing, Sonnet 73:

> *That time of year thou mayst in me behold*
> *When yellow leaves, or none, or few, do hang*
> *Upon those boughs which shake against the cold,*
> *Bare ruined choirs where late the sweet birds sang.*
> *In me thou seest the twilight of such day*
> *As after sunset fadeth in the west,*
> *Which by and by black night doth take away,*
> *Death's second self, that seals up all in rest.*
> *In me thou seest the glowing of such fire*
> *That on the ashes of his youth doth lie,*
> *As the death-bed whereon it must expire,*
> *Consumed with that which it was nourished by.*
> > *This thou perceiv'st, which makes thy love more*
> > *strong,*
> > *To love that well which thou must leave ere long.*

The poet's sickness culminates in these lines. In the two poems that precede it Shakespeare urges his friend not to mourn him after he has become the fare of "vilest worms." Such is his love for the youth that he does not wish his death to cause him the slightest grief. He would prefer it if the friend forgot him at once "for I love you so / That I in your sweet thoughts would be forgot / If thinking on me then should make you woe." Shakespeare may have been dangerously ill at this point. If Sonnets 71–74 record a time when he nearly died, Sonnet 75 manifests a distinct change of tone or mood away from death toward convalescence, sustenance, and life: "So are you to my thoughts as food to life, / Or as sweet seasoned-showers are to the ground." Shakespeare's sickness may have been connected to the plague that struck London in the summer of 1592. Perhaps, like Simon Forman, he survived an attack of it. His incapacity may have given the rival poet an opening, because that rival enters the fray at just this point.

The house in Henley Street in which Shakespeare was born and where he lived from 1564 until he left Stratford in the late 1580s. *(Sarah Lee)*

An animated street scene from the period, showing a central gutter, a tavern, a waste collector with horse and cart, and a woman publicly fouling the pavement, to the delight of a pig and the amazement of all the other onlookers. *(University of London Library)*

The recently identified house of Shakespeare's mother, Mary Arden, in the Warwickshire village of Wilmcote. *(Sarah Lee)*

Anne Hathaway, Shakespeare's future wife, spent her childhood in this large farmhouse in Shottery near Stratford. *(The Governors of Stonyhurst College)*

The revered Jesuit Edmund Campion, shown here in a contemporary sketch. Above his head can be glimpsed an angel with a martyr's crown. *(Sarah Lee)*

An original Tudor mural still to be found in the White Swan in Stratford-upon-Avon. It shows Tobias with the archangel Raphael to his left, parting from his parents to redeem his father's bond in a far-off city. *(Sarah Lee)*

In this chapel at Billesley, near Wilmcote, Shakespeare's granddaughter, Elizabeth Hall-Nash, married John Barnard in 1649, perhaps as a tribute to her grandfather, who may have married Anne Hathaway here in 1582. *(Sarah Lee)*

The old entrance to Billesley chapel through which William and Anne Shakespeare may have left as husband and wife in 1582. *(Sarah Lee)*

Clopton Bridge was called "great and sumptuous" in Shakespeare's time; trade and traffic between Stratford and London have passed across it since the Middle Ages and still do so today. *(Sarah Lee)*

A putative portrait of Christopher Marlowe from c.1585; he may have been the rival poet of the Sonnets. *(The Master and Fellows of Corpus Christi College, Cambridge)*

Richard Burbage acted in the same company as Shakespeare and played many of his most important tragic roles. *(The Bridgeman Art Library)*

The Lucys' manor on the Avon at Charlecote, from inside the same grounds in which Shakespeare may have been caught poaching in the late 1580s. *(Sarah Lee)*

The 1588 "Armada" portrait of Queen Elizabeth I, painted in the year of the naval battle from which England emerged victorious. *(The Bridgeman Art Library)*

St. Paul's cathedral still boasts its spire in this detail from a famous Tudor map of London (the so-called Copperplate). Blackfriars, the Fleet river, Bridewell prison, and Baynard ("Benams") Castle are clearly visible. *(Die Anhaltische Gemäldegalerie Dessau)*

Claes Jan Visscher's view of London as it was around 1600. In the foreground to the west of London Bridge are St. Mary Overy, the palace of the Bishop of Winchester with the Clink prison, and the first Globe theater and the Bear Garden. *(The Folger Shakespeare Library)*

Left: Robert Devereux, the second earl [of] Essex, from a 1596 portrait at just the t[ime] when Shakespeare was clashing with t[he] licensing authorities over using the nam[e] Oldcastle. *(The National Portrait Galler[y])*

Below: In this miniature by Nicolas Hill[iard] of Henry Wriothesley, third earl of Southampton, the young earl's mane and androgynous good looks are evident. *(The Bridgeman Art Library)*

Below: The 1596 Shakespeare coat of arms from a draft copy surviving in the College of Arms, displaying the motto *"non sanz droict"* and showing the transversal spear that runs across the escutcheon. *(The College of Arms)*

The Swan theater on Bankside was drawn in 1596 by the
Dutch visitor Johannes de Witt and copied by his friend
Arend van Buchel. It may show a performance of
a play by Shakespeare. *(The University Library, Utrecht)*

A "perspective view" by John Jordan in the eighteenth century with, on the left, New Place, the Gild Chapel, Shakespeare's school, and the medieval almshouses. Jordan's New Place dates from c.1702, when the Clopton family extensively rebuilt the old stone and timber house in which Shakespeare had lived. *(The Folger Shakespeare Library)*

The same view today with the Falcon inn on the right of the picture. *(Sarah Lee)*

The inside of the Gild Chapel in Stratford with faded traces of the Last Judgment on the arch across the nave; the images were whitewashed in the year of Shakespeare's birth when his father, John, served as borough chamberlain. *(Sarah Lee)*

New Place once occupied this open space, but now the well and a few foundation walls are all that remain; the neighboring Nash house, into which Shakespeare's granddaughter, Elizabeth, married, is extant. *(Sarah Lee)*

Looking west toward the Gild Chapel from the inside of the gardens of New Place. *(Sarah Lee)*

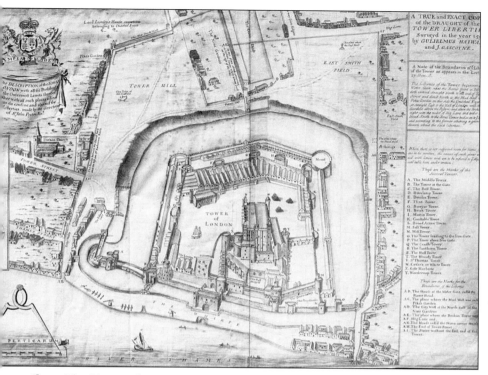

Above: The Tower of London as it was when John Gerard escaped from it in 1597. *(The Society of Antiquaries of London)*

Right: The frontispiece of the First Folio showing Shakespeare as he was in around 1600 at the age of thirty-six. *(Sir John Murray)*

Mr. WILLIAM

SHAKESPEARES

COMEDIES,
HISTORIES, &
TRAGEDIES.

Published according to the True Originall Copies.

LONDON
Printed by Ifaac Iaggard, and Ed. Blount. 1623.

Wenceslaus Hollar's view of Bankside looking toward the Strand and showing the second Globe theater of 1613 and the Bear Garden, with the labels reversed. *(The Guildhall Library, Corporation of London)*

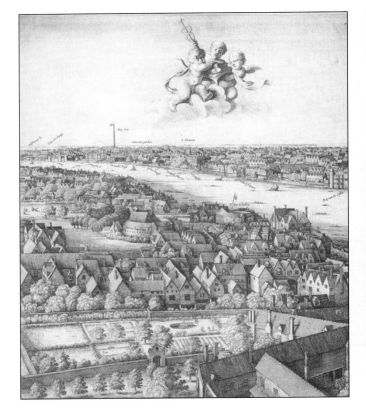

Hall's Croft, an impressive property that was erected in c.1614, probably by John Hall for himself and his family. *(Sarah Lee)*

Above: The chancel of Holy Trinity in Stratford, with the Shakespeare bust on the left wall overlooking the graves of Anne Shakespeare, William Shakespeare, Thomas Nash, John Hall, and Susanna. *(Sarah Lee)*

Right: Shakespeare's face may have been molded from a life or death mask toward the end of his life; the monument was in place by the time the First Folio was published in 1623. *(Sarah Lee)*

The inscription on Shakespeare's grave, which urges posterity to let his bones rest in peace. *(Sarah Lee)*

A Stratford lithograph by C. F. Greene from 1820, showing Market Cross and the corner house in High Street where Judith Shakespeare lived with her husband, Thomas Quiney; it had been the town's medieval prison (hence the name "Cage") and it still stands today. *(The Shakespeare Birthplace Trust)*

Left: Ben Jonson, painted in the year after Shakespeare's death. *(The National Portrait Gallery)*

Below: The contrasting signatures of Susanna Hall and her daughter, Elizabeth Nash, on a document of 1647. *(The Shakespeare Birthplace Trust)*

10

The Rival Poet: 1592–93

e are more than halfway through the cycle when the rival poet enters. It is in Sonnet 78 that Shakespeare first refers to "alien" pens seeking out the patronage of the young man. By the next poem their number has contracted to one, when the poet concedes that his "sick muse" must yield to "another." Almost immediately afterward, in Sonnet 80, the other poet has become the rival poet. The rhetoric of this poem, its similes and metaphors, contain important clues to the rival's identity.

> *O, how I faint when I of you do write,*
> *Knowing a better spirit doth use your name,*
> *And in the praise thereof spends all his might,*
> *To make me tongue-tied, speaking of your fame!*
> *But since your worth, wide as the ocean is,*
> *The humble as the proudest sail doth bear,*
> *My saucy barque, inferior far to his,*
> *On your broad main doth wilfully appear,*
> *Your shallowest help will hold me up afloat,*
> *Whilst he upon your soundless deep doth ride;*
> *Or, being wrecked, I am a worthless boat,*
> *He of tall building and of goodly pride.*
> > *Then thank him not for that which he doth say,*
> > *Since what he owes thee thou thyself dost pay.*

The marine imagery—"ocean," "proudest sail," "broad main," "soundless deep"—anticipates the other major poem referring to Shakespeare's rival, which starts with "Was it the proud full sail of his great verse / Bound for the prize of all-too-precious you?" (Sonnet 86). Before asking why the poet chooses to convey the relationship between himself and the rival in terms of barks, shallow drafts, and stately ships negotiating the deep ocean of the fair friend's generosity, let us take up a single word that may contain a clue, *the* clue perhaps, to the identity of the other poet: "might."

Shakespeare's use of the word "might" to render the distinct tenor of the rival poet's verse points to Marlowe more than to any other writer of the period. Many years later, in an elegy to his dead friend Shakespeare in 1623, Ben Jonson compared him to his peers, and concluded that Shakespeare did "our Lyly outshine, / Or sporting Kid, or Marlowe's mighty line." It's suggestive that in searching for an epithet for Marlowe's verse Jonson hit on "mighty," and that to praise Shakespeare even over mighty Marlowe was the supreme literary tribute he could pay to his friend. It may also have been the last salvo in the literary rivalry between the two greatest dramatists of the age by, as it happens, the third greatest, Jonson. It may well be that "mighty" was the word applied by the poets and dramatists, the cognoscenti of the period, to Marlowe's verse.

Shakespeare rarely refers to his contemporary dramatists, but he tips his hat to Marlowe in *As You Like It,* written seven years after the latter's death. On falling in love with Rosalind, Phoebe exclaims "Dead shepherd, now I find thy saw of might, / 'Who ever loved that loved not at first sight?'" She has, it seems, read Marlowe's *Hero and Leander,* for she quotes line 176 from the first sestiad. This is not the only reference in this highly discursive literary play to the poem. In the very next scene, Rosalind laughingly dismisses the idea that men might die "in a love-cause." Leander, she notes, "would have lived many a fair year though Hero had turned nun if it had not been for a hot midsummer night, for, good youth, he went but forth to wash him in the Hellespont and, being taken with the cramp, was drowned." Her spoof of *Hero and Leander* further suggests that Shakespeare is commemorating Marlowe in this play. Contemporary writers and players would instantly have recognized the famous quotation from the poem. Most important for us, though, is that Shakespeare, like Jonson, uses the word "might" to characterize Marlowe and thus links the usage with the idiom of the sonnets about the rival poet. When Shakespeare thought of Marlowe's rhetoric, the word "mighty," meaning "above a mortal pitch," sprang to mind. Marlowe, "might," and "mighty" were as conjoined as "Artful" and "Dodger" would be for generations reared on *Oliver Twist.*

There are two further significant links between Marlowe and *As You Like It,* which (not by the way) features a country yokel called William and is set in Shakespeare's own backyard in the Forest of Arden. The first one, a cryptic reference to Marlowe's violent death in Deptford, comes from Touchstone, the play's clown. Apropos of almost nothing, he remarks that "When a man's verses cannot be understood, nor a man's good wit seconded with the forward child, understanding, it strikes a man more dead than a great reckoning in a little room." The phrase "strikes a man more dead" is oddly anticipated in the second of the rival-poet sonnets, when the poet wonders whether it was the rival's supernatural gifts that so intimidated him: "Was it his spirit, by spirits taught to write / Above a mortal pitch, that struck me dead?" (86) *As You Like It*'s "great reckoning" is now commonly read as an allusion to the events of May 1593 and specifically to the wording of the coroner's report, which noted that Marlowe and his fellow diners "could not agree about the sum of pence, that is, le recknynge." A row ensued, which, according to the inquest, resulted in Marlowe's death at Ingram Frizer's hands.

Alone among his contemporaries writing about the death of Marlowe, Shakespeare uses the coroner's unusual key word "reckoning." This would seem to point to some inside knowledge of the event. It would have been easy enough for him to ask Southampton; the Cecils must have known what happened, and what the Cecils knew Southampton might find out. Indeed, I suggest that that is how Shakespeare discovered the facts of Marlowe's death, even if the version he was given may only have been the official one: that a senseless brawl over money robbed him of a close friend and the country of one of its greatest and most promising writers. The official version may just conceivably be true, notwithstanding the elaborate and overly convoluted statements about where the parties sat and how the killing of Marlowe could be twisted and turned until it became a legitimate act of self-defense. After all, a fight over traded insults was just the kind of impulsive behavior that stalked Marlowe throughout his short life.

There may well be another bow to Marlowe in *As You Like It*: Rosalind's transvestite alter ego, Ganymede. When she and Celia set out on their quest into Arden, Celia asks her what she should call her friend now that she will be disguised as a man. Rosalind replies: "I'll have no worse a name than Jove's own page, / And therefore look you call me Ganymede." The connotations of Ganymede were well known; Shakespeare is taking a chance here in having his resourceful tomboy heroine call herself the equivalent of a queen. The play toys with homoeroticism and explores homosexual attraction, as when Phoebe falls in love with Rosalind, and when Rosalind steps out of the fiction in the Epilogue to tease the audience about her androgynous status. Still, *As You Like It* is hardly a full-fledged gay work like Marlowe's *Edward II*.

There are cogent reasons for considering Marlowe seriously as the rival poet. After all, if the Cecils still wanted to woo their theater-obsessed ward through poetry, there was no one better or more famous than the cobbler's son from Canterbury. Since the late 1580s, he and friends of his like Edward Alleyn, the star in his company and the player of Tamburlaine and indeed of all the major Marlovian roles, had been the unchallenged masters of the English stage up at the Curtain and latterly down at the Rose on Bankside. Marlowe was known to the Cecils, since their Privy Council had intervened on his behalf when Cambridge University threatened to withhold his degree because of his papist connections. Wearing his hats of chancellor of the university and of Lord Treasurer and Privy Councilor, Burghley must have been partly responsible for the decision in Marlowe's favor. The council's confidence in the good service Marlowe had done the state may have been grounded in a briefing by Sir Francis Walsingham, the head of the Elizabethan intelligence service and the father-in-law of Sir Philip Sidney. It is an open question whether Marlowe was enlisted by the powers that were, or whether he volunteered his services.

Among his exemplary tales of lovers, Clapham's poem "Narcissus" includes that of Hero and Leander. Marlowe runs with this same story in his *Hero and Leander,* an inventive and scintillating Ovidian poem about first sexual love between a boy and a girl separated by the sea. It includes a brilliant scene of Neptune as an old lecher who in a moment of erotic abandon fondles Leander's perfect contours as the boy swims across the Hellespont. The homosexual encounter is portrayed with at least as much gusto as the love affair of Hero and Leander. Marlowe's choice of mythological motif would hardly have been influenced by Clapham's poem, which he almost certainly did not know. He probably chose Hero and Leander because the story was brilliantly bisexual and thus provided a perfect paradigm for an erotic pitch to the androgynous Southampton. *Hero and Leander* may constitute Marlowe's attempt to woo Southampton away from Shakespeare, throwing down a literary gauntlet to his friend and rival, daring him to match it, casting himself as Neptune and Southampton as Leander (who, like the young earl, has flowing locks).

Hero and Leander first crop up in Shakespeare's early solo play *The Two Gentlemen of Verona,* but they also feature in three plays on which Shakespeare probably collaborated: *A Shrew, King Leir* (c. 1592–93), and *Edward III* (c. 1592–93). The reference in *King Leir* is the most immediately intriguing as far as Marlowe is concerned. Gonorill welcomes Cornwall with "As welcome as Leander was to Hero, / Or brave Aeneas to the Carthage queen." Two lines, two mythic allusions, and two literary works by Marlowe, who had written *Dido, Queen of Carthage* while still at Cambridge. In *Edward III,* the sex-crazed king woos the countess by telling her that she is fairer

> *by far than Hero was,*
> *Beardless Leander not so strong as I;*
> *He swom an easy current for his love,*
> *But I will through a Hellespont of blood*
> *To arrive at Sestos where my Hero lies.*

The tale of Hero and Leander with its aura of risqué sexuality may have been one with which both Shakespeare and Marlowe toyed in the years before the plague forced the theaters' closure.

They may have made it theirs as two madcap twentysomethings over in Shoreditch in the late 1580s. If Shakespeare was indeed bisexual, at least in temperament if not practice, the odds are that he found his relationship with Marlowe liberating, if not downright exhilarating. For Marlowe, brilliant and gay, everything was up for grabs, and he probably got away with it in the arty communities of the 1580s because they recognized his extraordinary talent. Will Shakespeare likely became his bosom buddy, if not his lover. If anyone could bring out the glover's son from Stratford it was Marlowe. The real-life plot here seems barely submerged in the poetry. In Shoreditch, Shakespeare and Marlowe quite probably became close friends and dramatic collaborators before Shakespeare was drawn into the Southampton circle. It may even have been Marlowe who introduced them when the sixteen-year-old Southampton joined Gray's Inn. He may have watched from the sidelines as the relationship between them deepened, before himself joining the band of Wriothesley's declared suitors along with his Cambridge contemporary Thomas Nashe.

Nashe addressed to Southampton the first edition of his picaresque novel *The Unfortunate Traveller,* which was completed on June 27, 1593. The dedication, which takes the shape of a convoluted epistle, does not survive in later versions of the text, probably because it was unwanted. Nashe and Marlowe undoubtedly knew each other at Cambridge, where they overlapped for six or seven years, Nashe graduating in 1586 from St. John's and Marlowe in 1587 from Corpus Christi. The young Southampton turned up at St. John's in 1585 at the age of twelve and stayed there until 1589. It is inconceivable that he would not have known Nashe, who was then in his late teens, and he probably also knew Marlowe at Corpus Christi a few minutes' walk down the road. In 1585, the twenty-one-year-old Marlowe had two years to run before graduating. He may already have enjoyed a reputation among the literati as a poet and classical translator, though the university annals do not mention it. Some scholars believe that *Dido* may have been written in collaboration with Nashe while they were both at Cambridge—that is, around 1586. (Both their names appear on the 1594 publication.) The diamantine rhetoric and verbal pyrotechnics of *Tamburlaine* did not spring fully formed from Marlowe's head. To forge such a distinctive voice he must have been writing and experimenting steadily during his last years in Cambridge. The question is whether this Cambridge literary coterie consisted of ganymedes (or catamites; "Catamitus" is the Latin form of Greek "Ganymede"). If Marlowe knew Southampton in Cambridge (the Earl was still only thirteen when Marlowe left), he may have been attracted to the young aristocrat just as everybody else seems to have been. Perhaps Southampton was a willing catamite and thus served as a model for the "female wanton boy" Ganymede who partners Jove in the opening scene of *Dido*; or he might have been a "bedfellow," to use another term attributed to Marlowe in describing, not without blasphemy, the relationship between Christ and St. John the Evangelist.

In the summer of 1592 Marlowe must have been looking for sources of money. The plague and the Privy Council between them had cut the players and writers off from their lucrative livelihood. It is true that they would have earned something by touring. We know this to have been the case with Marlowe's company, since some of Edward Alleyn's correspondence with his wife and his father-in-law Henslowe has survived from the period when he was touring in the country after being forced out of London by plague. The closure of all major London playing venues lasted from the summer of 1592 until roughly the same time in 1594. Southampton and, perhaps, a serious illness of Shakespeare's prompted Marlowe to strike; *Hero and Leander* may well have been his first salvo in a bid for patronage. Shakespeare's *Venus and Adonis* was entered on the Stationers' Register on April 18, 1593, which suggests that Shakespeare wrote it earlier that spring or during Lent. If *Hero and Leander* was composed in competition with Shakespeare's poem, as is likely, it would date from around the same time. It is almost certainly Marlowe's last work.

If we had only the poem itself, Shakespeare's repeated tributes to Marlowe, and the use of the word "mighty," it would be harder to pin the tag of rival poet on Marlowe. But another clue consolidates the argument. It occurs in Sonnet 86, where the rival is said to be mentored by "spirits" and thus striking dumb the poor poet:

Was it the proud full sail of his great verse
Bound for the prize of all-too-precious you
That did my ripe thoughts in my brain inhearse,
Making their tomb the womb wherein they grew?
Was it his spirit, by spirits taught to write
Above a mortal pitch, that struck me dead?
No, neither he nor his compeers by night
Giving him aid, my verse astonishèd.
He nor that affable familiar ghost
Which nightly gulls him with intelligence,
As victors, of my silence cannot boast;
I was not sick of any fear from thence.
>*But when your countenance filled up his line,*
>*Then lacked I matter; that enfeebled mine.*

The gist is that the rival poet moves in mysterious, perhaps even dangerous circles and that this could be thought to cow the poet. Not so, Shakespeare retorts. Rather, the reason for his "silence" is that the fair friend has willingly lent himself to becoming the subject of the rival's verse and thus robbed Shakespeare of any reason for writing. We are given here circumstantial information about the rival's set of friends, "his compeers by night." It has long been suspected that in Sonnet 86 Shakespeare is having a dig at what was then called the "school of atheism" or "school of night," perhaps in response to a pamphlet by the leading Jesuit Robert Parsons.* In 1592, Parsons had written of "Sir Walter Ralegh's school of atheism" and accused Ralegh of presiding over a "school wherein both Moses and our Saviour, the Old and New Testaments are jested at, and the scholars taught among other things to spell God backward." While Parsons is clearly partisan, the thought of a school of atheism echoes the wild and iconoclastic views attributed to Marlowe by Baines and by Marlowe's former roommate and fellow playwright Thomas Kyd.

---

*By a strange twist of fate, Parsons was visited in Madrid in the late 1590s by the eventual publisher of Shakespeare's sonnets, Thomas Thorpe, who may have been a Catholic sympathizer (*Oxford Dictionary of National Biography,* Thomas Thorpe entry).

The "school" in question was headed by Henry Percy, the ninth Earl of Northumberland (he was Marlowe's exact contemporary), and Sir Walter Ralegh. It comprised writers, scholars, poets, and dramatists like Marlowe, George Peele, Thomas Watson, George Chapman, John Florio, and the poet Matthew Roydon, as well as two *magi,* the mathematician Thomas Harriot and the scientist Walter Warner. In 1595, Northumberland married the sister of the Earl of Essex, which suggests that Southampton may also have been close to members of this club. The fact that the most famous lyric of Elizabethan England, Marlowe's "Come live with me and be my love," was countered by Ralegh with a lyric of his own on the same topic indicates that the group was probably intimate as well as exclusive. It may have been distinctly Catholic in its orientation through the Earl of Northumberland, whose family, like Southampton's, traditionally aligned themselves with the old faith. The famous Italian occultist Giordano Bruno may have been associated with the school during his stay in England; it also counted as an adherent Ferdinando Lord Strange, the very patron of players whom Marlowe claimed to know when he was summoned before the governor of Flushing.

What renders it probable that "compeers by night" alludes to the "school of night" is that Shakespeare uses the latter phrase in Act IV of *Love's Labour's Lost,* and in a context that at once brings to mind the Sonnets. *Love's Labour's Lost* was probably written in late 1594 or early 1595. In the passage in question, the King tells the young nobleman Berowne that Rosaline his love "is black as ebony," which provokes the young man to a paean to blackness, despite the King's protest that "black is the badge of hell, / The hue of dungeons and the school of night."* The similarity to the Sonnets is immediately apparent: the rhetorical texture is very similar. Above all, these lines encourage us further to anchor the rival-poet sonnets in the time span 1592–94.

The rival poet puts in the briefest of appearances before vanishing from the cycle. No reason is given in the poems for his disappearance; he is simply there one moment and gone the next.

---

*Woudhuysen, p. 216.

Shakespeare barely has a chance to engage with him. If anything, he surrenders to the rival's superior talent almost at once, as if he could not possibly compete with such a poetic heavyweight. Then, nothing. It is as if the rival had never existed. We are not told that the youth returned to the poet, or that the rival found another object of adulation. Nothing in the sequence gives the slightest hint of any further development regarding the other poet. The reason for this is, probably, because he was killed at Deptford in May 1593. The case for Marlowe as Shakespeare's rival is further reinforced by the fact that in the late summer of 1592 both men were targeted by a savage invective by one of Marlowe's Cambridge contemporaries, Robert Greene. Greene's posthumously published pamphlet is one of the most famous documents of Elizabethan theater history. It remains to this day our first undoubted London notice of Shakespeare—and it is not flattering. "Greene's Groatsworth of Wit bought with a million of repentance" was entered on the Stationers' Register on September 20, 1592, and the passage concerning Shakespeare reads:

> there is an upstart crow, beautified with our feathers, that with his tiger's heart wrapt in a player's hide, supposes he is as well able to bombast out a blank verse as the best of you: and being an absolute Johannes *factotum,* is in his own conceit the only Shake-scene in a country.

The general meaning of this is clear, namely that Shakespeare is a devious, importunate, and bumptious literary thief. Greene is quite specific in his use of metaphor and simile, because the crow has since antiquity been associated with mimicry, just as the magpie has traditionally been with thieving. In Aesop's fable the crow is tricked by the fox, who appeals to her vanity. This sense may be submerged in Greene's broadside, but perhaps more to the point is the story of the actor Roscius and the "cobbler's crow," from Macrobius. Greene had earlier used this very fable in *Francesco's Fortune,* an attack on Edward Alleyn whom he mockingly called Roscius after the legendary Roman actor of that name. Greene challenged "Roscius" to admit that, like Aesop's crow, he was decked in the glory of Marlowe's feathers, that he had nothing to offer but what the cobbler taught him: "and if the cobbler hath taught thee to say *Ave Caesar,* disdain not thy tutor because thou pratest in a king's chamber."*

There may be a clue here to a more barbed and specific interpretation of Greene's famous attack on Shakespeare than is commonly assumed. It depends on inside knowledge that we happen to possess. Like Roscius/Alleyn, Shakespeare is alleged to beautify himself with others' feathers, but Greene may also be comparing him more specifically to the cobbler's crow who cannot sing anything by himself. Alleyn depended wholly for his great parts on Marlowe, the son of the cobbler from Canterbury, and was therefore a cobbler's son's crow. Similarly, Greene may be casting Shakespeare as a cobbler's crow, a versifying imitator who owes everything to the much more accomplished Marlowe. Shakespeare the crow is usurping Marlowe the cobbler, Greene implies, thereby providing further circumstantial evidence about the rivalry between the two chief playwrights of the age or, as Greene saw them, the mercurial flawed genius of the theater and a pushy literary thief who had not gone to university. As if this were not bad enough, the phrasing of Greene's charge of plagiarism and theft might hide a glancing blow at the one thing in Shakespeare's past that he must have been most troubled by, his stealing deer from the Lucys. Shakespeare would later refer to Greene's sniping as a "vulgar scandal," but he must have smarted from the attack and the damage to his reputation. Shakespeare was keen to preserve his good name, and while the esteem of one's peers was critical in a culture that valued "honor" above life, to the Shakespeares of Stratford it may have meant more than to most, given their history of debt and (probably) small-scale felony.

Besides, Greene had a point. One of the more disconcerting features of Shakespeare's works is that he often "borrows" his plots from other writers, and sometimes follows them very closely indeed. In accusing Shakespeare of plagiarism, predatory ambition, and arrogance, Greene quite intentionally lifts a phrase from Shakespeare's third play about Henry VI, one of the early masterpieces of the fledgling Elizabethan theater. As the Duke of York, the father of the future Richard III, stands captive on a mole hill, Queen Margaret

---

*Schoenbaum (1975), p. 116.

taunts him with the blood-soaked handkerchief of his young son Rutland. The grief-stricken and doomed father responds to this perversion of feminine nature by apostrophizing the Queen thus: "O tiger's heart wrapped in a woman's hide."

Greene was clearly not happy with Shakespeare. But neither was he with Marlowe. It is sometimes overlooked that in "Groatsworth" he tore into Marlowe for the second time in four years, and this time he directly accused him of atheism and political cynicism: "Why should thy excellent wit, His gift, be so blinded that thou shouldst give no glory to the giver? Is it pestilent Machiavellian policy that thou hast studied?" Machiavelli, of course, speaks the Prologue to Marlowe's *The Jew of Malta,* and in moving from the play to the life Greene was leveling serious charges against Marlowe. Greene died before the pamphlet appeared; it was left to his publisher, Henry Chettle, to face the fallout alone. Three months later, Chettle apologized. Here is the text in full:

> About three months since died M. Robert Greene, leaving many papers in sundry booksellers' hands, among other his Groatsworth of wit in which a letter written to divers playmakers is offensively by one or two [Marlowe and Shakespeare] of them taken; and because on the dead [Greene] they cannot be avenged, they wilfully forge in their conceits a living author [Chettle]; and after tossing it to and fro, no remedy but it must light on me. How I have all the time of my conversing in printing hindered the bitter inveighing against scholars it hath been very well known; and how in that I dealt, I can sufficiently prove. With neither of them that take offence was I acquainted, and with one of them [Marlowe] I care not if I never be; the other [Shakespeare], whom at that time I did not so much spare as since I wish I had, for that as I have moderated the heat of living writers and might have used my own discretion (especially in such a case) the author being dead, that I did not, I am as sorry as if the original fault had been my fault, because myself have seen his demeanour no less civil than he excellent in the quality he professes. Beside, divers of worship [that is, people of high rank] have reported his uprightness of dealing, which argues his honesty and his facetious grace of writing that approves his art.

Marlowe was alive when this was written, and although Chettle professed not to care about being acquainted with him he did point out in his own defense that he had edited out parts of the attack on Marlowe. These were probably charges of homosexuality. Chettle can have had little or no idea about Marlowe's political double life; even Cambridge officialdom did not until the Privy Council and the university's chancellor enlightened it. But Marlowe's sexuality would have been much harder to hide or shroud from cliquish gossip. If the actors knew, as they must have done, then publishers like Chettle could also find out. The "divers of worship" who called on Chettle— or, more likely, summoned him to explain his reasons for publishing the scurrilous charges in Greene's "Groatsworth"—must give one pause for thought. They can only have been noblemen from either the Privy Council or Cecil House, which would have come to the same at the time, or from Southampton himself.

As it happens, a striking image in the Sonnets may indicate that it was indeed Wriothesley and his friends who pressured Chettle. Sonnet 112 is one of a triad of poems in which Shakespeare laments the inequities of his lot as an actor (110–112). Fortune, he protests, is the guilty goddess that "did not better for my life provide / Than public means which public manners breeds." His name, he claims, "receives a brand" from acting and "almost thence my nature is subdued / To what it works in, like the dyer's hand" (111). The use of "brand" is quite strong, until we remember the lowly social status of players, who were little more than vagabonds unless they wore the livery of a particular lord. "Brand" is usually read in just these terms: the poet is seen as rueing the fact that he is little more than a licensed vagrant. But the sonnet that follows suggests that "brand" may refer quite specifically to the attack by Greene. In 112, the poet acknowledges his friend's support over a "vulgar scandal" and slander, which in the end failed to touch him thanks to that loyalty. The poet cares only, he affirms, about his friend's opinions, be they good or bad; others' are of no consequence:

> *Your love and pity doth th'impression fill*
> *Which vulgar scandal stamped upon my brow;*
> *For what care I who calls me well or ill,*

> *So you o'er-green my bad, my good allow.*
> *You are my all the world, and I must strive*
> *To know my shames and praises from your tongue—*
> *None else to me, nor I to none alive,*
> *That my steeled sense or changes, right or wrong.*
> *In so profound abysm I throw all care*
> *Of others' voices that my adder's sense*
> *To critic and to flatterer stoppèd are.*
> *Mark how with my neglect I do dispense:*
> > *You are so strongly in my purpose bred*
> > *That all the world besides, methinks are dead.*

The word "vulgar" then still retained the meaning of Latin *vulgus,* meaning public or published and in the public domain. "Scandal" meant variously moral lapse, damage to reputation, injurious rumor, slander, or malicious gossip. The gist of Sonnet 112 is that there was a public attack on the poet, in response to which the aristocratic youth rose to his rescue and, by "o'er-greening" the poet's "bad," championed his innocence, or "good." The use of "o'er-green" has caused editors of the Sonnets to seek similar usages elsewhere in Shakespeare, but to no avail. Whatever the roots of this coinage, it must mean something on the lines of dressing in a pleasant leafy cover and thus rendering harmless the "bad" done to the poet. The image may conjure up a vision of spring and rebirth, but it may also be a more specific, submerged allusion to Robert Greene.

There is only one reference in all these 154 poems to a public scandal and to bad-mouthing of the poet and it is here: "calls me well or ill." That it occurs alongside a coinage that happens to contain the name of Shakespeare's chief detractor from this period can hardly be a coincidence. There may be a prima facie case for reading "so you o'er-green my bad, my good allow" as something like "so long as you, unlike my detractor Greene, focus on my good parts," where "over" is read as "over and against, in the teeth of"; or "o'er-green" could signify turning Greene's slander into praise. We should not be surprised to find here a punning allusion to Greene's name. Shakespeare is returning a compliment, since in "Groatsworth" Greene called him "Shake-scene." Sonnet 112 is nothing less than an act of homage and gratitude by the poet to Southampton for his role in *l'affaire* Greene.* That Shakespeare was upset by Greene's attack is not in doubt. Why else would people in authority have dressed Chettle down? That Southampton and his friends put Chettle in his place with regard to Shakespeare but not necessarily Marlowe should give us pause. The attack on Shakespeare had been literary above all, on Marlowe personal, political, and theological—a much more inflammatory cocktail. The fact that the maverick spy and crypto-Catholic atheist died in the house of one Eleanor Bull, a cousin of one of the Queen's confidants and a relative of Burghley, may have a sinister logic. There were many reasons for Marlowe getting into serious trouble: he had a fiery temper and got into too many quarrels. They may all have converged at the so-called reckoning in Deptford in May 1593. We will probably never discover what really happened and why, but the fact that he died in a house with tentacles stretching to the Cecils at a time when they were promoting Southampton's marriage makes one wonder whether Marlowe and Southampton enjoyed "ganymedic" relations, neither of them for the first time and in Southampton's case probably not for the last.† Perhaps the Cecils felt it was bad enough having a pedophiliac homosexual son-in-law in the Earl of Oxford, and he moreover the father of the young woman whom they had tried to marry off to Wriothesley. It is unlikely that Marlowe was killed because of his sexuality, but if he was wooing the young Earl and threatened to compromise him it would not have endeared him to the Elizabethan powers.

---

*After writing this, I discovered that Fripp makes much the same point (*MA*, vol. 4, p. xlviii) when talking about Shakespeare and Greene. Although he takes the argument further than I do, I entirely concur with his refusal to separate the plays and life artificially.

†Akrigg (pp. 181–82) reports that during the Irish campaign Southampton was seen hugging and playing "wantonly" with Piers Edmond, Corporal General of the Horse.

 A Twenty=first=Birthday Poem: October 6, 1594

In a number of sonnets, the poet talks of absenting himself from the fair youth. This can hardly refer to anything other than Shakespeare taking off for Stratford-upon-Avon periodically to see his family, or touring for prolonged spells with the company during prohibition periods. It is clear from the Sonnets that by the time he was writing them Shakespeare no longer walked but rode between London and Stratford. He tells us with how heavy a heart he leaves his friend (Sonnet 50):

> *How heavy do I journey on the way,*
> *When what I seek–my weary travel's end–*
> *Doth teach that ease and that repose to say*
> *"Thus far the miles are measured from my friend."*

These must sometimes have been Shakespeare's thoughts as he sat in Henley Street thinking, even if guiltily, of Southampton. His young children were growing up and would have been changed at every visit. Of course he would have been excited at the thought of seeing them, but he was sowing his wild oats in London when, perhaps, he ought to have been a local glover and a good father. Such thoughts may explain why he never settled in the capital. The poem that has been understood as Shakespeare's first sonnet of leave-taking from Stratford begins, "How careful was I when I took my way / Each trifle under truest bars to thrust / That to my use it might unused stay / From hands of falsehood, in sure wards of trust."* The cadence here is remarkably similar to that of the opening lines of Sonnet 50, just quoted; perhaps the echo in the later lyric, when the poet is traveling in the opposite direction, is intentional.

The three main poems of separation, Sonnets 97, 98, and 99, all postdate Marlowe's death in May 1593 and are artfully structured around the seasons. The poet remarks that his absence from his friend has been "like a winter" with "old December's bareness everywhere" around him; this standard conceit, in which the missing lover turns the very seasons into their opposite by his absence, need not automatically detract from the poems' evidential value. If the chronology of the cycle is valid, and if we accept that Marlowe was the rival poet, then the separation to which Shakespeare refers in Sonnets 97–99 occurred some time in the summer and autumn of 1593. The rival poet has been out of the frame for the span of ten sonnets. Shakespeare was now probably home in Stratford-upon-Avon to sit out the closure of the theaters and to work on *The Rape of Lucrece*. As far as we can determine he was not touring.

It so happens that during the late summer 1593 Edward Alleyn, who was touring, and his father-in-law, Philip Henslowe, conducted a vivid correspondence in which they describe what life was like for those who remained in the city. Henslowe sent the actor greetings, particularly from Alleyn's wife, his "mouse," whose "commendations comes by itself which, as she says, comes from her heart and her soul praying to God day and night for your good health." After reassuring Alleyn that their house "on the Bankside right over against the Clink" had been spared, he relates that the plague was very severe, killing the entire household of one Robert Brown, including his wife and children, over in Shoreditch. These were presumably friends from Alleyn's days at the Theatre before 1591. Henslowe then cuts, without apparent change of register, from the horrors of the plague to domestic matters: he mentions Alleyn's furniture, notably his "bedstead," and, having noted that the garden and spinach are thriving, rues the fact that, while Alleyn's "orange-coloured stockings" had been dyed, there was "no market at Smithfield neither to buy your cloth nor yet to sell your horse for no man would offer me

---

*Wood, p. 131.

above four pound for him therefore I would not sell him but have sent him into the country till you return back again." Both men's letters use "mouse" and "good sweetheart and loving mouse" as terms of endearment for daughters and wives, as Shakespeare later used "mouse" in *Hamlet.* The prince urges his mother not to "let the bloat king [Claudius] tempt you again to bed, / Pinch wanton on your cheek, call you his mouse." Will may well have called Anne his loving mouse—the nickname was clearly current, as was Alleyn's affectionate use of "Jug" for his wife, "Joan."

On August 1 1593, Alleyn urged his family at home in London to take special precautions against the plague by keeping the house "fair and clean." At night, Joan should throw water before both the front and back doors and "have in your windows good store of rue and herb of grace." Alleyn was obviously a keen gardener, for he also finds time to remind her that "all that bed which was parsley in the month of September you sow it with spinach for then is the time." He would do it himself, he writes, but cannot because he will not be home until All Hallows. On August 14, 1593, Henslowe and Joan reply, addressing their letter "To my well-beloved husband Master Edward Alleyn one of my Lord Strange's players this be delivered with speed." Henslowe reproves his son-in-law for not writing:

> for we heard that you were very sick at Bath and that one of your fellows were fain to play your part for you which was no little grief unto us to hear ... we feared it much because we had no letter from you *when the other wives had letters* sent which made your mouse not to weep a little but took it very grievously thinking it you had conceived some unkindness of her because you were ever wont to write with the first and I pray you do so still for we would all be sorry but to hear as often from you as others do from their friends for we would write oftener to you than we do but we know not whither to send to you ... your garden and all your things doth prosper very well thanks be to God for your beans are grown to high hedge and well codded [bearing pods]. . . .

We learn from this that a lively correspondence culture evidently operated between touring actors and their spouses back in London.

Moreover, Joan was in touch with the wives of other players and got news from them. As well as providing a paradigm for the letters Shakespeare must have written to his family, the Alleyn-Henslowe correspondence ought perhaps to have shed light on Marlowe's fate. Perhaps oddly, it does not; perhaps almost everyone who knew Marlowe also appreciated that this business was best left alone. The written record is not helpful here, but the fact that the eventual publication of Marlowe's *Hero and Leander* coincides with the death of Burghley should perhaps point to a link. It is not impossible that Marlowe had toward the end of his life made an enemy of the most powerful man in the land, the same man probably who had earlier leaned on Cambridge to award him his degree.

What Shakespeare did in the summer and early autumn of 1593 we cannot be sure. He probably assisted with farming the land and rearing the children. It is most likely that he was helping out in his father's shop; an intriguing trace in the documentary record may well add substance to this hypothesis. It concerns Alexander Aspinall, the headmaster of the King's New School who succeeded John Cottom in 1582 and who would serve longest of any of its masters. Aspinall had been successful over the years in sending boys from Stratford up to Oxford. Two of them, George Quiney and Henry Sturley, both the sons of parents whom Shakespeare knew well, eventually returned to teach at their old school. Shakespeare would turn Aspinall into Holofernes in *Love's Labour's Lost* and allude to him in *Henry V*.

In 1594, the year of *Lucrece,* Aspinall married Ann Shaw, the widow of a wool driver by the name of Rafe Shaw. The Shaws' son, July, was a friend of Shakespeare's from their days together in Henley Street, when the Shaws had lived at the country end of the street near Henley Lane. Many years later, July Shaw would witness Shakespeare's will. Not long after Shakespeare's death, a rumor started in Stratford that when Aspinall gave Ann Shaw a set of gloves as a betrothal present the verses that came with it were written by Shakespeare: "The gift is small, / The will is all: / Alexander Aspinall." Certainly there may be a pun on "will": such puns are one of Shakespeare's favorite signature tunes in the Sonnets. Not only may he have written the verse, but he probably made the gloves, too.

Aspinall and Will Shakespeare must have been friends by 1594, and probably earlier, since he was teaching Shakespeare's children. Too, Shakespeare was almost certainly in Stratford at the time of the wedding, because of the prolonged closure of the London theaters. The dates line up. If Shakespeare was to make a betrothal present for anyone in his hometown it had to be then, and gloves are the present he would have made. Aspinall's gift of a book to his school, which bought a chain especially to secure it, suggests that the master may have been a bit of a bibliophile, another thing that he and Shakespeare had in common.

Alexander and Ann Aspinall and July Shaw moved to 21 Chapel Street, next door but one to where Shakespeare would eventually live. (Their back garden bordered on Nash's and New Place, and their house survives.) Aspinall joined his new wife's lucrative business of malting and trading in wool. No more teaching and living in the master's house above the council chamber, where he had spent so many years that long after his departure it was still known as "the Chambers over our Council Chamber wheare Mr. Aspinall dwelled."

While making gloves and penning pithy epigrams for wedding gifts Shakespeare was also writing *Lucrece* and his separation sonnets, which he may have posted to Southampton in London, through William Greenway and perhaps through Field when the latter visited the Midlands. During this time, Shakespeare seems to be rediscovering nature. Sonnet 98: "From you have I been absent in the spring/When proud-pied April, dressed in all his trim" has brought the world to life. The glorious, almost Romantic evocation of spring that follows is dashed by the wintry feel of the friend's absence. But not even winter can restrain the sheer pleasure that flows from the poet's pen at the sights and scents of rolling carpets of spring flowers, which is precisely why Sonnet 99 continues with flowers—lilies and York and Lancaster roses and, perhaps, the occasional apothecary rose, "a third, nor red, nor white, had stol'n of both."

One is tempted to say that this is pure Warwickshire, meaning that Shakespeare drew strongly on the countryside in these poems precisely because he was living in it at the time of writing. He is the most lyrical rural dramatist of the age, truer perhaps to his country roots by some distance than any other writer of the period. Who but the author of *A Midsummer Night's Dream* could start a sonnet with "The forward violet thus did I chide: / Sweet thief, whence didst thou steal thy sweet that smells, / If not from my love's breath?" and conclude, "More flowers I noted, yet I none could see / But sweet, or colour, it had stol'n from thee." The poet who compares his poetry with the "mournful hymns" of a nightingale that "hush" the summer nights (Sonnet 102) shares more with Keats than with almost any of his contemporaries; and, unlike the Cockney poet who avidly attuned himself to nature, Shakespeare knew nature from growing up in it. Had he not been Shakespeare he might have become Wordsworth, as far as the inherent magic of nature as a subject matter is concerned. From 102 it appears that the poet's ardor has cooled off a little; or so it might seem to the youth, the poet notes apologetically. Perhaps the calls on him of family life temporarily dampened his enthusiasm for the youth in London, but shortly afterward, in Sonnet 104, Shakespeare feels the need to take stock of his friend. He is reunited with him and the young man's beauty is once more in the foreground.

If nothing else, Shakespeare's enforced plague break from the London stage granted him extra time with the children. It may not have seemed so precious there and then, but it would surely become so in heartsick retrospect, and all too soon. Yet one can readily see why Southampton had become so dear to Shakespeare: not only was he one of the most dazzling stars in the Elizabethan firmament, but also he had been, by all accounts, exceptionally generous. If the gift of £1,000, or any sum near it, was made, then Southampton had rescued Shakespeare from indigence and persecution by the Lucys, and had raised his stock immeasurably in the eyes of his contemporaries in both Warwickshire and London. He had given him back his life and elevated him above his dreams, and all this in recognition of Shakespeare's talent for poetry.

In Sonnets 102, 103, and 104 Shakespeare and Wriothesley are reunited. Shakespeare was now living in London again, so these poems must date from after the summer of 1594, when the theaters reopened. Southampton seems to have been worried about his looks. He can hardly have aged much during their few months' separation, so there must be another reason; his twenty-first birthday, on October 6, 1594, suggests itself. If the chronology of the poems is correct, it is quite possible that Sonnet 104 was a gift to the Earl on his coming of age. Here is 104:

> *To me, fair friend, you never can be old,*
> *For as you were when first your eye I eyed,*
> *Such seems your beauty still. Three winters cold*
> *Have from the forests shook three summers' pride;*
> *Three beauteous springs to yellow autumn turned*
> *In process of the seasons have I seen,*
> *Three April perfumes in three hot Junes burned*
> *Since first I saw you fresh, which yet are green.*
> *Ah, yet doth beauty, like a dial hand,*
> *Steal from his figure and no pace perceived,*
> *So your sweet hue, which methinks still doth stand,*
> *Hath motion, and mine eye may be deceived;*
> > *For fear of which, hear this, thou age unbred:*
> > *Ere you were born was beauty's summer dead.*

We already think we know that Henry and Will first met in 1590 and that the first seventeen sonnets were written for the Earl's seventeenth birthday in October that year. That the young man's eyes feature so insistently in the poet's reminiscence may be of particular interest, for Southampton's luminous blue eyes were as commonly remarked on as his hair. That the poems refer to the seasons as they do may be sheer convention—or it may not: just around this time, the country experienced three of the wettest summers in recorded history. The weather in 1594 was spectacularly bad, and not just during the summer months. Rainstorms in March were followed by hailstorms and more rain in May, and "it commonly rained every day or night" throughout June and July. After a lull in August, the wet weather returned in September, in time to rot the crops; as a result, prices for rye and wheat rocketed. This must be the natural catastrophe behind Titania's speech in *A Midsummer Night's Dream,* which depends for its effect partly on the audience's recognizing the allusions to bad weather.

Under the circumstances it is painfully ironic that in the spring of 1594 Stratford-upon-Avon suffered the worst fire in its entire history. The conflagration started at nine on the morning of May 13 and burned down more than a hundred houses and barns. It destroyed two thousand pounds' worth of the town's most precious commodities, barley, grain, and malt: a disaster for one of the chief malting places in the Midlands. According to the record, the cause was "the negligence of an old woman [who was] put in trust to tend the fire of a brew house and fell asleep." The wind played its part and so did the absence of a fire brigade. Instead of attending to the fire by fetching water and detaching houses from one another with firehooks kept at Market Cross for just this purpose, the men of Stratford were "occupied for the most part in carrying out their stuff out of their houses into the fields and into the midst of the street." Only toward nightfall was the fire put down. Somewhat surprisingly, it does not feature as prominently in the minutes of the borough council as one might have expected. It is mentioned in a Michaelmas petition of 1594 by the borough to the Chancellor of the Exchequer ("we which by the late casualties of fire are so greatly impoverished"), but primarily to support the case for repairing the chancel and south aisle of Holy Trinity. The 1594 fire does seem to have triggered a mini–building boom, which produced at least two very fine town houses, Harvard House and the "Shrieve House," both near the epicenter of the 1594 fire. Although neither house can be said to be representative of a borough that by now counted a substantial underclass of poor and vagrants, it seems that the town carried on business almost as usual.

Fortunately, neither the 1594 fire nor another in 1596 damaged the Birthplace, although they got close. The first raged right opposite Shakespeare's home and destroyed the Cox and Cawdrey houses, while the 1596 blaze was stopped, it seems, by the Mere, but not before laying waste to the substantial holdings of the whittawer William Wilson. His "eight bays of housing" were "consumed to the ground." The westernmost space before the Mere on the north (Birthplace) side of the street was a garden belonging to Wilson. In 1596 it and the brook together may have provided a firewall. These fires could have taken place only during two of the few warm, dry spells in those years; how the locals must have cursed their fate.

One might expect Shakespeare to allude to these events in the writing that he was doing at the time, but there is nothing to be found in the Sonnets. If the "three hot Junes" of Sonnet 104 are more than mere stylization then they probably refer to the last full-blown proper summers, including that of 1593.* One corollary of dating Sonnet 104 to shortly before October 6, 1594, is that the proposed "Greene" poem with its allusion to the "vulgar scandal," Sonnet 112, must therefore be dated to after October 1594. This makes good sense, since the poems follow a chronological sequence and 112 concerns Shakespeare's reputation as an active playwright; he probably returned to this unhappy episode now to thank Southampton once more. We are in the autumn of 1594; the plague has abated, playing has resumed, and Chettle's apology has not only safeguarded and consolidated Shakespeare's theatrical career but also cleared his name. Shakespeare found himself joining the new Lord Chamberlain's Company, headed by Lord Hunsdon, which drew into it some of the best talent in the London theater: Burbage, Condell, Heminges, Kemp, and other eminences are listed among the "cast" of the First Folio. The Lord Chamberlain's included most of the stars of the time, except for those in the Admiral's, who stayed with Alleyn and Henslowe at the Rose on Bankside and farther south of the river at Newington Butts near Elephant & Castle. As for the company's chief writer, there was none better now that Marlowe was dead. Shakespeare would do for the Lord Chamberlain's what Marlowe had done for Alleyn, and then some.

---

*For a cogent and invigorating exposition of the European and British climate during just this period, see Le Roy Ladurie, pp. 246–48.

12.

Taming the Dark Lady: 1594—

he Dark Lady enters the scene in Sonnet 127, that is, some time after October 1594, and just where she ought to, since she probably became Shakespeare's mistress that autumn, during the first playing season after the two-year closure period. Her appellation derives from her complexion and makes her sound exotic, a Queen of the Night or Cleopatra figure rather than a dark-skinned woman of flesh and blood. The details that the poet marshals appear to point to a real-life woman rather than a generic one: she plays the virginals; Shakespeare repeatedly refers to her "raven-black" eyes and her dark skin; her lover finds her speech both alluring and irritating: "Nor are mine ears with thy tongue's tune delighted," he writes, echoing and contradicting his earlier "I love to hear her speak." Or perhaps he is thinking of her singing as she accompanies herself on the virginals. The poem starting "How oft, when thou, my music, music play'st / Upon that blessèd wood ... Do I envy those jacks that nimble leap / To kiss the tender inward of thy hand" carries an erotic charge reminiscent of the poetry of John Donne.

The most plausible candidate for the Dark Lady has long been Emilia Lanier (née Bassano), the daughter of Baptista Bassano, a renowned court musician. The Bassanos were a Venetian Jewish musical dynasty. Emilia's skin would probably have been olive rather than English "white." She was five years younger than Shakespeare, and four years older than Southampton. In October 1592, she married a French musician, Alfonso Lanier, and thus her son Henry, by her aristocratic former lover, was born legitimate in 1593.* If she was the Dark Lady, then her affair with Shakespeare started after her marriage; in one of the very last poems, 152, he accuses her of breaking her marriage vows and, by having an affair with the fair youth, her more recent pledge to the poet:

> *In loving thee thou know'st I am forsworn,*
> *But thou art twice forsworn to me love swearing:*
> *In act thy bed-vow broke and new faith torn . . .*

The poet's confession that he is "forsworn" must refer to his marriage vows. This particular poem about breaking faith, being late in the cycle, would have been written sometime after the affair started. It is likely that Shakespeare first saw Emilia Lanier in the company of the man who kept her as his mistress, Lord Hunsdon. A superb portrait of Hunsdon, dated 1591 and signed "by Mark Gerards," survives. Hunsdon is sixty-six years old in it. The face that looks out at us is that of a handsome, grand patrician. He was first cousin to the Queen, the son of Anne Boleyn's sister, and, of course, the founder of the Lord Chamberlain's Company. Although Emilia was undoubtedly Hunsdon's paramour, the relation ceased after her marriage to Lanier. It was then that she met Will Shakespeare, whose sonnets to young Henry Wriothesley may have already have been circulating in London. The occasion for this fateful tryst may have been, as we shall see, a performance of the greatest play ever to be put on at the Theatre, *Richard III.*

We know that by the summer of 1592 Shakespeare had written the audacious history play *3 Henry VI,* because Robert Greene's diatribe quoting from it appeared shortly afterward. Now *Richard III,* Shakespeare's second longest play after *Hamlet,* can have left no one in any doubt about who would be king of the London stage—even if Marlowe went on writing plays, Shakespeare would overtake him. In Tennyson's words, Marlowe was the "morning star" to Shakespeare's "dazzling sun."

---

*One of the best-informed discussions of the Dark Lady and Emilia Bassano is in Lasocki and Prior.

Shakespeare may have finished *Richard III,* with its brilliantly witty and resourceful crook-backed hero, before the closure of the theaters, but if not he was probably at work on it during the first few months of prohibition. The two years of the interdiction gave him plenty of time to fine-tune the play; it is not impossible that *Richard III*'s sheer length may be due to the fact that it was written in large part away from the playhouse and could not be rehearsed or revised on the stage until it was all written. When the houses reopened in 1594, the play was ready. It was quite probably the first production by the newly constituted Lord Chamberlain's Men, put on to celebrate their launch late that summer. Shakespeare knew that it was brilliant and so did they. And London audiences seem to have concurred.

The character of Richard Gloucester emerges as early as *2 Henry VI* and then inexorably bears down on us like a "usurping boar" as the Wars of the Roses plays draw to an end. Richard's very deformity is repeatedly and unsentimentally apostrophized: "foul stigmatic," "heap of wrath," "foul indigested lump." He joins with gusto in joking about his crippled spine, but his chief pleasure, along with killing and the pursuit of power, is women. He revels in his seductive abilities, which are considerable despite the instinctive abhorrence one would expect to greet such a man. In Richard III, Shakespeare created a radical character whose moral shortcomings are simply swept aside by his huge dramatic presence.

Audiences have always been entranced by Richard. In this connection, a story has come down to us over four hundred years, and there are sound reasons for thinking that it may be true. We are told that *Richard III* was playing in London, with the young Richard Burbage in the lead:

> Upon a time when Burbage played Richard III there was a citizen grew so far in liking with him that before she went from the play she appointed him to come that night unto her by the name of Richard III. Shakespeare, overhearing their conclusion, went before, was entertained and at his game ere Burbage came. The message being brought that Richard III was at the door, Shakespeare caused return to be made that William the Conqueror was before Richard III.

So John Manningham, a barrister at Middle Temple, recorded in his diary on March 13, 1602, some eight years after Burbage played Richard III. Burbage, Shakespeare's junior by four years, was the only actor in London who could compete with Alleyn. His Shakespearian roles included not only Richard III but also Hamlet, Lear, and Othello. Women frequently attended plays, and it was noted how freely they comported themselves: after attending a court entertainment in January 1618, Orazio Businio, the chaplain to the Venetian embassy, remarked that "the plump and buxom display their bosoms very liberally, and those who are lean go muffled up to the throat." The rumor recorded in Manningham's diary would seem to confirm English women's relative sexual freedoms. Here, after all, is a citizen's wife making herself freely available to a player, behavior that the twenty-first century may well be happy with but that sits doubtfully with the society of the 1590s.

And yet none of the participants in this miniature sexual comedy seems to be unduly troubled by it, nor for that matter is the narrator. Manningham portrays Shakespeare as a sexual opportunist but his report reads like an adaptation of Chaucer's "Miller's Tale." "At his game" is the equivalent of "having sex" and about as neutral. It is the stuff of young men behaving badly. Burbage was a bachelor at the time (he married his wife, Winifred, around 1600), but Shakespeare of course was not. The question is whether we can say anything at all about the identity of this "citizen," whether she was a widow of independent means who had the run of her house at night, or the wife of a husband in the country, or a wealthy prostitute. Whoever she was, she clearly loved the theater and had independent means of some sort. Nor is this the full story, since the tale of Shakespeare, Burbage, and the citizen's wife exists independently of the diary entry by Manningham. It is found in an eighteenth-century pamphlet by Thomas Wilkes called *A General View of the Stage* (1759):

> One evening when *Richard III* was to be performed, Shakespeare observed a young woman delivering a message to Burbage in so cautious a manner as excited his curiosity to listen to. It imported that her master was gone out of town that morning, and her mistress would be glad of his company

after the play; and to know what signal he would appoint for admittance. Burbage replied "three taps at the door" and "It is I, Richard the Third." She immediately withdrew and Shakespeare followed 'till he observed her to go into a house in the city; and enquiring in the neighborhood he was informed that a young lady lived there, the favourite of an old rich merchant. Near the appointed time of meeting, Shakespeare thought proper to anticipate Master Burbage and was introduced by the concerted signal. The lady was very much surprised at Shakespeare's presuming to act Master Burbage's part, but as he, who had wrote *Romeo and Juliet*, we may be certain did not want wit or eloquence to apologize for the intrusion, she was soon pacified, and they were mutually happy till Burbage came to the door and repeated the same signal. But Shakespeare popping his head out of the window, bid him be gone, for that William the Conqueror had reigned before Richard III.

According to this version, then, Shakespeare followed the woman "into a house in the city" from, presumably, Curtain Road in Shoreditch. The fact that the "young lady" was the mistress of a rich old man fits Hunsdon well enough, since he was in his late sixties at the time of his affair with the young Emilia Bassano. If this story does indeed allude to her, then the address in the city may be Blackfriars: this is where Hunsdon lived, directly south, in fact, of the hall that two years or so later Shakespeare's company tried to acquire for a new theater. By the autumn of 1594, Emilia Lanier was the married mother of a baby boy called Henry after his father, Henry Carey Hunsdon. Something of her bond with Hunsdon clearly survived their separation since she was keen that her son should carry his blueblood father's name. If she is indeed the lady in Wilkes's account, then she may still have lived in Blackfriars after her marriage.

It would be curiously fitting if Shakespeare's first sexual encounter with his mistress after an afternoon's showing of *Richard III* took place inside the former Dominican precinct, which was also coincidentally where his printer friend Richard Field lived and worked at the time. Blackfriars is sandwiched between two places that feature prominently in the play, Ely Place to the north (where Richard spotted the famous strawberries) and Baynard Castle directly south of it, on the site of today's almost equally grim multistory "Baynard Castle" car park. Wilkes's account has been dubbed "embellished," but we could call it so only if we had proof that he based his account on Manningham. But he could not have done so, since Manningham's diary only came to light in the nineteenth century. The diary is unlikely to be a forgery; the major Shakespeare forgeries began only with William Henry Ireland (1777–1835) and John Payne Collier (1789–1883). Manningham may have heard the story about Shakespeare and Burbage from his roommate Curle and jotted it down later that night; or else he had it from a senior Inner Templarian by the name of Towse. The most recent editor of Manningham's diary favors the latter provenance. If Manningham's source was William Towse, a senior bencher who later held the highest office at Inner Temple, then the story's credibility is enhanced. As for Wilkes, he seems to have gleaned his version from a printed (or handwritten) source that is now lost.

The jaunty reference in both versions of the story to William the Conqueror is suggestive, considering Shakespeare's fondness for toying with names. There is a passage in one of the plays that may connect to this story of Will Shakespeare the Conqueror and Richard Burbage. If the link could be proven—and the date of the play certainly fits—then we could confidently claim that the story of Burbage and Shakespeare was current in London by the mid-1590s and a source of fun for actor and writer alike. The play in question is the one that we know from its title in the First Folio as *The Taming of the Shrew*. In the mid-1590s it may have been known by another title altogether, as we will see shortly, one tantalizingly suggestive of this story of adulterous love and sexual triangles. The opening lines of the induction feature the following exchange between Sly and the hostess Marian Hacket:

> SLY I'll feeze you, in faith.
>
> HOSTESS A pair of stocks, you rogue!
>
> SLY You're a baggage. The Slys are no rogues. Look in the Chronicles—we came in with Richard Conqueror, therefore *paucas palabras,* let the world slide. Sessa!

This is the only direct reference in all of Shakespeare's works to the Norman conqueror. The joke on Sly depends for effect on the audience's instant recognition that the conqueror was William and not Richard. Perhaps Shakespeare is indulging in a private joke with Richard Burbage, who probably played both Petruchio and Sly. "Richard Conqueror" would have added piquancy if spoken by an actor called Richard, particularly since, as the emerging star of the London stage, he was undoubtedly the "conqueror" of the Theatre. Who knows, he may even have enjoyed the stage sobriquet "Richard Conqueror" during just this period, when his rocketing fame started to compete with Alleyn's and may even have threatened to eclipse it: when he was a Richard playing a Richard in a play named *Richard III*. And yet here we have a story of this very Richard Conqueror being pipped to the lady, as it were. If the anecdote quickly became part of London gossip, perhaps Shakespeare is alluding to it here a few months after it happened. This in turn may hint that *The Shrew* was written in late 1594, shortly after *Richard III*, that it alludes to the real-life seduction of one of Burbage's fans by Shakespeare, and that at the time Shakespeare relished his reputation for madcap sexual behavior. This need not surprise us: spectacle was his business, and why not include self-exhibition?

Shakespeare was probably galvanized into writing *The Shrew* by the publication in 1594 of *A Shrew*. Perhaps he felt indignant at the thought of one of "his" plays being thus printed without acknowledgment of him, and by a rival company; or perhaps he saw an opportunity here, to rewrite the play, make it his own, show them what he could do. Hence the utter Warwickshireness of the Induction. Few things could be more personal than that. When *A Shrew* was first published in 1594 it was advertised as "A pleasant conceited history called The Taming of a Shrew As it was sundry times acted by the Right honourable the Earl of Pembroke his servants." Both Shakespeare and Marlowe were associated with Pembroke's company; it put on Shakespeare's *Titus Andronicus* and *3 Henry VI* at just the time, around 1592, when Marlowe was giving them *Edward II*, which suggests further that Marlowe and Shakespeare were still very much in touch, if not actively collaborating, as late as 1592. *The Shrew* was Shakespeare's first engaging with Marlowe since the latter's death eighteen months earlier. While Shakespeare was keen to flag up his independence from Marlowe, he also pays homage to him. Grumio's "Beloved of me, and that my deeds shall prove" archly echoes one of Marlowe's most famous lines, Tamburlaine's "I am a lord, for so my deeds shall prove." Grumio's pitch for Bianca is similarly an elegy to the rhetorical glory that was Marlowe. His house, he claims, is "richly furnished with plate and gold," the walls covered with "Tyrian tapestry," and his "cypress chests" full of "fine linen, Turkey cushions bossed with pearl, / Valens of Venice gold in needle-work." As in the earlier play, one Christopher Sly starts off the action: "I am Christophero Sly. Call not me 'honour' nor 'lordship.' I ne'er drank sack in my life, and if you give me any conserves, give me conserves of beef." This plea for solid English fare fails to deter the Lord from willfully mistaking Sly for one of his betters as part of an elaborate farcical joke. So Sly resorts to the big guns and drops all pretense, starting with that aristocratic-sounding "o":

> SLY What, would you make me mad? Am not I Christopher Sly—old Sly's son of Burton Heath, by birth a pedlar, by education a card-maker, by transmutation a bearherd, and now by present profession a tinker? Ask Marian Hacket, the fat alewife of Wincot, if she know me not. If she say I am not fourteen pence on the score for sheer ale, score me up for the lyings't knave in Christendom.

The Shrew follows the main plot line of *A Shrew,* retaining the name Christopher and also calling the shrew Kate, but almost everything else is different. The setting shifts from Greek Athens to Italian Padua and the Induction is set in, of all places, Warwickshire. So specific and local is it that this play could only ever have been written by someone from Warwickshire, someone who knew about Wilmcote or Barton-on-the-Heath. The play is populated with English dogs called Merriman, Clowder, Silver, Belman, and Echo. It is informed by a knowledge of hunting that seems very country—as, for example, in the reference to "the hedge-corner, in the coldest fault." The multiple afflictions of Petruchio's ride display the playwright's intimate knowledge of horses. Shakespeare needed only to pop out of his parents' home in Stratford and call on the Hornbys, or Greenway across the street, to learn all about horses.

By reframing the revised version of the play with two Warwick-shire scenes, Shakespeare, the butt of an angry charge of plagiarism two years earlier, is signaling ownership of the text. He does so by aligning his identity with the family villages back in Warwickshire. Perhaps after the plague closures, which must have seemed inter-minable, he felt that he had to put his stamp on his new, but not quite new, play. His recasting of the Induction reveals a man eager to prove himself, clearly proud; in the days before his writings for the stage were printed and published, he was determined to show the world that these were *his* works, and nobody else's. Later, when he wrote *King Lear* (1605–1606), in the immediate wake of the publication of *King Leir,* he may no longer have felt this need to assert himself; after all, from 1598 on his published works had overtly advertised them-selves with his name on their title pages.

While many of the names are anglicized—Nathaniel, Joseph, Nicholas, Philip, Walter, Sugarson—three names in particular are not: those of Grumio and Tranio and of Kate's father, Baptista. They provide important clues about Shakespeare's intellectual develop-ment and life during this period. Grumio and Tranio step straight out of the Plautus' comedy *The Ghost* (*Mostellaria*), which Shake-speare clearly knew but does not seem otherwise to have used. To the extent that the sex scandal of Shakespeare, Burbage, and the bourgeoise may have found its way into *The Shrew,* the Dark Lady entered the play indirectly from the very start. But it is the much more revealing detail of Kate's father's name that helps identify her with Emilia Bassano Lanier. In *A Shrew,* the father was called Al-fonso, like Emilia's husband, but in *The Shrew* in 1594 he becomes Baptista, like Emilia's father. If the name Alfonso was one that Shakespeare happened to hit upon in *A Shrew,* in the second version of the play the name is no longer just a literary Italian fillip; it is now grounded in an imaginative reality that conflates the worlds of fiction and fact. The name Baptista affords presumptive evidence that the Dark Lady was Emilia Lanier—and it suggests, furthermore, that Kate Minola of Padua, daughter of Baptista, is based on Emilia Lanier, daughter of another Baptista.

The Induction to *The Shrew* opens with a clash over broken glasses between Christopher Sly of Burton-on-heath and his unnamed Hostess. The stage directions do not specify the location of the scene, but clues in the text enable us to identify it. The Hostess is "Marian Hacket the fat alewife of Wincot." With Cicely Hacket, the "woman's maid of the house" (she is really Marian's daughter), Marian runs an alehouse in Wincot. That Wincot stands in for Wilmcote, the home village of Shakespeare's mother, Mary Arden, was forcefully advocated by Halliwell-Phillipps, who also noted that "Marian Hacket, the fat ale-wife, was probably a real character, as well as Stephen Sly, Old John Naps, Peter Turf, and Henry Pimpernell." All these are named in the Induction; all we need to do is to find them in the parish records. Halliwell-Phillipps knew those records better than most people, and 130 years on from his groundbreaking work on the Warwickshire and Stratford archives nothing more has turned up. But we should not rule out the possibility that there were Hackets who ran an inn at Wilmcote.

Most, though not all, commentators agree on the identity of Wincot and Wilmcote. A Stratford Corporation minute of November 11, 1584, about Wilmcote refers to "the tythes of wyncote." There may be a further reference to this place-name in *2 Henry IV,* when Davy asks Shallow to adjudicate a dispute between "William Visor of Woncot against Clement Perks o' th' Hill." Woncot is probably Wilmcote, especially since Perkses were thick on the ground in the neighboring village of Snitterfield, the home of Shakespeare's paternal grandfather.* Shakespeare would have been aware of Snitterfield Perkses by September 1581 at the latest, when his "cousin"

---

*Chambers disagreed with Halliwell-Phillipps, over believing that the Wincot of *The Shrew* was the Wincot at Clifford Chambers, a few miles south of Stratford, because the name Hacket is actually recorded here once, with reference to the baptism of one Sara, daughter of Robert Hackett, on November 21, 1591. Since there are no other Hacket(t)s recorded in the Quinton register, Sara's parents may have been married elsewhere. The name Hacket(t) does occur in Stratford, but it is not common, even allowing for the parish registers' errors and incompleteness. The scene is set in Gloucestershire and since the nineteenth century it has been argued that the two litigants of *2 Henry IV* may have lived in Gloucestershire in the area around Dursley and the adjoining Stinchcombe Hill. The name Visor was common in the

Robert Webbe married Mary Perks of Snitterfield. The couple took over Shakespeare's grandfather's leasehold farm on the corner of Bell Lane after Richard Shakespeare's death. The details of the Webbe-Perks-Snitterfield links are perfectly clear from the minutes and accounts of the borough, where we also find information on one William Cook from the same hamlet.* Cook was closely involved in various transactions with Shakespeare's father and uncle as well as his Webbe cousins and Edmund Lambert, Mary Arden's brother-in-law. Moreover, he stood as godfather in 1586 to Robert Webbe's son William. He matters to us because the very scene in *2 Henry IV* that features Perks also makes much of a certain William Cook.

If Woncot is Wilmcote and the Perkses and Cooke are from Snitterfield, then "o' th' Hill" could also refer to a particular location in Snitterfield, which sits on two different levels, up by the church and down the hill near Bell Brook. While the Aston Cantlow parish registers, which cover Wilmcote, include the names Perkes, no Hackets or Visors are listed; still, Shakespeare may not have simply invented the names. Given that Wincot, Woncot, and Wilmcote are probably one and the same, Shakespeare seems to be setting the Induction of *The Shrew* on the edge of the forest of Arden and in front of his maternal grandparents' house of Glebe Farm. Any alehouses, taverns, or inns would have stood on or near the green then as now, with the Arden house next door to a tavern, or opposite it, or both, as is the case today.

The title of this play in the First Folio, *The Taming of the Shrew*, may be the original one. But it would have been rather confusing and perhaps commercially foolhardy if, on the playbill, all that differentiated the new Chamberlain's play from the old Pembroke's was the change to the definite article. *The Shrew* may, though, have been known by a different title, and one that may fit peculiarly well with Shakespeare's personal circumstances at the time. We know that a

---

region at the time, but Perkes is seldom found here. Stinchcombe Hill affords a good view right across to Berkeley castle on a hill four miles away so that the phrase "by yon tuft of trees" in *Richard II* may be evidence of Shakespeare knowing this area. Wood makes the same point and connects it back to John Shakespeare's career in brogging.

*MA, vol. 3, pp. 60–61.

Shakespeare play entitled *Love's Labour's Won* once existed, for in 1598 it was attributed to Shakespeare in a list in which other titles of his plays are given accurately.* The list appears in Francis Meres's *Palladis Tamia,* and it includes twelve plays by Shakespeare although only four, possibly five, had yet been published in quarto. Even with respect to those, Meres had no printed evidence of authorship, because it was only in the year he himself published that those quartos were attributed to Shakespeare. That he had inside information is also suggested by the fact that he knew the Sonnets *eleven years* before Thorpe published them in 1609.

The most striking feature of Meres's list is the absence from it of *The Taming of the Shrew* and the inclusion of *Love's Labour's Won* alongside *Love's Labour's Lost.* There is no conceivable reason why Meres would replace a play that happens to have survived, *The Taming of the Shrew,* with one that is lost, *Love's Labour's Won.* Nor did he do any such thing. Rather he included *The Taming of the Shrew* by the title it had in performances in 1594 and in a now lost quarto version: *Love's Labour's Won.* That *Love's Labour's Won* existed in the 1590s as a Shakespeare play is not in doubt, for Meres's reference to its existence is supported by the listing of a quarto with just that name in a 1603 stationer's book catalogue that was discovered in 1953. That catalogue also features *The Taming of a Shrew* (but not *The Taming of the Shrew*) as a separate entry. The logical conclusion to draw from the joint evidence of Meres's 1598 survey and the 1603 sales list is that *Love's Labour's Won* and *The Shrew* are one and the same, that in the 1590s there existed a quarto called *Love's Labour's Won* and corresponding to the play we know as *The Shrew.* This quarto still existed in 1603, when it was for sale, and the play in question was being performed under the title *Love's Labour's Won* at least up to 1598, when Meres saw it. Further support for this comes, indirectly, from the entry on the Stationers' Register of November 8, 1623, for the

---

*Although it omits the *Henry VI* plays and *The Merry Wives of Windsor.* Since *The Merry Wives of Windsor* appears to have been commissioned for a court performance, Meres may not have been aware of its existence when he wrote *Palladis Tamia,* although it's difficult to square this with the idea that he had inside information. It is worth noting that scholars used to argue for a rather later date, one after 1598, for *Merry Wives.*

First Folio. Among the plays listed there "as not formerly entered to other men" one would expect to find *The Shrew,* if it had never been published before the First Folio, but there is no trace of it. The reason is that it had already appeared in quarto, just like all the other plays that are not listed in this entry. If a quarto of *The Shrew* by the title *Love's Labour's Won* were ever to turn up, it might contain the part of the Induction that seems to be so oddly missing at the end of the comedy in its present state in the First Folio.

Shakespeare probably wrote *Love's Labour's Won* on his return from Warwickshire in 1594. It may have been his first contribution after *Richard III* to the newly formed Lord Chamberlain's Company and follows hard on the heels of the publication of the Pembroke play *A Shrew,* which was in all probability also mostly his. Soon afterward, and perhaps because of the success of *Love's Labour's Won,* he launched into another play, which was written as its twin: *Love's Labour's Lost.* The period of these two plays, 1594–95, coincides with the height of Shakespeare's involvement with the young man of the Sonnets and the Dark Lady.

Love's Labour's Lost is one of Shakespeare's rhetorically most brilliant and opaque plays. It ends, famously, on a note of irresolution: the various pairs of lovers are instructed that their unions will be postponed for a year—in Berowne's words, "Our wooing doth not end like an old play: / Jack hath no Jill." This, of course, is not the accepted idiom of romantic comedy. "An old play" here could signify the venerable genre of romantic comedy itself, but it may instead allude to *Love's Labour's Won,* which concludes with the subjugation of Kate and her triumph over her sister Bianca. The very title of *Love's Labour's Lost* would refer back to "an old play" if that play was called *Love's Labour's Won* and was still reasonably fresh in the audience's minds.

Just as he does in the Induction to *The Shrew,* so Shakespeare here gives us a recognizable slice of English countryside. Even the seasons spring and winter are represented in the play's final song. As the cuckoo and owl swap roles, we are treated to springtime meadows decked with daisies, violets, lady-smocks, and cuckoo-buds, while in winter icicles hang from the wall, "Dick the shepherd blows his nail, / And Tom bears logs into the hall, / And milk comes frozen home in pail." Roasted crab apples hiss in the bowl "while greasy Joan doth keel the pot": in such details, the play paints the domesticity of an Elizabethan home, one like Shakespeare's own. Although the name Joan is conventionally applied to any wench, as in "groan for Joan" or "Some men must love my lady, and some Joan," it was also the name of two of Shakespeare's sisters—the firstborn, who died in 1558, and the one who at the time of *Love's Labour's Lost* was twenty-six and living in Henley Street.

Like *The Shrew, Love's Labour's Lost* exhibits a raw sexuality—for example, in its barely coded talk of young women making their boyfriends come by hand. Perhaps it's as well that they do so, since full sexual intercourse may have dire consequences, as when Costard informs Armado that Jaquenetta is pregnant by him: "she is gone, she is two months on her way ... unless you play the honest Trojan the poor wench is cast away. She's quick. The child brags in her belly already. 'Tis yours." It was nearly thirteen years since Will Shakespeare had to play the "honest Trojan" to Anne Hathaway.

One of the distinctive features of both *Love's Labour's* plays is their smattering of Italian: Shakespeare now has enough Italian to pun in the language. Thus, when Bianca's father in *The Shrew* asks, "Is not this my Cambio?" she replies "Cambio is changed into Lucentio." The Italian word *cambiare* means "to change"; *cambio* can mean both transformation and exchange of currency.

It is a pleasant fantasy to think that Shakespeare might have picked up Italian from traveling to Italy, perhaps during the closure of the theaters. After all, the ersatz Italy of *The Two Gentlemen of Verona* (c. 1591) could hardly be more different from that of *Romeo and Juliet* (1596–97), *The Merchant of Venice* (1598), and *Othello* (1604). There is no documentary evidence that Shakespeare traveled abroad in the early 1590s, although we don't know that he never did. He so powerfully evokes the sheerness of the cliffs at Dover in *King Lear* that he probably saw them from the sea at some point, perhaps while touring with his company. In the summer of 1596, for example, they played at Rye in August and at Dover in September. Queen Margaret in *2 Henry VI*, which certainly dates from before 1592, bids the winds blow "towards England's blessed shore" noting that "As far as I could ken thy chalky cliffs, / When from thy shore the tempest beat us back, / I stood upon the hatches in the storm." Shakespeare may at the very least have popped across to France at some point, as Marlowe did to Flushing. The marine imagery in his plays suggests that he knew something about sailing. Perhaps at some point the Privy Council even issued him a passport to go abroad, as it did Marlowe. He undoubtedly knew French—he would write an entire scene in *Henry V* in French; and not just French, but punning French. In *The Merry Wives of Windsor,* he affectionately parodies French accents and mistakes in English. But Shakespeare may have come by his knowledge of French culture without traveling, notably through his friendship with Richard Field (who married a Huguenot) and his lodging, eventually as we will see, with a French Huguenot family.

Alas, the picture of Shakespeare touring Europe won't stand up to scrutiny. Such travel was unavailable to people from his class and background; he could have visited Florence, Padua, Venice, Verona, or Rome only in the retinue of a great lord, such as Southampton or one of the Cecils (none of these were on the Continent at that time). Rather than Shakespeare going to Italy, perhaps Italy came to him, in the shapes of Emilia Lanier and John Florio. Giovanni Florio (c. 1553–c. 1625), the English-born son of an Italian Protestant refugee, is best known to us for a famous translation of Montaigne's *Essays,* which Shakespeare used in *The Tempest.* He became Southampton's tutor in 1591 and turned the young Earl into a keen and accomplished speaker of Italian. By 1591, Florio had produced two grammars of Italian, *Florio's First Fruits* and *Florio's Second Fruits.* It is from the first of these that Shakespeare is quoting in *Love's Labour's Lost,* when Holofernes intones, "I may speak of thee as the traveller doth of Venice, *'Venezia, Venezia, Chi non ti vede, chi non ti prezia'* " (Venice, Venice, he who has not seen you does not value you). Florio could have taught Shakespeare about Italian customs and geography. He was, according to Ben Jonson, a keen lover of the theater and it is quite possible that the play-addicted Southampton and his tutor would have gone to see Shakespeare's plays in Shoreditch. Perhaps Florio took Shakespeare aside after a performance of *The Two Gentlemen of Verona* to tell him that Milan and Verona are not, in fact, separated by water. It may have been Florio who first described to Shakespeare those hotheaded young men spoiling for fights in the midday sun—the *bravi*, as Alessandro Manzoni would one day call them in *I Promessi Sposi*, a nineteenth-century Italian *Romeo and Juliet*. Perhaps Florio described for Shakespeare the country of *amore*, of sonnets, and of the *dolce stil nuovo*.

However Florio and Shakespeare met, Shakespeare's take on Italy was radically transformed by his exposure to Italian culture. This happened demonstrably before he wrote *The Shrew* and *Love's Labour's Lost*, and in good time for *Romeo and Juliet*, *The Merchant of Venice*, and *Othello*, the latter two, of course, set in Emilia Bassano's home city. From *The Shrew* on, all things Italian in Shakespeare may have been inspired by his relationship with an Italian lover who also happens to have been Jewish.

Emilia was a talented, beautiful, dark-eyed, and mysterious woman. Perhaps occasionally she was less than sweet-breathed, for the poet refers to "the breath that from my mistress reeks." She may have been eating garlic; in *A Midsummer Night's Dream*, Bottom warns his "most dear actors" to "eat no onions nor garlic, for we are to utter sweet breath," and the phrase "the breath of garlic-eaters" is the greatest insult that Menenius can hurl at the plebeian mob whom he blames for exiling Coriolanus.

The mistress until recently of one of the most powerful men in the land could not be content with a mere player, particularly not when his best friend was the beautiful Earl of Southampton. She knew her mind and was not afraid to take the initiative; indeed, she did so repeatedly in her busy seventy-six years of life, proceeding from the relationship with Hunsdon to marriage with Alfonso Lanier, then starting an affair with Shakespeare and, eventually and at first behind Shakespeare's back, with Southampton, before returning to her husband sometime before 1597.

13.

A Will "Made Lame by Fortune's Blows"

he identity of the Dark Lady can be teased out from the Sonnets, *The Taming of the Shrew*, *The Merchant of Venice*, and *Othello*. And in the Sonnets there may lie the clue to another Shakespearian secret, one that has been unnecessarily shrouded in mystery largely because some of the most influential commentators on the poems insist that a particular set of words must be read metaphorically. These words—"limp," "lame," "disabled," and "halting"—are all applied by the poet to himself. Some, finding the idea of a limping or even clubfooted Shakespeare too much to contemplate, have played down the subjective quality of those poems. Literal readings of the "lame" sonnets are even less popular than the allegedly "hydrocephalic" Droeshout portrait in the First Folio or the balding bust in Holy Trinity. We sometimes assume that if Shakespeare had suffered from a disability his contemporaries would surely have told us so—after all, they poked fun unblinkingly at lunacy in plays like Thomas Middleton's *The Changeling*. They were hardly squeamish about that kind of thing. But then Ben Jonson, who had a good deal to say about the Stratford playwright after his death, tells us next to nothing about his appearance except to express his approval of the portrait in the First Folio. The Sonnets are the most personal and immediate lyrics that Shakespeare ever wrote; perhaps we ought to be more sanguine about the evidence they afford.

Sonnets 37, 66, 89, and 90 all allude to disability. The poet was "made lame by fortune's dearest spite" (37); he despairs that his "strength [is] by limping sway disablèd" (66); he instructs his friend to speak "of my lameness, and I straight will halt" (89); he challenges the friend to "join with the spite of fortune, make me bow" (90). These references are almost always read figuratively. Verse, after all, often "halts," and "lame" retains this secondary meaning to this day. But the references have the ring of authenticity and there is no reason why they should not be literally true. At the very least we need to consider that Shakespeare, like Byron, may have limped owing to polio, or spina bifida, or an accident, such as a fall from a horse. In the Sonnets, Shakespeare is addressing someone who knows him well, and the rhetorical framing of his condition suggests that the speaker and his addressee both *know* that this matter troubles the poet.

The first intimation comes in Sonnet 37:

> *As a decrepit father takes delight*
> *To see his active child do deeds of youth,*
> *So I, made lame by fortune's dearest spite,*
> *Take all my comfort of thy worth and truth;*
> *For whether beauty, birth, or wealth, or wit,*
> *Or any of these all, or all, or more,*
> *Entitled in thy parts do crownèd sit,*
> *I make my love engrafted to this store.*
> *So then I am not lame, poor, nor despised,*
> *Whilst that this shadow doth such substance give,*
> *That I in thy abundance am sufficed,*
> *And by a part of all thy glory live.*
> > *Look what is best, that best I wish in thee;*
> > *This wish I have, then ten times happy me.*

"Made lame by fortune's dearest spite" means that the speaker was crippled by Fortune at her most cruel and injurious. His lameness is congenital; no one is to blame for it and no guilt attaches to it. But in watching the fair youth, he compares himself with a "decrepit" father who miraculously recovers the use of his limbs through the sheer delight he takes in watching his animated child play and run about. The young man's plenitude fills the poet's sad lack. If this imagery were an isolated instance in the Sonnets and the works generally, we might want to read it as having no external reference. But other references in the Sonnets and in the plays make plain that Shakespeare was keenly interested in lameness, in limping, in malformation of the spine. This latter powers *3 Henry VI* and *Richard III,* whose crippled hero, the "valiant crook-back prodigy / Dicky," loves being nature's freak (or so he claims when gibing about how dogs bark as he passes). A crookback he may be, but he successfully woos a widow in front of the coffin of her husband, whom he has murdered. This widow, like Shakespeare's wife, is named Anne; one wonders whether Shakespeare was equally jubilant after having overcome his Anne's resistance.

Several years later, Hamlet tells Horatio that the native custom of drunken revels damages the reputation of the Danes:

> *So, oft it chances in particular men*
> *That, for some vicious mole of nature in them—*
> *As in their birth, wherein they are not guilty,*
> *Since nature cannot choose his origin,*
> *By the o'ergrowth of some complexion,*
> *Oft breaking down the pales and forts of reason,*
> *Or by some habit that too much o'erleavens*
> *The form of plausive manners—that these men,*
> *Carrying, I say, the stamp of one defect,*
> *Being nature's livery or fortune's star,*
> *His virtues else be they as pure as grace,*
> *As infinite as man may undergo,*
> *Shall in the general censure take corruption*
> *From that particular fault. The dram of evil*
> *Doth all the noble substance of over-daub*
> *To his own scandal.*

Hamlet is talking about damage done unjustly to the whole physical and moral human fabric by a single prominent flaw, such as a birthmark. There is a note here of special pleading, of heartfelt frustration that a small blemish should have the power to ruin the beauty of the whole body. Never mind a person's many other virtues, "be they as pure as grace" or otherwise infinite; the "mole" will override them, like a mark on an otherwise pristine canvas. Shakespeare is making a general moral point. The "mole of nature" speech is a huge, elaborate, and excessive simile for what it is intended locally to illuminate. What Hamlet says, we know to be true. It was ever thus. Few children are complimented in the school yard for their wholesomeness; many are taunted for small physical blemishes. Shakespeare is talking here as much as Hamlet is.

The playwright and protagonist may converge in these lines, spoken just before the entry of the Ghost (on the cue "scandal"). There are reasons to believe that Shakespeare himself played the Ghost; Rowe notes that Shakespeare's

> name is printed, as the custom was in those times, amongst those of the other players, before some old plays, but without any particular account of what sort of parts he used to play; and though I have inquired, I could never meet with any further account of him this way than that the top of his performance was the ghost in his own *Hamlet.*

If this is true, then in *Hamlet,* in which a son cannot come to terms with the death of his father and the remarriage of his mother, the dead father was originally played by the father of a real-life boy called Hamlet. But in real life, it was the son who died; the ghost was young Hamlet. My immediate concern here is to ask whether the appearance of the ghost merely coincides with Hamlet's protest about the mole of nature, or whether the timing is more deliberate, artful, and local. In other words, Shakespeare wrote this scene knowing that he would play the role of the ghost. He was visualizing his entrance: that thought may have triggered the lines about the mole of nature. One of the most famous passages in the most iconic work of English literature may be autobiographical; Shakespeare may be reverting to the predicament that had exercised him profoundly in the Sonnets. The ghost may limp, and the "mole of nature" may be a clubfoot or spinal deformity.

We cannot be sure, of course, but further support for the idea that Shakespeare had some skeletal anomaly derives from yet another role that Shakespeare played. Our informant this time is the eighteenth-century editor Edward Capell, whom we have already encountered in relation to Shakespeare's poaching and the subsequent ballads. Capell reports that Shakespeare played Old Adam in *As You Like It*:

> A traditional story was current some years ago about Stratford that a very old man of that place, of weak intellects but yet related to Shakespeare, being asked by some of his neighbours what he remembered about him, answered that he saw him once brought on the stage upon another man's back; which answer was applied by the hearers to his having seen him perform in this scene the part of Adam. That he should have done so is made not unlikely by another constant tradition, that he was no extraordinary actor and therefore took no parts upon him but such as this; for which he might also be peculiarly fitted by an accidental lameness, which, as he himself tells us twice in his *Sonnets*, v. 37 and 89, befell him in some part of life; without saying how, or when, of what sort, or in what degree; but his expressions seem to indicate— latterly.*

In the play, Old Adam reveals that his "old limbs lie lame," and Orlando describes him to the exiled court in the Forest of Arden as "an old poor man / Who after me hath many a weary step / Limped in pure love." It is impossible to determine who might have been the seventeenth-century Stratford relative, although if he existed he had to be one of the Harts of Henley Street. That they would have seen a performance of *As You Like It* is unlikely but not impossible. Descendants of Shakespeare's sister Joan Hart lived in Stratford until the end of the eighteenth century.

Capell's source for the "traditional story" of Shakespeare being carried onstage is independent of Rowe, for he goes on to mention "another constant tradition" that *is* Rowe (the phrase "no extraordinary actor" is borrowed from Rowe's 1709 *Life*). As in the case of Sonnet 37, the language here need not refer to the poet's own state

---

*Chambers (1930), vol. 2, p. 289.

of health. After all, old men do become lame and slow. But there is more lameness in the plays, notably in *King Lear,* and this may clinch the argument that Shakespeare was lame.

Sonnet 37's "made lame by fortune's dearest spite" is closely echoed in *Lear,* when Edgar replies thus to Gloucester's question about his identity:

> *A most poor man, made lame by fortune's blows,*
> *Who by the art of known and feeling sorrows,*
> *Am pregnant to good pity.*

This is the sixth scene of Act IV, where Edgar as poor Tom encounters two old men, one of them the octogenarian king, the other the adulterous Gloucester, on a heath above the cliffs of Dover. In the immediate context, Edgar claims to be a person who readily embraces compassion because he has known and felt sorrows, having been made *lame* by Fortune. That, at least, is the reading in the first published version of the play, the quarto of 1608, which appeared some two years after the play was first written and performed. It is widely accepted that behind this printed text lies Shakespeare's own autograph manuscript for the play, produced during the spring of 1606. Shakespeare therefore wrote "lame," or something looking very much like it.

"Lame," however, expresses a very odd train of thought, because it seems so specific: that is, "lame" is precise in a way that "humble" or "sad" or any other adjective to fit naturally with a melancholy state of mind induced by fortune's blows is not. It is therefore not at all surprising that the second version of the play to be published in the period, the Folio *King Lear* of 1623, should replace "lame" with "tame" and, incidentally, also change the preposition, so that the line reads "A most poor man, made *tame to* fortune's blows" (emphasis mine). The change is not inconsiderable. "Tame" offers a wider, more generally moralized, and indeed flatter reading than "lame." No one knows how the differences between the quarto and Folio *King Lear*s came about, although some scholars argue that Shakespeare himself revised the play after the first publication. If he did, then the change from "lame" in the quarto to "tame" in the Folio would be proof that he felt uncomfortable with the somewhat unnatural train of thought here. But others, notably W. W. Greg, the famous bibliographer and librarian of Trinity College, Cambridge, have argued instead that a number of the most striking discrepancies show that different compositors and proof correctors guessing at ambiguities in the manuscript came up with different answers. This may in some ways be a more promising line of approach here, at least as far as this local textual difficulty is concerned.

Shakespeare wrote a widely used Elizabethan longhand, Secretary, which we today find hard to read. It appears in many Elizabethan documents and was only gradually superseded by what was then called italic, the hand that we use today. In Secretary, "lame" and "tame" are almost indistinguishable, as they may of course also be in italic. In other words, the different readings in the quarto and Folio of *King Lear* probably arose from variant readings of the same manuscript line. But the phrasings in Sonnet 37 and in the quarto of *King Lear* are nearly identical—"made lame by fortune's dearest spite / blows"—strong evidence that Shakespeare wrote "lame." Shakespeare, it seems, identified the most senseless blows of Fortune with congenital lameness, and the most likely reason is that he himself suffered from it. Lameness is an obsession with Shakespeare because of his own experience of life.

Take a further example from the Sonnets, this time from 89, which also puns on the poet's first name:

> *Say that thou didst forsake me for some fault,*
> *And I will comment upon that offence;*
> *Speak of my lameness, and I straight will halt,*
> *Against thy reasons making no defence.*
> *Thou canst not, love, disgrace me half so ill,*
> *To set a form upon desirèd change,*
> *As I'll myself disgrace, knowing thy will....*
> > *For thee against myself I'll vow debate;*
> > *For I must ne'er love him whom thou dost hate.*

At the top of the list of things that give offense to the glamorous youth the poet places his "lameness," which he offers, tongue-in-cheek and punningly, to suspend forthwith, "to halt" meaning both "to stop" and "to limp." Of course, he cannot do that in real life, he is saying; only at the level of language can he cease to halt, to stammer, to sound pedestrian. If necessary, he will take the youth's side against himself, for "I must ne'er love him whom thou dost hate." The poet knows the youth's wishes—or perhaps that should be his "will," which is also the poet's will, and the poet is Will Shakespeare who is himself. Sonnet 90 resumes with the "hate" from the preceding poem and almost immediately reverts to the subject of disability:

> *Then hate me when thou wilt, if ever, now,*
> *Now, while the world is bent my deeds to cross,*
> *Join with the spite of fortune, make me bow . . .*

Once more the particular phrase works at literal and metaphorical levels simultaneously. The poet may be bending from congenital damage to his spine, or he may be bowed by misfortune. Or "bent" and "cross" in the preceding line may between them generate "bow," as in "cross-bow." Such instinctive, associative rhetoric is a striking feature of Shakespeare's verse generally, so there may be no more here than the inner abandon of Shakespeare's language, a free play of sound patterns and resonant phrases.

In the end, though, there is considerable evidence that in his plays and poems Shakespeare was deeply preoccupied by having a limp. He was as frank about the anguish this caused him as he was self-advertising about his first name in Sonnets 135 and 136, which stand out for their obsessive play on "will." These two poems are intimately linked in other ways as well, not least by their obscenity in, for example, describing the woman as having a will that is "large and spacious" while accusing her of not allowing the speaker "to hide my will in thine." As may be apparent from the foregoing, "will" was sixteenth-century slang for both male and female sex organs. There are no fewer than thirteen uses of "will" in Sonnet 135, and one "wilt." The poem concludes:

> *So thou, being rich in Will, add to thy Will*
> *One will of mine to make thy large Will more.*

Let no unkind no fair beseechers kill;
Think all but one, and me in that one Will.

The next poem continues the theme with its obscene salvo "Will will fulfil the treasure of thy love, / Ay, fill it full with wills, and my will one." It concludes in barbed magnanimity: "Make but my name thy love, and love that still; / And then thou lov'st me, for my name is Will." That is, he urges her to engage in autoeroticism because in doing so she will love him, too: after all, his name and her genitals' are the same. The rhetorical tricksiness of these two poems is impressive if rather chilly and seemingly pointless. In a much gentler mode, the poet reverts in Sonnet 143 one more time to reminding her and us explicitly that his name is Will. The sonnet is brilliantly structured around the conceit of a busy housewife and mother setting down her baby to catch a runaway chicken; "her neglected child holds her in chase." This time the poet is not a sexual predator but rather in the condition of a bewildered toddler. Once his lover has caught the fluttering object of her desire she will return to the poet

And play the mother's part: kiss me, be kind.
So will I pray that thou mayst have thy Will
If thou turn back and my loud crying still.

The question the biographer wants to ask here is why the poet should be so free with his name. We know who he is, and so did the people to whom he addressed these lines. True, plays on his name allow him to joke liberally on men's and women's "wills," but he is not in the theater, trying to please the masses. There is no need to try to score points in poems meant, one imagines, for private ears. Or perhaps Shakespeare suspected all along that his poems would be distributed; he may even have wanted it to happen. Whatever his reasons, he clearly loved playing with his name, and his play, as the nature of the puns makes clear, is nothing short of self-induced sexual pleasure. Both the poet and his mistress are somehow at it together, the poet implies, as we lurch ever further away from the world of the youth, until (Sonnet 144) she finally gets hold of the young man and buries him inside her own will: "I guess one angel in another's hell," he is forced to admit when he realizes that they in turn are now involved.

The Will poems collapse the artificial barriers that have been set up to keep Shakespeare and the poet carefully apart. While a measure of artistic decorum is maintained in the "fair youth" poems, it is abandoned here. The poet tells us that the speaker is himself, Will Shakespeare. Another name, one very close to Shakespeare's life, may feature as well, and in ways that significantly illuminate the story behind the cycle and its likely publication history. The name of Anne Hathaway has been found in the penultimate line of Sonnet 145, where "hate away" is its homonym:

> *Those lips that love's own hand did make*
> *Breathed forth the sound that said "I hate"*
> *To me that languished for her sake;*
> *But when she saw my woeful state,*
> *Straight in her heart did mercy come,*
> *Chiding that tongue that ever sweet*
> *Was used in giving gentle doom,*
> *And taught it thus anew to greet:*
> *"I hate" she altered with an end*
> *That followed it as gentle day*
> *Doth follow night who, like a fiend,*
> *From heaven to hell is flown away.*
> > *"I hate" from hate away she threw,*
> > *And saved my life, saying "not you."**

Shakespeare, who so loved playing with language, cannot have been unaware of his own pun.

If Sonnet 145 is an early love poem to Anne Hathaway, it would have to date from the 1580s. The poem certainly feels very different from any other in the post-126 series, and not just because of its unique use of octosyllabic lines. It is written in an altogether gentler mode and idiom than the Dark Lady poems, and it lacks

---

*The poem has been known as the Anne Hathaway poem since Gurr (1971).

their aggressive edge. Even if there were no Hathaway connection in this light and conventional lyric, it is out of place here, while yet being unmistakably Shakespeare's. The only possible source for the manuscript would be Shakespeare himself, since only he or Anne would have owned a copy; that he probably kept the manuscript is in itself interesting, because it suggests that even as a seventeen-year-old he took his writing seriously enough to want to preserve it.

Of all the sonnets, the one immediately preceding the Anne Hathaway poem is the most scandalous. Sonnet 144 was published in *The Passionate Pilgrim* in 1599 and openly contrasts the poet's two illicit lovers and their gender:

> *Two loves I have, of comfort and despair,*
> *Which like two spirits do suggest me still.*
> *The better angel is a man right fair,*
> *The worser spirit a woman coloured ill.*

Shakespeare's most insensitive act of all may have been to counterpoint the most nakedly adulterous of all his poems with one addressed to Anne Hathaway by his youthful self years earlier. Between them, the twenty-eight lines of 144 and 145 probably distill Shakespeare's entire love life up to August 1596.

We have seen "Will," "Hathaway," and even "Greene" written into the Sonnets; Emilia Lanier's maiden name, Bassano, may also have appeared, notably in Sonnet 151, which ends with a tribute to his mistress "for whose dear love I rise and fall." This deeply erotic poem about the Dark Lady is constructed around the dichotomy of body and soul; inevitably, the body wins out. The moment it is given the green light by the soul to love, the speaker has an erection at the mention of the woman's name:

> *My soul doth tell my body that he may*
> *Triumph in love; flesh stays no farther reason,*
> *But rising at thy name, doth point out thee*
> *As his triumphant prize. Proud of this pride,*
> *He is contented thy poor drudge to be,*
> *To stand in thy affairs, fall by thy side.*

This may be no more than the general rhetoric of sexual intercourse, but the fact that the poet's flesh specifically rises "at thy name" might give us pause, since he has already made such play of his *own* name. The poet's rising at his lover's name and then falling by her side after standing in her affairs may suggest that there is something specifically rising or falling about that name. In Italian the poet would go from *alto* to *basso,* from high to low; *basso* and "Bassano" are, of course, cognates. At least, the evocation of the mistress's name and the particular local phrasing suggest that "Bassano" *may* be putting in an appearance here.

The early 1590s must have been among the most exciting in Shakespeare's life. His deepening friendship with Southampton could hardly fail to exhilarate and inspire him. The story of the Sonnets runs from 1590 to, probably, August 1596, when Hamnet Shakespeare died. By 1598, members of a London clique of literati had access to the bulk of the Sonnets, and a year later two poems from near the end of the cycle were published in *The Passionate Pilgrim.* At no point is there a major disparity between the chronicle of the Sonnets and the lives of their presumed real-life characters. These protagonists are Shakespeare, Southampton, Marlowe, and Emilia Lanier. For reasons that we can only guess at, Shakespeare was roped in sometime before October 6, 1590, to persuade the glamorous young Southampton to marry. A strong bond grew up between the two men, who were born nine years apart. When Shakespeare was attacked by Greene, Southampton seems to have called on Greene's publisher, perhaps accompanied by the large retinue for which he was known. In his retraction, the publisher, Chettle, acknowledged that important people had remonstrated with him. Two years later, when playing resumed in London, Shakespeare thanked Wriothesley in a sonnet for his intervention. During the 1592–94 closure of the theaters, Shakespeare seems to have returned home to Stratford, for there is no record of his touring during those two long years. He was now safe from the Lucys, thanks to the protection of Southampton.

During the interdiction period Shakespeare wrote two brilliant long poems, *Venus and Adonis* and *The Rape of Lucrece.* From Henley

Street, he could easily have sent them to his London printers and publishers through the offices of his neighbor the Stratford carrier, Greenway. We know from the correspondence of Shakespeare's friends Quiney and Sturley that a "pony express" delivered mail between London and the Midlands in under seventy-two hours. But there was an even easier and more obvious way of conveying his precious poems to London, and that was by passing them to his friend Richard Field directly whenever the latter visited Stratford during those two years.

Shakespeare and Marlowe were probably friends as well as collaborators and competitors at the Theatre, the Curtain, and perhaps even the Rose. During the spring of 1593, their literary rivalry extended to Southampton; Marlowe wrote *Hero and Leander* and thus provoked Shakespeare to write *Venus and Adonis*. Marlowe probably knew the young Wriothesley at Cambridge; the young Earl was apparently irresistible, and in any case Marlowe was not usually one to resist temptations. He may have homed in on his target at a time when Shakespeare was quite ill. But the brilliant "mighty" rival soon vanishes from the cycle, for Marlowe was killed in May 1593, shortly after the writing of Sonnet 86, which evokes "the proud full sail" of his verse.

The length of the Shakespeare-Southampton relationship is suggested by the poet's repeated references to "three years," which would suggest a time between 1590 and 1593, if the first seventeen poems were indeed a birthday gift for Southampton. Shakespeare was at most thirty-five years old when he wrote the last sonnets; we can set this cutoff date with reference to 138 and 144, which were both published in 1599. Meres's *Palladis Tamia* makes the date another year earlier, 1598. Sonnet 138 was quite probably written no later than 1597, so that when Shakespeare called himself old in it he may have been thirty-three.

Thanks to the timing of the Sonnets, and the accounts by Manningham and Wilkes of the "citizen," Burbage, and Will the Conqueror, we can reasonably assume that the Dark Lady and the young mistress of an old merchant are one and the same. Shakespeare became involved with her in the autumn of 1594, while the newly constituted Lord Chamberlain's Company was performing *Richard III* and before he wrote *The Taming of the Shrew*. The Dark Lady was twenty-five, married, and a mother. She had been the mistress of the man who now ran the company for which Shakespeare was acting. We know from the poems that Shakespeare's mistress was dark-skinned, musical, and sensuous. In the chronology of the Sonnets, we have reached 127 before she appears on the scene in late 1594 or early 1595. Shakespeare and Emilia Lanier are now sexually involved, but then she makes a play for the young Southampton. She and the Earl start an affair. The poet knows about it but rationalizes it: his lovers love each other because they both love him. He is torn between sex with his sensuous mistress and his deep Platonic love for the young man.

14.

𝒮The Catholics and Oldcastle: 1594–96

n 1594, the year in which Shakespeare returned to the London stage, the country was in an uneasy state of truce. Six years had passed since the Armada, and another eleven would go by before the Gunpowder Plot once more convulsed the nation. But the Catholic resistance was in ferment. The presence at the death of Marlowe of Robert Poley suggests that the same agents policed the country who several years earlier had helped bring down Mary Queen of Scots. After the deaths of Campion and the Babington plotters, and the arrest in 1592 of Robert Southwell, it might have seemed to most of Protestant England that the snake had been both scotched and killed (to borrow from *Macbeth,* in which Shakespeare alludes to the Catholic struggle). But the authorities knew better. They were relentless in their search for Henry Garnett, John Gerard, Edward Oldcorne, Nicholas Owen, Robert Parsons, William Weston, Henry Walpole, and others. In the mid-1590s Burghley was growing weaker politically; the Catholics had their sights set on Essex and those around him. With both Leicester and Walsingham dead by 1590 and Robert Cecil not yet anointed as Burghley's successor, the Privy Council, the country's chief executive organ of government, was wide open. Essex tried throughout this decade to achieve ascendancy over the Cecils, although his political skills would never match Robert Cecil's. Perhaps it was these emerging fault lines that the Jesuits were hoping to exploit, for they certainly had good intelligence about the inner workings of the Privy Council. There are no better or more intimate

guides to what divided the nation at the time than Gerard, Weston, and Garnett. The latter makes it into *Macbeth*; in the intelligence jargon of a later age, he was Control.

The Jesuit missionaries shadow Shakespeare's life. Neither they nor any of his contemporaries could have guessed at the greatness with which they shared the city on the Thames; if they had, they might have construed it as a sign that their country more than ever deserved to be saved. For they seemed to be all deeply patriotic. In spite of the severity of the persecutions, none of the missionaries voice the slightest animosity against any of their gaolers or enemies—with one exception: Topcliffe. He was a sadist. The Catholics called him a butcher and the loyalists do not seem to have thought more warmly of him. (Even they jailed him for corruption.) In his house in Westminster churchyard he had, under warrant from the Privy Council, equipped his own torture chamber in a room with blacked-out windows. Unlike the Tower, this dwelling lay outside the official control of the organs of state. Here was the chief persecutor of the Elizabethan age, a cruel, corrupt minor nobleman who took the trouble to buy and gleefully annotate a published Catholic record of their martyrs. Topcliffe's marginalia include a little figure dangling from the gallows.* He was the swamp thing of sectarianism. His authentic voice can be heard in a macabre note that he wrote from the Marshalsea where in 1595 he briefly joined his victims on a charge of libeling privy councilors. Petitioning the Queen, he noted that because of his misfortune "the fresh, dead bones of Father Southwell at Tyburn and Father Walpole at York, executed both since Shrovetide, will dance for joy." And yet he failed to intimidate many of his victims, notably Gerard.

In the middle of the night April 23, 1594, near enough to Shakespeare's thirtieth birthday, Gerard and Owen were rudely woken in their room in Golden Lane in Holborn by a raiding posse. A few days later, Gerard was interrogated for the first time by Richard Young and by Topcliffe, who was wearing his court dress with a sword at his side. "He was old and hoary and a veteran in evil," Gerard would write later. Topcliffe glared at him and told him that he

---

*Kermode (2004), p. 129.

was Topcliffe: undoubtedly Gerard had heard of him? To make his point more emphatically, he flung his sword on the table, as if to suggest that he might use it. Gerard did not flinch.

Gerard was twenty-nine years old during this interview. For six years, he had repeatedly given the slip to various search parties, most recently on Easter Monday, 1594, at a place called Braddocks, a Catholic manor in Essex situated between Thaxted and Saffron Walden. The owner was a family by the name of Wiseman and their near neighbors included Penelope Rich, the sister of the Earl of Essex. Gerard was trying to convert her, as eventually he succeeded in doing. While the raiders were swarming all over Braddocks, Gerard absconded into one of Nicholas Owen's most ingenious priest holes, underneath the grate of a top-floor fireplace whose flue extended down into the room below. Even though the chapel where he was hiding was betrayed halfway through a four-day search, Gerard was not found. At one point two guards of the search party sat so close to the grate that he overheard everything they said. When they decided to light a fire, it burned a hole through the wooden floor of the grate, over which bricks had been loosely laid, and thus exposed Gerard's cubbyhole. "If they had entered," Gerard writes, "they would have seen me, for the fire had burned a hole in my hiding-place, and I had to move a little to one side to avoid the hot embers falling on my head." The cubbyhole at Braddocks was inspected as late as the 1930s and its brickwork then "looked as fresh as if Nicholas Owen had quarried it out only the week before."*

Gerard arrived in the Clink in the summer of 1594. This was a small structure built on to the western side of the palace of the Bishop of Winchester. The regimen varied in severity, but by all accounts the Clink was a surprisingly liberal penal institution. Indeed, the Catholics seem largely to have had the run of the place, with mass being said regularly and on important feast days, and some prisoners managing to get keys to their cells and almost freely visiting other internees. There is even a record of one Catholic priest, Father Thomas Leak, frequenting the Bankside theaters on day release while serving his sentence. The taverns, stews, and of course bear-

---

*Quoted in Caraman (1965), p. 278.

and bull-baiting venues of Bankside lay within a few minutes' walk of Clink Street. A brothel called Little Rose, at the top end of Rose Alley on Bankside, belonged to the entrepreneurial Philip Henslowe, who also owned the theater of that name. South of the Clink, a passage cut across between Dead Man's Place and New Rents. It formed the southern boundary of gardens that belonged to the Bishop of Winchester. The Clink was only the start, and during the three years that followed, John Gerard would endure the rigors of the Elizabethan prison system in London.

As for Shakespeare, he moved back to London in the summer of 1594 and probably lodged initially in Shoreditch where, for the time being, the newly constituted Lord Chamberlain's Men were marooned at the Theatre and Curtain. After writing *The Shrew* and *Love's Labour's Lost* for the company, Shakespeare gave them *Richard II* and *A Midsummer Night's Dream,* respectively a dazzling history play, which also happens to be a tribute to Marlowe's *Edward II,* and one of the greatest comedies ever written. At the time he was being pulled in three different directions: toward the Dark Lady, Southampton, and Anne Hathaway. That is probably why he followed the key poem about his sexual and spiritual infidelities, Sonnet 144, with the so-called Hathaway lyric. These are the poles of his private life. His extraordinary candor in writing about them, with at times barely a hint of disguise or screening out of the self, reveals Shakespeare to be as defiant now as he had been eight years earlier when he crossed swords with the Lucys. His is a personality as intrusive and powerful as Marlowe's, which is presumably why the two got on so well and also why they irritated Greene so much. Shakespeare's subjective "I" is everywhere. Not for him the role of an elusive dramatic genius mysteriously suffused through the works and diluted in the process. His voice demands to be heard; he wants us to know that he is from Warwickshire and that it was he, the friend of the brightest young things in the country, who wrote *The Taming of the Shrew.* Perhaps he was irked that a rival company dared lay claim to his earlier play. He showed Pembroke's Men by "out-shrewing" them with the revised version of the farce, just as many years later he would return to *King Lear* in the wake of the publication of *King Leir.* There is a pattern here of a writer who, far from not caring about the status or authorship of his plays, is deeply territorial about his intellectual property. This may be exactly why he rushed the "good" quarto of *Hamlet* into print after the egregious first quarto hit the bookshops.

The scope of the imagination is severely tested in Shakespeare's *Richard II.* It is the most lyrical, poetically self-conscious, and bisexual of all of Shakespeare's English histories. We are in a world of spoiled young men here, and this in a play written at the height of the affair with Emilia Lanier. Shakespeare may have been as high on the elixir of love and success as Richard II is drunk on language (this is the only play in the canon to be entirely in verse). When all is lost, Richard yearns to engender an imaginative kingdom through the mating of his female brain with his male soul. He could almost be Shakespeare's double, since this is exactly what Shakespeare did, create a world from airy nothings. Always he is present in his work—as poet-king Richard II, as crookback-clown king Richard III. Perhaps the yeoman glover felt that he could take on all these roles now that he had himself moved close to the center of power through Southampton. How ready he was cheerfully to impersonate kings we saw in his "Will the Conqueror" fling at Burbage's expense. In *Richard II,* however, he trespassed on forbidden territory when he wrote the deposition scene. Somehow he escaped censure when the promptbook of the play was submitted, as it had to be by statute, to the Lord Chamberlain's office for vetting. The play was duly performed. It would be a while before these particular chickens came home to roost.

At some point between 1594 and 1596, Shakespeare moved to St. Helen's Bishopsgate. A tax levy from 1597 lists him as a defaulter, thus implying that he had lived there until recently. The parish of St. Helen's was close to Houndsditch and in the surrounding area resided the bulk of London's small Jewish community. Emilia Lanier's father, he who may have lent his name to Kate's father in *The Taming of the Shrew,* was laid to rest here in 1576. He had lived near Charterhouse, but his burial is recorded in St. Botolph's, the church immediately south of Bedlam at the western end of Houndsditch.

Shakespeare probably followed *Richard II* with *A Midsummer Night's Dream,* which he may have written for the marriage on

February 19, 1596, of Lord Hunsdon's daughter Elizabeth. Although the writing of specifically nuptial plays was rare in the period, plays were certainly sometimes presented as wedding entertainments. If the play is indeed connected to this particular wedding, as has been argued from time to time, then it had to have been commissioned well in advance. Shakespeare must have written it in late autumn of 1595 or over the Christmas period 1595–96. In the play's magicked wood near Athens, Bottom is allowed to join the Queen of the fairy kingdom in her bower for a night of oblivion and sheer bliss. Anything goes in the lunar forest. The seeds of Bottom's dream were sown in the two *Shrew* plays. Male desire and fantasies were there exploited to brilliant dramatic effect, and how much more freely now that the mischievous lords of the earlier Inductions have become Oberon and Puck. *A Midsummer Night's Dream* is a benign fantasy about love from a time when Shakespeare's love life was deeply complicated. It knows no imaginative bounds and it manifests almost naked pride in the power of art. The play is as confident of its imaginative reach as *The Tempest* would be many years later. Oberon controls the unconscious dark, and his power over the irrational forces unleashed in the "wood" (which, in the idiom of the time, means "mad") in the end usurps the authority of reason and paternalism, which are symbolized by Athens. Here is the same confidence that wishes to confer immortality on the young man of the Sonnets through the act of writing.

It was probably during Lent of 1596 that Shakespeare started work on *King John,* the play where Stratford is conjured in a tailor and blacksmith trading gossip. *King John* may connect with Shakespeare's domestic circumstances in other ways; consider a simile that seems to step straight out of Henley Street. We are at the parley before Angiers. The Bastard, the exuberant illegitimate son of Richard the Lionheart and Lady Faulconbridge, protests that the city's defender, Hubert, has "a large mouth indeed" and that he "talks as familiarly of roaring lions / As maids of thirteen do of puppy-dogs." There is something irresistible in the picture of thirteen-year-old girls talking "familiarly" of puppies. The Bastard, of course, is poking fun at Hubert; as the Lionheart's true heir, he takes umbrage at Hubert's leonine similes and inflated Marlovian rhetoric. Yet the image is characteristically Shakespearian: warm, affectionate, and possessed of an imaginative life that transcends its function in the dramatic context. I suggest that Shakespeare is thinking of thirteen-year-old girls because he wrote this play in the spring of 1596, when his own daughter Susanna turned thirteen. Perhaps there were puppies in the Henley Street house, a new generation of Crabs or perhaps even the offspring of the unsentimental Crab himself who so offended by not mourning his master's parting. The age of thirteen is the most discussed age in Shakespeare because of Juliet, whose age he lowered to thirteen although in his source she was sixteen. Shakespeare may have linked Juliet's age to thirteen for good reasons, as we shall see later. Time and again it is in his similes that Shakespeare is at his most revealing and autobiographical.

The portrayal of childhood in *King John* ranks among Shakespeare's most powerful. There is a brilliant parody of baby talk, when young Arthur is caught in the middle between his mother, Constance, and his grandmother Queen Eleanor. Eleanor beckons the little boy to come toward her, coaxing him with "Come to thy grandam, child." Constance replies in a mocking parody of infant prattle with "Do, child, go to it grandam, child. / Give grandam kingdom, and it grandam will / Give it a plum, a cherry, and a fig. / There's a good grandam!" In tears Arthur protests, "I would that I were low laid in my grave." He is not "worth this coil that's made for me." To be prematurely "low laid" in his grave is precisely the fate that awaits him, as it does little Macduff, and Mamillius in *The Winter's Tale.*

When Constance believes that she may have lost Arthur forever after the boy is taken prisoner by his uncle, she launches into the most heartrending lament by mother over son in all of Shakespeare. She turns to the Pope's envoy, Cardinal Pandulpho, and, clutching at the Catholic promise of a resurrection in the flesh, she wails, "I have heard you say / That we shall see and know our friends in heaven. / If that be true, I shall see my boy again." But he will not be the same. Instead his "native beauty" will have vanished; the person she meets in heaven will be marked and scarred by life. "Therefore never, never / Must I behold my pretty Arthur more." To the French king's admonition that she rein in her grief, Constance replies,

Grief fills the room up of my absent child,
Lies in his bed, walks up and down with me,
Puts on his pretty looks, repeats his words,
*   Remembers me of all his gracious parts,*
Stuffs out his vacant garments with his form. . . .
O Lord, my boy, my Arthur, my fair son,
My life, my joy, my food, my all the world,
My widow-comfort, and my sorrows' cure!

Perhaps the Shakespeares learned in the spring of 1596 that their little boy was incurably sick; perhaps Constance, mourning for her son *before* he kills himself, reflects a response to their imminent loss. But whether one reads Constance's lament this way or not, there is too much in *King John* about a mother's grief for a son for us not to see a kinship with Anne Shakespeare's loss of her boy.

King John dramatizes conflicts from the reign of John Lackland, the brother of Richard Coeur-de-Lion. This same John was forced into a showdown with Rome, and eventually with his own barons over Magna Carta. It was quite impossible for a dramatist of the time to touch on the historical infallibility of Rome and the papacy without being acutely aware of the momentous implications of the 1534 Act of Supremacy declaring the monarch the supreme head of the Church of England. In *King John*, Shakespeare shows himself to be soundly Protestant: England gallantly defies the Pope's unctuous envoy, Cardinal Pandulph. In the two plays that follow *King John*, the *Henry IV*s (probably written between May 1596 and August 8, 1596), he gives us the ultimate lord of misrule, Sir John Falstaff. This oversized old reprobate shares his boozy kingdom with the red-nosed dipsomaniac Bardolph; bombastic, Marlowe-spouting Pistol; mine hostess Quickly; and the tart with a heart, Doll Tearsheet. Although the *Henry IV* plays are set in the early fifteenth century, they give us the flavor of a tavern like the Board's Head in Shakespeare's day, with its waiters, its named rooms, the itemized cost of sack and food, Falstaff in a drunken stupor behind an arras overnight, and a general atmosphere of crapulous brawling and playing. The *Henry IV* plays are plays of London life and politics, bursting at the seams with vitality and linguistic inventiveness.

It is easy to forget that they were written for the Holywell Theatre and would have been put on there or, perhaps, at the Curtain;
the Globe did not yet exist. But there was a tavern called the Boar's
Head in Southwark, well known to players, Edward Alleyn among
them. This has tended to make us think of the *Henry IV* plays as
Bankside saturnalia above all. The same applies to Sir John Fastolfe's
associations with the Surrey side of the Thames. Fastolfe—the resemblance to "Falstaff" is no accident—was an iconic figure in fifteenth-
century Southwark, where he vied with the Bishop of Winchester for
supremacy. He owned considerable property there, including moated
beerhouses opposite the Tower of London in Horsleydown Lane
and the Boar's Head brewhouse in Long Southwark, now the Borough High Street. Whatever else he was, Fastolfe was a major brewer
of what Falstaff excelled at consuming.

At first Shakespeare did not call his mountain of language, wit,
subterfuge, and corruption Falstaff at all, but Oldcastle; the change
was forced by outrage in the highest circles. The epilogue to the second part of *Henry IV* acknowledges the mistake and apologizes for it,
stressing that the real Oldcastle was a (Protestant) martyr while the
character in the play is only a cheerful maker of mischief. "For Oldcastle died martyr, and this is not the man" are the exact words that
distance Shakespeare's intentions from the dangerous world of sectarian politics. However hard some writers on Shakespeare have
tried to prove otherwise, Oldcastle-Falstaff remains resolutely apo-
litical. It is inconceivable that Shakespeare would have called the
character Oldcastle after August 8, 1596, because on that day the
sixty-nine-year-old Sir William Brooke, the tenth Lord Cobham and
father-in-law of Robert Cecil, assumed the office of Lord Chamberlain. He thus became the Queen's chief licenser of plays through the
Office of the Revels, and he held that post until his death seven
months later, on March 5, 1597. The Cobhams were directly descended from Oldcastle, Henry V's proto-Protestant Lollard companion, whom the King had in the end publicly burned in Smithfield.
In Foxe's *Book of Martyrs*, the chief Protestant primer and a book that
Shakespeare knew very well, Oldcastle occupies a huge section under
the rubric "The Trouble and Persecution of the most valiant and worthy Martyr of Christ, Sir John Oldcastle, Knight, Lord Cobham."

Shakespeare had undoubtedly read the long section on Oldcastle in Holinshed, one of his favorite sources.

But Shakespeare could not have anticipated that the Queen would name Cobham Lord Chamberlain. It is hard not to detect Cecil's hand in this. Like his father, Robert understood power and the need to control the arts. For him they may have been mere *circenses,* or circuses, to entertain the people and thus keep them quiet. With his father-in-law pliantly orchestrating the revels, Cecil must have hoped to enhance his power base at the court. And he succeeded, at least in the short term.

Shakespeare was clearly fascinated by his own national history in a way that (despite *Edward II, The Massacre at Paris,* and, perhaps, the Marlowe-Shakespeare collaboration *Edward III*) Marlowe was not. Marlowe was too deeply engaged in actively helping to shape his country's history to be able to stand back. Shakespeare never went down that road. In the period 1595–96 he wrote no fewer than four English histories. They do not allow us to rule either way as far as his allegiances are concerned: on the one hand, he lampoons a famous Protestant martyr; on the other hand, there is no mistaking his stand regarding the conflicting authorities of Rome and England in *King John.* Why in *Henry IV* he chose a name that risked causing dangerous offense we will never know, but in doing so he demonstrated his restless and difficult-to-subjugate nature. He hit upon "Falstaff" through "Fastolfe" in the first instance, but the name may in the end owe as much to the fact that "Fall-staff" evokes "Shakespear" as to the landowning brewer from Southwark. That Falstaff's name has roots in reality makes it clear that Shakespeare was committed to some version of historical truth in the *Henry IV* plays, certainly where major players were concerned.

The two plays also echo Shakespeare's life: the relationship between youthful Hal and elder Falstaff reflects the discrepancy in age between the poet and the fair youth; indeed, the dating of the *Henry IV* plays coincides with the latter stages of the Sonnets. And in the Gloucestershire settings of *2 Henry IV* there is the strongest sense of Shakespeare drawing on his own experience. We have already encountered scenes from the road in *1 Henry IV,* where the carriers and travelers are immediately recognizable from life in England toward the end of the sixteenth century. In *2 Henry IV,* Shakespeare takes us into Warwickshire's backyard, the neighboring county of Gloucestershire. He might have chosen Warwickshire, just as he could have set the scene involving Shallow, Silence, and the hapless ragamuffins Mouldy, Shadow, Wart, Feeble, and Bullcalf in a rural town called Stratford. And why not, since there were drill parades in Stratford in the sixteenth century and archery practice on the riverside common called the Bancroft? This Shakespeare never did, and the absence of Stratford or Warwickshire by name is a somewhat surprising facet of his works when his home county's flora are everywhere in them.

That there may be a more specific overlap between the Gloucestershire scenes and Shakespeare's life has been argued from time to time. In his 2003 BBC programs *In Search of Shakespeare* the British historian and television journalist Michael Wood showed the name of Visor in a local cemetery in Gloucestershire. The Visors were dealers in wool whose name also occurs in the second part of *Henry IV* where it seems to be associated with just this part of the country. This strongly suggests that Shakespeare knew parts of Gloucestershire, perhaps through his father's extensive wool dealings in the 1570s, which went as far afield as Lancashire. In *Brief Lives* (1681), John Aubrey, who was born three years after the publication of the First Folio in 1623 and a mere ten after Shakespeare's death, remarked that Shakespeare "understood Latin pretty well, for he had been in his younger years a schoolmaster in the country." The source of this information was William Beeston, whose father, Christopher Beeston, had acted alongside Shakespeare and the Lord Chamberlain's at the Curtain in Shoreditch, in Jonson's *Every Man in his Humour* in 1598. The idea that Shakespeare was a schoolmaster has a promising pedigree, but it seems intrinsically more likely that if Shakespeare did get to know this part of the country it would have been because as a teenager he accompanied his father on business trips. Aubrey appears to be skeptical of the schoolmaster hypothesis: Beeston notwithstanding, he notes that "[t]his William being inclined naturally to poetry and acting came to London I guess [at] about 18 and was an actor at one of the playhouses and did act exceedingly well."

Such contradictions convey the flavor of Aubrey's account,

tantalizing because it is so close in time to the poet and yet so hugely prone to error. Hardly anyone now believes Aubrey's claim that Shakespeare returned home to Stratford only once a year; his statement that Shakespeare's father was a butcher is demonstrably wrong. Disconcertingly, Aubrey claims to have gotten his information from some of Shakespeare's neighbors, who told him "that when he was a boy he exercised his father's trade, but when he killed a calf he would do it in a high style and make a speech." Since Aubrey was a younger contemporary of Shakespeare's family and their neighbors, it is puzzling that his sketch should be so patchy and flawed, especially considering that he had interviews with both William and Robert Davenant. We need to weigh and choose every bit of Aubrey's information very carefully indeed.

A more promising line of inquiry involves Shakespeare's use of names. There are no fewer than four Williams in *2 Henry IV*: "Will Squeal, a Cotswolds man"; Shallow's "cousin William," who is a good scholar and at Oxford before heading for the Inns of Court; William Cook the cook; and William Visor of Woncot. The last two appear toward the end of the play, in a scene that clearly draws on Shakespeare's own experience of life in the country. Here petty and venal justices of the peace rule the roost as they reminisce, fantastically, about their sexual exploits as students in London. Old Shallow is foremost among them. Like Shakespeare's "cousin" John Greene, Shallow "was once of Clement's Inn, where I think they will talk of mad Shallow yet . . . we knew where the bona-robas [best tarts] were, and had the best of them all at commandment." Although Shallow is often played indulgently, Shakespeare's view of the character is in fact contemptuous. Shallow may not be as culpable as Falstaff, but he is complicit in the latter's abuse of the king's levy of troops, and the audience cannot help but side with Falstaff as he prepares to fleece Shallow. Shakespeare's sympathies did not automatically lie with the country at the expense of the big city.

There is a country Davy in this scene as well. The matter is rural, domestic, and local, not an idyll but an inside view of country life, its administration, the sowing of headland with certain kinds of wheat, the lay of the fields, the settling of a blacksmith's bill for shoeing the horses and for his coulters, the docking of the cook's wages for losing sack (an expensive sweet Spanish wine bought at Hinckley Fair, some thirty miles northeast from Stratford), and the impromptu and unprincipled settling of a lawsuit. Here is the country reality behind the matter-of-fact entries in the minutes and accounts of the Stratford Corporation. The scene provides detail that we might have expected to find in farmers' diaries or letters of the period, had there been any.

Another passage in *2 Henry IV* may be linked to a specific event in Shakespeare's life, the purchase of New Place in the spring of 1597. He may at first have thought of building from scratch, however, if we are to judge from his preoccupations of the time. In *2 Henry IV* he employs an extensive and elaborate architectural analogy for the planning that must go into any attempt to bring down a king and government. He refers to surveys, foundations, architects' models, costings, and the danger of running out of cash halfway through the project and being forced to abandon the house to the elements:

> *When we mean to build,*
> *We first survey the plot, then draw the model;*
> *And when we see the figure of the house,*
> *Then must we rate the cost of the erection,*
> *Which if we find outweighs ability,*
> *What do we then but draw anew the model*
> *In fewer offices, or, at last, desist*
> *To build at all?*

Shakespeare probably also knew, while he was writing the play, that the Underhills of Stratford, who then owned New Place, were in deep trouble financially.* By the mid-1590s New Place needed

---

*From the chamberlains' yearly accounts and from litigation over land in Wilmcote in 1584, between the Underhills of Stratford and Stephen Burman of Shottery (Burman had earlier supervised the will of Shakespeare's father-in-law Richard Hathaway), it appears that the Underhills owned or leased property in Wilmcote (SBTRO ER 82/11/2/24). The Underhills and Wilmcote Ardens probably knew one another and years later Shakespeare may have had advance notice about their intentions to sell New Place.

considerable repairs, it seems, but it remained a local status symbol. It is not impossible that, like others among the Stratford oligarchy, Shakespeare had his eye on their property in Chapel Street, and that his sudden interest in houses was triggered by rumors about the Underhills' straits.

In July 1596 came Stratford's second devastating fire, this one not quite as bad as the huge blaze of two years previous. Across Henley Street from the Birthplace lay scorched ruins; reconstruction was slow.

It may have been the 1596 fire that caused Shakespeare to rethink his plans for building a house in Henley Street; perhaps the plot he had in mind was burned, or the foundations had been incinerated. Too, Stratford now needed to rebuild extensively. Shakespeare's project may have become too complicated, and because he could not be on site to supervise the new structure he may instead have decided at that point to buy rather than to build. By now, New Place had probably come up for sale.

Another aspect of the construction simile in *2 Henry IV* is that Shakespeare may well have written the passage after seeing the damage in Stratford. The simile occurs only in the Folio text of 1623, not in the quarto of 1600 set from Shakespeare's own manuscript. In other words, the reconstruction of Stratford after July 1596 is echoed only in the second version of the play. Although that version was not printed until 1623, it is very nearly contemporary at source with the text in the quarto. This suggests that Shakespeare wrote the conflagration of July 1596 into the already completed play shortly after the event. As it happened, the text behind the Folio had to be revised anyway because of the Oldcastle fiasco; Shakespeare took the opportunity to reflect on it in the aftermath of the fire. Indeed, the insertion affords further proof that Shakespeare could not resist inserting real life into his plays.

One would expect the most poignant link between the life and *2 Henry IV* to be in the famous scene in which Bolingbroke lies on his deathbed in the Jerusalem chamber in Westminster. Hal is at his bedside; they are alone. There comes a point when Bolingbroke seems to have died. Hal, as the Prince of Wales, removes the crown from his father's head and leaves. He has not seized the crown out of naked ambition, but has assumed it with the full knowledge of the responsibilities its possession entails. But Bolingbroke wakes one last time, and finding the crown gone he panics and calls for help.

The reunion of father and son on the king's deathbed is unique in Shakespeare. Holinshed's treatment of the episode is perfunctory; Shakespeare expands on him hugely and infuses the scene with sorrow and solemnity. He is not interested primarily in death, separation, and loss but rather in the emergence of the self-redeemed heroic king. For the succession to be legitimate and untainted it has to be *seen* to be so, and that is why Shakespeare takes us right into the royal bedroom to witness it. We also need to hear the dying king's repentance of his usurpation of Richard II. An overriding imaginative and political logic works against the scene's value as evidence about Shakespeare's life. If it bore the imprint of Shakespeare sitting at the bedside of his dying son, we would expect it to be full of loss and pain, but there is little domestic sentiment in the scene. Instead the politics of succession and past usurpation loom large. Shakespeare seems to have reserved his grief for *Romeo and Juliet*, the play after *2 Henry IV,* a play about dead children.

In the spring and summer of 1596, Shakespeare wrote three plays; perhaps he was trying to keep busy because his son was dying. He had reached the height of his profession in the mid-1590s and he would never surrender his preeminence. He chose to risk much, addressing tricky historical topics such as the character of Oldcastle and the deposition in *Richard II.* Little wonder that the histories landed him in trouble. But he could hardly have anticipated that, six years after its writing, *Richard II* would be commandeered to become part of a daring yet amateurish bid for power. Similarly, Cobham's appointment as Lord Chamberlain was wholly unexpected, so it is hard to infer from *Henry IV* that Shakespeare set out on a crusade against the Protestants when it is quite possible that the name Oldcastle would readily have passed muster under another licenser of plays. It is as if Shakespeare was destined to become a Catholic dissentient in spite of himself.

In any event, Shakespeare's work in 1596 may have owed something to what was shaping up in Stratford. Perhaps the two *Henry IV* plays were his own counterblast to his anti-Roman *King John.*

Perhaps friends such as Southampton, whose family had a long tradition of supporting the Catholics, leaned on him to redress the religious balance in his work.

Shakespeare's father seems to have died a Catholic, if we can trust the evidence of the will found in the roof of the house; as to Shakespeare himself, we have Richard Davies's famous claim that he died Catholic too. It is possible that the crypto-Catholic character of the two *Henry IV* plays was inspired by the most poignant of all reasons, the fact that Hamnet lay dying. The Shakespeare family may have turned to Catholicism in extremis. Shakespeare may have sought solace through immersion in work as well; he wrote more during the period from Lent 1596 to Lent 1597 than at any other time of his life. In what may have been Shakespeare's darkest hour, his company could not afford to stand still, and the Burbages now made a move that would have far-reaching repercussions for the players, the audiences, and the shape that drama would assume.

$\mathcal{F}rom$ Blackfriars to Bankside: 1596–99

he Burbages did not own the site on which their precious Theatre sat, but their investment in the building itself and in the entire Holywell plot of land was huge; by 1596, when the lease of the building came up for renewal, they were the plot's major rent collectors. It seems that they anticipated that the freeholder, one Giles Allen, might refuse to discuss terms in an attempt to force them to surrender the land, and with it the Theatre. Provident as ever, the builder patriarch James Burbage set out to acquire a site in the middle of the City of London: the refectory, or *frater,* of the former Dominican monastery of Blackfriars (so called for the order's black and white habit). The entire area had become Crown property after the Dissolution of 1536. As such it constituted a "liberty," meaning that the City had no jurisdiction over it. This was the point, of course, since the town council harbored Puritan leanings, whereas the court keenly patronized the players—who were, moreover, represented on the Privy Council by Lord Hunsdon.

The old Blackfriars had grown and evolved into a privileged part of London over nearly 250 years until the Dissolution, when Protestant profiteers developed it by tearing down its former ecclesiastical buildings. By the time Shakespeare purchased the eastern gatehouse, Blackfriars had become a desirable residential area. Burbage paid six hundred pounds for the refectory, which was destined, twelve years later, to become Shakespeare's winter playing venue. The whole neighborhood vanished in the Great Fire of London, in 1666. Luckily, the "Agas" map represents the Blackfriars as it was in Shakespeare's time, and a bit more detail appears on a recently discovered and very clear third sheet of Copperplate. The prior's garden or cloister is the convex bulge on the northeastern edge with the gallery crossing over into the King's Wardrobe, while the inner cloister is the square marked as a colonnaded cloister walk on the map. The Blackfriars theater comprised the buildings that run north to south on the west side of the inner cloister. The exact dimensions of the refectory were sixty-six feet by forty-six feet. The entire Blackfriars precinct was on a slope, so that the top, at Carter Lane, and the bottom, at Shoemaker Row, were out by thirty feet. The upper part of the *frater* was therefore on two floors, the southern edge, which verged on Lord Hunsdon's property, on three. In 1629, Hunsdon's residence became the King's Printing House. About a hundred feet above the *frater* stood Lord Cobham's house; Cobham was not as close to the projected theater as Hunsdon, but he was not far off. As the crow flies, the distance from the *frater* to St. Andrew's-by-the-Wardrobe and what would eventually be Shakespeare's gatehouse measures seventy-two yards.

The Burbages acquired the new venue early in 1596, but in November of that same year local residents successfully petitioned the Privy Council against their putting on performances. They drew attention to the amount of noise a theater would generate, its unbecoming proximity to St. Andrew's-by-the-Wardrobe, and the fact that the lords Cobham and Hunsdon would have their peace shattered by this enterprise in their backyard: "near adjoining unto the dwelling houses of the right honourable the Lord Chamberlain and the Lord of Hunsdon . . . and besides that the same playhouse is so near the church that the noise of the drums and trumpets will greatly disturb and hinder both the ministers and parishioners in time of divine service and sermons."* The *frater* was not quite so near St. Andrew's as they made out, but even so, who wanted players in their backyard? However, Cobham—the same who had required Shakespeare to change Oldcastle's name—did not sign the petition, but George Carey, the second Lord Hunsdon, did, an act of NIMBYism

---

*Chambers (1923), vol. 4, pp. 319–20.

avant la lettre by this keen patron of the performing arts. He would, of course, have sat right underneath the noise coming from the players. Within a few short months he would succeed Cobham as Lord Chamberlain and therefore licenser-in-chief of plays.

If Hunsdon's signing comes as a surprise, it is still a lesser one than the fact that Shakespeare's lifelong friend Richard Field also put his signature to the document, this barely two years after publishing Shakespeare's two long poems. The Vautrollier family, into which Field married at St. Anne's Blackfriars in January 1589, had of course long lived in the precinct, and both *Venus and Adonis* and *The Rape of Lucrece* were probably printed right here. It is possible that the Fields had come under pressure from their Huguenot and Calvinist neighbors and friends. One wonders whether Shakespeare knew that Field had signed the petition or whether this betrayal—if betrayal it was—remained secret. Securing the Blackfriars playing space was a matter almost of survival for the Lord Chamberlain's, as their drastic action with regard to the Theatre would shortly demonstrate. For the Blackfriars to come to nothing, at least for now, must have been a huge blow, and even if the company mitigated its financial losses by subletting the premises, things must have looked bleak. In the end, if they had not been thwarted over the Blackfriars venue they might never have built the Globe, so this story has a kind of happy ending. Perhaps that ending made Shakespeare forgive Field, if he ever knew of the signature. He may well have done, since of course there were leaks from the executive and Shakespeare's ears may well have reached into the Privy Council through Southampton and Essex.

The Burbages had hired Peter Street to convert the *frater* in 1596 and old Burbage had himself moved into the Blackfriars precinct in anticipation, presumably, of the conversion work. The air of urgency about all this makes clear how big a business the theater really was, the various prohibitions notwithstanding. Indeed, a beautiful and ambitious playhouse had just risen right across the river from Blackfriars. Called the Swan, it cost an estimated one thousand pounds to build; it must have been a taunting presence to the Burbages as they watched audiences boarding their water taxis at Puddle Wharf for the five-minute hop to Paris Garden or Falcon stairs on the Surrey side of the river. The Swan stood right in the northeastern corner of Paris Garden Manor and can be seen on a 1627 map of the area, where it is called "Old Play house," presumably because by then it was thirty-one years old.*

The ghosts of the three major Bankside theaters hug the local bridges: the Rose (1587) and the Globe (1599) on the west and east sides of Southwark Bridge respectively, and the Swan (1596) on the eastern edge of Blackfriars Bridge. Of the four London theaters that a Dutch traveler named Johannes de Witt saw in 1596—the Theatre, Curtain, Rose, and Swan—the two on Bankside seemed to him the most impressive, particularly the brand-new Swan: "Of all the the-atres, however, the most magnificent and the largest is the one whose sign is a swan . . . for the reason that it can accommodate 3000 people."† Clearly Shakespeare's company needed a new venue if it was to keep up with the competition; the thought of an audience of three thousand is awesome.

De Witt dutifully sketched this rare and, for him, exotic play-house, which, like an inn or a tavern, was identified by a pictorial sign. His friend Arend van Buchell made a copy of the drawing, and this copy survives in the library at the University of Utrecht. For once, we can see a theater almost as Shakespeare saw it; the De Witt drawing afforded significant clues for reconstructing the Globe on the South Bank today.

The success of the Bankside theaters was due in no small mea-sure to the river taxis, for which the theaters in turn constituted a bo-nanza. By the time the Globe opened, in 1599, the houses on the Surrey side of the river at peak times could, taken together, hold up to ten thousand people, most of whom would arrive by boat. The various interdictions on playing inevitably affected the river econ-omy. On one occasion, when Henslowe's Rose was closed, the wa-termen petitioned the Privy Council pointing out the symbiotic relationship between them and the playgoers and pleading that it

---

*The street grid in this area remains the same as in Elizabethan times. The Swan was at the northwestern end of Hopton Street, slightly recessed toward the railway track that crosses to Blackfriars here.

†Chambers (1923), vol. 2, p. 362.

may "therefore please your good Lordships for God's sake and in the way of charity to respect us your poor watermen, and to give leave unto the said Philip Henslowe to have playing in his said house during such time as others have according as it hath been accustomed."[*] The watermen hustled for business at their many mooring points. There were no queues and passengers could pick whichever boat they fancied. Many of the wherries had comfortable cushioned seats, usually for two, and a number boasted canopies to protect their customers from rain or hot sunshine; but the arrogance and bumptiousness of the taxi rowers were legendary.

The Swan was built by an entrepreneur and loan shark called Francis Langley, whose moated manor stood nearby in a park. Shakespeare and Langley knew each other and both are mentioned in a writ of attainder in the year following the aborted Blackfriars venture. The charge may have arisen as a retaliatory writ against Langley by one William Wayte with whom Langley was litigating just then. It is possible that Shakespeare was included in Wayte's writ because he was associated as a chief player with Langley at the latter's Swan theater in the autumn of 1596. Above all, Wayte's writ places Shakespeare south of the river at just the time when the Lord Chamberlain's Men are thought to have been playing in Southwark. Perhaps the company wanted to test the waters on Bankside before trying to find another property. Despite Langley's unenviable reputation, the company may have enjoyed performing there, for the playhouse was new and well appointed. It may well have been their spell at the Swan that set them thinking about the Globe.[†]

If the Lord Chamberlain's Company did play at the Swan in 1596, then the scene in the De Witt drawing could well be from a Shakespeare play. It is the sparsest of scenes: two women characters interact while a man holding a spear seems to bow in the foreground as he looks on. One of the two women is standing; she seems to be talking rather insistently to the other one, who sits on a bench. The standing woman is holding what appears to be a bonnet, perhaps removed out of deference to the seated lady, whose hat is on her head.

---

[*]Chambers (1923), vol. 4, p. 312.
[†]Schoenbaum (1975), pp. 146–47; Ingram, pp. 139–50.

The only Shakespeare play in which two characters regularly appear alone on the stage is *The Two Gentlemen of Verona*. The drawing cannot be of a Silvia-Julia scene, because Julia is disguised as a boy during her encounter with Silvia, whose attendant Ursula is present anyway. If this is a scene from *The Two Gentlemen of Verona,* then, it has to be one of the encounters between Julia and her waiting woman, Lucetta. The most likely scene is the first one between them: the two women are alone and Proteus's servant has given Lucetta a letter from Proteus, which she offers to her mistress with "Peruse this paper, madam." Out of faux maidenly modesty, Julia refuses, though she is sorely tempted: "What fool is she, that knows I am a maid, / And would not force the letter to my view," she remarks to herself. Lucetta is well aware, of course, that Julia wants the letter, and as she leaves she archly lets it fall. Julia recalls her, Lucetta picks up the paper, and then the following exchange takes place:

> JULIA What is't it that you took up so gingerly?
>
> LUCETTA Nothing.
>
> JULIA Why didst thou stoop then?
>
> LUCETTA To take a paper up that I let fall.
>
> JULIA And is that paper nothing?
>
> LUCETTA Nothing concerning me.
>
> JULIA Then let it lie for those that it concerns.

After a bit more of this, Julia snatches the letter from Lucetta.

Perhaps this very scene was being acted when De Witt visited the Swan, with the standing woman, Lucetta, not holding a hat but flaunting Proteus's letter. The spear carrier, who sports a beard just "like a glover's paring-knife," could be Proteus's servant, Speed, who leaves the stage a mere three lines before Julia and Lucetta enter and may be looking on while the two women quibble. As in the scene in *Twelfth Night* when Malvolio peruses Maria's cod letter while being watched onstage, so a mere two scenes later Speed eavesdrops on the encounter between Silvia and Valentine, commenting on it in a series of asides. Perhaps De Witt conflated the two scenes when he drew the stage of the Swan from memory.

In 1596 the Lord Chamberlain's Company was probably playing part-time south of the river at the Swan while the Theatre in Shoreditch was into its last season. Shakespeare may still have been living in St. Helen's Bishopsgate, perhaps not far from his brother Gilbert, who by 1597 was listed as a haberdasher in St. Bride's in Fleet Street in the City of London.* That in London Gilbert stuck close to his roots is evident from his standing bail, for a huge amount, in Queen's Bench in 1597 for a Stratford clockmaker, William Sampson. It is not possible to determine when Gilbert fetched up in London, but the brothers must have been close, for Will trusted Gilbert with his financial affairs in Stratford. Gilbert's presence in London in 1596–97 (and perhaps even earlier) also suggests that Will's secrets, notably his affair with Emilia Bassano, at just this time were probably known to Gilbert. But it does not follow from Gilbert's being family that he would have kept quiet about Will's behavior if it was indeed reprehensible. Sibling relationships in the plays are notoriously complex, and Shakespeare's portrayals of brothers in *Hamlet, King Lear,* and *The Tempest* are disturbing. Shakespeare's private London life may be largely a closed book to us since, like most private lives, it left little trace in the official records. At least, though, we can say that the presence in London of Stratfordians close to him—his brother, the Greene brothers, Richard Field, and eventually Richard Quiney— suggests that his *public* life was well known in Stratford. His Warwickshire family and friends would surely have reported that the native son was the talk of the town, the main reason people flocked to the playhouses in their thousands.

Conceivably, Shakespeare had already moved to Bankside by 1596; if so, it would have been to be nearer to the Swan. The reason for considering the possibility is that in the eighteenth century, the great Shakespearian Edmond Malone encountered and owned a document "which formerly belonged to Edward Alleyn" and which showed that Shakespeare lived in Southwark, near Bear-Garden, in 1596. This document has since vanished, but it may resurface someday. That Malone would have invented it is inconceivable. He did not commit forgeries; he exposed them. If ever there was a searcher

*Halliwell-Phillipps (1887), vol. 2, p. 298.

for the truth in the century of great Shakespeare forgeries, it was he. Malone's lost document placed Shakespeare's residency in the liberty of the Clink, and somewhere in the vicinity of the Bishop of Winchester's palace and jurisdiction, which is why the sheriff with responsibility for Bishopsgate was instructed to start looking for Shakespeare on Bankside after he failed to pay taxes, probably by default, in Bishopsgate.*

When the Swan opened in Paris Gardens, the area enjoyed a dim reputation, which is somewhat surprising given that the royal barge was moored here, at Barge House stairs or Old Barge Stairs. One imagines the Queen's barge watchmen on duty at night anxiously peering into the fogbound banks of Paris Gardens—an image suggested by contemporary accounts of this part of Bankside, which is now the home of the Tate Modern. Burghley's intelligence agents reported that the place was sparsely inhabited and densely wooded, therefore a favorite spot for clandestine meetings between foreign ambassadors and their spies. The riverside was so thickly overgrown with trees and willows that even on moonlit nights one man could not see another.† On the Hollar and Wyngaerde drawings, the wooded character of the area clearly stands out. It is one of the marked differences between this and the northern part of the town. For Elizabethan villains, the stretch of Bankside from the Clink to Narrow Wall, the path that skirted the arch of the river on its westward bend, was a haven. That refuge from prosecution and punishment lay a bare five-minute water ride away on the Surrey shore was known throughout London, and a bone of contention between the City and the Bishop of Winchester.‡

Toward the end of July 1596, Shakespeare was riding the crest of success with acclaimed poems and plays, a major share in the new Lord Chamberlain's Company, and the prospect of performing at a better and more central venue. He was making an impressive amount of money and his social aspirations, to become "gentle," are

---

*Chambers ([1930], vol. 2, p. 88) reports Malone.

†Ingram, pp. 83–84; Carlin, p. 32.

‡In this part of Southwark the writ of the Bishop of Winchester ran, who wielded jurisdiction over smaller offenses, excluding murder and treason, which were prosecuted in the Royal Courts.

entirely understandable. He may already have had his sights set on New Place, if we believe that the architectural references in *2 Henry IV* indeed echo his plans to buy it. Then the bottom fell out of his world. On July 22, the theaters were temporarily closed by a decree of the Privy Council due to a plague scare; on August 8, Cobham took over as Lord Chamberlain; and on August 11, Hamnet Shakespeare was buried in Stratford-upon-Avon.

"Alack, My Child Is Dead":
Wednesday, August 11, 1596

n August 11, 1596, Shakespeare almost certainly stood at his son's grave—in the churchyard of Holy Trinity or perhaps in the church. He was thirty-two years old. The date of the funeral suggests that Hamnet died the weekend of August 7–8. His elder sister, Susanna, was thirteen, his twin, Hamnet's sister Judith, just eleven. This would have been the first death in their immediate family: before now, they had been spared some of the sorrows their grandparents' family faced in the 1550s and 1560. Among the mourners with William and Anne and their daughters would have been Shakespeare's parents and Hamnet's godparents, along with other family and friends. We don't know exactly where in the churchyard (or inside the church) Hamnet Shakespeare's remains were committed to the earth; eventually, his bones would have found their way into the charnel house that connected with the northern end of the chancel through a small door almost directly under the bust of William Shakespeare today. According to Robert B. Wheler, who was fifteen when the ancient charnel house was demolished in 1799–1800, the building was by then severely dilapidated and contained an "immense quantity" of bones. These were carefully covered over and may still rest deep under the lawn to the north of the chancel.

That the charnel house exercised Shakespeare considerably is clear from the curse on his gravestone that dares anyone to transfer his bones into the house of shanks. A charnel house features prominently in only one of Shakespeare's plays (the term occurs twice), and that is also the play perhaps most intimately connected with the death of Hamnet: *Romeo and Juliet. Romeo and Juliet* is Shakespeare's most anomalous tragedy, a play about two teenage victims of fate and of the rash behavior of their elders and friends. It was written well before *Hamlet,* and Shakespeare may have acted in both. If *Romeo and Juliet* was inspired by the death of Hamnet, it must come after August 1596, as a number of significant clues indeed imply. One is the publication of the first quarto of the play in 1597, where the title page notes that the play "hath been often (with great applause) played publicly by the right Honourable the Lord of Hunsdon his Servants." So a version of the play was in existence by 1597 and was performed by a company whose patron was the younger Hunsdon. The Lord Chamberlain's Men were known as Hunsdon's Servants only from July 22, 1596, to March 17, 1597. They were renamed the Lord Chamberlain's on March 17, 1597, roughly a fortnight after old Cobham's death and in time for the younger Hunsdon to take over as Lord Chamberlain on April 14. Just over a week later, on April 23, Hunsdon was nominated a Knight of the Garter. *Romeo and Juliet* was therefore written after July 22, 1596; by April 17, 1597, it had been performed "often" by the players under Hunsdon. We can further narrow down the date of the play thanks to the seizure of the printing press used for the first quarto of *Romeo and Juliet.* Among its printed work at the time of the raid were the first four sheets of the first quarto.* As the confiscation took place sometime between February 9 and March 26, 1597, the play self-evidently existed in some form by the later of those dates. Can an earliest possible date also be deduced?

In March 1596, Essex attacked Cadiz, which fell and was looted in June. News of the English success had reached London by the end of July; according to Stow, "great triumph was made at London" on Sunday, August 8. Mercutio may be referring to the Cadiz expedition when he claims that Queen Mab sometimes "driveth o'er a soldier's neck, / And then dreams he of cutting foreign throats, / Of breaches, ambuscadoes, Spanish blades, / Of healths five fathom deep." That this alludes to Cadiz becomes more plausible when it is

---

*For more about the raid on John Danter's press, see Levenson, pp. 107–11.

realized that Shakespeare seems to allude to the same expedition in *The Merchant of Venice*, where he mentions the "wealthy *Andrew*." The captured Spanish galleon the *San Andreas* and the saga of the Portuguese carrack *Madre de Dios* and the great diamond ensnared both Cecil and the owner of the Swan, Francis Langley, in a web of lies and deceptions.* Both Cadiz and the Azores adventure of 1597 would have been much on Shakespeare's mind, because Southampton participated in both. And given the young man's closeness to Essex, who led the two expeditions, it would come as no surprise if Shakespeare knew a great deal about them.

Shakespeare must have started work on the play sometime in the aftermath of Hamnet's death. *Romeo and Juliet* is potentially an intensely interesting document for the biographer. The action takes less than a week and is set toward the middle of July, hence the references to Lammas Eve and Lammas Tide, July 31 and August 1. Both dates denote ancient English harvest festivals, and July 31 is also Juliet's birthday. In choosing to set his play in the middle of July ("a fortnight and odd days" before August 1), Shakespeare departs from his source. This is notable because *Romeo and Juliet* is one of several plays in which Shakespeare follows a source text so closely that he must have worked with a copy of it open on his desk. In perhaps a more surprising departure, he also lowers his heroine's age from sixteen to a mere thirteen. Juliet is the youngest of Shakespeare's heroines, and the play repeatedly alludes to her youth. Since she is to marry, one way or another, she will not only have sex but may become a very young mother. When the man to whom she is betrothed, County Paris, remarks to her father, Capulet, "Younger than she are happy mothers made," Capulet replies, "And too soon marred are those so early made. / Earth has swallowed all my hopes but she; / She's the hopeful lady of my earth." Shakespeare underlines

---

*The ship was plundered before the Crown and the Cecils laid their hands on it. The great diamond was rumored at the time to be worth about "half a million ducats" and became the hottest stolen property in England. Its many tribulations, from its disappearance into, eventually, the Queen's possessions, involved a number of shady goldsmiths, financiers, and dealers, including the owner of the Swan, Francis Langley. Its recovery became Robert Cecil's private crusade. For a riveting account of it, see Ingram (pp. 98ff).

the pathos of his young lovers' predicament by turning them, and Juliet in particular, into near children.

I have pointed out that the play is set in mid July. Not only did Hamnet Shakespeare die around Lammas, but his sister Susanna turned fourteen in May 1597 and was thus the same age in real life as Juliet is inside the play when her father was writing it. The line separating the worlds of fiction and reality comes close to erasure when we remember that Juliet's double in the play is called Susan. As a baby, Juliet was suckled by Nurse, who had milk because she and Lady Capulet bore baby daughters at the same time. But Nurse's daughter died in infancy. Wistfully remembering her dead child, for whom Juliet has now become a substitute, Nurse muses that at "Lammas-eve at night" Juliet will turn fourteen:

> *Susan and she–God rest all Christian souls!–*
> *Were of an age. Well, Susan is with God;*
> *She was too good for me.*

One naturally wonders whether Shakespeare did not comfort his wife and surviving children, and perhaps himself, with the thought that Hamnet had been too good for them and had therefore gone to God. The name Susan, strikingly, occurs *nowhere* in Shakespeare outside this play; his only other Susan is Susan Grindstone, a servant in the Capulet household. This is not all. If Nurse and Shakespeare both have daughters called Susan, daughters of exactly the same age, then Shakespeare and Nurse may be one and the same. There is a hint of identity early in the play, when Juliet awaits Nurse's return from her embassy of love to Romeo. Nurse is late and, hardly able to contain herself, Juliet exclaims, "O, she is lame!" I have argued that lameness and limping are more than just metaphors in the Sonnets. Maybe Shakespeare played Nurse, so that the limping playwright with a thirteen-year-old daughter called Susanna played the part of the lame Nurse whose daughter called Susan would have been thirteen had she lived. It is Nurse who reminisces affectionately about Juliet's infancy and childhood upsets, although the teenage Juliet finds her observations and jokes acutely embarrassing. Nurse on Juliet's tumble, and her husband's ribald teasing of the little girl about one day falling backward (having sex) rather than forward are the stuff of comedy and parenting.

It is Nurse who leads the lament for the "dead" Juliet after trying innocently to wake her with "lady," "slug-abed," "love," and "sweetheart," endearments that could come straight out of any household. The expressions of grief by Nurse, Capulet, and Lady Capulet over the dead child are raw and heartrending. When the bereaved mother wails, "O me, O me, my child, my only life! / Revive, look up, or I will die with thee!," may this not reflect Shakespeare's memory of his own child's death? So, too, the father's "O child, O child, my soul and not my child! / Dead art thou, alack, my child is dead, / And with my child my joys are burièd."

The last scenes of *Romeo and Juliet* play in a graveyard and in the charnel house or family vault of the Capulets, where Juliet's kinsman Tybalt now rests. Juliet's vision (in Act IV, Scene 3) before she swallows the draft that sends her into a deathlike stupor is the most powerful glimpse of such a mausoleum in Shakespeare. It forcefully articulates his view of what elsewhere he called the "secret house of death." It is hard not to think of the ossuary at Holy Trinity where the bones of generations of Stratfordians were stacked, especially when Shakespeare wrote these lines at a time when his eleven-year-old son was newly laid in his winding sheet. Juliet trembles at the thought of waking alone in the Capulets' tomb; she dreads being "stifled in the vault / To whose foul mouth no healthsome air breathes in." In this place haunted by night spirits her ancestors have been "packed" for hundreds of years, being joined just recently by her cousin Tybalt, "but green in earth" and "fest'ring in his shroud":

> *Alack, alack, is it not like that I,*
> *So early waking what with loathsome smells,*
> *And shrieks like mandrakes torn out of the earth,*
> *That living mortals, hearing them, run mad—*
> *O, if I wake, shall I not be distraught,*
> *Environèd with all these hideous fears,*
> *And madly play with my forefathers' joints,*
> *And pluck the mangled Tybalt from his shroud,*

And, in this rage, with some great kinsman's bone
As with a club dash out my desperate brains?

What renders the play so poignant is the contrast between the defiant vitality and daring of its young lovers, their passionate innocence and physical desires, and the starkness of death. Only in *King Lear* are we left with a comparable sense of waste. For Shakespeare to conjure up a lively, funny, maverick like Mercutio at a time when he was overwhelmed by grief testifies to an iron resolve. *Romeo and Juliet* becomes an act of solace and perhaps of atonement, a determination to create children in the teeth of adversity and death, children who, unlike his son, are resurrected every time the Chorus steps out to begin another performance. Too, however great the grief Shakespeare felt, he had a family to support. The resulting work was a triumph and the company loved it: hence its many performances for Hunsdon.

Shakespeare probably stayed on in Stratford for a while after Hamnet's death, to comfort the family, to pursue business interests, and to see through his father's imminent gentrification. All we know about how the Shakespeares grieved is that in the wake of the boy's death his father wrote a gut-wrenching tragedy about two teenagers. The pain of Nurse and of the two sets of parents at the end of *Romeo and Juliet* may be the Shakespeares' pain.

While his friends in London were trying to clinch a deal for the Blackfriars playing space, Shakespeare's father became *armiger*, someone entitled to a coat of arms. John Shakespeare had applied as long ago as 1568 but had not been successful. This time there was no stopping him. The grant of arms to the Shakespeares by Sir William Dethick, Garter King-of-Arms of the College of Arms in London, survives in two paper drafts, the grant itself, from 1596, and a confirmation and follow-up, from 1599. The Shakespeares would have been issued letters patent on parchment; these must have been one of the family's most cherished acquisitions and proof positive that the glover, magistrate, and mayor, John Shakespeare, was a man who could hold his head high again. This precious document has vanished along with so much else from the Shakespeare story. It must have accompanied the future Lady Barnard when she finally left Stratford; if it ever resurfaces, it will tell us something about the movements of the Shakespeare family in the seventeenth century. But it would not reveal much else about them: we do, of course, have the text of the grant, which is remarkably reticent about the family even though it includes information they presented in support of their claim.

According to the grant and its confirmation, the Shakespeares proudly stressed their association with the Ardens of Wilmcote and tried to foreground the possibility that Mary Arden was related to the prestigious Ardens of Park Hall. In the end Dethick was not convinced, although it appears from the text of the 1599 issue that he at first considered letting the Shakespeares quarter the famous Arden arms. The Shakespeares' claim to arms was grounded in their family's distinguished service under Henry VII and also in John Shakespeare's service as a Stratford magistrate and justice of the peace. But the documents have little or nothing to say about the more distant origins of the Shakespeare family in Warwickshire, only that they had been resident there at least since the reign of Henry Richmond, that same king whose emergence at Bosworth Field in 1485 Shakespeare dramatized in *Richard III*.

The wording of the 1599 grant does enlarge importantly on the Warwickshireness of the Shakespeares: it notes that John Shakespeare's great-grandfather was rewarded by Henry VIII "with lands and tenements given to him in those parts of Warwickshire where they have continued by some descents in good reputation and credit." The word "continued" may not sound quite accurate if, as is usually assumed, John Shakespeare was hiding away from debtors in his fortress in Henley Street in the 1580s. But the 1596 award confirms that John Shakespeare "hath lands and tenements of good wealth and substance: £500"—that is, he was worth at least five hundred pounds. Clearly, then, Shakespeare had not only redeemed his father's debts but also secured the family stock. Perhaps this was known, and it may have been precisely this that caused the York herald Rafe Brooke, who queried the Shakespeare arms during an audit of Dethick's work, to scoff at the grant of arms to a player rather than an alderman. Southampton's rumored loan of a thousand pounds may well have done its part.

With the death of Hamnet, the male Shakespeare line had become extinct ten weeks or so before plain Will metamorphosed into Master, a title that became the butt of several jokes by his peers, and particularly by Ben Jonson. But no one could take the grant from him now, and the fact that the drafts for the document are extant in a drawer at the College of Arms in London is proof of it. When the family was notified of the elevation, in October 1596, Shakespeare had probably returned to London, so it is likely that he himself collected the grant from Derby Place (the College of Arms was housed on the same site then as today).

There must be a reason why the York herald in his complaint against Dethick's grant of arms to John Shakespeare noted on his drawing of the Shakespeare escutcheon, "Shakespeare the player by garter." In none of the extant documents about the grant of arms is there a reference to William Shakespeare the player, so that information must be in one of the lost ones, or else Brooke heard of the connection between John Shakespeare and Will Shakespeare the player elsewhere and took it as proof of the inappropriateness of the grant. Clearly John Shakespeare could hardly apply for arms on the grounds that his son had earned the right to them, but we may be sure that it was his son who conducted the negotiations.

The grant of arms would have provided Shakespeare with a sound pretext to head back to the Midlands that autumn, as he must have been anxious to do now that one of his children had died. He may therefore have set his sights firmly on New Place, a house that required a fair amount of restoration and tender care, but that would befit the new Master and his family. Henceforth, the Shakespeares were like the Quineys and John Sadler, local meritocracy and big fish in a small pond. Whatever Will may or may not have done at Charlecote, there was no gainsaying his standing now in the community. Alone among the self-made burghers of Stratford—the Aspinalls, Badgers, Bakers, Barbers, Cawdreys, Fields, Greenways, Perrots, Phillipses, Rogerses, Sadlers, Shaws, Smiths, Sturleys, Tylers, Quineys, and Whateleys—only Will Shakespeare moved in the top London circles.

Not that the upper crust were always the safest of allies, as Shakespeare must have discovered just then. In the very month when his family had reaped the social rewards of claiming kinship with the famous Ardens of Park Hall, the Ardens once more became news in London and England, this time through one Edmund Neville. Neville, the nephew of Edward Arden of Park Hall, had been held in the Tower since 1584 on charges relating to the so-called Parry plot, another murky conspiracy that may not have been anything of the kind. For Neville, the Tower became his Colditz: he tried to escape no fewer than three times. Of course, Shakespeare would have heard about these, for heralds cried every escape all over town to enlist the population's assistance in the chase. In October 1596, after two earlier failures, Neville made a most daring bid for freedom. He started to ignore his warders altogether, not greeting them or looking at them, only staring out of the window with his back turned. Then came the day of his flight. He had created a mock-up of himself, which he placed in the window and topped with a hat. In the meantime, he had disguised himself as a blacksmith, complete with tools dangling from his belt. When the warder came with dinner and left it for the silent and unmoving figure, as he usually did, the prisoner slipped out from behind the door.

He did not get very far. He was spotted by a woman who knew that at that time prisoners' cells were strictly off limits even to workmen, and that was that. The adventure ended almost amicably, with the warder remarking to Neville, "Will you never stop trying your tricks? Now get back with me." One wonders whether the warder was in on the scheme, as this all sounds a bit too "Boys' Own" to be entirely convincing. Certainly in a famous prison break the following year, the warder came under immediate suspicion and went into hiding with his family, while being fully funded by the Catholics.

Since the Shakespeares had just recently enhanced their standing in society through the Arden connection, Will Shakespeare, the writer of English histories, would probably have been acutely conscious of Neville's presence in the Tower. By sheer coincidence, the next break from the Tower also involved an Arden. The Catholic John Arden was not, it seems, a relative of the Warwickshire family. Oddly, his life and Shakespeare's may touch at the margins: John Arden's confiscated lands had been surrendered to John Lanier, one of the Queen's musicians and the father-in-law of the Dark Lady.

In December 1596, not long after the Shakespeares' social elevation, John Shakespeare's brother Henry died, to be followed in February 1597 by his widow, Margaret. Henry Shakespeare had not
covered himself in glory; he spent most of his life farming in and
around the ancestral Shakespeare village of Snitterfield and in Ingon,
a few miles north of Stratford on the way to Warwick. He also enjoyed the sad distinction of having been jailed for trespass in 1591 at
the suit of the baker Richard Ainge from Bridge Street, a relative of
the Henley Street Ainges. Whatever Henry's faults, though, his
brother can hardly have been indifferent to his death or Margaret's.
We tend to assume that in those days everyone had to learn to live
with death as we never do. There is some truth in that, but the grief
would not necessarily be less. That much is clear from the rhetoric of
loss in *King John, Romeo and Juliet,* and *King Lear.*

17.

Merry Wives and New Place: 1597

n the spring of 1597 something happened that caused Shakespeare to spar one more time with his old nemeses the Lucys. Clearly his rancor against the people who had humiliated him years earlier had been simmering, for he chose to revisit the scene of his crime, and in the highest literary court of the land. Perhaps his bitterness was increased if he felt that by forcing him out of Stratford they had cost him time with his dead son.

In any event, the incoming Lord Chamberlain, George Carey, the second Lord Hunsdon, probably asked Shakespeare to write a play especially for himself, as a homage to the Queen. During Cobham's tenure, Hunsdon had acted as patron of Shakespeare's company; he was now about to join the Order of the Garter. To show his gratitude and in his new role as the Lord Chamberlain and patron of Shakespeare's company, he was especially eager to please the Queen, and she reportedly adored Falstaff.

What Shakespeare delivered was *The Merry Wives of Windsor,* a knockabout comedy in which Falstaff chases a couple of bourgeoises. Shakespeare had clearly not anticipated this evolution in the dramatic life of Falstaff: in *2 Henry IV,* he had announced that Falstaff's next move would be to accompany Henry V to France. The persistent rumor that *Merry Wives* reflects the Queen's yearning to see Falstaff in love quite probably has some basis in fact, particularly since Windsor was the very same place where Hunsdon would be elevated to the Garter in the Queen's presence on St. George's Day, 1597.

Shakespeare was probably working on short notice; the play's composition likely spanned the weeks between March 17 and April 23, 1597. Perhaps that is why it is largely in prose. Its comic timing is flawless. Scenic and dramatic thinking came naturally to Shakespeare, but verse may have been a different matter: its scarcity in *Merry Wives* suggests that when Shakespeare wrote fast he did not instinctively slip into meter. This although, admittedly, his facility was legendary and seemingly effortless. In a poem addressed to Jonson, Francis Beaumont offered to relinquish any "scholarship" in order to keep his lines "from all learning . . . as clear / as Shakespeare's best are." In his famous elegy, Jonson also made much of Shakespeare's "nature," while conceding that his friend had plenty of art. The First Folio, which includes Jonson's tribute, also comprises a preface by Shakespeare's fellows and friends Heminges and Condell. In their famous address "To the Great Variety of Readers," they note that Shakespeare's fluency was such that "[h]is mind and hand went together, and what he thought he uttered with that easiness that we have scarce received from him a blot in his papers." This harmonizes remarkably with one of Ben Jonson's late statements about Shakespeare, in his notebook called *Timber, or Discoveries Made upon Men and Matter,* which postdates the Folio:

> I remember the players have often mentioned it as an honour to Shakespeare that in his writing, whatsoever he penned, he never blotted out line. My answer hath been would he had blotted a thousand, which they thought a malevolent speech. I had not told posterity this but for their ignorance, who chose that circumstance to commend their friend by wherein he most faulted.

Since Jonson clearly echoes the use of "blot" in the First Folio, and in an almost identical context, one may assume that the "players" who so praised Shakespeare's facility were Heminges and Condell and the rest of the King's Men. Jonson was notoriously defensive about his own slow pace of writing and keenly resented the charge of pedantry. Shakespeare's never blotting a line implies that his scripts were generally clean, so if we were to find an autograph by

Shakespeare we could legitimately expect it to be "unblotted," clean, relatively easy to read, fair, and "natural." Just such a manuscript probably does exist, the famous 164 lines of Hand D of *Sir Thomas More*. It shows a fluid, cursive, and attractive Secretary longhand and there is a very wide, though not universal, consensus that it is by Shakespeare. But the *More* lines contain a number of longhand corrections and false starts; entire lines are crossed out. This is of course only a tiny fragment from a huge body of nearly forty plays. The story that Shakespeare never corrected may reflect a fictive memory spawned by the prodigious brilliance of his work.

Merry Wives came at the end of a particularly turbulent and traumatic period for Shakespeare. As Rowe noticed long ago, with this play he was settling old scores. He had already touched on Charlecote in the portrayal of Shallow in *2 Henry IV,* which immediately precedes *Merry Wives.* But now he chose to reengage with the Lucys in a play at just the time when he was set to return more permanently to Stratford.

At the very start of *Merry Wives,* Justice Shallow, Slender, and Sir Hugh Evans are gathered in Windsor. Shallow is determined to bring a Star Chamber case against Falstaff: "Knight, you have beaten my men, killed my deer, and broke open my lodge." To this Falstaff mischievously replies, "But not kissed your keeper's daughter?" One is entitled to wonder whether the keeper at Charlecote had a daughter. The action against Falstaff hinges on a business similar to the one that may have pitted Shakespeare against the Lucys, but the differences are striking too. In *2 Henry IV* Shallow is shown up as an ineffectual, venal, weak, and bragging sexual fool. Thomas Lucy of Charlecote will have been a very different character and none of the glimpses we get of Shallow's biography, as for example his training for the bar at Clement's Inn, comport with Lucy's life. Yet the Shallow of *Merry Wives* may be a parody of the real-life local grandee. In the opening lines of the play, Shallow and Slender are in full flow about Shallow's ancestry and coat of arms. According to Slender, for the last three hundred years all the Shallows have been *armiger*: "They may give the dozen white luces in their coat." It is with this that Shallow and the Welsh parson Evans now engage, playing on "coat," a garment as well as a coat of arms, and on "louse" and "luce," just as Shakespeare had done a decade earlier in his lousy-Lucy ballad:

> SHALLOW It is an old coat.
>
> EVANS The dozen white louses do become an old coat well; it agrees well, passant: it is a familiar beast to man, and signifies love.
>
> SHALLOW The luce is the fresh fish; the salt fish is an old coat.

The luce is the pike, the most aggressive of predators among freshwater fish. To this day, the visitor to Charlecote is greeted by a village sign with the ancient arms of the Lucy family on it, three luces or pikes. Shallow's coat of arm goes the Lucys' much better, bearing a dozen. (One of the Lucy tombs in Warwick does feature the three luces quartered, for a total of twelve.)* To dare this, Shakespeare must have felt that he was beyond the Lucys' reach now, thanks to his alliances with some of the most powerful people in the land. Something of him, too, informed Falstaff, anarchic, relentless, perhaps even (for all his success) self-destructive. Not that he was in a position to play Falstaff to Shallow's Lucy, but a private dimension clearly resonates just beneath the surface of the play. Slender intriguingly swears by his gloves and Mistress Quickly inquires concerning him, "Does he not wear a great round beard, like a glover's paring-knife?" Together these details conjure up a rural community of irate country justices, stolen deer, park lodges, and gamekeepers or warreners. Rowe was the first to draw attention to the overlap of play and life and the parallels between Shallow and Sir Thomas Lucy:

> Falstaff is allowed by everybody to be a masterpiece...
> amongst other extravagances, in *The Merry Wives of Windsor*
> he has made him a deer-stealer that he might at the same
> time remember his Warwickshire prosecutor under the name
> of Justice Shallow; he has given him very near the same coat

---

*Schoenbaum (1975), p. 80.

of arms which Dugdale, in his antiquities of that county, describes for a family there.

Rowe's use of the word "extravagance," which he had earlier applied to Shakespeare's poaching, puts the playwright's taunting of the Lucys on a par with the other "extravagance" that led to his flight from Stratford to London.

Merry Wives, which features a schoolboy by the name of William, also has much to reveal about the syllabus at Shakespeare's school. Too, *Merry Wives* gets in a dig related to Shakespeare's run-in with Cobham over Oldcastle. Lord Cobham was, of course, William Brooke; Shakespeare has the needlessly jealous and ridiculous Ford take the alias Brooke. It is worth noting that in the Folio text of the comedy "Brooke" has become "Broome." Cobham was dead; Shakespeare could afford to be rather bolder than he ought. But that he would take on the authorities within six months of his gaffe over Oldcastle is intriguing, for Robert Cecil would not have taken kindly to further lampooning of his now dead wife's ancestry. Cecil knew Shakespeare and in general probably rather approved of him. Perhaps he was swayed by the sheer comedy of *Merry Wives*, one of Shakespeare's funniest and perhaps most ingenuous plays, in which political barbs are subordinate in the text to its comic genius. This must be why it passed muster, even if "Brooke" had to be changed to "Broome."

The first performance of *Merry Wives* was probably in Windsor on April 23, 1597. Of course Shakespeare would have played in it himself. A month later he signed the contract that made New Place his. He was officially living in Stratford again.

There is no record of Shakespeare's brothers being involved in the purchase, but we can be reasonably certain that Gilbert and perhaps also Richard kept their brother informed of the property's availability. How else could he secure that coveted house when others, such as the Cawdreys, Quineys, Smiths, and Sadlers, some of whom held land and barns in the adjacent orchards and gardens off Chapel Lane, must have been circling around it too? That it was sold in the end to the London-based playwright with no apparent presence or allies on the town council is remarkable. It would have been impossible without the local support of his family. In 1596–97, Gilbert Shakespeare resided in close proximity to his brother in London. He may have doubled as Will's agent and business partner. We do not hear of Gilbert, Richard, or Edmund Shakespeare owning property separately in Stratford. In this respect, the family is unusual in the town; the logical conclusion is that Will's brothers either moved into New Place with him in 1597 or else stayed put in Henley Street.

New Place made a public statement for him in Stratford. The house had been singled out in the most famous sixteenth-century survey of the kingdom, that made by John Leland in the 1530s. The town, he wrote, boasted "two or three very large streets" as well as "back lanes" and was "reasonably well built of timber." There was, moreover, "a right goodly chapel in a fair street toward the south end of the town, newly re-edified by Hugh Clopton"; the same Clopton had "built also by the north side of this chapel a pretty house of brick and timber, wherein he lay in his latter days and died." This was New Place, a name it acquired sixty-five years before Shakespeare bought it. After Clopton's death the house passed through several owners until the family called Underhill sold it to Shakespeare in May 1597 for a paltry sixty pounds. This sum, declared in the so-called foot of fine, is so low that scholars have tended to discard it as notional and to argue that the real price must have been considerably more than the sum declared in the contract.*

The Underhills were a tortured clan but had been rich enough to be among the few Stratford families required to provide arms for the defense of the realm in 1588. William Underhill was an Inner Temple lawyer, clerk of assizes at Warwick, and an important local landowner. But the family's fortunes had declined and the large house may have come to present too much of a financial strain. There is some evidence to suggest that Shakespeare had to spend

---

*Fripp ([1928], p. 44) claims that it cost twice that (£120) and Schoenbaum notes that such contracts, known as foot of the fine, were often largely fictitious: "For Sir Hugh Clopton's Great House, however decayed, the figure may well seem absurdly low; but in fines of this period the consideration mentioned is customarily a legal fiction. We do not know how much Shakespeare actually laid out" (Schoenbaum [1975], p. 173).

money on restoring it. Thus, when the year after the sale the Stratford Chamberlains record that the Corporation paid Shakespeare ten pence "for one load of stone," this is usually interpreted as a reference to stone left over from the renovations at New Place, which he sold to the Corporation for work on Clopton Bridge.*

Shortly after selling New Place to Shakespeare, old Underhill died in suspicious circumstances. His eldest son, Fulke, was hanged at Warwick in 1599 for poisoning him. The domestic tragedy of the Underhills could almost be a paradigm for *Hamlet.* Perhaps Shakespeare thought so, too, when, like old Hamlet, he rested after lunch in his orchard or gardens in New Place. The property included barns, a cottage, and eventually two gardens and two orchards. It ran a goodly length down past "Dead Lane," the name usually given at the time to Chapel Lane, which was also known as Walker Street or Dead Man's Lane. The gardens of New Place are today an idyllic spot. Westward, they afford one of the best views of Elizabethan Stratford, with the back of Nash House, the Gild Chapel, and the Falcon Hotel; even though New Place itself is no more, the Falcon had an upper floor added in around 1645, and the White Cross, which stood outside the entrance to the chapel and was the second of the three main Stratford crosses, has long since disappeared. The 1590 survey of manorial property in Chapel Lane lists closes, orchards, barns, and gardens here. This especially rural part of town rolled gently down to the Bancroft and the Avon.

The purchase of New Place marked a milestone in Shakespeare's life. The decision to return to Stratford must have been triggered by Hamnet's death: his domestic life would henceforth center on Stratford. That he may have been looking to build there the year before suggests as much. If he had ever harbored thoughts of leaving his wife, these were probably shelved when Hamnet died. It would henceforth be much harder to enjoy carefree sex—if he ever did, for even in London he did not have living quarters conducive to sexual liaisons. The evidence we have suggests that he usually lodged with people; he may never have been anything but a lodger, away from his real home.

---

*Chambers (1930), vol. 2, p. 96.

New Place included ten hearths; its master bedroom was probably at the back, overlooking the garden and orchards. We have a fairly good idea of the house's external appearance in Shakespeare's time from two sketches by the famous engraver George Vertue during his visit to Stratford in October 1737. In making his drawing of the timber-and-stone five-gabled New Place, Vertue followed instructions from a source who remembered what it had looked like. He did not name his informant; remarkably, though, he is corroborated by another testimony from the eighteenth century, a description of New Place compatible with his drawing. This oral reminiscence was recorded and published by the Reverend Joseph Greene. It is possible that Greene's source, one Richard Grimmitt, was the same as Vertue's, although a descendant of the Harts, Shakespeare's only surviving family in Stratford in the eighteenth century, has also been suggested. By the date of Vertue's drawing New Place had long reverted to the Cloptons, who had radically rebuilt the house toward the end of the seventeenth century, effectively pulling down the mansion that Shakespeare knew and replacing it with a brick house. When Sir John Clopton settled the property on Hugh Clopton and his intended wife in September 1702, the building was called "New House," and it was this new house that stood when Vertue visited. This brick mansion survived for over sixty years but was long gone by the time John Jordan made a drawing of it, in 1793. Jordan, who lived locally, was a reasonably accomplished draftsman; he was thirteen years old when the brick-clad New House was demolished in 1759. In other words, the 1737 Vertue and 1793 Jordan drawings afford fairly accurate views of New Place as it was during Shakespeare's tenure and the new house after the Clopton makeover.

The New Place that Shakespeare acquired in 1597 boasted a three-floor frontage and a fine porch and gables. We know from local ground-rent records that its frontage measured about fifty-eight feet (a single burgage), and a Stratford rent roll of 1561 calls it "domum vocatam *the newe place*." All the other houses in town, including the Birthplace, are described in the same document by the term *tenementum*. New Place, in other words, was grander. It was much larger than two of the best-preserved 1590s houses that survive in the town, the Harvard House in High Street and the Shrieve House in Sheep Street. The former with its remarkable carvings is a perfect example of the town's new architecture after the fire of 1594. Shakespeare undoubtedly knew it and its owner, Thomas Rogers, the grandfather of the founder of Harvard College (now University). As for the Shrieve House, it belonged to William Rogers and then his widow, Elizabeth Walker Rogers, at a time when Shakespeare resided not far away in New Place. The Shrieve House doubled as a tavern and was well stocked with hogsheads, large casks for storing beer and wine. Its inventory included fourteen pounds of liquorice and six pounds of aniseed, neither a common commodity in rural sixteenth-century England. It also must have enjoyed a certain cachet for the sheer amount of glass in its hall and stairwell. New Place similarly had leaded glass panes.

It is frustrating that this house, probably the most important in Shakespeare's life, should not now be standing. Instead, there is a gaping hole in the ground with a few foundation walls and a well. In the twenty-first century, the Stratford creche is exhibited here at Christmas. One of the most intriguing features of the Vertue drawing is the courtyard in front of the house. Even the best Stratford houses at the time were not usually recessed that way, as the Harvard and Shrieve Houses demonstrate. Neither are other ancient houses in Stratford of the same vintage—the Falcon Hotel, or Mason's Court, or the White Swan, in Rother Street. The New Place courtyard on Chapel Street contained, as Vertue notes, "a long gallery" intended "for servants." Even this detail, a courtyard with servants' quarters before a recessed house, suggests that New Place was designed as a small manor, as befits its privileged position so close to the Cloptons' chapel.

That the courtyard opened on to Chapel Street rather than Chapel Lane is clear from Vertue's 1737 drawing. In October 1767, the Reverend Joseph Greene's source, Richard Grimmitt, who was born in January 1683, told Greene that in his youth he had been a playfellow of Edward Clopton and "had been often with him in the Great House near the Chapel in Stratford called New Place." Grimmitt recalled that "there was a brick wall next the street, with a kind of porch at that end of it near the Chapel, when they crossed a small kind of green court before they entered the house, which was

bearing to the left and fronted with brick, with plain windows consisting of common panes of glass set in lead, as at this time."* Another
source provided Greene with the most tantalizing and poignant detail of all about New Place in Shakespeare's time. Greene learned
from Sir Hugh Clopton, who was born in 1672, that when the Cloptons acquired New Place back toward the end of the seventeenth
century,

> several little epigrammes on familiar subjects were found
> upon the glass of the house windows, some of which were
> written by Shakespeare, and many of them the product of his
> own children's brain: the tradition being, that he often in his
> times of pleasantry thus exercised his and their talents, and
> took great pleasure when he could trace in them some pretty
> display of that genius which God and Nature had blessed
> him with.†

If only one could prove that at home in Stratford Shakespeare affectionately engaged with his children in educational word and
spelling games! Hamnet, of course, never lived in New Place, so the
children in question are Susanna and Judith. Shakespeare's decision
to grieve for his son by writing his *daughter* into *Romeo and Juliet* reveals something about a father who passionately loved his daughters,
and never more than now that they were all he had left. The anecdote hints, too, that the girls might have inherited some of his great
talents. That the bond between the poet and his two surviving children was deep seems to me undeniable in light of the almost obsessive attention to father-daughter relationships in the last plays.

---

*Halliwell-Phillipps, who misread "near the Chapel" as "next the Chapel" and
wrote "where" instead of "when," noted that the main entrance to the house "was
then in Chapel-lane." This is highly unlikely in itself as well as being incompatible
with the Vertue sketch, which clearly shows the courtyard giving on to Chapel
Street. That is exactly where one would expect to find it. The transcripts of Greene
in Fox ([1956], p. 159) and Chambers ([1930], vol. 2, p. 99) are accurate; Halliwell-
Phillipps ([1887], vol. 2, p. 120) is not.

†Fox (1956), p. 81. New Place returned to the Cloptons through the daughter of
Sir Edward Walker, who bought it from the estate of Lady Barnard. See Chambers
(1930), vol. 2, pp. 98–99.

A clue in a later document may help ground and consolidate Sir Hugh Clopton's story while at the same time casting light on the business of Susanna Shakespeare's literacy. Two of Susanna's signatures have survived, on documents from 1639 and 1647. She was fifty-six when she signed and put her seal to the first one, sixty-four when she signed the second. This may be the reason why the 1639 signature seems a little more forceful. It also bears the well-preserved imprint of her signet, which quartered the Hall and Shakespeare arms. The exquisitely etched Shakespeare spear is clearly visible in the wax as it traces a slender transverse line across the miniature escutcheon. Susanna wrote a Secretary hand, almost certainly like her father's but unlike that of her daughter Elizabeth, whose distinct, attractive, and predominantly italic signature, "*Eliza: Nash*," appears alongside her mother's on the 1647 document. It may be that fathers in the Shakespeare and Hall families taught their daughters to write or, if they had been to ABC school, continued to tutor them beyond school. If so, Clopton's assertion might well turn out to be true. Elizabeth Nash wrote an italic hand because her father, John, did, just as her mother used Secretary learned from Will. Toward the middle of the seventeenth century, English handwriting was moving in the direction of italic anyway, but one other aspect of Susanna's hand may, just possibly, point directly at her father.

Susanna twice signs herself "*Susanna Hall*." In her 1639 signature the first "a" could easily be misread as a "u," and the third one is not quite closed at the top either. The middle "a," which ends her first name, is an entirely commonplace and unmistakable "a." This matters because Shakespeare's "a"s seem to have been unusually open and were mistaken for "u"s. In printed versions of his plays set from his own longhand drafts, the two vowels seem frequently to be at odds as most famously in the opening line of Hamlet's first great soliloquy, "O that this too too sallied flesh would melt." This is the reading of the second quarto, which most editors of the play use as copy text ("sallied" meaning "assailed"), but the First Folio has "solid," and Shakespeare may well have written "sullied." If both father and daughter left the letter "a" open, it is because either Shakespeare taught his daughter to write, thus passing on his idiosyncrasies, or she copied him, or both. If Susanna was literate, then Judith presumably was, too, so we ought to wonder why she did not sign her name when she witnessed a deed of sale for her future mother-in-law.

With New Place William Shakespeare acquired another very public status symbol for the Shakespeares: a designated pew in Holy Trinity. As the son of the mayor, little William would have enjoyed a place alongside his father and mother in the front pews of the Gild Chapel and Holy Trinity. Now, nearly thirty years on and the son of an *armiger* father, he was entitled to a pew on the south side of the nave, "near the point where the present pulpit now stands"—that is, two thirds of the way down the south aisle.* By 1633, when Shakespeare's son-in-law John Hall with Susanna and their daughter also lived in New Place, the pew had migrated to the first arch of the north aisle, next to the Clopton chapel. The Halls worshipped henceforth "adjoining unto the seat of William Combes, esq., and unto an arch in the said church on the north side." This was evidently a particularly prestigious pew, for the Corporation objected to Hall's tenure, pointing out that "from time immemorial" its use had belonged to the aldermen's wives. That the occupants of the Clopton mansion in Chapel Street should be sitting close to the ancestral Clopton chapel makes sense, but the borough council did not see it that way. During Shakespeare's residence, if not earlier, the owners of New Place were probably moved from the northern aisle precisely because they were no longer Cloptons.

By the time the Shakespeares moved into New Place, some ten months had elapsed since Hamnet's death. At the age of thirty-three and with a number of important plays behind him, Shakespeare would now write in a study of his own. Perhaps while doing so he enjoyed looking out over his orchard of apples, quinces, pears, cherries, and grapevines. That vines grew in the great garden of New Place we know for a fact, because some fifteen years after Shakespeare's death a baronet by the name of Sir Thomas Temple requested vines from New Place. His sister-in-law, who had lived opposite the Shakespeares in what is now the Falcon, had highly commended them. At the time, Susanna and John Hall with their twenty-three-year-old daughter lived here, and the house and gardens

*Lewis, vol. 2, p. 595.

will have been as Shakespeare left them. The produce of his orchard had clearly impressed his neighbors.

New Place was big enough to accommodate the immediate family several times over. We know that Shakespeare's parents and his sister Joan stayed put in Henley Street, but nothing is recorded about the whereabouts of his brothers Gilbert, Richard, and Edmund. In 1597, Edmund, the youngest brother, was in his late teens, probably working in John Shakespeare's business in Henley Street and living in the house. Eventually, he would make his way to London. About Richard, who was twenty-three in 1597, we know very little other than that he probably stayed in Stratford, where in 1608 he turns up in a "Bawdy Court" summons. We do not know what this was about. As for Gilbert, he was thirty-one now, a bachelor, and probably residing in New Place.

Shakespeare's life in 1596–97 was hectic. If he wrote *A Midsummer Night's Dream* for the Carey wedding in February 1596, then in the fifteen months between that and Carey's elevation to the Garter on April 23, 1597, he wrote *King John,* the two parts of *Henry IV, Romeo and Juliet,* and *The Merry Wives of Windsor,* the latter probably in mere weeks. In August 1596 he buried his son; that October he oversaw the granting to his father of a coat of arms; in December 1596 and in February 1597, he would have been somehow involved in his uncle's and aunt's funerals; and in the spring of 1597, while writing *The Merry Wives of Windsor* to order, he also conducted and concluded the purchase of New Place. Clearly Shakespeare was a man of exceptional energy, but there is something compulsive about the pace of his activities during this period. It makes one wonder, again, how much of a release the theater provided for him.

In the eighteen months from May 1597 to the start of 1599, however, Shakespeare seems to have written only two plays, *The Merchant of Venice* and *Much Ado about Nothing.* Perhaps he was exhausted, or perhaps he and the company were busy searching for a new permanent house now that the Theatre was silenced and the Blackfriars *frater* had fallen through. We do know that Shakespeare was acting during this period, because he appeared in Ben Jonson's *Everyman in His Humour* at the Curtain in 1598. In the folio of his own works that Jonson published in 1616, he is listed among the play's principal actors—indeed, he gets top billing, ahead even of Burbage and Kemp. We may want to remember this when considering Shakespeare's surmised roles in his own plays, for example *Othello* and *King Lear.*

Shakespeare must have settled into a completely different way of life after becoming master of New Place. His value to the company as writer-in-chief was henceforth unchallenged. He probably could afford to stay away more and to write whatever he wanted, above all to write plays that originated to some extent directly in his own experience. On his birthday in 1597, he was quite probably with his company at the Garter celebrations in Windsor, putting on *Merry Wives.* Perhaps it was her former lover's recent successes, with his grand new mansion in Stratford and a special play commissioned from him for one of the grandest occasions in the country, that prompted Emilia to seek out the fortune-teller Simon Forman within a few weeks of the Garter Feast of 1597. The purpose of her visit was to find out about Lanier's prospects for advancement, though her concern for his career did not stop her from letting Forman touch her intimately, as we know from Forman's notorious diary (where indeed we get most of our information about her). Forman was the king of shysters and charlatans in Shakespeare's London, a quack, an astrologer, and perhaps an abortionist. He is the man behind Jonson's con man Subtle in *The Alchemist.* In real life, Jonson cheerfully cashed in sexually on Forman's reputation as a diviner. Once, according to his friend William Drummond of Hawthornden, Jonson posed as a soothsayer in order to seduce a woman, meeting her in a house in the suburbs where he was "disguised in a long gown and a white beard at the light of dim-burning candles, up in a little cabinet reached unto by a ladder." The incident brings to mind Shakespeare's encounter with Burbage's admirer.

A number of women from Shakespeare's immediate circle visited Forman, who turned up many years later at three of Shakespeare's plays and left us fascinating eyewitness accounts of them. When Emilia Lanier visited Forman in May 1597, it was specifically to inquire about her husband's prospects for a knighthood. John Shakespeare had gotten his coat of arms the previous autumn, so perhaps Emilia was taking a cue from her former lover. Perhaps she missed the thrill of being the lover, first of the Queen's cousin, then of the darling of the London theater, and latterly of both Shakespeare and the glamorous Southampton. If Forman's diary can be believed, she was ambitious, keen to improve her standing in society, and suggestible, not only with respect to astrology but also in allowing him to seduce her. With his habitual devil-may-care candor, Forman records that when he visited Emilia on September 20, 1597, at her house in Longditch in Westminster, he felt "all parts of her body willingly and kissed her often."* But she refused him sexual intercourse. Earlier he had helped her cause a three-month-old fetus to miscarry. The fetus was already dead, it seems, if that is what his statement about its not kicking means, and as far as the context allows us to determine, the intervention was not an abortion so much as an attempt to ease Emilia Lanier's pain. She had complained to him about, among other things, her inability to carry pregnancies to full term.

Forman's huge popularity with women—including both of Shakespeare's likely mistresses, the Dark Lady and the English Lady (about whom more later)—may not be entirely unconnected to Forman's ability to provide certain services such as termination of pregnancy. As far as Emilia Lanier was concerned, his diary establishes that in the spring of 1597 her marriage was physically still alive. She spoke to Forman with remarkable frankness about her affair with Hunsdon, who had died the year before, and Forman duly recorded her talk in his diary. He did not note any mention of her affairs with a player and his dearest friend; she may not have wished to advertise her licentiousness. After all, the affair with the Lord Chamberlain dated from before her marriage and so was not adulterous; besides, Hunsdon was of far too high a rank to be brought down by a mistress. Perhaps she told Forman about Hunsdon to impress him. She obviously enjoyed the quack's company, for she paid him several visits over five months.

It was probably between spring 1597 and Emilia's final visit to Forman in September that year that she and Shakespeare split. One wonders whether she ever talked to Forman about her affair with the king of London playwrights. It is a curious fact though that in the

---

*Lasocki and Prior, p. 103.

year of his death, 1611, Forman should heave himself off to the Globe to see no fewer than three Shakespeare plays, *Macbeth, The Winter's Tale,* and *Cymbeline,* the last two of which were new that year. Many years earlier he had visited the Curtain in the course of an amorous pursuit, but he was not a habitual theatergoer and no one knows why he suddenly became so interested that he wrote the most detailed accounts of performances to have reached us from the entire period. Perhaps he was drawn to the theater by watching himself played by Burbage in *The Alchemist* (1610).

Forman knew London players and playwrights through their wives, and in his den in Philpot Lane off Eastcheap, near where the Great Fire started, he gathered around him a motley clientele of Londoners including members of the rising bourgeoisie. Among his coterie was Marie Mountjoy, a French Protestant woman whose husband, Christopher, had fled to London from the persecutions that began on St. Bartholomew's Day—August 24—of 1572. The Mountjoys were "denizens" or naturalized aliens. Mrs. Mountjoy thought she was pregnant, but her baby seems to have been dead in her womb already, unless Forman lent a helping hand. Believing herself to be pregnant, Marie Mountjoy first called on Forman on September 16, 1597, just when Emilia Lanier stopped seeing him, and according to Forman's diary she also conducted an amorous liaison with him. This would not matter much to us except that Shakespeare started living in the Mountjoys' home in around 1602. There he was drawn into a minor domestic drama that was eventually adjudicated in the Court of Requests, a local court set up to recover small debts. The significance of this episode and how it left a trace in one of Shakespeare's most famous plays will be seen in due course.

There is a link, too, between Marie Mountjoy and Jane Davenant, the mother of the future playwright William Davenant and the woman long rumored to have been Shakespeare's mistress. Jane's brother Thomas Sheppard was a royal glover, and Christopher Mountjoy made headgear for the court. Both men were on Queen Anne's payroll in 1605, by which time Jane Davenant and her husband had moved to Oxford. Jane Davenant seems to have sought out Forman for the same reason as his other women "patients," namely some malfunction of her reproductive system. Her pregnancies repeatedly ended in stillbirths. Throughout this period, Forman was involved in a passionate and violent love affair with a married Catholic woman, Avis Allen. He chronicled the affair in some detail in his diary, employing an obscure code including the bizarre coinage "halek" for having sex. The record of this relationship and his treatment of his young wife, Anne Baker, whom he calls Tronco, show Forman up for an amoral chancer. Avis Allen died of puerperal fever in June 1597, at just the time when he was also seeing Emilia Lanier.

$\mathcal{F}$light from the Fortress

hile Shakespeare settled into New Place, his contemporary Gerard settled into the Tower of London. After his arrest in Holborn in 1594, Gerard had embarked on a three-year tour of London's prisons. These, the underbelly of the Elizabethan city, held large numbers of people who were guilty only of loyalty to their Catholic faith. At some point, Gerard was moved from the Counter in the Poultry to the Clink on Bankside, a transfer that he compared to a move from Purgatory into Paradise. He may have tried to escape, for on April 12, 1597, he was shunted into the Tower, while one of his servants ended up in the dreaded Bridewell. This prison sat directly west of what is now Blackfriars Station and stretched all the way up to St. Bride's in Fleet Street.* The fastidious Gerard called it "the most loathsome of all the prisons." His servant suffered solitary confinement there, almost starving in a narrow cell with thick walls and no bed so that he slept crouching in a window ledge. He could not change his clothes "for months," and the little straw on the cell floor was crawling with vermin so that he could not rest on it. "Worst of all, they left his excrement in an uncovered pail in that tiny cell, and the stink was suffocating." Gerard's experience of the Counter was similar: he had a tiny garret for a cell, his bed was soaked whenever it rained, and the only latrine for that entire wing of the prison was

---

* The Unilever building occupies part of its site today.

next door. "[T]he stench from it often kept me awake at night or even woke me up," he later wrote.

Gerard's new home was the Salt Tower, in the southeastern corner of the Inner Ward, and his cell was the same one once occupied by Father Henry Walpole to whom Topcliffe referred in his memo. According to Gerard, the morning after his arrival he inspected his cell and in its dim light spotted the name Henry Walpole "cut with a chisel on the wall." (The name can still be seen today.) Nearby in a narrow window had been Walpole's little oratory, a makeshift shrine. Gerard felt greatly comforted to be in a cell that he felt had been "sanctified" by the martyr Walpole, who had been tortured as many as fourteen times. His own fate would not be quite so grim: unlike Walpole, Gerard lived to tell the tale.

Father William Weston's, and particularly Gerard's, accounts of their stays in the Tower rank among the most important to have come down to us. They experienced the place and all it stood for from inside, and thus convey its atmosphere as a detached account, such as Platter's, could never do. True, the traveler Thomas Platter does mention seeing the big rack and its ropes in the basement of the Tower and he comments briefly on them. But he hardly saw what Gerard did the day that he was marched to the torture chamber from the lieutenant's lodgings. The details provided by the Jesuits remain among our principal sources of information on the Tower.*

Gerard's fate was sealed when he refused to reveal to the attorney general, Sir Edward Coke (a Cecil protégé), where his superior Henry Garnett was hiding. Garnett was an enemy of the state, Gerard was told, and "you are bound to report on all such men." His interrogators then produced the warrant for the torture, signed by, among others, Francis Bacon. Gerard persisted in his silence and was therefore led away, "in a kind of solemn procession," through an underground passage that opened into a vast dungeon

---

*Anna Keay notes that the Tower "was also used, on occasion at least, for the torture of prisoners: John Gerard's account of his incarceration describes his torture in a large dark room with 'wooden post which held the roof of this huge underground chamber,' all of which is consistent with the basement of the building before the insertion of the brick vaults in the eighteenth century" (Keay, p. 41).

under the White Tower. The place was full of instruments of torture and they told him that he would have to endure all of them. He was suspended by his hands from one of the huge support pillars, but because he was so tall his feet still touched the ground, so they dug away the earth from under him. He steadfastly refused to confess in spite of the pain that started to spread through his body. He felt, he later wrote, his blood "rush up into my arms and hands and I thought that blood was oozing out from the ends of my fingers and the pores of my skin"; his suffering was so intense that he thought he could not possibly endure it. But he did endure it, and even managed, as they took him back to his cell, to pass on a message to his friends on the outside, reassuring them that he had not betrayed them.

For five months Gerard did not fully recover the use of his hands, but when he did it was to carry out the most audacious escape in Elizabethan England and the only major successful break from the Tower. Conditions in the fortress were generally bearable and although, for example, beds and linen were not provided, prisoners could pay to have such items sent in. Henry Garnett asked his loyal friend Mrs. Vaux to let him have a new pair of spectacles because he felt rather lost without his. Prisoners could receive visitors, too; they were allowed to stay until five P.M., when a toll announced the Tower curfew and all outsiders had to leave the building or else be locked in for the night. Even the warden of the Tower at the time of Gerard's stay there usually commuted to his home in Charing Cross overnight. For him the Tower was just a place of work. Prisoners were served dinner in their cells. Gerard mentions a daily ration of "six small rolls of very good bread" from, presumably, the fortress's bakery, and these could be supplemented with any other food that prisoners desired and could pay for.

This is where Gerard's famous oranges come in. In the summer of 1597 he repeatedly sent out the warder who looked after him to buy large oranges. The man was, it seems, partial to them, as, presumably, was Gerard. There must have been a ready supply in market stalls near the Tower, because the warder could hardly have spent much time searching for them. Even so, they may have been a bit of a novelty in the 1590s: Shakespeare first refers to the color orange in *A Midsummer Night's Dream* and to oranges (twice) in *Much*

Ado about Nothing, a play almost exactly contemporary with Gerard's incarceration.*

Gerard's account of his life in the Queen's prisons reads like something out of a Cold War novel. He was buying oranges because oranges lent themselves perfectly to secret writing and thus allowed him to communicate with his former fellow internees in the Clink. A letter written in lemon juice dries to invisibility and can be made legible by heating, but once it cools it becomes invisible again, so it can be intercepted, read, and resealed without the intended recipient ever knowing. Orange juice, however, remains visible once it has been brought out by heat, "so a letter in orange juice cannot be delivered without the recipient knowing whether or not it has been read." One can readily see why the Queen's secret service believed Catholic priests to be dangerous fifth columnists. This was the kind of knowledge that full-fledged secret agents could be expected to possess, but it is hard to believe that self-professed pacifist servants of Christ would just happen to know how to write invisible letters. It was orange juice that allowed Gerard to conduct the secret correspondence with a fellow prisoner that would eventually set him free. Even if the authorities had grounds for believing that Gerard was innocent of any direct plotting against the Queen, they also knew that he had links to all the major figures in the Catholic underground, including the Arundels, the Wisemans, and the Vauxes, all of whom knew Garnett and all of whom were waiting in the wings if a political or military bid for power came from within, as one would within a very few years.

One day, while Gerard was recovering from his ordeal in the Salt Tower, he spotted a man in the street outside who was repeatedly

---

*Oranges were also finding their way to Stratford now, through Greenway, who took them up from London in 1598 for Mistress Quiney. She was married to Shakespeare's friend Richard Quiney and was the future mother-in-law of Judith Shakespeare (Shapiro [2005], p. 261). An entry in the Stratford archives suggests that oranges were around almost a hundred years before Gerard, which the *Oxford English Dictionary* supports by citing a usage from 1490. The Stratford reference comes from the "Masters' and proctors' accounts 1500–1501" and reads, "Expenses of the Feast: 5 qrs. of malt; 2s for brewing the same; 12s for 5 calves; 7s paid to the cook from Coventry; 7s paid for fish and 'oranges,'" the word itself being thought bizarre enough to require quotation marks (SBTRO: BRT1/3/110).

covering and uncovering his head to attract his attention. Gerard signaled to him that he should desist, but he persisted. It was early May 1597 and hot. Given the southeasterly position of the Salt Tower and the excuse given by the man in question, that he enjoyed a daily constitutional stroll past the Thames, the street can only have been the wharf between Cradle and Well Towers, close to the modern Tower Bridge Approach. In the sixteenth century the wharf ran east toward Iron Gate Stairs south of St. Katharine's Street, just where Tower Bridge joins the river's northern shore. Here there were some slum houses on either side of the wharf. Gerard's unknown long-range visitor was a man called Francis Page, a devout Catholic who had resided at the Wisemans of Braddocks with Gerard and who had come to ask Gerard's blessing. He did so day after day, pacing up and down in full view of the Salt Tower, always hoping to catch a glimpse of Gerard and ready to receive his blessing. He was, of course, soon spotted, arrested, and interrogated in the Tower, and eventually confronted with Gerard.

But the authorities were more Dogberry than Smiley and were outwitted by the two dissenters, who steadfastly refused to admit that they knew each other. On one occasion Gerard was taken from his cell through a hall where a number of prisoners, including Page, were gathered. Gerard asked loudly whether there was anyone by the name of Page among them since such a person was foolishly claiming to know him. After that the authorities knew that they could get nothing out of them and Page was released shortly afterward. He was, however, determined to forge his destiny in martyrdom and this he grimly achieved at Tyburn a few years later after being received into the Society of Jesus. The memory of the faithful Page elicited one of Gerard's most poignant passages:

> "Like gold in the furnace he was tested, and was accepted like the victim of a holocaust: he washed his robe in the blood of the Lamb." Now he no longer walks up and down by the waters of the Thames watching me in the Tower, but serene and happy in heaven he looks down on me, still tossed on the waters by the winds and storms. But he is, I trust, anxious still for my safety.

The waters of the Thames and the shores of biblical Babylon merge here seamlessly in the writings of a man whose fearlessness was matched by his gift for narrative and pathos. He would write about the dead Garnett in much the same language, confident in the knowledge that these newly martyred saints were guarding his path in heaven and speeding him on his way to salvation. He himself had been found unworthy of martyrdom, Gerard noted sadly many years later when he wrote his autobiography, his God choosing not to choose him.

All of London was alert to the politics of the day. At the time of Babington's arrest in 1586, the bells of every London church were tolled to ring out the good news. Bonfires were lit throughout the city including in Clink Street where at that time William Weston was interned temporarily, in a building on the river opposite the Clink itself. When the men were transported under escort from the Tower upriver to Westminster for trial, a flotilla of small craft swarmed about them throughout the journey. They were the curious, the mob, and the hacks of the time. Every major state success against the Catholics was advertised publicly, as in the dragging of Campion through the streets with a large sign advertising his status as a recusant and traitor. Shakespeare could not have looked away even if he had wanted to—not in London and not in Stratford. But in his hometown at least there were no public executions, no grim prison fortresses, no heads stuck on spikes high above Clopton Bridge. We can never know what Shakespeare really thought of any of this, but we may wonder whether he did not share the deep revulsion felt in some parts of his country about the treatment meted out to recusants. When the warden of the Tower eventually resigned his position, it was rumored that he had done so because he could no longer face supervising the maltreatment of prisoners. That in this climate of violence and state terror Shakespeare should be writing controversial history plays shows quite how deeply he himself participated in this debate about who the English people really were, or imagined that they were. Perhaps in his most secret inner being he, too, wandered along the shores of the Thames and looked up at the Tower, a building that features in his plays more prominently than any other, and was troubled by what it hid from the people of

London. He could hardly ignore the fate of the grand Ardens of Park Hall, who had been so infamously traduced by the state and with whom he and his family claimed kinship. It is inconceivable that someone so steeped in history was not also acutely aware of the politics of the present.

The first news Londoners heard as they woke on Wednesday, October 5, 1597, was a proclamation about the escape from the Tower overnight of John Gerard and John Arden. By then Gerard was probably holed up at Father Garnett's house in Spitalfields. What had happened was this. Gerard had got wind of the fact that John Arden, whose case he knew, was held in the Cradle Tower. He could see Arden, who was under sentence of death, from his cell because Arden was allowed to exercise on the roof of Cradle Tower. This was not uncommon: William Weston similarly records sitting out in the sun on another tower. Cradle Tower and Gerard's cell in Salt Tower were separated only by the Queen's so-called Privy Garden. Gerard noticed that Arden's wife seemed to have unchecked access to her husband and thought that through them he might secure hosts and a pyx, the vessel for keeping the hosts, in order to celebrate mass. He wrote Arden one of his orange letters and, by bribing his warder, eventually got access to Arden's cell. The two men spent an entire day and night together. It was then that Gerard realized that from Cradle Tower, which hovers above the moat, they could probably abseil across to the outer wall of the moat and from there reach the wharf, and then take off in a boat down the river.

He smuggled instructions for a rescue mission out of the Tower. Finally, on the night of October 3–4, they were all set. But the three men who rowed up the river to assist their rescue were caught by the Thames tide and tossed against one of the massive starlings of London Bridge. Meanwhile the two prisoners were waiting in the dark on top of Cradle Tower. The current pinned the rescuers' light craft against the starling and threatened to break it up at any moment. In the autumn night the crew's screams for help could be heard nearly half a mile downriver. A number of people tried to launch boats to come to their rescue but could do little more than gather in a desperate circle around the three men wedged on the pillar. At last, two of the men were saved when a powerful seagoing launch intervened, while the third man was winched up to the bridge in the nick of time. What story they told the authorities we do not know, but earlier in the evening they had pretended to be fishermen.

The following night, which was the night of Tuesday to Wednesday, they were back and this time managed to throw over a rope as agreed with Gerard. This was far from the end of difficulties, because the outer wall turned out to be rather higher than they had thought, and consequently the incline of the rope was not steep enough to allow the men to glide down it. Instead they had to pull themselves along almost horizontally. For good measure, Gerard found that the rope had stretched and slackened after Arden, who preceded him, had passed down it, so that he now faced an uphill struggle, quite literally, as he hung over the moat. He had started out from Cradle Tower pulling himself along the top of the rope, but he got only a few yards facing downward when his body swung around and he almost fell. The rope was now quite slack and Gerard clung to it almost unable to progress. With much effort, he got as far as the middle of the rope but could go no further. Still weak from his torture, he thought it was all over, but one of the boatmen somehow heaved him up and over the outer wall to safety.

For the next nine years, Gerard would be a dedicated and tireless evangelist. The torturers in the Tower never dented his faith nor even intimidated him in the slightest. His underground ministry was a thorn in their sides until he left England in 1606.

The day of his departure from his native shores would be a day of horror, when Shakespeare, along with thousands of other Londoners, probably stood somewhere outside the western porch of St. Paul's Cathedral to witness another ritual slaughter, that of Henry Garnett. Perhaps in the intervening years Shakespeare had sometimes passed the tall and glamorous John Gerard in the Strand, a part of town that the Jesuit frequented and where indeed he had at least one, if not two, safe houses, with the Arundels and the Wisemans. In one of these he was very nearly apprehended in the summer of 1599. But although the authorities never again laid their hands on Gerard, the persecution of those who sheltered him intensified. Less than a year after his escape from the Tower, his friend Jane Wiseman was facing the ultimate penalty that the Elizabethan state could legitimately exact. When she was accused of treason for sheltering Catholic priests she refused to plead so as to avoid forfeiting her estate if she were found guilty; this gesture of defiance automatically carried the severest penalty in the land. Jane Wiseman was sentenced to pressing to death. This barbaric punishment was formally abolished only in 1827, by which time Dickens was already fifteen and the Great Reform Bill of 1832 was just around the corner. The sentence on Jane Wiseman would be carried out in the old Marshalsea Prison in Southwark near Mermaid Court off the Borough High Street, and directly south of Guy's Hospital, which today straddles the backyards of some of the most famous medieval and Elizabethan inns including Chaucer's Tabard, which stood in what is now Talbot Yard.*

The Marshalsea's yard was infamous as the place where people were pressed to death. For Shakespeare this punishment was the ultimate horror. That much is clear from a quip in *Measure for Measure*, when the irreverent and flamboyant Lucio objects that having to marry his pregnant prostitute girlfriend is a fate worse than pressing to death. Perhaps this was Shakespeare's way of coping with a reality that defied moral understanding. He lived, after all, in a society that on the one hand allowed his talent fully to blossom while at the same time constructing a judicial framework that could not be termed civilized by any stretch of the imagination. Here is Jane Wiseman's sentence, passed on July 3, 1598:

> The sentence is that the said Jane Wiseman shall be led to the prison of the Marshalsea of the Queen's Bench, and there naked, except for a linen cloth about the lower part of her body, be laid upon the ground, lying directly on her back: and

---

*By the time Dickens wrote his famous Marshalsea novel, *Little Dorrit* (1855–57), the prison had already closed, after first moving to its location north of St. George the Martyr on Borough High Street. Chaucer's famous inn was called the Tabard because of its sign of a jacket or sleeveless coat. Its "gallant host" in the late fourteenth century was Harry Bailey, who choreographed the pilgrims' journey from London to Canterbury. Rather like Shakespeare, Chaucer felt relaxed about importing real people into his fiction, for in a poll tax return of 1381 for twenty-two hostelers from Southwark we find one "Henry Bailif," none other than Chaucer's host (Carlin [1996], p. 48).

a hollow shall be made under her head and her head placed in the same; and upon her body in every part let there be placed as much of stones and iron as she can bear and more; and as long as she shall live, she shall have of the worst bread and water of the prison next her; and on the day she eats, she shall not drink, and on the day she drinks she shall not eat, so living until she die.

That Elizabethan England could not quite face up to its own darker side, however, is evident from the briefest comparison of this specific and graphic sentence to a woodcut from 1623. In it a fully clothed male figure looks almost relaxed as the weights sit on top of him in a tidy box. His facial expression is abstract and generic.*

Jane Wiseman's sentence was commuted to life in prison; in her friend Gerard's words, "But her position and her good name gave the Queen's councillors second thoughts. They did not want to shock London by their barbarity." Perhaps the unflinching acceptance twelve years earlier of the same fate by Margaret Clitherow, who was canonized together with Campion in 1970, had proven to the authorities that proceeding in this fashion could be counterproductive.

---

*The woodcut is the title page of a pamphlet called "The Life and Death of Grifin Flood Informer 1623" (*Riverside Shakespeare* [1997], p. 583).

19

The Moneylender of London: October 25, 1598

round the time of Gerard's escape from the Tower, an old acquaintance of Will's from Stratford turned up in London on Corporation business. This was Richard Quiney, whose son Thomas would one day wed Shakespeare's daughter Judith. Hamnet's death and the purchase of New Place suggest that Shakespeare was drawing closer to his fellow townspeople than he had been for over a decade. That he would see Stratfordians who visited London can be taken for granted; they would have provided him information about his family and friends as well as alerting him to business opportunities in his hometown. He in turn was able to show them the ropes in the metropolis.

Shakespeare and Quiney had grown up in Henley Street. As little boys they had probably ambled to the King's New School together. They may have shared memories of muffled walks out of Henley Street in deepest winter, each clutching a candle to light him on his cold way through the snow. Shakespeare was rich now and known to be so: no one in Stratford could have missed the statement made by New Place. This must be why Quiney was urged by his fellow Stratfordian Abraham Sturley in a letter of January 24 1598, to broach the matter of tithes over in Shottery with Shakespeare. Sturley pointed out that Richard's father, Adrian Quiney, thought that "our countryman, Master Shakespeare, is willing to disburse some money upon some odd yardland or other at Shottery or near about us." According to Sturley, Adrian Quiney was keen that Shakespeare should be approached about the tithes because it would procure him well-disposed business partners locally and was bound to be a win-win venture for all concerned: "If obtained it would advance him indeed and would do us much good."* There was strength in numbers and in good business partnerships in Stratford, and from now on Shakespeare would be broadening his base at home ever more. After a decade or so in the metropolis Shakespeare the adopted Londoner started to act as financier for transactions in Warwickshire, even if he was not quite ready yet to invest in the right to collect local taxes on produce and property.

The year 1598, which saw Southampton's marriage, the publication of Meres's *Palladis Tamia,* and Lord Burghley's death, also marked a watershed for Shakespeare: he now achieved literary closure with respect to his relationships with Emilia Lanier (née Bassano) and Southampton. The play in which he did so, *The Merchant of Venice,* also pays tribute to his murdered friend Marlowe; five years on from the tragic events in Deptford, it was apparently safe to do so. The publication, also in 1598, of Marlowe's last work, *Hero and Leander,* suggests as much. *Hero and Leander* was dedicated to Marlowe's patron, Thomas Walsingham, at whose country seat in Kent it was probably written.

It is peculiarly fitting that Shakespeare's sonnets were now mentioned in print for the first time, in *Palladis Tamia.* Its entry on the Stationers' Register on September 7 coincides almost exactly with the clandestine wedding of Southampton and Essex's cousin Elizabeth Vernon, which took place toward the end of August 1598. Meres refers to homoerotic sonnets addressed to Southampton at a time when the relationship between the two men had run its course, with no chance of resuming either the relationship or the poems, now that Wriothesley was married and about to become a father. Not that Southampton ceased to be prodigal and profligate after his marriage, although he was sufficiently afraid of the Queen's wrath— Elizabeth Vernon was one of her maids of honor—to try to stay on in France in defiance of her wishes. As a contemporary noted in a letter of November 8, 1598, "The new Countess of Southampton is

---

*Chambers (1930), vol. 2, pp. 101–2.

brought abed of a daughter, and to mend her portion the earl her father hath lately lost 18,000 crowns at tennis in Paris."*

Shakespeare now wrote a sexually penitent play that pits a homoerotic relationship against straight love and marriage. *The Merchant of Venice* was entered on the Stationers' Register in July 1598.
And why Venice, if not because Shakespeare's and Southampton's
mistress Emilia Lanier had been a Venetian? Besides, Venice resembled London far more in the sixteenth century than it does today.
The Grand Canal would readily have brought to mind the busy
Thames, just as the ornate and elaborate wherries evoked Venetian
gondolas, not to mention the correspondences between London
Bridge and the Royal Exchange, on the one hand, and the legendary
heart of Venice's business center, the Rialto and Rialto Bridge, on the
other. A powerful marine trading empire and bulwark against the
Turks, crisscrossed by canals and dark alleys: that was the Elizabethan view of Venice at a time when England itself was poised on
the verge of empire. The founding of that vehicle of early modern
English colonialism, the East India Company, was just around the
corner; *The Tempest* would be inspired by a colonial expedition that
prominently involved the Earl of Southampton. In Shakespeare's
plays, the maritime republic of Venice is not a place of beauty but of
economic might and governance. He and Emilia Lanier must have
talked of things Venetian. Both his Venetian dramas, *The Merchant of
Venice* and *Othello,* may echo their affair, and not only in his borrowing her names for characters in both plays.

The only hard documentary evidence for dating *The Merchant of
Venice* is its entry on the Stationers' Register in the summer of 1598.
The play was probably written shortly before then. As in *Othello,* the
characters' names are Shakespeare's rather than his sources'. The
play concerns two men who are very close: the merchant of the title,
one Antonio, and another businessman, Bassanio, whose fortunes
have hit a low ebb and who, at the start of the play, is set to embark on
a quest for a rich bride. Although it is not explicit in the text, Antonio
appears to be older than Bassanio. Antonio's antagonist in Venice is a
financier, the moneylending Jew Shylock, who is the father of a

---

*Chamberlain, vol. 1, p. 52.

daughter of marrying age. These two have in the past squared up to each other near the Rialto, Venice's traditional business center, and they confront each other again when Antonio guarantees a loan from Shylock to allow Bassanio to sail in style to Belmont where his future bride, Portia, lives. Shylock advances the money, but subject to a bizarre bond: the only security he requires from Antonio is a pound of flesh of his body should Bassanio default. The story of the pound of flesh has a long pedigree; as usual, Shakespeare makes it his so that today his version and his characters are those most associated with it.

Without recapitulating the plot of the play in any detail, we can see that its motifs bear striking similarities to Shakespeare's life and particularly to the story of the Sonnets. Portia quickly realizes that her new husband had a "bosom lover" before her and that their feelings for each other ran deep. Too deep, the play seems to suggest, as it sets in motion a mechanism to rescue Antonio from the clutches of Shylock and the Venetian law whose unbending nature he ruthlessly seeks to exploit while bringing Antonio's and Bassanio's relationship to a head in the trial scene and its aftermath. The exchange and movement of the rings between, particularly, Antonio, Bassanio, and Portia, suggest that whatever homoerotic subtext there may be here, Shakespeare advocates heterosexuality as the "natural" state. The imaginative logic of the play demands that Bassanio leave Antonio behind, painful though that may be; at the end of the play, Antonio is the last character left on stage after the others have paired off. He is as solitary now as Shylock, who has lost his daughter and his ducats and faces the prospect offstage of a forced conversion to Christianity.

Antonio ominously calls himself "a tainted wether of the flock, / Meetest for death." He is an outsider, melancholy at the thought of his best friend marrying a woman, yet prepared to offer his own flesh and blood to safeguard his friend's future and to secure for himself a loving memory in his friend's life and marriage. He wants Bassanio to commend him to his wife, to tell her of his supreme sacrifice: "And when the tale is told, bid her be judge / Whether Bassanio had not once a love." If the fiction of the play is matched to the narrative of the Sonnets, Shakespeare takes Antonio's role, while

Bassanio may be a version of Southampton, who probably told Shakespeare about his relationship with Elizabeth Vernon at some point during the summer of 1598.

Resonating beneath the surface of *The Merchant of Venice* is Marlowe's *The Jew of Malta,* which was first performed at the Rose theater in February 1592. Shylock recalls the play when in an aside he compares the men's eagerness to desert their wives for their friends. "These be the Christian husbands," he notes; "Would any of the stock of Barabbas [Marlowe's villainous hero] / Had been her husband rather than a Christian!" Marlowe's dark, witty, and outrageous farce, with its prologue spoken by Machiavelli, was periodically revived throughout the period, as Henslowe's diary demonstrates. It became grimly topical in June 1594 when the Queen's Portuguese-Jewish physician, Roderigo Lopez, was put to death for allegedly trying to poison the sovereign. The Queen did not believe in his guilt and neither did informed opinion of that time or this. One of Lopez's own former patients, the fiercely ambitious and unscrupulous Earl of Essex, had been pursuing a vendetta against the doctor and used him to enhance his own grip on power.

For Shakespeare to evoke Marlowe in 1598, for him to write the parts of Shylock and his daughter, Jessica, where Marlowe had Barabas and Abigail, is deliberately to invite comparison with his scornful dead friend and rival. Moreover, the play was entered on the Stationers' Register as *The Merchant of Venice, or otherwise called the Jew of Venice,* rendering the comparison explicit. The hard edges of Marlowe's black comedy are rounded out in Shakespeare's play, and the characters, particularly Shylock, assume a measure of humanity that invites compassion and understanding. Neither is a facet of Marlowe's play. As the father of a daughter, Barabas is a cipher, whereas Shylock is no different from any other Elizabethan father, rather like Shakespeare, who by the summer of 1598 must have expected to remain a father of daughters.

Marlowe's play is a brilliant piece of theater, as cheerfully anti-Catholic in its portrayal of fornicating friars and nuns as it is anti-Semitic. Shakespeare seems to pursue a different agenda altogether. By combining the Jewish plot with a play about men who are intimately bonded and whose union is wrenched apart by a young woman, he commemorates his own relationship with Southampton and even, perhaps, with his Anglo-Italian, Venetian-Jewish mistress. In a mellow, if not melancholic way, *The Merchant of Venice* may be Shakespeare's last contribution to the battle of poetic wits so abruptly ended five years earlier by the murder of the golden boy of the Elizabethan theater. Their rivalry was by now irrelevant, but Shakespeare would not let it go. He would prove that he also could deploy what he had once called "the proud full sail" of Marlowe's "great verse." Within the play's first few lines a fittingly marine and Marlovian chord is struck, when Salerio tries to explain to Antonio why he might be so sad:

> *Your mind is tossing on the ocean,*
> *There where your argosies, with portly sail*
> *Like signiors and rich burghers on the flood,*
> *Or as it were the pageants of the sea,*
> *Do overpeer the petty traffickers,*
> *That curtsy to them, do them reverence,*
> *As they fly by them with their woven wings.*

In returning to his old rival's play for his own sentimental leave-taking from Southampton and that entire homoerotic world, Shakespeare is paying tribute to Marlowe. Burghley's death on August 4, 1598, marked a watershed in Elizabethan England as a whole; for Shakespeare and the Southampton circle it seems to have sealed the end of a cycle of events. *The Merchant of Venice* is the last salvo in a contest of gay and straight sex that involved Shakespeare, Southampton, Marlowe, and Emilia Lanier, and to which Elizabeth Vernon, Portia to Shakespeare's self-sacrificing Antonio, now put a stop. The desire to surrender his entire self to the love of the fair youth is present, too, in Antonio. It is restrained at first, but in the trial scene it becomes transcendent and Antonio offers up his heart for Bassanio. In the play, the heart is both real and metaphorical; in the wider context of the Sonnets and the play, it is a metaphor for adoring love. Antonio's uncovering of his chest is also Shakespeare's baring of his soul, in the poems and perhaps also in real life.

We do not know where Shakespeare was in the summer of 1598;

most likely, he was living and working in London. Southampton had been carrying on with Elizabeth Vernon throughout 1598 and had made her pregnant as early as February or March. He was lost to Shakespeare, and had probably been so for over a year already, since the death of Hamnet. By the time of *The Merchant of Venice*, Emilia Lanier was reunited with her husband, Southampton was married, and Shakespeare had in more ways than one returned to Stratford. He chose to mark the end of a passionate love affair that lasted seven years, from 1590 to, probably, the summer of 1596, with an iconic play in the autumn of 1598. That he did so demonstrates his almost obsessive desire to view and understand his life through the prism of his works. Far from being the most impersonal of dramatists, he is the opposite. It is as if he had to tease the world with his life story, never quite telling it, but imparting to his contemporaries and to us tantalizing hints of what was going on inside him. Only this dramatist could ever have written the Sonnets. The Will Shakespeare of autumn 1598 was a very different man from the Shoreditch playwright who had probably been Marlowe's companion. In the England of that time, people grew up fast. Shakespeare packed a huge amount of living into his first ten years in London, but now it was time to take stock and, perhaps, to settle down. Since May 1597 he had been a substantial Stratford burgher with a high-profile investment in his hometown, a coat of arms, and disposable cash.

The Merchant of Venice must have been the hottest ticket in town, particularly if coteries at court and among the literati suspected it of hidden codes. It may have been playing at the Swan on Bankside or at the Curtain in Shoreditch when Richard Quiney of Stratford-upon-Avon sat in the Bell Inn writing a letter to Shakespeare. The timing was impeccable, for he wrote requesting a loan from the author of a play about moneylending. The Bell Inn stood in Carter Lane, which runs east to west between St. Paul's Cathedral and the river. Like so much else of Shakespeare's London, the Bell vanished in the Great Fire of 1666, and now, at the time of writing, the entire block south of Carter Lane is being redeveloped.

Quiney's note is the only surviving letter addressed to Shakespeare, hence its exceptional importance.

Loving countryman, I am bold of you as of a friend, craving your help with £30 upon Master Busshell's and my security or Master Mytton's with me. Master Ruswell is not come to London as yet and I have especial cause. You shall friend me much in helping me out of all the debts I owe in London, I thank God, and much quiet my mind which would not be indebted. I am now towards the court in hope of answer for the dispatch of my business. You shall neither lose credit nor money by me, the Lord willing, and now but persuade yourself so as I hope and you shall not need to fear but with all hearty thankfulness I will hold my time and content your friend, and if we bargain farther you shall be the paymaster yourself. My time bids me hasten to an end and so I commit this [to] your care and hope of your help. I fear I shall not be back this night from the court. Haste. The Lord be with you and with us all. Amen.

From the Bell in Carter Lane the 25 October 1598. Yours in all kindness, Richard Quiney.*

The letter is addressed, "H[aste] To my Loving good friend and countryman Master William Shakespeare deliver these." Two of the men it mentions, Mytton and Ruswell, were retainers of Sir Edward Greville from Warwickshire; in 1599, they would be summonsed on the same occasion as Gilbert Shakespeare. Richard Quiney, the Shakespeare brothers William and Gilbert, and some of Greville's retainers were clearly close enough to trust one another in financial affairs.

A Stratford Corporation minute of September 27, 1598, instructed Quiney "to ride to London about the suit to Sir John Fortescue for discharging of the tax and subsidy." Fortescue was the master of the Royal Wardrobe, next to Blackfriars. So Quiney was in the capital on Corporation business, almost certainly in connection with the new corn and malt legislation, which restricted the hoarding by

*Chambers (1930), vol. 2, p. 102. The letter is among the Quiney papers in the Stratford archives. Richard Quiney's firstborn, Adrian, married Eleanor Busshell in 1613, so that friendship at least endured beyond Richard Quiney's death. Richard Quiney, Jr., married Eleanor Sadler the same year, and Thomas Quiney married Judith Shakespeare in 1616.

private individuals of these commodities. A Stratford survey of February 1598 showed that the master of New Place had not been as civically minded as he ought: at a time of national shortages, the Shakespeares were officially hoarders of corn and malt.

By October 1598, Quiney was almost an old London hand. It was over a year since he had first visited the capital as his hometown's special envoy. So we may be somewhat surprised that within a month of arriving this time he had incurred substantial expenses and was asking Shakespeare for a loan. Security would be provided by the three named individuals. Meanwhile, he was in a hurry to get off to court about his business, from which he might not be back that evening. Perhaps his appointment with the Privy Council or even Robert Cecil himself was a late one, or maybe it was not in Whitehall but in Greenwich. The latter had been the case when Barber and Jeffereyes were in London on Stratford business a few years earlier. This is all rather confusing since Sir John Fortescue, whom Quiney was specifically delegated to see, lived in Carter Lane, just a few doors west of the Bell.

"I fear I shall not be back this night from the court" was an odd thing to say, as if he intended to tell Shakespeare not to trouble himself to visit the inn. If only Quiney had written an address on the letter rather than pass it to a messenger; an address would have told us exactly where Shakespeare lived on that date. Official documents still place him in Bishopsgate, but we know from a list of debtors to the Exchequer that by 1599–1600 he had moved south of the river, to Bankside, where he came under the jurisdiction of the Bishop of Winchester. The list of debtors and Malone's memo provide evidence that put Shakespeare south of the river in 1596 and that he had probably lived here for a while before October 1598. In any case, we may be reasonably confident that a messenger who set out in search of Shakespeare on this Wednesday would have gone south of the river and probably headed straight for the Swan, or, though this is less likely, to the Curtain in Shoreditch. Both were well-known London landmarks, of course. The fact that Quiney did not address his letter to a house or a ward can only mean that the bearer knew exactly where to find Shakespeare. We might guess that he knew him by sight, but he did not need to: he only had to turn up at the playhouse where the Lord Chamberlain's were performing and hand the letter in.

The carrier of Quiney's letter was probably a bellhop from the inn, which was patronized by councilors and businessmen from Warwickshire. How substantial it was can be gleaned from a map drawn shortly after the Great Fire of 1666. On it the space formerly occupied by the Bell spreads back deeply into a courtyard to the south of Carter Lane. It would have had a number of staff, just like any major modern hotel.

To muddy the waters, there was another Bell Inn nearby, also popular with Stratfordians. This second Bell stood in neighboring Friday Street, which runs toward the river east of Carter Lane and parallel to Bread Street, where Milton was born. Thus, about three weeks after Quiney's letter to Shakespeare, the closet Puritan and future adversary of playing, Daniel Baker, sat in Stratford writing to his "loving friend Mr. Leonard Bennet at the Bell in Friday Street."* On the same day, he dispatched another letter "to his loving uncle Mr. Richard Quiney of Stratford at his chamber at the Bell in Carter Lane." There seems to be no record of a Leonard Bennet in Stratford, but he must have been a visitor to London rather than a native: otherwise, he would not have needed to stay at an inn. Since Baker knew him, he was probably a Stratfordian or certainly from the area. Daniel Baker, who calls Richard Quiney his uncle, was related to him through the latter's marriage to Elizabeth Phillips, the daughter of Thomas Phillips. The Quiney-Phillips alliance created a powerful bloc from two of the most prominent families of Henley Street. Baker's mother was probably Richard Quiney's sister-in-law.

Quiney may have run up debts in London through circumstances that he had not anticipated. His family was wealthy and the borough had voted him a budget for going to London, though this may have been collected in arrears. In an emergency, cash could be

---

*"Daniel Baker to his kind and loving friend Mr. Leonard Bennet at the Bell in Friday Street in London, asking him whether he has paid iiij.li. vij.s to Mr. Edward Kympton, draper, at the sign of the Black Boy in Watling Street, and requesting him to leave x.li with Mr. Thomas Hacket, draper, at the signe of the ij. cats in Canninge Street" (Stratford, October 26, 1598; SBTRO: BRU15/1/127).

sought from moneylenders. Perhaps Quiney could not be fitted in when he was scheduled to be seen at court and therefore had to stay on in London, a potentially costly circumstance. In such a case one's townsman might come in very handy, particularly if he had deep pockets. That Shakespeare had been approached by the Quineys and Sturley earlier in the same year to underwrite the purchase of the Shottery tithes suggests he did indeed lend money, not unlike his alter ego Antonio.

Shakespeare may have pledged Quiney the money in person shortly after the letter was sent. When he did so, at the same time and for no known reason, he returned Quiney's letter. That is, if it was sent in the first place. That Shakespeare granted the loan the very same day is implied in a November 4 letter that Abraham Sturley addressed "To his most loving brother, Master Richard Quiney, at the Bell in Carter Lane at London give these." Sturley acknowledges receipt of Quiney's letter of October 25, sent home to Stratford through Greenway, who delivered it at Sturley's house on the night of Tuesday, October 31.

> Your letter of the 25 October came to my hands the last of the same at night per Greenway, which imported . . . that our countryman Master William Shakespeare would procure us money, which I will like of as I shall hear when, and where, and how . . . now to your other letter of the 1st of November received the 3rd of the same . . .

Quiney had written Shakespeare in a considerable rush—"My time bids me hasten to an end"—and hardly seems to have had time for another letter. Yet he did, and it trumpeted mission accomplished to Sturley. Perhaps his visit to the court that day was stalled or canceled at the last minute, after he had already written to Shakespeare, so that Quiney never left for Whitehall. Or perhaps he returned early, to find an emollient Shakespeare waiting. If he did not send the letter or leave the Bell after writing but instead waited for Shakespeare to arrive, that would explain why the letter went home with him to Warwickshire.

Quiney and Shakespeare probably shook on the deal there and

then in one of the convivial lounges of the Bell. After Will's departure, perhaps to catch a late boat home across the river, Quiney sat down, eager to impart his good news to Sturley and in time for Greenway to gather it in his mailbag for Stratford. What does not quite make sense is that Quiney's letter to Shakespeare implies that the money was for his own personal need, that the debts were his own. Sturley's letter, however, suggests that the money would be used for some joint business of himself and Quiney. Was Shakespeare tricked into lending money out of friendship to someone who had in mind a different purpose altogether from the one he presented? Too, paper was expensive then, and people did not as a rule write for frivolous reasons; yet we have here a letter that was probably never sent. It is worth noting that Quiney does not list Sturley as a guarantor of this substantial loan. Perhaps Shakespeare was not so well disposed to Sturley, who had long been associated with the Lucys and was in their pay in the late 1580s, at just the time when Shakespeare was caught poaching. In any event, the Quiney-Sturley correspondence does seem to suggest that Shakespeare was a loyal and generous friend, prepared to lend to those whom he knew well and particularly to old neighbors. Shakespeare's private reputation has occasionally suffered owing to his apparent appetite for litigation; the truth is that he was no more litigious than any other burgher of the period, and that he was capable moreover of impressive generosity.

In replying to Quiney's letter of October 25, Sturley referred to a *second* letter, posted by Quiney in London on Wednesday, November 1, and received in Stratford just two days later. A kind of express post must therefore have operated between London and the Midlands, and since the carrier Greenway had dropped off *his* London mailbag on October 31, it was somebody else who provided the expeditious two-day service. We have multiple "postmen" on this route, then, and some rapid travel—which means that even in London Shakespeare was never very far from his family. He could write to them frequently, and undoubtedly did. From the Quiney correspondence for this period, we may assume that a routine epistolary exchange between the two places was the norm.

It is almost inconceivable that Quiney would not have seen any of Shakespeare's plays during his several long spells in London between 1597 and 1602. Indeed, he probably went to the theater quite a bit, and would have reported in Stratford that Will was the talk of the town. Shakespeare's reputation was soaring: soon he would be fêted in Cambridge and, more intriguingly perhaps, pictures of him would become available to fans. Also in 1598 a quarto of *Richard II* appeared for sale, the second quarto of this play in two years. Quartos were not particularly prestigious publications—a Shakespeare quarto sold for between five and eight pence—but they brought in a bit of money. There was no other reason to publish a play when to do so was to court plagiarism. What makes the 1598 quarto of *Richard II* particularly significant is that Shakespeare's name appeared on it: that is, it advertised its pedigree in the hope of boosting sales. It was the first time that this had happened. The attributed quarto publication of *Richard II* was followed by a quarto of *Richard III* also bearing Shakespeare's name. He had become marketable. Quiney may well have picked up a *Richard II* quarto and taken it home to Stratford; as for the playwright, that he owned quartos of his own plays can be taken for granted, and he was bound to have shown them to his family and friends. These were *his* books. Many years later, he paid tribute to the extraordinary power of books in the figure of Prospero, whose very magic arises out of "books."

By the autumn of 1598 Shakespeare was a man of serious means. When his company looked for a permanent venue he was ready to contribute cash. We may remember that when the lease on the Theatre expired in April 1597, the Lord Chamberlain's became nomads, probably playing at the Curtain and the Swan. Meanwhile, the great Theatre lay empty: clearly news in London. In the words of the contemporary satirist Everard Guilpin, "but see yonder, / One, like the unfrequented Theatre, / Walks in dark silence and vast solitude."* The Lord Chamberlain's Men needed a home and the Burbages decided to build a new playhouse on Bankside, where they held a thirty-one-year lease on land near the Rose. When the Shoreditch

---

*Chambers (1923), vol. 2, p. 398.

freeholder Giles Allen persisted in his claim to the Theatre, on the basis that common law entitled him to everything that stood on his plot, the Burbages and their colleagues and friends started to dismantle the building. On December 28, 1598, a cold, snow-bound day, they took down all the timber and got it ready for transporting to Bankside.

A Stratford Alexander in Henry V at the Globe: 1599

The carpenter Peter Street, the future builder of the Globe and the Fortune, helped in the Theatre's dismantling. He had been involved two years earlier in the proposed conversion of the Blackfriars *frater*. He had grown up in the same part of the City of London as the Burbages and probably knew the joiner James Burbage as a young man. He may have been involved in the building of the Theatre in the mid-1570s. Expert guidance was required, because the timber had to be preserved for reassembly. We know from a later reference to the lease of the second Globe that the foundations of Globe I (1599) and Globe 2 (1613–14) were identical.* Shakespeare's three main theaters were therefore to all intents and purposes the same house, even though the second Globe was tiled and particularly splendid. (It was also vastly more expensive than the first Globe, presumably because all the timber needed to be new.)

The legal saga launched by the demolition ran for years. Pulling down the old house was a noisy affair and, as Allen's admittedly partisan deposition makes clear, unpleasant for the neighbors. Prolonged too, since every bit of timber had to be numbered. There would have been tens of cartloads to transport, and it is inconceivable that any of them passed across London Bridge, which was rather narrow, charged a hefty toll for transports, and was closed at night. It is much more likely that the wagons and carts trundled

---

*Chambers (1923), vol. 2, p. 426.

through the snowy City toward Street's timber yard on the wharf at Bridewell stairs. Street's was directly southwest of the present Unilever building and just above the Blackfriars underpass, probably in the area squeezed in between Watergate and the aptly named John Carpenter Street. The site was a timber yard already in the late 1550s; on a contemporary map the substantial wood yards of the Bridewell district are clearly sketched in. Street had been operating from these premises since 1596. From Bridewell stairs it was easy to convey the timber to Bankside on barges.

The first Globe probably cost between four and five hundred pounds to build. A few months after its completion, Peter Street was hired by the Lord Chamberlain's rivals to build another theater to almost the same specifications, but square rather than round. This playhouse, which was commissioned by Henslowe and Alleyn, would become the Fortune, in the liberty of Finsbury. Its site is commemorated today by Fortune Street, directly north of the Barbican. The reason Henslowe was eager to move his playing operations north of the river must have been to avoid competing with Shakespeare's company. The Lord Chamberlain's Men enjoyed a huge reputation and had the advantage now of playing at a brand-new venue very close to Henslowe's Rose, a smaller house that was then twelve years old. Also, audiences may have thought twice about crossing the river if they could walk to a play in the City instead. The outlay for the Fortune was estimated at £440 and seven months were allowed for building it, which suggests that rather less money and time may have been required for the Globe because once the foundations were in place the numbered timbers had only to be assembled. On May 16, 1599, a reference in the lease of the ground occupied by the Globe refers to it as "*de novo edificata*," newly erected, which means it took under five months to complete. It is worth noting that the second Globe, which cost a staggering fourteen hundred pounds, rose from scratch between the middle of February 1614 and the end of June that same year, four and a half months.

A considerable part of the money raised for the Globe in 1599 was apparently borrowed. We do not know what Shakespeare's share was, but in addition to the Burbages, who held 50 percent, there were several other shareholders, notably Shakespeare, Augustine Phillips,

Thomas Pope, John Heminges, and Will Kemp. When Kemp left the company in 1599, his share was merged into the other players' 50 percent holding, so that after 1599 four of them held half the shares and the Burbages the rest.

When the Lord Chamberlain's Men moved there, Bankside had already become a playground *extra muros* for Londoners. Not only were the Rose and Swan theaters here, but the area was also Londoners' favorite venue for bear and bull baitings. These were Sunday pastimes. The inquisitive Thomas Platter once again takes us right to the heart of 1599 when he was visiting the capital. Platter, who did not flinch at public executions in France and Catalunya, watched bear-baiting with detached curiosity. He records how a blind old bear was brought on and boys started striking at it with staves. But the bear broke lose and fled back into its cage. Afterward Platter and his companions went to inspect the English mastiffs that were set on bears and counted 120 of them as well as a number of bears and bulls. He was dismayed by the stench of the entire area of Pike Garden. The kennels and boxes for bears and bulls lay just a few yards south of the spot where today the Millennium Bridge touches the Surrey bank of the Thames. From here the kennels ran in parallel rows from north to south into where the eastern wing of the Tate Modern stands now.

Harry Hunks and George Stone were the stars of the bear world of late-sixteenth-century England, and Shakespeare would have seen them and known their names. Cockfighting and bull fighting as well as bear-baiting all formed part of Bankside culture, as did stews and taverns. The bear, the bull, the mastiff, the lion, and the lamb lay together on Bankside, which boasted several prisons including the Clink. The Clink was low-lying and damp and insalubrious because it was so near the Thames and because a sewer cut through Dead Man's Place to the west of the prison. The entire area to the west of Paris Garden was known as Lambeth Marsh. In itself the Clink was an insignificant prison; as has been mentioned, its regime was easy compared with that at other penal institutions of the period, perhaps because so many of the inmates were prisoners of conscience rather than hard-bitten criminals. Henslowe lived in the Clink's immediate vicinity. He did not seem to mind. He was a formidable entrepreneur: his interests on Bankside were boundless, inasmuch as they included theaters, taverns, and whorehouses. Eventually he also secured the franchise to become master of the royal game, which included bear-baiting. Henslowe's personality may be belied by the cozy and innocuous domestic chitchat in his correspondence with Alleyn.

Southwark became Shakespeare's place of work for the next nine years. The Globe stood near Maiden Lane, which is modern Park Street, so called because the Bishop of Winchester's park lay directly south of it. The theater's foundations are marked on the pavement at Anchor Terrace, in a spot directly southeast from where Southwark Bridge Road crosses over Park Street. The massive flyover disguises the fact that in the late sixteenth century the Globe stood no more than about eighty yards from its competitor the Rose. The latter occupied the southeastern corner of Rose Alley, which has linked Maiden Lane to Bankside since the Middle Ages. The players could undoubtedly hear one another across the distance between the houses.

Like its rival to the west, Langley's Swan, the new playhouse had received an emblematic name. Whether the Globe's banner really showed Hercules or Atlas propping up the world, as is sometimes alleged, we cannot say, but it did fly a flag; and if the Swan featured a swan, then it is quite likely that the Globe's emblem was the globe. The choice of the name may even have been Shakespeare's. He did, after all, write the speech that begins "All the world's a stage / And all the men and women merely players." This was in *As You Like It,* only the third play ever at the Globe. Prospero famously alludes to the Bankside theater when he declares that we may all be the stuff of dreams and that "solemn temples, the great globe itself" will dissolve alike in the end.

It is debatable which of Shakespeare's plays inaugurated the new playhouse. The Globe and the "wooden O" of the opening chorus of *Henry V* are probably one and the same,* and such is the excitement in the choruses of this play about the limitless ability of the stage

---

*Another school of thought maintains that the O is the stage of the Curtain in Shoreditch. See, for example, Shapiro (2005), p. 99.

imaginatively to re-create oceans and spaces that perhaps *Henry V,* rather than *Julius Caesar,* launched the Globe on its trajectory of fame. In Act V Shakespeare compares the welcome extended by Londoners to Henry V to that which the Romans granted to Caesar, or that which the people of London will accord the Earl of Essex on his victorious return from Ireland after crushing the Tyrone rebellion:

> *Were now the general of our gracious Empress–*
> *As in good time he may from Ireland coming–*
> *Bringing rebellion broachèd on his sword,*
> *How many would the peaceful city quit*
> *To welcome him!*

Given these triumphalist references, Act V must date from after March 27 1599, when Essex left London for Ireland. It must also have been completed before September 28 of the same year, for on that date Essex infamously rushed into the Queen's palace at Nonsuch after the campaign had failed. Since the Globe seems to have been fully operational by the middle of May that year, the theatrically celebratory, martial, and grandiloquent *Henry V* would seem to have been an obvious choice for an inaugural play.* We know that *Julius Caesar* was performed at the Globe in September 1599, because Platter saw it there on the twenty-first. *Julius Caesar* was probably a new play; heavily versified and marmoreal as it is, it stands to reason that Shakespeare would have needed some time to write it. He had probably written most of *Henry V,* up to the end of Act IV, during Lent of 1599, then reacted to Essex's departure for the Irish wars by putting him right into the chorus of Act V, apparently unable to resist the analogy between Henry's adventure and Essex's. It

---

*Shapiro (2005) argues the case for *Julius Caesar* and a later opening of the Globe, while Gurr ([1996], p. 291) believes that "*As You Like It* was almost certainly the first play Shakespeare wrote for the Globe." Henslowe's receipts (Foakes, pp. 92, 120) do not help, even though there is some evidence to suggest that they dipped considerably in the autumn of 1599 when the Globe was fully operational, which suggests that the Rose was feeling the impact of the competition from the newly opened Globe.

seems likely, then, that *Henry V* was finished by the middle of April 1599, if not before, and that it may have been intended to coincide with the opening of the Globe the following month. That Shakespeare might want to pay tribute to Essex in an English war epic written at just the time of the Tyrone conflict is entirely natural, for Southampton and Essex were the closest of allies, especially now that Wriothesley had married Essex's cousin. The two men were not only related, they were comrades-in-arms in Ireland. There is every reason to think that Shakespeare and Southampton continued as friends; it may have been this friendship that before long set Shakespeare and his company on a potentially deadly collision course with the Privy Council over a play involving the deposition of an English king.

The most intriguing biographical clue in *Henry V,* however, is neither its link to the Globe nor its allusion to Essex and the Irish wars, but Shakespeare's extensive use of French in the fourth scene of Act III, where Katherine, the princess of France, and an elderly lady-in-waiting named Alice rattle off an abundance of Franglais double entendres. From this linguistic hybrid the dramatist generates a thread of comedy that is picked up again at the very end of the play, when Henry of England woos Kate of France in "plain English" as well as in artfully halting French. We have no idea when Shakespeare became so accomplished in the language, which was not taught in grammar schools. The only plausible explanation is his friendship with Richard Field's French family. Shakespeare would not move in with the Mountjoys of Muggle or Monkwell Street until 1602. If his French can indeed be traced to the Fields, it follows that he must have seen much of them in their Blackfriars home. Moreover, though Emilia Bassano was a Venetian, she was married to a French musician. The French scenes in *Henry V* help, if somewhat obliquely, to consolidate Shakespeare's links to Field and Emilia. If he acquired French by osmosis from one of his best friends who happened to be closely connected to Huguenots, then he was blessed with exceptional powers of assimilation. Admittedly his ear for language was incomparable, but to be that gifted where other languages are concerned, even allowing for the spin-off benefits of a classical grammar school education, would be truly astonishing.

Yet it is suggested even by his sporadic references to Italian. One wonders whether Shakespeare picked up Italian from his mistress but chose not to use it in his plays because there was no audience for it. Where Italian settings are concerned he harbors no such anxieties after *The Taming of the Shrew,* which probably owes its relocation from Athens to Padua to the Italian mistress. People have long suspected that Shakespeare could read Italian; there is a famous moment in *Othello,* when the Moor challenges Iago to give him "the ocular proof" of Desdemona's infidelity. This is Shakespeare's only use of the word "ocular." Clearly he is thinking of the Italian text of his source, which has "vedere con gli occhi."* He must have read Italian, and furthermore his command of the language must have been good enough for turns of phrase to linger in his mind's ear before being transposed into English. Had Shakespeare used "ocular" more widely, this argument would fall, of course, but he did not; it appears, uniquely, in *Othello,* and at just the point where it also occurs in the source. Shakespeare borrowed endlessly; his mind absorbed everything he read to use for future reference. The word *occhi* had obviously struck a linguistic chord with him; his "ocular" is, remarkably, only the second recorded usage in English in this signification.

When Shakespeare moved into New Place he acquired a set of new neighbors. One of them was the high-profile Stratford schoolmaster and bibliophile Alexander Aspinall, for whom Shakespeare had probably made those famous gloves three years earlier. Shakespeare and Aspinall may have borrowed books from each other, or discussed books across the fence that separated their gardens. Shakespeare built up the library in New Place, and it must have been he who created the study that existed in the house many years after his death. He probably bought his books in St. Paul's Churchyard in London or else in the Strand. Richard Field, whose master printed Holinshed's *Chronicles* while Field did North's *Plutarch* and Ovid's *Metamorphoses,* three of Shakespeare's favorite texts, must have possessed an impressive library, even if it may have belonged to the

---

*The phrase does not appear in the French translation of the novella by the Italian humanist Cinthio, which some scholars argue Shakespeare used.

printing company rather than him. It is possible to list a number of the books that Shakespeare read and used in his works, and this is exactly what Geoffrey Bullough did in his nine-volume compendium of the sources of Shakespeare's plays. Bullough's four and a half thousand pages—his work is an enduring monument of Shakespearian scholarship—prove quite how bookish and literary Shakespeare really was. And Bullough cites only the books he demonstrably drew on, probably a fraction of his overall reading. He needed books in Stratford. The roads and tracks linking the Midlands to the capital in the late sixteenth century were busier than is now commonly imagined; packhorses and carts would have transported goods, including books, up to Warwickshire. That is how Shakespeare built up his library; he also probably brought books home in his own luggage. Again, his friend Field may have been collecting in his parental home in Stratford some of the books that he himself printed, and books could also be bought in Oxford, through which Shakespeare seems increasingly to have passed. For obvious reasons both Oxford and Cambridge enjoyed a thriving trade in books.

Shakespeare and Aspinall were not alone in owning books in Stratford, but home libraries as such did not exist at the time, at least not in Shakespeare's Warwickshire circles. There was, of course, John Brownsword, the master at the grammar school from 1565 to 1567 and assistant curate to Master John Bretchgirdle, who had baptised Shakespeare. Brownsword was the holder of a master of arts from Christ Church, Oxford; though no books are itemized in his inventory of 1565, he loved them and had an impressive library. Almost half of Bretchgirdle's estate, some ten pounds' worth, consisted of books, many of which he bequeathed to friends and godsons. As for Brownsword, he wrote Latin poems, which one of his pupils published in 1590, and he is included as a poet in *Palladis Tamia*. If Meres was in Shakespeare's circle, it might have been Shakespeare who alerted him to Brownsword's existence, thus doing the former teacher a good turn.

Among Stratford inventories only one features a library, that of John Marshall, clerk of Bishopton. Marshall's library comprised some 170 volumes, among them Latin grammars, Ascham's *Schoolmaster,*

Ovid's *Tristia*, Aesop's fables, Terence's plays, Cicero, and Castiglione, as well as a number of religious texts and tracts. Here, if he had lived to see it, was a man who might have bought the First Folio when it appeared. It might also be worth mentioning Clement Swallow of Shottery in this connection. He probably died in 1572, because his inventory was taken on March 24 of that year. The last item in it consists of "certain law-books and other books with other trifles of small value." One wonders whether Master Swallow owned law books because he was a justice of the peace; perhaps this Swallow was a Shallow. Perkes's first name in the famous country scene of *2 Henry IV* is the unusual (Catholic and papal) Clement, which leaves one wondering whether it might not have migrated from the life into the works by way of, in this case, Shottery and a man who owned books.

In Stratford, Aspinall was sometimes known as "Great Philip Macedon," because he called his son Alexander after himself.* The two Alexander Aspinalls also became known as Alexander the Great and Alexander the Little. It is only a short hop from the Stratford Alexanders two doors north of New Place to jokes about Alexander the Great-Big-Pig in *Henry V,* which contains other Stratford echoes in its references to the Welsh. The Welsh jokes are not surprising, for the Tudors were of Welsh extraction and Elizabethan Stratford numbered among its inhabitants an unusually large and prominent Welsh constituency, with names like "Edwards *alias* Welsh," Lewis-ap-Williams, Griffin-ap-Roberts, Fluellen (Llewellyn), Morris Evans, Jones, and others.

While translating Stratford names like Fluellen or indeed Bardolph (or Bardell) from real life into fiction can be done at the stroke of a pen, turning real characters into fictional ones is a very different matter. Moreover, the comic references to Alexander the Great in *Henry V* have a literary and historical pedigree. Shakespeare was reading Plutarch at around this time, in preparation for the next play, *Julius Caesar.* We know that he worked that way from his practice elsewhere. For example, he was demonstrably studying Plutarch for *Antony and Cleopatra* while he was halfway through writing *Macbeth.*

---

*Fripp (1924), p. 63.

When Macbeth claims that under Banquo his "genius is rebuked as it is said / Mark Antony's was by Caesar," Shakespeare is remembering Plutarch's "Life of Marcus Antonius," which makes this very point. He always kept an eye on the next project. In the final stages of *Henry V* he was reading not only Plutarch but also Holinshed. The two most important lives behind *Julius Caesar* are the "Life of Caesar" and the "Life of Marcus Brutus," and the Greek parallel life to Caesar is that of Alexander the Great.

So literature and Shakespeare's life in Stratford probably converge in the Alexander jokes in *Henry V*. In one of the play's most famous passages, Fluellen compares Alexander and Henry V. What really links Macedonia and Monmouth, he explains, are their two rivers, the clincher being that "there is salmons in both." This is a nonsense, of course, intended as a spoof of Plutarch. Then, at the end of the play, the rejection of Falstaff is poignantly recalled as if to undercut the cult of heroism:

> Alexander killed his friend Cleitus, being in his ales and his cups, so also Harry Monmouth, being in his right wits and his good judgements, turned away the fat knight with the great-belly doublet—he was full of jests and gipes and knaveries and mocks—I have forgot his name.

Something in Shakespeare was ever more Falstaff than Bolingbroke, more poacher than gamekeeper, more rebel than king, more Brutus than Caesar. Perhaps the two Aspinalls inspired him to take liberties with the name of Alexander, to treat legendary great men with comic irreverence. In being the butts of his indulgent laughter, Shakespeare's fellow Stratfordians may have shown him the way.

If the rousingly patriotic *Henry V* suits London's bellicose mood of the first half of 1599, *Julius Caesar* is much more skeptical of institutionalized power. The fact that it is a Roman play rather than an English history affords Shakespeare more room for maneuver, freeing him to question the scope of absolutism, to consider the role of the people. (But the notion of democracy as we understand it was probably alien to him.)

Thomas Platter saw *Julius Caesar* on September 21, 1599. His brief diary entry is that of a perceptive tourist and he records the kind of detail that we might otherwise not get. Writing up his notes some five years after the event, Platter recalled how after lunch, around two o'clock, he and his party crossed the Thames and "in the strewn-roof house saw the tragedy of the first Emperor Julius." There was a cast of "at least fifteen characters" whose acting skills impressed him greatly. The show ended with a very well executed dance, "two in men's clothes and two in women's in wonderful combination with each other."* This early performance apparently ended with Brutus and Caesar dancing with Portia and Calpurnia, since the latter are the only two female roles in the play. It is strange to think that when Platter saw the play all of its performances, ever, could probably still be counted on one or maybe both hands. Immediately after the stabbing of Caesar, Cassius remarks to his fellow conspirators that their "lofty scene" will be renacted countless times in the future, that the Caesar whom they killed will "bleed in sport" in countries and languages that have not yet been discovered, and that every time this happens Brutus, Cassius, and the other conspirators will be called "the men that gave their country liberty." A more resounding endorsement of republicanism is hard to imagine.

The association that started in 1599 between Shakespeare, the Globe, and Southwark would extend beyond his death, for both the monument in the chancel of Holy Trinity and the engraving that prefaces the First Folio have their origins in Southwark. In that hugely important year, Shakespeare pitched his tent in this hybrid area of town and country, a southern mirror of Shoreditch that now boasted the most splendid theater in the country. Although by living south of the river he cut out the daily commute across the Thames, this can't have been a major consideration, because by 1602–1603 he had moved back into the City of London. Throughout his career he only rented property in London and was thus more flexible and mobile about where he chose to live than most actors. In any case, he must have been spending a considerable part of his time at New Place.

---

*Chambers (1923), vol. 2, p. 365.

As fate would have it, there may well have been a pressing incentive to shuttle between London and Stratford more and more often, because by 1600, if not before, he had probably met the woman who was destined to play a crucial role in his life, and she had moved to Oxford by the turn of the century.

21

Picturing a Poet and a Pantomime Rebellion: 1600–1601

hakespeare's next play, his third Globe drama, was *As You Like It*. The character of the forest of Arden may reflect the fact that he finished the play in Warwickshire during the fiercely cold spell over Easter 1600. When we first see Arden, it is a place where the "penalty of Adam" has as little power to hurt "as the icy fang / And churlish chiding of the winter's wind." The whole spring that year was desperately cold. It snowed on Easter Sunday—March 23—and again from April 4 until well into May. *As You Like It* famously contains the only part attributed to Shakespeare in the seventeenth century apart from Hamlet's father's ghost, that of Old Adam. Autobiographical traces have been detected in its setting and in the character of a country yokel by the name of William. This is not to mention the repeated references to *Hero and Leander* and to Marlowe, perhaps even to Marlowe's death. The fact that the forest of Arden is probably intended, as in the play's source, to be a forest in Europe near Lyons, perhaps the Ardennes, which straddles Belgium and Luxembourg, does not necessarily gainsay this. Whether or not Shakespeare is pitting his lives in London (court) and Warwickshire (forest) against each other, the play further illustrates how he intermingles life and fiction.

As You Like It is remarkably relaxed. If it buzzes, it buzzes with inaction. It is one of Shakespeare's most discursive plays. Nothing much happens, but there is plenty of dazzling chat and lightning repartee about poetry and love, men and women, and women who have to act like men to transcend social restrictions. Shakespeare is uniquely fascinated by the boy-girl or "female page" motif. The donning of women's clothes by boy actors ran into biblical difficulties, because the Book of Deuteronomy specifically outlaws transvestism. The Puritans, who hated the stage, were quick to cast this back at the players, but they were as yet contained by Parliament and the Crown. It has become fashionable to think that Shakespeare was attracted to boy-girl transvestism because of a latent homosexuality, and there may be some truth in this. He uses the motif in no fewer than five plays, from the early *The Two Gentlemen of Verona* to *Cymbeline* twenty years later. But there may be a more obvious reason for his love of imaginative transsexuality: his own boy-girl duo. Put Hamnet in girl's clothes and you had Judith, while Judith disguised as a boy was Hamnet. Perhaps it really was that simple, and perhaps Shakespeare was now recalling Marlowe and *Hero and Leander,* and thus the time of the Sonnets, for related reasons. If he ever did consummate a homosexual relationship, it would have been with Marlowe.

At around the time of *As You Like It,* Marlowe's great gifts as a tragedian, as well as his death, atheism, and homosexuality, were mentioned in a play put on at St. John's College, Cambridge. This was Burghley's old college as well as Southampton's. In this play, called *The Second Part of the Return from Parnassus,* one Judicio remarks

> *Marlowe was happy in his buskind muse,*
> *Alas unhappy in his life and end,*
> *Pity it is that wit so ill should dwell,*
> *Wit lent from heaven, but vices sent from hell.*

His fellow Ingenioso replies, "Our *Theater* hath lost, *Pluto* hath got, / A tragic penman for a dreary plot." Two of literature's best-known references to Marlowe's death, by Shakespeare and the anonymous author of a Cambridge play, thus appeared close to each other, probably because censorship surrounding him was being relaxed now that Burghley was dead. Shakespeare was now famous, and the most powerful literary witness to his ascendancy comes from the three *Parnassus* plays, all anonymous closet dramas performed by students at St. John's College around 1600. Besides commemorating

Marlowe, if "commemorating" is the right word, they cheekily suggested that Jonson might have been well advised to stick to bricklaying because he was "so slow an inventor." (Others made similar remarks.)

The authors of the *Parnassus* plays repeatedly allude to *Romeo and Juliet* and they quote *Venus and Adonis* and *The Rape of Lucrece*. Almost all their Shakespeare material is connected to one particular character, a foolish courtier by the name of Gullio. After slightly misquoting the opening two lines of *Venus and Adonis*, Gullio exclaims, "O sweet Master Shakespeare, I'll have his picture in my study at the court," meaning the courtyard of St. John's.* The *Parnassus* picture of Shakespeare may well be the one in the First Folio that seems to show Shakespeare in his mid- to late thirties, as he was in 1600. Hamlet's invitation to his mother, "Look here upon this picture, and on this, / The counterfeit presentment of two brothers," may similarly be inspired by a picture of Shakespeare that had been drawn or painted around this time, if not by the same image to which Gullio refers. If Shakespeare played Hamlet's father's ghost, the subject of one of the two pictures, that would have rendered the lines especially poignant. If a picture of him did circulate at the start of the seventeenth century, we may be fairly certain that Shakespeare himself would have owned a copy.

Even if we were unaware of the approximate dates of the *Parnassus* plays, we would guess from the reference to "Master Shakespeare" that they were written after October 1596, when the Shakespeares acquired their arms. The author or authors were clearly familiar with the personnel of the Lord Chamberlain's Men, three of whose shareholders, Shakespeare, Burbage, and Kemp, feature in the plays, the last two as characters in the final installment, where they discuss their peers and the demerits of academic drama. There is more to Gullio, though. He appears only in the second play of the trilogy. Gullio is a bombastic fool who is besotted with Shakespeare and whose past career bears a close resemblance to

---

*Leishman, p. 185, lines 1032–33. Stanley Wells has called this "Shakespeare as pin-up." He reminds us that a portrait of Ben Jonson had been issued as an independent print in the 1620s and was later used as the frontispiece to two of his books.

Southampton's, particularly as regards his military service in Spain, Portugal, and Ireland and a visit to Paris.

Gullio quotes liberally from *Venus and Adonis,* which was of course famously dedicated to Southampton. This may be the playwright's main reason for according the poem such prominence, when he is clearly familiar with other works including *Romeo and Juliet.* We are told nothing of Gullio's love life, but his devotion to *Venus and Adonis,* with its intensely self-absorbed youth, points at narcissism, which would also fit Southampton. Gullio professes to value this most popular of Shakespeare's works in the period above all other literature. Let the rest of "this duncified world esteem Spenser and Chaucer," Gullio is for Shakespeare and *Venus and Adonis.* When Gullio remarks, "I stood stroking up my hair, which became me very admirably," one may be forgiven for thinking of Southampton's famous mane. The name of Gullio's love is Lesbia, phonetically not so different from Southampton's wife's name, Elizabeth (so often contracted to Lisbeth). Cumulatively, these coincidences make one wonder whether Gullio may not be identified with the Earl. So does his absence from the third *Parnassus* play, by which time Southampton was serving a life sentence in the Tower of London. Southampton was a St. John's man, a patron of the arts, a friend of Shakespeare's, and a soldier. He was also, briefly, the dedicatee of Thomas Nashe's *The Unfortunate Traveller*; Gullio's sparring partner in *Parnassus,* Ingenioso, is based on Nashe. The question is whether a parody of Southampton would be likely to be staged in his own college, an institution that enjoyed the patronage of the Cecils and which at that very time counted Robert Cecil's nephew among its alumni. Or maybe Southampton could be parodied at St. John's precisely because at just this time he found himself in the Tower: in that case, the second part of *Parnassus* postdates his February 1601 trial.

The satire of Gullio is not a vicious one; he is a gull and a literary glutton. Southampton was easily led and foolishly impulsive, qualities pleaded in mitigation at his trial by Robert Cecil, who argued that he had been led astray. That may well be true, because the usually benign Earl was also a hothead, capable of flaring up over nothing, as for example in his behavior in the Queen's antechamber when he defied court protocol over a game of primero. Unlike Hamlet, he was ever ready "greatly to find quarrel in a straw / When honour's at the stake." The Cecils may have blessed the *Parnassus* plays as a small cog in their machinery of propaganda, and they may as a by-product have left us some more tantalizing clues about Shakespeare and Wriothesley.

There are three references to Shoreditch in the *Parnassus* trilogy. Two of them flag it as a place of debauchery; the third puts Gullio there when Ingenios/Nashe reveals that he has arranged a meeting "at Gullio's chamber in Shoreditch." This could well refer to Southampton's rooms there. He was addicted to plays; after his return from Ireland in 1599 he was reportedly spotted at the theaters every day along with Lord Rutland, despite their duty of attendance at court. If he did have lodgings of some kind in Shoreditch in the 1590s, that would certainly help explain his easy familiarity with the players as a young man, and of course particularly with Shakespeare. Moreover, if he had been drawn into gay circles at Cambridge, it would make sense for him to gravitate toward Shoreditch, where some of his former Cambridge companions lived. The idea of Gullio doting on a picture of "sweet master Shakespeare" while studying at St. John's is, of course, ludicrous and meant to be so: Gullio is portrayed as engaged in a demeaning and socially dysfunctional act. An earl or courtier, however narcissistic, and a mere player—it hardly bears contemplating. But for the biographer of Shakespeare what matters here is the proof that "pictures" of Shakespeare circulated long before the one in the First Folio of 1623. By the end of the sixteenth century he was a star and, like his social betters, he was being drawn or painted.

As the old century drew to a close, England remained a deeply troubled society. In the years ahead the reign of Elizabeth I would eventually be seen as a golden age, but not while it was being lived. The Queen was old and fading now and the absence of an heir deeply preoccupied the nation and its executive. The tensions and factions at the heart of government are well known to us four hundred years on. They would have been common knowledge in 1600, when everyone knew about the fault line that ran between the younger Cecil and Essex.*

That rift would trigger the most cataclysmic event of Shakespeare's time in London: the attempted Essex putsch of Sunday, February 8, 1601. Someone who watched the unfolding events from inside the Tower of London was Father William Weston, who had been transferred there from Wisbech in 1598. His sight was failing and he felt lonely and abandoned. His faith had been severely tested by solitude and despair and there were times when he nearly lost his mind. One day, he recalled later, he was sitting listlessly in his cell when he heard the noise of men running about in what sounded like a frenzied stand to arms. Pikes, mail jackets, and muskets appeared and there was shouting, proffering of threats, and a general panic. Something dreadful had clearly happened, and he wondered whether it might not be an attempt on the Queen's life or an attack on the Tower itself. When his warder brought him his meal that evening, he was agitated and fully armed. He told Weston that they were all lost and betrayed because the Earl of Essex and many nobles had risen up against the Queen. But the commotion lasted only a few hours. A few days later, Essex was beheaded not very far from Weston's window in the Tower.

Essex's disorganized bid for power lasted just one day. It ended that evening with him holding some of the country's chief law officers hostage inside his mansion off the Strand. Essex Street and Essex and Devereux Courts today recall its presence south of St. Clement Danes and Temple Bar. An eyewitness account of the conspirators' shambolic attempt to breach the gates of the City of London at Ludgate sounds like a bad pantomime, as does the Essex

---

*Ever since his appointment to the Privy Council in 1593 Essex had sought to become the Queen's chief adviser and supplant the Cecils. He certainly became her favorite, but his hawkish attitude, among others, toward military intervention in Europe and his seeking an alliance with Henry IV of France set him on a collision course with the cautious diplomacy of the Cecils. His row with the Queen on July 1, 1598, and his subsequent estrangement from court and favor played into the hands of his enemies on the Council. The disastrous Irish campaign of 1599 and his undignified return to Nonsuch later that year effectively put the seal on his career as a major figure in English politics.

party's desperate boarding of boats at Queenhythe to ferry them back to the Strand. The only political agenda seems to have been Essex's own personal ambition.

Throughout this most turbulent day Southampton stayed at Essex's side, quite literally so when the two stood together on the roof at Essex House that afternoon trying to bargain with the Queen's forces. They were tried side by side in Westminster Hall on February 19, 1601. The trial lasted exactly one day.

We will probably never know whether Shakespeare had advance warning of the coup from his onetime boon companion. That something major was afoot would have become fairly clear to the Lord Chamberlain's Men when they were approached on the Thursday before the coup and urged by Essex's friends to put on *Richard II* that Saturday. In their defense the hapless spokesman for the company, Augustine Phillips, pointed out to Lord Chief Justice Popham that they had resisted the initial approach, on the grounds not least of this now being an old play, which might have them act to an empty house. They eventually gave in, partly because Essex's men offered the solid financial inducement of forty shillings above and beyond their normal fee, and also perhaps in response to behind-the-scenes lobbying by Southampton. The players escaped almost scot-free for what could readily have been construed as lèse-majesté. We know from the testimony of one of her contemporaries that the Queen saw herself as akin to Richard II, a monarch who was deposed by a pretender.

Barely three weeks after playing *Richard II* for the Essex cause, the Lord Chamberlain's Men performed at court before the Queen. It was February 24, 1601, the eve of Essex's execution. What play was put on that night is not known. The fact that Shakespeare's company were playing at all must have been intended by the Privy Council to stress that normality was restored, that it was business as usual, for playing had resumed. It was Shrove Tuesday, after all. The performance cannot have been easy for the actors, several of whom had been close to members of the Essex circle (to say nothing of Shakespeare and Southampton). Nor can the ailing Queen have been indifferent that night to the morrow when her former favorite would die. One wonders whether Robert Cecil was present and what his thoughts may have been. He had at last achieved the family's ambition to destroy the flashy Essex. The Cecils had built their lives and amassed a fortune by preying on others, and Essex had been one of their most powerful enemies.

Lent 1601 started with the execution of Essex on Ash Wednesday. Shakespeare must have been in London; his company had acted before the Queen the night before. His thoughts and his friends' must have been on Tower Hill where the hero of the chorus of *Henry V* was dying. The events on this violent Ash Wednesday may have reminded Shakespeare, if he needed reminding, of the dangers of the court world. Far better to enjoy quiet domesticity at home in Stratford. Lent traditionally was vacation time—even if it meant writing plays in preparation for the new season—reading, and helping out his father and siblings in their gloving business. In New Place he was comfortable, warm in front of his many large fires, and with enough time on his hands to play with his daughters, go for walks, and generally enjoy the life of a country gentleman.

On his return to Stratford he must have been mobbed by family and neighbors, who would have wanted to know what on earth was going on in London and what it was like to play before the old Queen on the eve of her favorite's beheading. If he answered such questions, he probably did so guardedly; he may have compared notes with other Stratfordians, but how many of the local burghers could have known that he had addressed sonnets to one of the two chief defendants in the most sensational treason trial of the age? For the time being, the wayward Earl was safe in the Tower—and, as Shakespeare probably knew too, he was quite comfortable there. Southampton had enjoyed a lucky escape.

A few months later, the author of *Henry V* wrote *Troilus and Cressida,* which lampoons Achilles and the whole heroic war ethos. Achilles and Patroclus, the only overtly gay characters in Shakespeare, are portrayed as cowardly. There can be little doubt that the play was inspired by the events of February 1601. The comparison of Essex with Achilles was not just in the air in the 1590s; it had been made directly by the author of the text that lies behind Shakespeare's *Troilus,* George Chapman. In his dedication of *Seven Books of the Iliad*

(1598), Chapman announced that in Achilles Homer had prefigured the Earl of Essex, the "now living instance of the Achillean virtues."* It follows that Patroclus, Achilles' lover, and Southampton may be linked as well. In Shakespeare's play, the railing one-man chorus, Thersites, spits poison at all the major characters, calling Patroclus "Achilles' male varlet" and "his masculine whore."†

If Shakespeare wrote *Troilus and Cressida* as a satire on martial values starring male lovers, Achilles/Essex and Patroclus/ Southampton, he was skating on thin ice. While an opportunistic anti-Essex play might be just what Robert Cecil and the Privy Council desired after February 1601, Essex still had many powerful allies, not least the King of Scots, James VI. As for Southampton, it seems almost inconceivable that Shakespeare would really have betrayed his friend this way, exploiting his sexuality for satirical purposes in a politically angled parable. Perhaps Shakespeare was handed a "plot" and ordered to fashion from it a work of propaganda. Henslowe records paying Ben Jonson an advance of twenty shillings in 1597 "upon a book which he was to write for us before Christmas next after the date hereof which he showed the plot unto the company." "Book" means a play and the "plot" is what we would now call a treatment, a short proposal for a script. The peculiar history of the text of *Troilus and Cressida,* and the fact that as late as 1609 it seems not to have been acted in the theater ("never staled with the stage, never clapper-clawed with the palms of the vulgar"), underlines the perception that this is a distinctly odd work. It is certainly a deeply cerebral one, and there has long been a suspicion that it may have been written for a particular social circle or an Inns of Court audience of lawyers. If the political agenda was mandated by the authorities, they in turn may not have wanted the people or populace to see the result, a satire on two prominent aristocrats, even though it may

---

*Quoted in Bevington, p. 12.

†The play was entered on the Stationers' Register in 1603, but it is usually dated to late 1601 because another one of its characters, the bombastic Ajax, may spoof Ben Jonson. Between September 1600 and May 1601, Jonson was writing for the Children of the Queen's Chapel (also known as the Chapel Children) in Blackfriars and by so doing seems to have given offense to some of his fellow writers for the adult companies.

have reflected their own agenda. *Troilus and Cressida* seems a treacherous work for Shakespeare to have written, unless the impetus for it originated with members of the Privy Council who may have been busy making sure elsewhere, notably in Cambridge, that Southampton would be seen for the fool he was.

The play's motifs and specific satirical targets were perhaps imposed on Shakespeare, but its skeletal story about two doomed lovers during the Trojan War originates in Chaucer's *Troilus and Criseyde*. And there may have been a more direct connection between Shakespeare and Chaucer just then, namely his residing in the City of London close to Chaucer's renowned editor at this time. Shakespeare himself told the court in *Mountjoy vs. Belott* that he met the Mountjoys of Muggle (Monkwell) Street in or around 1602. He does not tell us exactly when he moved there; in 1612 he said he had known them "ten years or thereabouts," which is vague enough. He may well have lived in their house before 1602, after only a short stay on Bankside. In Muggle Street he found himself quite near the best-known Chaucerian editor of the day, Thomas Speaght. Speaght's house perched at the top of the street, up against London Wall and next to St. James-in-the-Wall, whereas the Mountjoys' corner house stood at the northeastern intersection of Muggle and Silver Streets. Speaght as much as the authorities may have had a hand in persuading Shakespeare to write *Troilus and Cressida*. He may have sought out the company of the celebrated playwright, who was better connected now than most people, including Speaght's own friends.

Whatever anxieties and resentments the members of the Lord Chamberlain's Men may have harbored about the regime and what it asked of them, the players had families to support and lives to live. The acidic farce *Troilus and Cressida* is Shakespeare's retort to the tragic events of February 1601. If he was asked to write it, he probably had little choice, especially since the company had sailed so close to the wind with *Richard II*. They could not afford another confrontation with the authorities. Total compliance was in order, and if parodying their former friends and supporters in Achilles and Patroclus was the price of mending fences, it was a small one. Essex was dead and Southampton would probably regain his liberty and be reconciled again. He knew the rules of the game—and, indeed, he eagerly rejoined the social circle around the players after his release. Perhaps he was mollified by recognizing a kinder, much more flattering and complex portrayal of himself in another Shakespeare play, *Hamlet*, which would establish itself as one of the most acclaimed in the world.

As summer turned to autumn, Shakespeare had an idea for a new play. This one would be for himself only, or rather about himself and his family. It was a play about twins; its title was *Twelfth Night*, and its subtitle *or What You Will*.

$\wp$aughters and Sons
and Lovers: 1601–1602

 *welfth Night* was probably written over the summer of 1601, for it seems to echo Ben Jonson's *Poetaster*, which was put on by the Chapel Children of Blackfriars that spring. Shakespeare again uses a name from real life for one of his main characters, Orsino. This can only derive from the name of Virginio Orsini, the Duke of Bracciano, who sojourned in London during Twelfth Night 1601 and before whom Shakespeare's company performed on at least one recorded occasion. On Tuesday, February 2, 1602, the Feast of Candlemas, there was a performance of *Twelfth Night* at Middle Temple, possibly the play's first.* It has become famous because, remarkably, an eyewitness account of it has survived, and by the same John Manningham who gave us the story about Burbage, Shakespeare, and the theatergoing citizen.

> At our feast we had a play called "Twelfth Night, or what you will," much like the comedy of errors.... A good practice in it to make the steward believe his lady widow was in love with him, by counterfeiting a letter as from his lady, in general terms telling him what she liked best in him, and prescribing his gesture in smiling, his apparel, etc., and then, when he came to practise, making him believe they took him to be mad.

---

*In the best single study of the play to date, Edmondson ([2005], p. 1) disagrees: "Although almost certainly not the play's premiere, it [the Middle Temple performance] was no doubt an evening of high spirits."

Six weeks later, Manningham recorded the "Will the Conqueror" anecdote. He probably saw Shakespeare play in this special
indoor evening performance of *Twelfth Night*, and perhaps rumors
about the players had started to fly among the legal wits immediately
afterward; one does wonder, though, why Manningham waited six
weeks to write down the "Conqueror" story.

While the senior Templarian Towse is credited with telling
Manningham the story, we should also consider John Marston as a
source. He was a Midlander, an Oxford scholar, a poet, satirist, playwright, and lawyer, and eventually a priest. He had joined the Middle Temple in 1594, at just the time of the Burbage-Shakespeare
caper. At a Christmas dance in December 1601 he had cheerfully insulted the ingenue daughter of an alderman. Manningham reported
this on November 21, 1602, almost a year after it happened; perhaps
the prospect of Christmas had jogged his memory. In the mid-1590s,
Marston and his father, another Middle Temple lawyer, stood surety
in Middle Temple for their fellow Midlander Thomas Greene,
Shakespeare's "cousin." Greene kept chambers in London after being called to the bar in 1600. He was close to Shakespeare and he
ended up living in the Shakespeares' house, while naming two of his
children William and Anne. If he saw the Middle Temple Candlemas production of *Twelfth Night*, as he probably did, he would have
been present alongside the Marstons, Manningham, Curle, Towse,
and, perhaps, other relatives of Shakespeare's. The Greenes, Marston,
and Shakespeare do seem to connect, even if we cannot tease out the
precise links. And there is some circumstantial evidence that the
Greenes may have been rather more loose-tongued than they ought
to have been about Shakespeare and his family. It is probably just a
coincidence that a tawdry rumor that would one day threaten the
good name of Shakespeare's daughter may have originated with the
Greene brothers.

Shakespeare had used same-sex twins in *The Comedy of Errors* at
a time when his own twins were both alive; now he fielded a version
of his own family, diminished though it was. In *Twelfth Night* a providential recovery restores to wholeness an essentially indivisible
twain. Remarkably, the mother of Viola and Sebastian does not figure
at all; instead, the play contains a famous reflection that is sometimes

cited as proof of Shakespeare's estrangement from his own children's mother. Orsino urges Cesario to let his "love be younger than thyself" because female beauty, which holds "the bent" of men's affections, fades all too quickly: "for women are as roses, whose fair flower / Being once displayed, doth fall that very hour." The evidential value of these lines may be somewhat weakened by the fact that they are spoken by one of Shakespeare's romantically most self-obsessed characters. Orsino is hardly Hamlet or King Lear, and his views do not suggest the authorial self-projection that audiences and readers frequently detect in these two tragic heroes. Even so, there is no irony here, no feeling that at this point in the play Orsino is talking anything other than plain common sense. Orsino thinks that men should not marry women older than themselves; perhaps Shakespeare, who after all wrote the lines, thought so, too. In that case, the lines sound a note of retrospective regret, always assuming that Anne was indeed seven years older than the poet.

When Shakespeare wrote *Twelfth Night*, Judith was sixteen, about the right age for Viola and Sebastian. We are not given the twins' ages in the play, but we are offered a curious detail about their past: their father died on the day they turned thirteen. Perhaps something in Shakespeare died forever in 1596, when he wrote an elegiac play with the thirteen-year-old Juliet as its heroine. *Twelfth Night* is made bittersweet by the longing of brother and sister for reunion. Hence, perhaps, Sebastian's phrase "deity in my nature," since to reunite Judith and Hamnet would indeed have needed an act of God. Perhaps Shakespeare felt that he had written *Romeo and Juliet* for Hamnet and Susanna. *Twelfth Night* may well have been written for Judith. If this father, who saw his children only from time to time, a circumstance rare in Shakespeare's social circle, did indeed delight in their ability to read and write as Sir Hugh Clopton recalled hearing many years later, what would stop Judith from asking that her father write a play about boy-girl twins? Perhaps she had the idea after seeing an early performance of *As You Like It.*

Perhaps. It may also be relevant, since the Middle Temple performance took place on Candlemas, that Judith and Hamnet were baptised at Holy Trinity on that very same day seventeen years earlier. This could be a coincidence, of course: it was the Templarians who set the program for that night's entertainment in 1602. But it was Shakespeare who wrote the play and he chose this one, the only one among all his works to be constructed around boy-girl twins, because the performance coincided with the twins' christenings. It would be counterintuitive to deny the link here. The Middle Temple performance took place two or three days after Judith's seventeenth birthday, which might suggest that her father brought her down to see it as a treat. If so, it implies that Shakespeare was rather closer to Judith than is sometimes assumed. She has at times seemed to be the Cinderella of the Shakespeare family, but there are reasons for believing that she was immensely precious to her father, that the young women of the last plays are at least as much her as Susanna. Judith may be the young woman behind the heroine of *Twelfth Night.* The thought that she was the only survivor of the doublet must have been constantly on her father's mind. Viola is one of the most tenderly imagined and most feminine of Shakespeare's heroines. Whereas Rosalind in *As You Like It* is empowered by her disguise and bestrides the play with wit and mastery, Viola is trapped in her transsexuality. Rosalind may well be based on Susanna Shakespeare, who one day was famously compared to her father and called "witty above her sex" by those who knew her, who inherited most of her father's estate after marrying well, and who may even have looked after her more retreating and passive sister. There is every reason for Rosalind and Viola to have resembled Shakespeare's daughters. It is, of course, Viola rather than Rosalind who becomes the model for the daughters in the later plays, perhaps above all because she was the one left at home with her father when he was writing them.

Again and again Shakespeare's plays chime with details and events from his life. He emerges as someone who wrote compulsively, not only to earn a living but also to control and impose meaning upon contingent events. The works become a way of life, which is presumably why he wrote so much, and often so close to the bone. The transsexual Illyrian twin comedy and its transvestite Arden predecessor seem to pay tribute to Shakespeare's daughters. Moreover, in *Twelfth Night* Shakespeare indulges in the fantasy of resurrecting a lost male twin. When Viola's brother turns up, not only are the twins reunited but also the Duke and Olivia win their hearts' desires because Viola has managed to make "division" of herself. Instead of one, there are suddenly two, and of the right sexes for a proper heterosexual fit with their respective partners.

Earlier it was suggested that Shakespeare's interest in death by water might have grown from his early life on the Avon and that it connected with drowning as a literary motif in his first so-called new comedy, *The Comedy of Errors*. Almost every other example of this genre involves this theme. At its sources, "new comedy" revolves rather narrowly around children and parents split at birth, mostly by shipwreck. The roots of this preoccupation can be traced back to the seminal comedies of the great Athenian playwright Menander, who lived in the fourth century B.C. In dealing with recurrent motifs in Shakespeare's comedies, we find ourselves continually sifting convention from the possibility of genuine biographical nuggets. Thus Ophelia's drowning in *Hamlet* and Sebastian's presumed death by water in *Twelfth Night* may just happen to feature in these two chronologically contiguous plays; yet they also mesh intimately with particular names and aspects from Shakespeare's domestic life— especially, of course, the death of Katherine Hamlet in 1579. Then again, perhaps we ought to consider the possibility that Hamnet drowned in the Avon. The awkward witness of *The Comedy of Errors* must make us somewhat skeptical about any connection, however, for with all its marine imagery it predates the boy's death. And in *Twelfth Night* and *The Tempest*, both written afterward, the "drowned" youths survive. If not for that, one might feel more justified in seeing a drowned son hinted at in the plays.

In *Twelfth Night*, the boy is resurrected; in *The Winter's Tale*, the little boy, Mamillius, dies while his baby sister survives. Shakespeare the father of daughters cannot bring himself to let the daughters of a father perish. After *Hamlet*, relationships between fathers and daughters become the most important domestic relationships in the plays. Perhaps both *Twelfth Night* and *Hamlet* reflect a wish fulfillment. Perhaps Shakespeare wrote *Hamlet* to complete business left unfinished by *Twelfth Night*. The twin comedy may well include Judith, but Hamnet was not Sebastian; Shakespeare could not bring him back from the dead like the separated twin in the play.

It may be the ineluctable reality of loss that led him to write a play about his dead son Hamnet; the death of his own father would be the prompt. Nearly six years had passed since Hamnet's death. In *Hamlet* Shakespeare now explores a fictional father-son relationship and turns particularly to the young man's relationship with his mother, which is profoundly troubling and suggestive. Hamnet died before he reached puberty, so it would be quite wrong to align him too closely with the Prince of Denmark. The same could not be said, however, about the Earl of Southampton whose mother, Mary, remarried not once but twice. His parents' marriage had been a traumatic one, riven by, among other things, the passionate Catholicism that landed his father in prison. Southampton's father accused his wife of adultery and died when the young Earl was just eight years old. Wriothesley was twenty-one—just of age—when his mother married again in 1594, at the height of his friendship with Shakespeare; he was twenty-five when she married for the third time. The young man must have eagerly discussed the 1594 remarriage with his poet friend and may have found it hard to accept. It was the countess's third husband, Sir William Harvey, who after the Countess of Southampton's death in 1607 married Cordell Annesley, the woman behind Lear's youngest daughter.

Tuesday, September 8, 1601, may have been the darkest of Shakespeare's life since Hamnet's death, for he buried his father at Holy Trinity that day. Shakespeare had striven hard to restore John's fortunes and had returned the former mayor to a position of respect. Father and son were probably close. One of the few references to John Shakespeare in the seventeenth century, by someone who apparently met him "in his shop," describes him as "a merry-cheeked old man that said Will was a good honest fellow, but he durst have cracked a jest with him at any time."* Apparently old John Shakespeare was not intimidated by either his son's success or his way with words. Will had inherited his father's business acumen, but unlike John he never came unstuck or needed to hide from creditors. John Shakespeare must have been a frequent visitor to New Place. He was in his late sixties by the time of the purchase; his son probably modeled garrulous old men like Shallow on him.

---

*Chambers (1930), vol. 2, p. 247.

During one of those visits John Shakespeare may have brought up a delicate matter, perhaps not unconnected with the Oldcastle and Falstaff business in the *Henry IV* plays. He and his wife had both passed well beyond the average Elizabethan life expectancy; it was time to make a will. That this former keeper of the borough accounts did so we should not doubt, even though the document has so far not been traced. From the subsequent fate of the Birthplace, it appears that he left the bulk of his estate to William as the firstborn son, while probably allowing Mary and Joan to remain in their home.

What provision John Shakespeare made for his other three sons we do not know, but we *think* we know that he made a further will, which did not dispose of his worldly belongings but rather entrusted his soul to the Catholic church. This is the so-called testament of John Shakespeare, a handwritten document of six leaves, which had been entrusted to Edmond Malone by a young contemporary, the amiable Reverend James Davenport (1787–1841). Davenport had it from a Stratford alderman, with whom it had been lodged years earlier by the master bricklayer who found it in the rafters of the Birthplace on April 29, 1757, while retiling the roof. The testament remains one of the most controversial topics in Shakespeare studies. We no longer have the original, and Malone, who had held it in his hands, went from believing in it to promising to expose it as a hoax. Fortunately, he printed the text, so at least we know what it said. It was what is known as a Borromeo will—that is, a Catholic "contract and testament of the soul." Such a will was drafted first by the revered Cardinal Carlo Borromeo of Milan in the 1570s, and copies entered England with the Campion mission of 1580. The testament found in the Birthplace corresponds in all essentials to another Borromeo will in English that surfaced intact in 1966. By means of such a will, an outwardly conformist Protestant could die in the old faith: he simply inserted his name into the prepared formula.

There is no doubt that the documents are genuine. The workmen who discovered them are almost certainly above suspicion, and no commercial gain was sought from the discovery, neither by the bricklayer nor by Thomas Hart, a direct descendant of Shakespeare's sister Joan who had commissioned the retiling, nor even by the local poet, draftsman, and amateur Shakespeare sleuth John Jordan. Inevitably, perhaps, Jordan's role in the story—his eagerness to be published, and his proffering a forged version to Malone of the missing first leaf—has aroused suspicion of the whole document. If the testament from Henley Street was a hoax, the forger was someone who had access to a genuine version of the testament, wrote it out with John Shakespeare's name inserted at every juncture, and then somehow managed to plant it in the rafters. But why would anyone do such a thing? Jordan can be ruled out as a suspect: he was eleven years old when the testament was discovered. He copied it twenty-seven years later, in 1784. The fact that he subsequently tried to fob off on Malone a forged copy of the will's missing first leaf has no bearing on the authenticity of the original document, which Jordan never owned. On balance, it appears that John Shakespeare intended to die in the Roman faith. That the will was not buried with him, as was the usual practice, suggests either that he changed his mind or else that for some reason the document could not be retrieved for his funeral on September 8. If anyone other than John and Mary Shakespeare knew the whereabouts in the house the formulary was kept, it would have been their eldest son and executor.

The odds are that John Shakespeare first received a copy of the formulary during the Campion mission, when the Jesuits stayed in Lapworth and elsewhere in the Midlands, including Shottery, perhaps even at the Badgers' next door to the Shakespeares, or else with the Wheelers or Whateleys. John probably hid the will shortly after taking possession of it. As the 1580s turned ever more violent and oppressive, he probably signed it and then hid it where no one would think to look, in the roof of the house. Catholics had become expert at creating hiding places. It is inconceivable that John Shakespeare would have forgotten about the testament, but it is equally hard to believe that Will and his mother would not have put it in John's coffin or tucked it into his winding sheet. Perhaps the times were once again too dangerous. For all we know, coffins were checked by the authorities for just such documents before being committed to the earth. Most secret Catholics of the period seem to have evaded detection and taken the wills with them to their graves, one reason so few have come to light.

It was barely seven months since Shakespeare's friend Augustine Phillips had pleaded not guilty on behalf of the Lord Chamberlain's Men after their performance of *Richard II*. Had a Catholic will been found now on Shakespeare's father, the consequences might have been grim. But why the family did not dispose of the incriminating document, we do not know. Perhaps they hoped to use the formulary for Mary Arden but then did not do so after her death. Once the original house was leased to the Hiccoxes, the will in the roof was beyond the family's reach. One wonders whether it gave Shakespeare an occasional headache to think that this potential time bomb, with his father's name on every page and starting each paragraph, was ticking away in the roof of his ancestral home.

Paragraph XII of the formulary is of particular interest for its doctrinal implications:

> *Item,* I John Shakespeare do in like manner pray and beseech all my dear friends, parents and kinsfolks, by the bowels of our Saviour Jesus Christ, that since it is uncertain what lot will befall me, *for fear notwithstanding lest by reason of my sins I be to pass and stay a long while in purgatory* [emphasis added], they will vouchsafe to assist and succour me with their holy prayers and satisfactory works, especially with the holy sacrifice of the mass, as being the most effectual means to deliver souls from their torments and pains; from the which, if I shall by God's gracious goodness and by their virtuous works be delivered, I do promise that I will not be ungrateful unto them for so great a benefit.

The wording and sentiment are utterly Catholic, as is the plea for intercessory prayers. The ghost of Hamlet's father returns to haunt his son from just such a prison house. The doctrinal confusion in *Hamlet*, between the Protestant student from Wittenberg and the restless Catholic soul of his father's ghost in Purgatory, is often seen as symptomatic of its period—rightly so, for Catholicism had been the one and only faith of a spiritually united country only two generations earlier. It seems, though, that Shakespeare had an intensely personal stake in the play, and not just because the old anonymous play *Hamlet,* which may have been the main source for Shakespeare's drama, happened to have a hero with the same name as his dead son.* Shakespeare must have seized on that in the first instance, of course, and then realized that it would allow him in some way to converse with his father across the grave. Perhaps, and even more radically, *Hamlet* may serve as Shakespeare's vehicle to come to terms with his own spiritual betrayal of his father. John Shakespeare did *not* take the Borromeo testament with him into eternity: perhaps that was because his son William refused, and perhaps he did so for ideological reasons as much as out of political astuteness. John Shakespeare's son may not have shared his faith, so that while John saw himself in Purgatory, his son's beliefs may have chimed much more with the powerful Anglican orthodoxy that prevailed in London. Protestants rejected purgatory, claiming that it lacked scriptural authority. Doctrinally, therefore, *Hamlet* performs a balancing act between the old and new faiths. Shakespeare's Prince is famously at "school in Wittenberg," the cradle of Protestantism, where Martin Luther had nailed his polemical theses to the door of the Schlosskirche in 1517. There is nothing of this in the source; it deliberately muddies the religious waters in the play.

Whatever doctrinal disputes he and his beloved father had in the privacy of the house in Henley Street, Shakespeare here is revisiting such scenes in a long play's journey into night, a play perhaps of old sorrows. Shakespeare's way of dealing with the tremendous loss of his father was to write a play in which a father's ghost appears to a son who is named after Shakespeare's own dead son. That the play was written after the summer of 1601 may be confirmed by the famous "little eyases" passage: when Rosencrantz refers mysteriously to "an aery of children, little eyases, that cry out on the top of the question and are most tyrannically clapped for," he is alluding to the competition for audiences in the summer of 1601 between the child companies and Ben Jonson on the one hand and the adult actors or "common players" and their writers on the other. This was the so-called War of the Theaters, a murky spat that pitted John Marston

---

*This play is commonly called the *ur-Hamlet* (that is, the original *Hamlet*) and was around as early as 1589. It is usually attributed to Thomas Kyd, the author of *The Spanish Tragedy*.

against Ben Jonson while also involving the dramatist Thomas Dekker. Shakespeare's reference to "little eyases" (fledgling hawks) seems to be his modest contribution to it. Rosencrantz's reference to the child actors is triggered by the arrival in Elsinore of "the tragedians of the city," who used to be Hamlet's favorites. When Hamlet inquires why they are touring, since they were better off staying put in the city and, presumably, at a permanent venue like the Globe, Rosencrantz replies: "I think their inhibition comes by the means of the late innovation." "Inhibition" means a prohibition from playing at their former venue, a circumstance with which Shakespeare was all too familiar. Decrees of inhibition issued by the Privy Council were rather more than a professional hazard. At the stroke of a pen, the Council could strip the players of their livelihoods, although it rarely did so because the players were well connected at court and the Lord Chamberlain in 1601–1602 sat on the Privy Council. It is quite possible that the "innovation" in *Hamlet* refers to a real episode, such as, for example, the Council's attempt on December 31, 1601, to enforce its earlier statute limiting the number of playhouses to two.

Hamlet was entered on the Stationers' Register on July 26, 1602, as "A book called the Revenge of Hamlet Prince of Denmark as it was lately acted by the Lord Chamberlain his servants." The second quarto, on which all modern texts are based, appeared in 1604, the same year as Marlowe's posthumously published *Dr. Faustus,* a play whose intellectual restlessness chimes with the moral chaos of *Hamlet.* Shakespeare's great tragedy voices deep anxiety about the human condition, particularly about how all human life inextricably entails its own cessation, so that death is the one and only absolute certainty about life, and how death may indeed be the alpha and omega. Crammed with allusions to the Bible, *Hamlet* is yet relentlessly secular. It is a deeply radical work, a humanist tragedy. When Hamlet mourns for his father, Gertrude comforts him with the thought that "all that lives must die, / Passing through nature to eternity," while Claudius remarks that the "common theme" of humankind and nature is the "death of fathers." Claudius is good on the loss of fathers.

As regards traces from real life, it is of some interest that the plot of the murder, the poisoning of Hamlet's father in his orchard, should echo, though perhaps not directly, the murder of the person who sold New Place to Shakespeare. Shakespeare probably wrote *Hamlet* in New Place, or else in a room backstage at the new Globe, or perhaps even in his lodgings at the Mountjoys'. Lent of 1602, which was probably when most of the writing was under way, started on February 17, with Easter falling on April 4. A fortnight earlier, Shakespeare had probably played in *Twelfth Night* before an audience that contained members of his family. Now he would have time to complete the hugely long *Hamlet,* whose sheer scale may be linked to its commemorative drive. The iconic status of Shakespeare's great tragedies should not distract from their location in time, which alerts us that three of them almost certainly constitute responses to personal bereavement, *Romeo and Juliet* to the loss of Hamnet, *Hamlet* and *Coriolanus* to the deaths of his son and his parents. The links between Shakespeare's life and literary productions could hardly be more direct. Far from these being the exceptions, they are the norm. That this writer rather than any other dramatist of the period should have written an autobiographical cycle makes perfect sense. His plays follow the same pattern of self-expression. No writer of the period was more anxious than Shakespeare to be heard. One wonders whether, like his friend Ben Jonson, he kept a commonplace diary.

There was a time when the line "To be, or not to be, that is the question" did not exist. We do not know on what day Shakespeare wrote it, let alone what hour. It could have been in the winter of 1601–1602, perhaps over Christmas, when all of Christian England was ritually pondering the birth of Jesus or the meaning of all human life; or on December 31, 1601, when Shakespeare might have been taking stock, perhaps in amazement and alarm at quite how much had happened since "this time last year." One day, Shakespeare wrote the most quoted line in English poetry. Since it was first spoken by Burbage on the stage of the Globe, it has gone around the world, until it no longer belongs to Shakespeare any more than his plays do. They have acquired their own histories of performance and interpretation and are now almost totally divorced from the moment of their imaginative conception. And yet common sense tells us that these timeless plays also bear, buried beneath the surface, historical traces that belong firmly to the moment when they were written, traces from both the wider history of the nation and Shakespeare's life.

Such contingent data need not detract from the plays' imaginative integrity any more than Leonardo da Vinci's famous soup getting cold detracts from the validity of his geometry. Shakespeare wrote at a desk, surrounded, presumably, by books. He would have broken off from writing to eat and drink, just as Leonardo da Vinci left off his geometric meditations at some point to eat his cooling soup. The fact that Leonardo actually jotted this down on the same piece of paper that contained his mathematics brilliantly collapses the quotidian world and the timeless zone of creation. Everything that has ever been written, painted, or sculpted was made somewhere in time. If we could know exactly when "To be, or not to be" was written, we would hardly decline that knowledge on the basis that it might strip the mystique from great literature. We would love to know what Shakespeare had just eaten, where he was sitting, what was piled up on his desk, and all the other contingent details of that point in time. Whether Shakespeare wrote the most famous literary line in the language late at night or first thing in the morning, or at 11:14 A.M., it should matter to the biographer and the literary scholar alike. In 1602, Shakespeare's father had recently died, his son, Hamnet, was dead, and his closest friend languished in the Tower while that friend's master, the most glamorous soldier in the land, had lost his head on Tower Hill. Little wonder that *Hamlet* is soaked in darkness and pain.

It is also drenched in angst about middle-aged female sexuality. Hamlet's mother, Gertrude, mysteriously marries Hamlet's uncle quickly after her first husband's death and thus becomes the most sexually imagined woman in Shakespeare. Hamlet provides an unsettling amount of detail about his mother's sexual behavior, all of which he has to conjecture, though he cruelly hits the mark with those wanton pinches, "reechy kisses," paddling in necks, and words of endearment. He urges his mother desist from living in "the rank sweat of an enseamèd bed," from living "stewed in corruption, honeying and making love," from dwelling in "the nasty sty" that is Claudius's bed. It does not get much more graphic than this, and nowhere do we come closer to middle-aged sex in an Elizabethan bed than in the fourth scene of Act III of *Hamlet*. Since Shakespeare is forever breaching the boundaries between life and art, one may wonder whether the mother of the younger Hamlet having sex with the elder Hamlet's younger brother might reflect a real event. In other words, we should consider the possibility that the other Hamlet's mother, Anne Hathaway, may have betrayed Shakespeare sexually with one of his younger brothers, so that when Hamlet remonstrates with Gertrude Shakespeare may have imagined his son arguing with Anne.

That Shakespeare committed adultery in London is almost universally accepted; that Anne in turn might have cheated on him during his long absences, and perhaps with his own wayward brother, should not be ruled out. Perhaps one of his brothers made a pass at her during one of Will's prolonged absences. Perhaps Mrs. Shakespeare turned him down, which would rhyme with the ghost's instructing Hamlet not to hurt his mother. Rowe reports that in an early performance of the play, Shakespeare himself played the vengeful ghost of the old King dispatched while sleeping in his orchard. There is no reason to doubt this; by having a character who shared his own son's name address the lines hurled at Gertrude by Hamlet in the closet scene, Shakespeare may have raised the stakes considerably. Whatever lies beneath all this, Shakespeare must have been keenly aware of a special burden attaching to the fact that these words were spoken by Hamlet. There is of course also considerable affection for Gertrude in the play, and her "adultery" is so only in a strictly biblical sense, since the Bible prohibits sex with a sister-in-law. English common law did not. This is not the place to develop ideas about the understanding of adultery in *Hamlet*, or to consider whether Claudius and Gertrude were sexually involved before the death of old Hamlet, whose ghost calls Claudius "adulterate beast." Nothing in the play leads one to believe that any such relation ever existed. If anything, the love affair or marriage of Claudius and Gertrude, not only its unexplained speed, is one of the play's mysteries, as the obsession with sex and adultery is a mystery of *King Lear*.

Younger brothers are cast as villains in Shakespeare after *Hamlet*.

Whereas in *As You Like It* an elder sibling persecuted Orlando, it is the other way around in *King Lear* and in *The Tempest*. Prospero, an unmistakable alter ego for Shakespeare even in the most cautious interpretation, is betrayed by a cruel younger brother who remains completely unredeemed. Edgar in *King Lear* is double-crossed by a younger brother, who moreover carries the name of Shakespeare's baby brother, Edmund. It is surprising that Shakespeare did not make more earlier of relationships between brothers, given that he was one of four. That he was close to Gilbert seems clear from the way he delegated business affairs to him; Edmund may still have lived in Henley Street as a twenty-two-year-old glover at the time of *Hamlet* in 1602. This leaves us Richard to consider, Will's junior by ten years. Unlike the other Shakespeare brothers he appears in no London record to have surfaced so far. He crops up once in the so-called Stratford Bawdy Court files in 1608, but, though this would seem like a gift to the biographer, we don't know his offense. He may have done no worse than fail to receive the sacrament, or not cease to trade in time for church. He was fined twelve pence, the money to go to the poor of Stratford.

At the time of *Hamlet,* Anne Hathaway was around forty-six years old, if we read her gravestone right, and Richard was twenty-six. The Shakespeares had now lived in New Place for five years; it is reasonable to think that Richard, Gilbert, and perhaps Edmund also lived there then. Joan, as we know from the documentary record, stayed on in Henley Street, perhaps to look after her widowed mother; also in Henley Street was Joan's husband, William Hart, whom she had married around 1599. Their first son, William, was born in 1600; three more were to come. As the firstborn male of the family, Shakespeare had inherited the Henley Street house. It was too big for the few people who lived there now and he apparently decided to lease out the eastern parts of the premises, what is now called the woolshop. First, however, and perhaps with a future let of the west side of the house in mind, he seems to have added a house to the back of the western edge of the main rectangular frame. This is known today as Joan Hart's cottage. It may indeed have been intended to create enough space to keep the remaining family comfortable while surrendering a large enough house to the new tenants.

To build, expand, or convert with a view to letting seems to have been common practice at the time. Shakespeare needed to look no further than James Burbage's conversion into a boardinghouse of the Great Barn in Holywell for a paradigm. (But Burbage's project caused Giles Allen to complain about its shoddiness.)

Whatever reconstruction Shakespeare carried out, it seems to have taken some time. Perhaps his mother and sister were reluctant to surrender the big house in which they had lived all their lives. What happened next was that Shakespeare let out part of Henley Street to Lewis Hiccox. He had inherited the Hiccoxes, Lewis and Thomas, as tenants on May 1, 1602, when Gilbert, acting on his behalf, paid out a vast sum of money for land and tithes in Old Stratford. Shakespeare spread his local investments further, toward the end of September, when he bought a quarter acre of land with a cottage down from the King's New School and opposite the New Place gardens from the manor of Rowington, held by the countess of Warwick. By 1603 Hiccox had been granted a license to earn his living as a publican and innkeeper in the house in Henley Street. He called his establishment the Maidenhead and eventually the Swan and Maidenhead. "Swan" was clearly something of a selling point, since there seem to have been at least two other Swan tavern-inn combinations in town. By the time Lewis Hiccox opened in Henley Street, his kinsman Thomas (perhaps his brother) had moved to premises opposite the Birthplace. He had earlier (October 31, 1599) been granted a lease to build "a fair house" on the ground where the Shakespeares' neighbor John Cox had lived for forty-one years, on condition that the house in this fire-ravaged area would be standing by the autumn of 1602. When the Maidenhead opened in 1603, Lewis and Thomas Hiccox were neighbors across the street, and Shakespeare had become the landlord of an inn and public house.

At least there does not seem to have been any unseemly rush to "maximize" the use of the Henley Street house. The passage of time suggests that there had been major alterations to the property, as there would have to be to make the place into a functional inn. Probably all of Shakespeare's family except for his mother, his sister, and his sister's husband and children moved to New Place. Large though the house was, it would have been virtually impossible to keep an affair hidden. The house was now occupied by Anne, her two daughters, and, probably, three uncles, one of whom was only three years older than Susanna; most likely, there were servants, too. If the analogy with the play holds up, it suggests that Anne stayed loyal to her husband and family, since Gertrude clearly has no idea that Claudius murdered old Hamlet. If one of his younger brothers betrayed Shakespeare's trust, Richard is the most likely suspect.

With *Hamlet,* Shakespeare seems to want to move on from the "sweet prince" his son; to commemorate his adored father; to pay tribute to the glass of fashion and nobility incarcerated in the Tower; and, perhaps, to come to terms with a domestic drama in New Place. Adultery becomes a defining feature of Shakespearian drama now, and particularly in *Othello, King Lear,* and *Antony and Cleopatra*—this last gloriously cutting loose from any traditional moral anchorage, and in ways that defy rational understanding. After *Hamlet,* Shakespeare launched into a series of dark and obsessive plays in which female sexuality is confronted as something dangerous and destructive. Several plays from around this time, including the late comedies *All's Well That Ends Well* and *Measure for Measure,* show a fascination with complex and confused forms of desire, as in the so-called bed trick. A male character expects to find a sexually desired woman in a bed in the dark of night and to possess her illicitly, but in each case the object of desire is replaced by his intended wife. He experiences the thrill of bad behavior, but the sex is retrospectively legitimated by the marriages that conclude the plays. Sexual passion is, of course, a leitmotif of Shakespeare's comedies; *All's Well* and *Measure for Measure* are no exception. Nevertheless, the latter, Shakespeare's very last comedy, is the most unusual. Much of its action takes place in a prison, and some on death row. It ends with a man disguised as a friar marrying a young woman who was a novice of the Clares, one of the strictest monastic orders and bound by a vow of silence. The other unions are forced: Lucio weds his prostitute girlfriend, Mistress Kate Keepdown, who "was with child by him in the Duke's time," and poor Mariana marries Angelo, who first jilted her and then possessed her in a "moated grange" while mistaking her for someone else.

Most important, the play's plot revolves around a young man,

Claudio, who is sentenced to death for impregnating a young woman, Juliet. Claudio and Juliet are engaged to marry, in what Claudio calls "a true contract"—that is, they have pledged their troth in front of witnesses, and are therefore legally bound in marriage, although the union requires church sanction before it can be sexually consummated. As Claudio puts it, "You know the lady; she is fast my wife,/Save that we do the denunciation lack/Of outward order." Claudio is sentenced to death for following legitimate natural instincts. Shakespeare is dramatizing a version of his own past sexual life, and well may one ask why he was doing so exactly now. The answer is that he was almost certainly engaged in a clandestine love affair, and it may have brought back memories of an eighteen-year-old boy becoming a father years earlier, before he had had time to become a man.

Audiences and readers are in no doubt that Claudio and Juliet merit our compassion, and particularly by comparison with the play's two fundamentalists, Claudio's sister, the novice Isabella, and Angelo, the "precise" deputy of the Duke. Their views of sexuality are extreme; Isabella's is steeped in the rhetoric of Catholic martyrdom. When she is asked to "lay down the treasure of your body," she replies that she will under no circumstances surrender her "body up to shame." Rather, she would prefer to "strip myself to death as to a bed/That longing have been sick for," and to wear as rubies "th' impression of keen whips." This is the rhetoric of John Gerard, of William Weston, and of Catholic poets like Richard Crashaw. Shakespeare seems to be deeply suspicious of it; though he grants Isabella the need to preserve her dignity, her absoluteness frightens him, while the fallible sexuality of Claudio and Juliet acknowledges the enormous and inescapable importance of the human body. It is with them that the author empathizes.

Isabella is the only major character in Shakespeare to be so named. In Shakespeare's source, a play by George Whetstone, she is called Cassandra. Shakespeare either plucked her name out of the world at large or drew from his own family's history. Wroxall Abbey, a few miles north of Stratford, had had a prioress by the name of Dame Isabella Shakespeare toward the end of the fifteenth century. It is hard not to imagine that there must have been some link in

Shakespeare's mind between the absolute and saintly Isabella of *Measure for Measure* and this presumptive ancestor. In Shakespeare's own lifetime, Dame Joan Shakespeare was sub-prioress of the same abbey; she had died in 1571, when he was seven. He must have known of the Shakespeare abbesses, he who was so keenly interested in English history and his own family. If the Shakespeares of Henley Street and Snitterfield were related to the Shakespeares of Wroxall, as seems likely, then the family of the future dramatist must have felt bereft of an important part of its heritage by the Reformation. This may help explain his choice of the name Oldcastle a few years earlier.

23

Affairs of the Body and Heart: 1602–1604

o complicate his life further, Shakespeare proba-
bly began a love affair around this time with a
woman named Jane Davenant. How they first
met is not documented, although it is likely that they became acquainted while he played on Bankside in the late 1590s before she
moved to Oxford in 1601.* Jane Sheppard, or Jennet as she was also
known, was baptised at St. Margaret's in Westminster on November
1, 1568. She married John Davenant, a prominent wine merchant, in
1593 at age twenty-five and, according to parish records, suffered
several miscarriages between then and the move to Oxford. She was
Shakespeare's junior by four and a half years.

In the 1590s, the Davenants lived up from the Vintry at Three
Cranes Wharf, directly east of the famous inlet of Queenhythe,
which survives to this day. Three Cranes was the prime site in London for the unloading of wine barges. A notable tavern, also called
the Three Cranes, stood here; Jonson mentions it in the same breath
as the Mitre and the Mermaid in *Bartholomew Fair*. It may well have
been a watering hole for players crossing the river homeward after
their shows in Bankside. Three Cranes Wharf and its church of St.
James Garlickhythe stood in a straight line across the river from the

---

*Perhaps Shakespeare met her through the Mountjoys, since Marie Mountjoy
and Jane Davenant's brother Tom were in the same branch at court and Shakespeare
may already have been on friendly terms with the Mountjoys through his friend
Richard Field. This would be long before he moved in with the Mountjoys.

Globe; the Davenants' house was directly across the Thames from the Rose and Globe.* Living near the Thames and immediately south of the church of St. James, the Davenants must have been acutely aware of the traffic across the water and of the Bankside playing venues. Contemporary rumor had it that while they lived in London the Davenants keenly supported the theaters, and Shakespeare in particular.

There are two important seventeenth-century witnesses to the story of Shakespeare and Jane Davenant: John Aubrey and the antiquarian Anthony Wood. Both men knew the Davenant children, who were born in Oxford after 1600. Aubrey (1626–97) was twenty years younger than the playwright William Davenant, Wood (1632–95) twenty-six years younger. Aubrey famously wrote in 1681 that

> Sir William Davenant Knight Poet Laureate was born in . . . the City of Oxford, at the Crown tavern. His father was John Davenant a vintner there, a very grave and discreet citizen. His mother was a very beautiful woman, and of a very good wit and of conversation extremely agreeable. . . . Master William Shakespeare was wont to go into Warwickshire once a year and did commonly in his journey lie at this house in Oxon: where he was exceedingly respected. [I have heard parson Robert D{avenant} say that Master William Shakespeare here gave him a hundred kisses]. Now Sir William would sometimes when he was pleasant over a glass of wine with his most intimate friends . . . say that it seemed to him that he writ with the very spirit that did Shakespeare, and seemed contented enough to be thought his son. He would tell them the story as above [in which way his mother had a very light report, whereby she was called a whore].

Anthony Wood did not disagree with much of this, although it may be he who crossed out the reference to Robert Davenant's being kissed by Shakespeare and the reference to Jane Davenant being

---

*Today Southwark Bridge thrusts out south over the Thames from what used to be Three Cranes Lane.

called a whore.* Wood adds, in his rehash of Aubrey, that William's father, John Davenant, was "an admirer and lover of plays and play-makers, especially Shakespeare, who frequented his house in his journeys between Warwickshire and London." This information may have come from one of the Davenants, since Wood later frequented the tavern that the Davenant family had owned for the first twenty years of the seventeenth century. Aubrey paints a woman of impressive personal magnetism, who may in her own way have been as accomplished as the musical Emilia Lanier.

We saw how in January 1598 Jane Davenant, like Emilia Lanier, sought out Forman. At the time he lived in Lambeth. Jane had recently lost a baby and wanted to know whether she could become pregnant again. Perhaps after several miscarriages she was growing desperate, particularly now that she was nearly thirty. It is unlikely that her affair with Shakespeare had begun yet, though he had extricated himself from both Southampton and the Dark Lady well before.

He was based in Stratford again, but by an ironic twist it may have been just this new domesticity and Stratford that brought him and Jane Davenant together. After buying New Place in 1597, he must have wanted to live there as much as possible, for it was his house and his family home. As well as returning for Lent Shakespeare may have stayed for shorter breaks. He was rich now; he could afford the best horses and, as the Candlemas timing of *Twelfth Night* seems to indicate, he may have brought his family down to London from time to time to entertain them with his art, a Prospero showing off tokens of his vanity. Also his septuagenarian father may have been ailing for a while before dying in September 1601. Will was always close to his father. It is unthinkable that he would not have wanted to see more of him at just the time when he stood to lose him. He now had the means after all to ride to Stratford almost whenever the mood took him.

Shakespeare had a choice of routes to Stratford; in the year of his

---

*Chambers (1930), vol. 2, p. 254. The brackets in the quotation are in Chambers and are his way of signaling that these passages are scored out in the original (*Bodleian Aubrey MS*. 6 f.46); "perhaps by Anthony Wood," according to Chambers's headnote to the extract.

father's death, the Davenants moved to Oxford, and Shakespeare began traveling through it. This now probably became his only route, and there is no reason for thinking that he stayed anyplace but where seventeenth-century rumor put him, at the Davenants' Crown Inn on Cornmarket. When the King's Men performed *Hamlet* at Oxford and Cambridge, Shakespeare and his fellow players must have met up with the Davenants on the occasion of the Oxford premiere. In return, this apparently debonair couple of theater lovers would undoubtedly have continued their support for the company they knew from Bankside. The Davenants had chosen their location well: the preferred venue of players on tour in Oxford was directly opposite their new home. It seems that players usually "lodged at the galleried King's Head inn in Cornmarket almost opposite Davenant's inn" and then staged their plays in the inn yard.*

It was around this time in 1602 that Shakespeare moved in with the Mountjoys. That the Mountjoys, the Davenants, the Sheppards, and the Fields all knew one another, that Marie Mountjoy was having an affair with a silversmith and consulted Forman at just the time when Emilia Lanier stopped seeing him—this suggests that they all belonged to the same London circle of writers, actors, publishers, printers, and craftsmen attached to the court, and that is why Shakespeare took lodgings with the Mountjoys. Within a year or so, Shakespeare's friend Ben Jonson started a five-year spell of residence in Blackfriars, so that he and Shakespeare henceforth lived in almost the same neighborhood. Jonson's play *Sejanus*, which dates from around 1604, starred Shakespeare, who is mentioned prominently in its cast list and that of *Every Man in His Humour* in the Jonson Folio of 1616. In the months and years after 1602, Shakespeare's journey from London to Stratford, with its stopover in Oxford, may have become something eagerly to anticipate, particularly if his landlords in London were close friends of the hosts of the Crown in Oxford.† Perhaps

---

*Edmond, p. 23.

†Malone notes that he had "Another curious document in my possession, which will be produced in the History of his Life [Malone's projected biography of Shakespeare], affords the strongest presumptive evidence that he continued to reside in Southwark to the year 1608" (Chambers [1930], vol. 2, p. 88). Unlike Malone, however,

Shakespeare needed just that kind of sustenance when so much else in his life was threatening to fall apart.

Shakespeare wrote *Othello,* his brooding tragedy about the dark side of human sexuality, while living with the Mountjoys. A small but significant strand of the play's plot reaches back right into his landlord's household. For once we have hard documentary evidence: Shakespeare's own testimony in a lawsuit concerning a dowry, the records of which survive in the papers of the Court of Requests. Ten years after the event, Shakespeare testified that he had lived with the Mountjoys in 1602 and that Marie Mountjoy had enlisted him as a go-between in the proposed marriage between her daughter Mary and the Mountjoys' apprentice Stephen Belott. The legalese of the relevant passage sounds as dry as sawdust:

> And further this deponent [Shakespeare] sayeth that the said defendant's wife [Marie Mountjoy] did solicit and entreat this deponent to move and persuade the complainant [Belott] to effect the said marriage and accordingly this deponent did move and persuade the complainant thereunto.

So here we have the thirty-eight-year-old William Shakespeare wooing Stephen Belott on behalf of his landlord's wife. Presumably she had picked him for this delicate errand because he had a way with words and, of course, because by now he was no ordinary lodger but a renowned dramatist. From their address in the City of London we may be fairly certain that the Mountjoys were comfortably off and that the master of New Place did not lodge in a garret

---

we know from Shakespeare's own testimony given during the Belott-Mountjoy lawsuit that he lived at the Mountjoys' in the City of London by probably 1602. Malone was unaware of any documents placing Shakespeare in the City of London in the early seventeenth century, because those concerning the Mountjoy dispute were discovered in the National Archives only in 1910. These findings do not impugn Malone's integrity; instead we should seriously consider the likely existence in the eighteenth century of a document that placed Shakespeare in Southwark, even though he may not have lived there. Perhaps it was another set of tithe requests, or perhaps a "token book" that listed the names of those in the borough who were expected to attend church.

but probably had an entire floor to himself.* The arid language of the documents and their practical concerns about the size of the dowry and also about a promissory note regarding the estate expected after old Mountjoy's death are of their time. Somewhat disconcertingly for a trained actor and intellectual magpie, Shakespeare ten years on could not remember any details about the sums that were involved.†

A writer who recycled his work because its motifs and rhetoric stayed in his mind, a man with flair for business and a good head for figures, ought to have been able to cast his mind back accurately to ten years earlier, when the negotiations with young Belott involved the vast sum of two hundred pounds. The fact that the written record includes two occasions on which Shakespeare failed to provide an answer after being consulted for information, when his very profession for twenty years consisted of remembering lines as well as writing them, is baffling. It almost suggests that he did not want to cooperate in either case, and it leaves an uncomfortable impression of someone who seemed disengaged from real life when it suited him to be so. "What, Michael Cassio, / That came a-wooing with you?" Desdemona gently chides Othello when she is trying to coax him into restoring Cassio's command, and here we have Will Shakespeare in real life wooing the man Belott on behalf of someone else, another crossover from life into art. We know of this only because Shakespeare was asked to testify in a minor lawsuit a decade later. Stephen Belott married Mary Mountjoy on November 19, 1604. Having been instrumental in bringing about the wedding, Shakespeare probably attended it. The Belotts ended up living in the house of the very same George Wilkins who would go on to collaborate with Shakespeare on *Pericles,* and who also testified during the Mountjoy-Belott suit.

The Belott-Mountjoy tug-of-war and marriage coincide almost exactly with *Othello,* which was performed at court in November 1604. In the Italian source, Giraldi Cinthio's *Hecatommithi,* the blame

---

*For the kind of house that Shakespeare may have lodged in while at the Mountjoys', see Wood, p. 249.

† Shapiro (2005), pp. 215–16.

for the tragedy is laid partly at least at the door of Disdemona's father who, we read, "had given her a name of unlucky augury": Disdemona in Greek means "unfortunate." The ill omen is compounded by the Italian resonance of the young Venetian's name, *démona* meaning female devil (whereas Shakespeare's plangent "-demona" seems to chime mournfully with the character of Othello's wife). Shakespeare supplied all the other names in the play. In *Hecatommithi*, the Othello character is called the Moor or *il capitano Moro*, while Iago is simply the Ensign; Bianca, Michael Cassio, and Emilia are all Shakespeare's. Juliet's ingenuous question about the arbitrary link between external reality and linguistic signifier—"What's in a name? That which we call a rose / By any other word would smell as sweet"—applies more widely to Shakespeare's works. His names, unlike those in Jonsonian comedy, are rarely generic, except for the Marinas, Perditas, and Mirandas of the last plays. There are few Subtles, Faces, Volpones, or Corbaccios in Shakespeare. The nomenclature of *Othello*, a play in which Shakespeare supplied all the names except one, might therefore not only guide our perception of the plays but also contain clues about his life. The names in *Othello* cut both ways: on the one hand they are literary, imaginative, and internal, in that the Moor and his Venetian wife seem to be doomed to tragedy by their names, while on the other hand Emilia may step into the play from the real world and thus participate in an internal dialogue between Shakespeare and himself.

The most mystifying and revealing cross-over from real life, however, connects the play back to Stratford. It occurs in one of Iago's replies to Desdemona. Desdemona has asked him about what kind of praise he would heap on a deserving woman. He answers with "She that was ever fair and never proud," and then, among the attributes of feminine virtue, he includes "She that in wisdom never was so frail / To change the cod's head for the salmon's tail." This passage is commonly labeled obscure, because it seems to evoke a lost fishy idiom. Clearly a bawdy joke is concealed by the locution, "tail" being a word Shakespeare repeatedly uses for the female genitals, as in Petruchio's "What, with my tongue in your tail?" Cods' heads similarly carry specifically masculine sexual meanings. Heaven forbid that the passage should allude, as it seems to do, to lesbian aberrations, to fair women sometimes preferring tail of salmon to head of cod. The word "salmon" occurs three times in Shakespeare, including the famous salmons in the rivers of Monmouth and Macedon in *Henry V.* He would have associated "salmons" first and foremost with a part of sixteenth-century Old Stratford known as Salmon Tail and Salmon Jole, to the west of Bull Lane and verging on today's Sanctus Street. The history of these place-names is obscure. There may have been salmon ponds here in medieval times, when this entire area was farmed by monks from Old Stratford and the former priests' house, the College, near Holy Trinity. In Middle English, and still in Shakespeare's time, the word "jole" denoted the head of a fish, and hence "the head and shoulders of salmon, sturgeon, or ling" (*Oxford English Dictionary*). In Stratford, therefore, the tail and head of salmon sat side by side.

Shakespeare may be substituting a Stratfordism for a common English idiom of the period. Since almost no one would understand a reference to Salmon Tail, it may be meant to identify the speaker with a private mnemonic signature. Shakespeare might have inserted such a signature if he himself decided to play Iago, that most intellectually manipulative role, ever orchestrating, pulling strings, deviously destructive, consumed by envy and sexual obsession. Toward the end of the play, when Othello realizes the enormity of what Iago has made him do, he says: "I look down towards his feet, but that's a fable. / If that thou be'st a devil, I cannot kill thee." The devil was commonly thought to be cloven-footed or clubfooted. Othello's lines suggest either that Iago has a clubfoot and that Othello should therefore have guessed that he was the devil, or that he is expecting to see a cloven foot because to be so wicked Iago surely had to be the devil incarnate. If Shakespeare was lame and cast in the role of Iago, Othello's bewildered remark would carry a special resonance for him, beyond that of the role in the play of the sex-obsessed Iago. Iago's creator may have felt the pangs of conscience over his sexual relationship with a friend's wife, Jane Davenant.

Iago is famously all of twenty-eight years old, whereas Shakespeare was forty when he wrote *Othello.* It is worth noting this, because in that most flamboyant play about guilt-free middle-aged adultery, *Antony and Cleopatra,* Shakespeare and the Roman *imperator* are exactly the same age, forty-two. If the rhyming of Antony's age with Shakespeare's were to guide our perception of what role Shakespeare played in *Othello*, it would make him the Moor rather than Iago. As it happens, we know that the star of the company, Richard Burbage, played Othello. It is unlikely that anybody else would assume that demanding part during his lifetime, which outlasted Shakespeare's.

Another aspect of Iago may connect guiltily with Shakespeare: his latent homosexuality. When Othello requests "a living reason" from Iago to expose Desdemona's betrayal, Iago relates a fantastical tale: "I lay with Cassio lately," he starts, and then explains how he was kept awake by toothache and thus overheard Cassio talking in his sleep. Convinced that the body lying next to him was Desdemona's, Cassio gripped and wrung Iago's hand, kissed him hard "as if he plucked up kisses by the roots" from Iago's lips, then laid his leg over Iago's thigh and, while sighing, kissed him and cursed the fate that gave her to the Moor. Othello's response to this perverse fiction is to exclaim "O, monstrous, monstrous!," as Iago's recital indeed is. Heterosexual intimacy is not Iago's forte. Instead, he is the play's chief peddler of pornographic fantasies. It is significant that his marriage to Emilia has not produced offspring although in *Hecatommithi* the Iago character is the father of a three-year-old daughter, whom Disdemona adores. One day the Ensign takes the daughter to her and, while she presses the little girl to her breast, he steals her delicately embroidered handkerchief, a present from the Moor. Iago's barren marriage and his aura of homosexuality further set him apart from benign nature. *Othello* resembles *The Merchant of Venice* to the extent that both plays feature men who cannot move in harmony with the natural heterosexual order of being: Antonio is not allowed into the magic circle of coupledom symbolized by the rings that he extracted from Bassanio, while Gratiano (who in *Othello* returns as Desdemona's uncle) gave his wife Nerissa's ring to Nerissa disguised as a lawyer's clerk. The last two lines of the play are Gratiano's "Well, while I live I'll fear no other thing / So sore as keeping safe Nerissa's ring." That is, he will be on guard lest someone else get hold of Nerissa's ring (her vagina) and cuckold him. Antonio's final line in *The Merchant of Venice* is "I am dumb," that is, silent, while

Iago's last two lines similarly promise that the rest will be silence: "Demand me nothing. What you know, you know. / From this time forth I never will speak word." The silent stoicism of gay men in normative heterosexual cultures may be all that Antonio and Iago share—except, perhaps, for the fact that both parts were written by Shakespeare for himself, or inspired by his own ambiguous sexual self, or both. If Shakespeare wrote the part of Iago for himself, he chose a hugely demanding role. His acting career may have been underestimated thanks to Rowe's comment that he distinguished himself "not as an extraordinary actor." He obviously played throughout his career; and though he never climbed the peaks of Burbage and Alleyn, neither, it seems, did anybody else except famous "clowns" of the period like Tarlton, Kemp, and Armin.

If we accept for a moment that Shakespeare may have played Iago, then calling Iago's wife Emilia acquires a logic and momentum of its own. Though we must concede the intrinsic circularity of the deductive process, Emilia in *Othello* reflects aspects of the character of Shakespeare's mistress as we reconstructed her from the Sonnets and Forman's diary. What there is of Emilia Lanier in the Forman papers from 1597 suggests clearly that she was hugely ambitious, ostensibly for her husband but ultimately for herself, too, of course. Her proceeding to become one of the first English women poets in the seventeenth century marks her as independent-minded and suggests that to some extent she lived by her own rules. Shakespeare's choice of name for Iago's wife was probably inspired by the one Venetian woman he knew, who happened to be called Emilia and whose views on married faith may have chimed with the views the character Emilia expresses to Desdemona. We are in the scene of the willow song, toward the end of Act IV, and Desdemona has just asked Emilia whether she would commit adultery, "do such a deed for all the world." Emilia's response is that she would "not do such a thing for a joint ring, nor for measures of lawn, nor for gowns, petticoats, nor caps, nor any petty exhibition; but for all the whole world? Ud's pity, who would not make her husband a cuckold to make him a monarch? I should venture purgatory for't." Emilia speaks the most pragmatic lines about sex and adultery of any woman in Shakespeare.

It may be dangerous to draw close analogies between reality and fiction, but when there are good reasons for suspecting that they exist we should not shy away from acknowledging them and pondering their implications. In the case of the two Venetian plays, *The Merchant of Venice* (1598) and *Othello* (1604), we may well wonder whether Shakespeare would have chosen different themes had he not been involved with a Jewish Venetian woman. Emilia was, moreover, a musician, which may have contributed to the preoccupation with music as the lovers rest in Belmont at the end of *The Merchant of Venice*. In *Othello* the maritime city of Venice, which was mapped for us in the earlier play with regard to the Rialto and its customs, business traditions, and ethnic mix, is revisited, again with careful attention to social and political detail. Venice for Shakespeare is a real place, one that he seems to know intimately. If Shakespeare had traveled to Italy, it is Venice that he would have visited: that much is clear from the plays.

The use of Emilia Lanier's name in *Othello* and the fact that she is married to Iago makes one wonder further about him. The character clearly comes from somewhere inside Shakespeare's head in the first instance, but the name is perplexing. It is notoriously hard to pronounce in English, whether as a trisyllabic "I-a-go" or as two syllables starting with an "ia" dipthong. The most famous Iago is Santiago, as in Santiago de Compostela, the revered Catholic shrine in northwestern Spain dedicated to the Apostle James. The year in which *Othello* was written also heralded the era of King James I. Shakespeare would engage the new Stuart dynasty in *Macbeth* two years later, but for him to use the first name in the kingdom in his first play of the first full year of the new reign and apply it to a pornography-spewing, psychopathic schemer seems reckless. If we are right about Iago's homosexuality, then Shakespeare's use of Iago/James becomes downright defiant, since all the actors must have known from their contacts at court that the new King was at least bisexual.

Its awkward pronunciation makes Iago's name as elusive as the character is opaque. Even so, one wonders whether the King did not balk during the play's first recorded court performance, in November 1604. It was not so long ago that the company had a brush with the law over *Richard II.* James I's response to *Othello* is not recorded; perhaps he was mollified by the play's homage to his poem "Lepanto," about the famous naval defeat of the Turks in 1571. The poem had been published in a new edition in 1603. Within two months of his accession to the throne of England, James had turned the Lord Chamberlain's Men into the King's Men by royal patent. Now they were safer from the City of London's occasionally heavyhanded regulation. Also, James's first act as England's monarch had been to free Southampton, a further indication perhaps of a sympathetic disposition toward players. For whatever reason, Iago did not trigger another Oldcastle fiasco; *Othello* slipped comfortably and unchallenged into the Shakespeare canon and Folio.

On the royal license of the King's Men, Shakespeare follows only Lawrence Fletcher (a former "comediane serviteur" to King James in Scotland); he precedes Burbage, Phillips, and the other members of the company. This prominence may have been due to the intercession and renewed patronage of the newly released Southampton. Within less than a year of their licensing, the King's Men were issued with four and a half yards of "red cloth," enough for a doublet and breeches each to be worn while processing in James's coronation. In the Account by the Master of the Great Wardrobe, Shakespeare is listed first, ahead of Phillips and Fletcher, Heminges and Burbage. These royal charters and accounts demonstrate that Shakespeare had truly arrived.

He and Southampton, both of them older and wiser now, probably picked up where they had left off. Certainly the Earl's time in the Tower had not dented his enthusiasm for theater: that much is evident from a letter addressed in 1604 by a harassed-sounding Sir Walter Cope to Robert Cecil and relating to a proposed entertainment laid on by Southampton for the new Queen. Cope had spent all morning searching for players and entertainers but with little success. Burbage claimed that the King's Men had "no new play that the Queen hath not seen" but that they would revive "*Love's Labour's Lost* which for wit and mirth he says will please her exceedingly; and this is appointed to be played tomorrow night at my Lord of Southampton's."*

Whether or not Shakespeare undertook the role of Iago/James,

---

*Chambers (1930), vol. 2, p. 332.

the play constitutes a most intense meditation on the devastating power of human sexuality. Why Shakespeare wrote such a work at just this time, no one knows. It is hard to see what in Cinthio's anodyne *Hecatommithi* fired his imagination, other than perhaps the play made of Disdemona's name in an otherwise name-free narrative. The anxieties about sexual betrayal and desire in *Othello* verge on mania. If Shakespeare and Jane Davenant were involved at this time, then the play may reflect the moral chaos into which Shakespeare was plunged by the affair. Cassio's wooing of Desdemona on Othello's behalf, and Shakespeare's acting for Mme. Mountjoy in the business of Belott, ran on twin tracks. One wonders whether Shakespeare's and Brabantio's lives did too, since in 1604 Shakespeare's daughters were twenty-one and nineteen years old. It would be a while before he lost Susanna to another man and had to be told, like Brabantio, that she saw a "divided duty."

If Susanna's future husband had not arrived in town by 1604, the Jesuits certainly had. Catholic stirrings were inevitable in the wake of the 1603 Stuart accession, when hope ran high among the oppressed majority that their cause might find a sympathetic ear in the new Scots King. They became bolder now in Stratford, which as noted earlier lay close to the Jesuits' regional headquarters in nearby Worcestershire. Shakespeare would have known that something was afoot locally when in January 1604, the year before the Gunpowder Plot, a priest in disguise was spotted in Stratford. He bolted to safety. It was not clear to the people who encountered him that he was indeed a Jesuit, but the authorities had little doubt on this point. Two residents, "Joan Ange spinster" and an otherwise unidentified "boy" who was nearly knocked over by the stranger, gave statements. Both recalled that the man was wearing high shoes with stockings and green breeches, and the boy testified that he had gone up to the Reynolds house. The stranger "had run so of knavery to overthrow him and so [the boy] gave him way, and looked after him to see whither he would, and he saw him stay his hand upon the cheek post of Mr Reynolds's door and so stand still, and so the said boy turned and went his way." Even if Shakespeare was not in Stratford at the time, he would have heard about the incident, especially since it happened nearly on his doorstep. Reynolds's large property sat on the site of the present Shakespeare Hotel—that is, a few yards north of New Place. He also owned a farm over in Old Stratford, near Holy Trinity, but it seems more likely that the foppish-looking visitor fetched up in Chapel Street. As diehard Catholics, the Reynoldses found themselves on the same 1592 recusancy register as the Debdales and the Cawdreys, whose son George was officially listed by the recusancy commission as a "seminary priest or a Jesuit." They were as deeply implicated as it was possible to be.

It is unlikely that the priest in question was George Cawdrey, since Joan Ange would have recognized him. He was probably one of the Jesuits sheltering at Hindlip Hall over in Worcestershire. This ancient manor house would shortly achieve tragic fame throughout the Midlands when Father Henry Garnett was caught in one of its priest holes. At some time or other most of the major Jesuit players, including John Gerard, Nicholas Owen, Thomas Stanney, and Edward Oldcorne, who had disembarked in England with Gerard, passed through the house. The conspicuous and inept fop of Stratford could have been almost any of these but the elegant Gerard, who was a master of disguise. Oldcorne kept up a high profile in the Midlands and had operated out of Hindlip for sixteen years; or perhaps the priest was Oldcorne's assistant, Father Thomas Lister. This wavering, neurotic, and claustrophobic character greatly tried Garnett's patience and was back in England at the time of the incident in Stratford.

Whoever the priest was, what really matters is that he was there at all. One naturally wonders whether he called on the Shakespeares. His hosts in Stratford obviously included the Reynoldses and probably the Cawdreys, the Badgers, and other local Catholics. It is highly likely that he also called on the Debdales of Shottery, among the most stubborn of all recusant local families, particularly now that their son had been put to death in London. In all likelihood the priest's mission was to prepare the local faithful for the accession of a new monarch in hopes of securing a better deal for the Catholics. (When they failed, as they would do shortly, they decided to take another route, one more dangerous and violent.) The Midlands were as important in this risorgimento as Lancashire, the traditional citadel of Catholicism.

The Reynoldses were on intimate terms with the Shakespeares. The son of the family, William Reynolds, was a neighbor and friend of William Shakespeare who left him a gold memorial ring in his will. Reynolds was the poet's junior by eleven years.

Of course Shakespeare knew that Jesuits were active in Stratford and the neighboring villages, but the record shows that in his hometown he was always a businessman first and foremost. In the space of three years he invested the awesome sum of £760. His outlay on July 24, 1605, of £440 for a share in local church tithes, is the equivalent of the projected entire cost of the Fortune theater in London. We may be sure that the father's bitter experience had taught the son to be prudent and that this huge sum was only part of his assets. He sat on New Place and its barns and gardens, his share in the Globe, and much cash, one imagines, since otherwise he could hardly have afforded his further investments and his purchase a few years later of the Blackfriars gatehouse. As ever his investments were shrewd and sound, and light-years away from the redistributive and egalitarian ethos of the play on which he would embark shortly: *King Lear.*

A passage from John Aubrey quoted earlier raised the possibility that Shakespeare fathered a baby with Jane Davenant. William Davenant was christened at St. Martin Carfax in Oxford on March 3, 1606, and was therefore conceived in June or July 1605. No extant records place Shakespeare in Oxford during those months, but there is no earthly reason why they should. The huge financial transaction he conducted in person in Stratford on July 24, in connection with the church tithes, places him in the Midlands at just the right time, and he would certainly have had the opportunity to see Jane Davenant. The King's Men were probably playing in London then; it is interesting that Shakespeare was allowed to take off for Warwickshire in mid-season. Perhaps major shareholders were granted leave for occasional visits home, or perhaps he gave himself leave: he was by far the company's biggest asset, as he and they would, of course, have known. Each such break would have meant a spell of perhaps as much as ten days or even a fortnight away, since the journey alone took at least two days in each direction. Some of the lead players probably could go home and attend funerals or sit at sickbeds. One of the many advantages the King's Men enjoyed was that their undisputed star was a Londoner, Burbage, and his immediate family lived in the capital. On balance, we should, perhaps, accept that Shakespeare's comings and goings were relatively unconstrained thanks to his importance to the company.

Shakespeare may have stayed on in Stratford until nearly the end of August, since it was then that the King came to Oxford. There, on August 27, he was treated to a work called *The Three Sybils*, in which his lineage was acclaimed and his descent was traced from the fruitful line of Banquo. At least one distinguished historian argues that Shakespeare was present on this occasion, which would have provided an obvious prompt for *Macbeth*.* The thought that Shakespeare stayed in Oxford in August 1605 in the wake of the royal party is intriguing, even if the evidence is tenuous. He may have been up again in October, because the King's Men performed *Othello* in Oxford on the ninth. By then, Jane Davenant was four or five months pregnant. One wonders whether she and her husband attended the performance. If they did, she would have seen a play that was quite possibly inspired by her relationship with the rich player and dramatist who may himself have played Iago. If he was the father of the baby she was carrying, she may have told him the truth about it then.

---

*Fraser, p. 161.

24

"My Father's Godson":
1605–1606

As a newcomer in Shoreditch, Shakespeare may have had a hand in the old *Leir* play, which had very recently been printed. It contains some of the raw materials for the main plot of Shakespeare's masterpiece but nothing for its subplot about the price the Gloucester family must pay for old Gloucester's adultery, which produced the illegitimate Edmund. Scholars have tried to trace the Gloucester material back to texts Shakespeare knew, for example Sidney's *Arcadia,* but to no real avail ultimately. This is for the simple reason that Shakespeare lifted it from his own life.

As for the main plot of *King Lear,* the sorry history of the Annesleys anticipates it while also involving Southampton and his family. Brian Annesley was a wealthy Kentish father with three daughters. The two eldest were married, and when he developed senile dementia they wanted to have him declared insane and committed accordingly. Chief of the two harpies was his daughter Lady Wildgoose, whose name may be echoed in one of the Fool's jingles: "Winter's not gone yet if the wild geese fly that way," he says, and goes on, "Fathers that wear rags / Do make their children blind, / But fathers that bear bags / Shall see their children kind." After divesting himself of both authority and wealth, the Fool promises, Lear will suffer nothing but grief at the hand of his thankless daughters.

Wild geese heading south at winter's approach will not stay behind, any more than Lear's selfish daughters will. Shakespeare did not necessarily need a greedy Lady Wildgoose for the Fool's song. But in the Annesley story as also in Shakespeare's play, it was the youngest sister who would not stand for her father's abuse and successfully petitioned Cecil for help. Her name was Cordell. When Brian Annesley died in July 1604, she inherited most of his estate. She had been assisted in her struggle by Sir William Harvey, one of the executors of her father's will. We have met Harvey, as the third husband of Southampton's mother and therefore, of course, as the Earl's stepfather. When Southampton's mother died in 1607, Harvey married Cordell Annesley—perhaps because, like Lear, he wanted to "set his rest on her kind nursery." Shakespeare would have heard about the Annesleys through Southampton.

The strands that converge in *Lear* are the contemporary domestic tragedy of the Annesleys, literary texts such as the anonymous *Leir* play and Spenser's *Faerie Queene,* which tell versions of the story of the main plot, and events from Shakespeare's own life, which probably become the blueprint for the Gloucester subplot. It is impossible to know precisely when he embarked on writing *Lear,* but it must have been after the partial eclipse of the moon on September 27, 1605, and the total midday eclipse of the sun on October 12 following.* Gloucester is unmistakably referring to these when he says that the "late eclipses in the sun and moon portend no good to us" but instead augur the cooling of love and friendship, division between brothers, "in cities mutinies, in countries discords, palaces treason, the bond cracked between son and father." The play can be dated to after the eclipses, but not too many months after, or the allusion to the "late" eclipses would eventually become a solecism. When *King Lear* was acted at court on St. Stephen's Day of 1606, it must have been in existence for a while. In addition, the theaters were closed in July 1606 by another plague scare. We can narrow down the time even further. There is a defining moment in the play when, on the verge of madness, Lear confronts the unleashed elements, raging against nature, asking it to flatten "the thick rotundity of the world" and to crack its own mold and thus

---

*Respectively, at 3:37 A.M. and 1:06 P.M. NASA Eclipse homepage, http:// sunearth.gsfc.nasa.gov/eclipse.

annihilate all future generations at source: "all germens spill at once / That make ingrateful man." Kent stands appalled, for he has never seen "Such sheets of fire, such bursts of horrid thunder, / Such groans of roaring wind and rain." No man can endure such an onslaught, he claims.

The storm scenes in *King Lear* are the most powerful that Shakespeare ever wrote. Although the tempest that rages during the night of Duncan's murder in *Macbeth* is rendered almost as memorable by its unforgettable images of perverted nature, the storm in *Lear* is unequaled for sheer imaginative drive. It is hardly a coincidence that the two plays with the most powerful storm scenes in Shakespeare follow each other closely in 1606, for extraordinary and devastating storms had hit England and northern Europe early that spring. In the words of an eyewitness, "The nine and twentieth, and thirtieth of March [1606], the wind was so extraordinary great and violent, that it caused great shipwreck . . . it also caused the sea, and divers rivers to overflow their bounds, and drowned many people, and much cattle."* The third act of *King Lear* was almost certainly written after this; the scene is directly topical. There is no gap here between the historical present of the moment and the timeless world of literature.

The dating of the play through natural phenomena so far suggests a span of up to six months, with the first two acts being written sometime between October 12, 1605, and March 30, 1606. That seems much too long even for a work as extraordinary as *King Lear*, especially when the period includes the four weeks of Lent, which Shakespeare would have exploited for concentrated writing at New Place. For this and other reasons, a later starting date seems likely. When Gloucester describes the portentous character of the eclipses, omens of "mutinies," "discords," and "treason," Shakespeare is speaking to a nation that at that moment was coming to terms with the aftermath of the Gunpowder Plot of November 5, when a group of well-connected Catholics attempted to blow up Parliament. The response of Cecilian England was swift, savage, and efficient. The details of the plot are amply documented elsewhere, as is the fate of the chief conspirators

---

*Stow and Howes, p. 883.

including of Guy Fawkes.* What may be less well known is the depth of penetration of the Catholic Midlands and of parts of Warwickshire that were in the vicinity of Stratford. It was nearly twenty years since the similar failure of the Babington plot to enthrone Mary Queen of Scots and thus restore the country to Catholicism.

News of the near catastrophe reached Stratford the next day. Posts tore through the night to alert the local authorities in Warwick, Charlecote, and elsewhere. Within hours of the discovery of the plot, the mayor of Stratford, one William Wyatt, led a raid on Clopton House where one of the conspirators, Ambrose Rookwood, was hiding out. In ordinary circumstances, Wyatt would have been out of his league tangling with the Cloptons and their friends and allies. In 1605 he lived as a mere burgher in Sheep Street opposite what is now the "Cordelia Cottage." Clashing with a fellow citizen over the rental of a horse was more his style. The mayor knew what to look for at the Cloptons', and he found it: vestments, chalices, chasubles, and other traces of an active Catholic cell. Most, but not all, such materials had been shifted successfully to the Badgers of Henley Street, the Shakespeares' next-door neighbors. It had taken a few hours only for the fallout from the Gunpowder Plot to arrive, and before long the Badgers in turn were arrested.

If Mary Arden still lived here rather than at New Place, then the fate of the Badgers might have struck a painful chord, recalling the persecution of her extended family under the previous regime. Robert Debdale of Shottery had been a prominent local victim, and he and Mary's larger Arden family were featured in the tract "A Declaration of Egregious Popish Impostures," whose publication coincided with the Stuart accession of 1603. The tract described a notorious case of exorcism in a place that Shakespeare might well have passed through on his way between London and Stratford, Denham in Buckinghamshire. "A Declaration" had been commissioned by the Privy Council and written by Samuel Harsnett, a militant Cambridge-educated Protestant who was chaplain to the Bishop of London. He eventually became Archbishop of York.

---

*Fraser tells the story of the Fawkes plot with considerable panache.

Shakespeare probably read "A Declaration" because of the Gun-powder Plot, which is to say only after November 5. That he knew it by the time he wrote *Lear* is certain, because several of the devils in Poor Tom's catalogue of spirits step straight out of Harsnett, includ-ing the famous "foul fiend Flibbertigibbet," a nocturnal spirit who "gives the web and the pin, squinies the eye, and makes the harelip, mildews the white wheat, and hurts the poor creature of earth." Harsnett's pamphlet is a tirade against Campion, Weston, Debdale, and other Jesuits, characterized as lecherous and obscene disciples of the devil. Luckily for the good and enlightened people of England, Harsnett notes, Tyburn has a way of dealing with them. Never mind their blood-soaked girdles (Campion) or hoses (Debdale) on the quartering block: these are relics only to benighted fanatics. Throughout his lewd account of the exorcism, more *Tom Jones* than history, Harsnett hints that a devious sexual subtext ran through it. This may well have been so, and it is true that Jesuits performed ex-orcisms on poor Sara Williams of Denham, who eventually testified against them. Harsnett reports with relish Sara's claim that "the priests did pretend that the devil did rest in the most secret part of my body" and would also issue from that same part. This allowed them to fondle her genitals, Harsnett notes, or, better yet, have other women do so.

The tract teeters on the verge of pornography and it does so with exemplary savagery, thrilling to the word "tail" in a particularly poisonous swipe at the revered Campion. Any reader would have known what was meant: the execution ordered the ripping off of the "privy member," which was thrown into a fire or large seething cauldron to be followed by the entrails of the victim, whom the law required to be kept alive and "seeing" at that stage of the proceed-ings. The horror and the outrage to the dignity of the human body speak for themselves. "A Declaration" is a piece of vicious propa-ganda with an effective rhetorical punch. As the greatest student of Shakespeare's sources remarked, "If Shakespeare was a Roman Catholic would he have drawn so much from Harsnett's book?" Again we are confronted by the paradox of Shakespeare reading and ingesting a text that he must have execrated, not least because of its hostile treatment of the Ardens and of Debdale. (We are assuming, of course, that because the Debdales, Burmans, and Hathaways were all neighbors in Shottery, Shakespeare was also close to them.)*

"A Declaration" is not for the fainthearted. Shakespeare's parade of Harsnett's devils may suggest that in the wake of the Gunpowder Plot he had become more hostile to Catholic defiance. His use of the word "rip" comports with this idea: it is hard not to hear an echo from treason trials in Edgar's line about reading the letter by Goneril found on the dead Oswald: "To know our enemies' minds we'd rip their hearts; / Their papers is more lawful." The word occurs in *Macbeth*, when Macduff reveals that he was "from his mother's womb / Untimely ripped," and only twice more in all of Shakespeare's plays. The fourteen months between November 5, 1605, and the end of 1606 were among the darkest and bloodiest in the country's history. On Friday, January 31, 1606, Guy Fawkes and a number of other conspirators were put to death; to render the whole business more spectacular, scaffolds were erected at certain key locations in London, notably at the western end of St. Paul's Cathedral and in Old Palace Yard in Westminster, close to where people queue today for admission to the House of Commons, in full view of Westminster Abbey and Westminster Palace. Londoners could choose not to attend executions at Tyburn, but it was much harder to avoid them when they took place in the City itself.

In borrowing from Harsnett's splenetic text, Shakespeare connects *King Lear* to the political context of the day. Already George Badger had been taken down to London for interrogation about his collusion with the Cloptons. Then, on Thursday, January 23, 1606,

---

*Bullough, vol. 7, p. 419. Bullough quotes Harsnett telling his readers that the powers of exorcism ("devil-killing virtue") "did not lie in the priest's head only, as the poison of an adder doth; nor yet in his tail alone, as the light of the glow-worm; but was universally diffused over all and every part of his body, and so transfused into all and every part of the apparel that came near his body. Campion's girdle that he wore (as seems) at Tyburn, (and I wonder how they missed the rope that embraced his holy neck) being enriched with an outlandish grace that it came from Jerusalem (as Father Edmunds tells us) and had there girded about the sepulchre of our Saviour Christ, shall tell you stranger news than Debdale's stockings did" (ibid., p. 418; spelling and punctuation modernized).

Henry Garnett, Edward Oldcorne, Nicholas Owen, and Ralph Ashley were all captured at Hindlip.

Perched on top of a hill near Worcester with commanding views over the surrounding countryside, the manor of Hindlip was owned by Thomas Habington, a friend of Antony Babington's and a considerable antiquarian scholar. It was one of the safest Catholic refuges in the country. Hindlip Hall and its warren of secret passages and priest holes have long since gone and the site has become the headquarters of the West Mercia Constabulary: such are the long-range ironies of history. When the priests were arrested, Garnett and Oldcorne had been cowering in a cramped hole for seven days and nights. Garnett's legs had started to swell badly, but there was no chance of relief. If only they could have shifted the books and other "furniture" to gain just a little more space to sit. In the meantime neither of them went "to the stool" at any point, although they did pass water. Garnett claimed that they were in good heart throughout, although they heard the searchers above them and were convinced that they would be found sooner or later. When eventually the two men emerged from their hiding hole, the stench nearly overwhelmed the searchers.

Shakespeare could be under no illusion about the scale of local Midlands involvement in recusant activity. If he was shifting or questioning his allegiances at just that moment, then these events may well have consolidated his sense of a real threat to the commonwealth. Although leading Jesuits repeatedly protested their aloofness from political chicanery in open letters to the Privy Council, people at the time found this hard to credit. After all Father Oswald Tesimond had confessed Robert Catesby's seditious intentions to Garnett only a few days before November 5. (Catesby was the principal conspirator.) To the new Protestant mind-set, and under extreme political pressure just then, the seal of the confessional lacked biblical authority and credibility.

One of Garnett's various cover names was Farmer. In addition to being the chief Jesuit in England he was famous, or infamous, for a treatise on equivocation, which he had written in defense of Southwell's use of it at his trial in February 1595. It is through this that he enters *Macbeth* in the drunken Porter's speech, which alludes both to his alias and to his equivocations at his own trial, which was staged at the Guildhall on Thursday, March 27, 1606. By then, one of the Jesuits' most loyal and most necessary followers, Nicholas Owen, had perished under torture in the Tower of London. Although the official version was that he had committed suicide, Owen probably died on the rack. English law forbade the racking of men and women who suffered from hernias, but the rule appears to have been disregarded in Owen's case. In the words of his friend and sometime roommate John Gerard, "his bowels gushed out with his life."

He had been Garnett's ally and companion for nearly twenty years. Gerard describes him as "the chief designer and builder of hiding-places in England," who could therefore, if he succumbed, hand over more priests and their supporters than almost anyone else. Nicholas Owen did not succumb, and he must have died in unimaginable agony. He is revered by Catholics as a true hero of the Elizabethan underground and in 1970 he was canonized by Pope Paul VI among the Forty Martyrs of England and Wales. His death would have been a desperate blow to Garnett, whose own terror at the thought of torture is well documented in his correspondence. At the time of Southwell's detention, he had clung to the hope that his own physical body would be able to endure what Southwell must be suffering at that moment because it formed part of the wider mystical body of Christ. Surely He would help his disciples by assuming some of the pain inflicted on them by their blind and misguided countrymen. In the end, Garnett was racked only once. When they came for him a second time, he pleaded with them not to make him suffer again. He promised to provide all the answers that they desired to their questions, just as if he had been racked. It seems that the Privy Council acceded to his pleas for justice or mercy.

All this was going on while Shakespeare was writing *King Lear,* a play every bit as obsessed with adultery and female sexuality as *Othello*. But whereas the adultery in *Othello* is a hallucinatory fiction, here it is real, jauntily acknowledged by the chief offender, Gloucester. The play opens with him bragging to Kent about his younger son Edmund's illegitimacy. When Kent replies, "I cannot conceive you," Gloucester cheerfully replies

Sir, this young fellow's mother could, whereupon she grew round-wombed and had indeed, sir, a son for her cradle ere she had a husband for her bed. . . . Though this knave came something saucily into the world, before he was sent for, yet was his mother fair, there was good sport at his making, and the whoreson must be acknowledged.

Gloucester's punishment for his sexual misdeed and his shamelessness is swift and terrible: his illegitimate offspring betrays him and he is cruelly blinded, in the single most violent onstage scene in Shakespeare. Cast on the mercy of his rightful son and heir, Edgar, he dies of a broken heart. Almost everything to do with the Gloucester plot seems to be Shakespeare's invention; at least, it has no known sources. If, however, Shakespeare was involved sexually with Jane Davenant while he was writing *Lear*, then we would surely be right to detect a subtext of guilt, even downright fear of retribution, in the role of Gloucester.

We must ask whether there is anything in the play to connect it with the Davenants, and as it happens a key word points quite specifically in that direction. On a purely literary level, it acts as a bridge between the two plots and has dynastic implications. It occurs in the first scene of Act II, when Regan and Gloucester are discussing Edgar's heinous readiness apparently to usurp his father. "Madam, my old heart is cracked, is cracked," Gloucester complains, to which Regan replies, incredulously, "What, did my father's godson seek your life? / He whom my father named, your Edgar?" This is, remarkably, the only use in all of Shakespeare's plays and poems of the word "godson." It would be an extraordinary coincidence for "godson" to occur in Shakespeare's complete works at just the time when the only person on record who was reputed by his contemporaries to be Shakespeare's godson, if not his son, was born, someone who moreover occasionally seems to have boasted about being Shakespeare's son. At the very least, we have to consider seriously the claim that Davenant was Shakespeare's godson; there is no reason why the Davenant boys, parson Robert and dramatist William, should lie, to Aubrey or anyone else, about knowing Shakespeare. The claim that Davenant was Shakespeare's biological son is of a different order altogether. Assuming that Jane Davenant's pregnancy did result from a sexual liaison with Shakespeare in the summer of 1605, he would have found out by October at the latest. No wonder that Gloucester refers to the recent solar and lunar eclipses—Shakespeare, too, might have thought of them on hearing the news.

Gloucester's adultery produced a boy. If the parallels between Shakespeare's life and plays are as intimate as has been argued here, then the writing of *King Lear* got under way after Jane Davenant's baby was born and its sex was known, in early March 1606. Shakespeare now had all the materials that he required for the subplot. The consolidated evidence of the storm in Act III, the sex of the illegitimate offspring, and the use of the word "godson" therefore place the writing of *King Lear* sometime after March 3, 1606. Shakespeare could rely on his audience's remembering the eclipses of the past autumn; they were etched in people's memories because of the Gunpowder Plot, which came shortly after and which people at the time connected directly with these omens. The day after Shakespeare may have stood as godfather to William Davenant in Oxford was Shrove Tuesday, March 4, 1606, which was, of course, followed by Ash Wednesday and the four weeks of Lent. This must always have been Shakespeare's peak writing time. His plan would probably have been to complete the play in time for the reopening of the London theaters after Easter—April 20 that year—perhaps to be ready for performance by May or early June. In light of his likely use of the March storms in the second scene of Act III, one might want to be more specific still and suggest that he wrote the first two acts of the play during March 1606 and Acts III–V during April and May, hence perhaps the springtime cuckoo-flowers in the mad Lear's crown of weeds toward the end of Act IV.

Rumors about Shakespeare and Davenant had spread by the eighteenth century. Thus the Reverend James Davenport of Holy Trinity, who became Malone's trusted helper in Stratford, acknowledged in a letter to Malone in late May 1788 that he had "heard . . . of the tradition that Sir William Davenant was a natural son of our poet." Davenport's use of "heard," so like the Reverend John Ward's 126 years earlier about the local tradition of Shakespeare's vast earnings, demonstrates that Stratfordians eagerly discussed the private life of the town's most famous son, especially in its more sensational aspects. Shakespeare did have at least one legitimate godson, young William Walker of Stratford, who was left money in his will. Shakespeare probably stood as godfather to him in Stratford in around 1609. Many years earlier he may also have stood as godfather to Ben Jonson's son, Benjamin, whom Jonson called his "best piece of poetry" in a poem addressed to him. Benjamin died, aged seven, in 1603. There may have been other godchildren. Shakespeare's "cousin" Thomas Greene called his first two children William and Anne, but neither is mentioned as Shakespeare's godchild, nor is either of the Greenes remembered in Shakespeare's mysterious will. William Davenant, who was eleven when Shakespeare died, also does not feature in the will. He hardly could, since to include him might have amounted to a posthumous acknowledgment of adultery. If Davenant was Shakespeare's son or godson we may be sure that Shakespeare had made provision for him, probably by giving money to his mother (if she needed any; the Davenants were wealthy).

Edgar is Lear's godson, but as with *Othello*, the most immediate and necessary intersection of play and life lies in the casting. We know that Burbage played Richard III, Othello, Hamlet, and Lear, just as we can confidently pronounce on certain roles that fit Will Kemp (Falstaff, Peter), Robert Armin (Touchstone, Feste), John Lowin (Henry VIII), and others. A crude matching of the cast of *King Lear* and the personnel of the King's Men might suggest that the middle-aged Will Shakespeare was well equipped to play Gloucester. Shakespeare may have written the part with himself in mind, as a middle-aged adulterer who had recently become the father of an illegitimate son, but it does not follow that he actually played it. Rather, if Shakespeare played the twenty-eight-year-old Iago with a limp or a clubfoot he may have played Gloucester's legitimate son, Edgar, who describes himself as "made lame by fortune's blows."

The two plays were written and performed close in time; each features a character who may limp. In staring down at Iago's foot, Othello may supply one of the most important visual clues that Shakespeare left us about the character. Perhaps on the stage of the Globe Iago limped, and contemporary audiences would have been troubled by this and wondered about it until Othello's bewildered question at the end spelled it out for them. Shakespeare seems to be drawing attention almost compulsively to his disability and to want to generate theatrical capital from it. The part of Edgar, like that of Iago, is a substantial one, the second longest in *Lear*. If we could prove that Shakespeare played those two parts, we could also assert categorically that he undertook major roles in his plays, rather than bit parts as is sometimes assumed. If the Gloucester plot in the play and the birth of William Davenant are directly connected, it would be fitting for the boy's real-life godfather, William, to play the godson in the play. It would have an imaginative logic comparable to his playing the slow and limping Nurse, whose lost daughter, Susan, would have been the same age as Juliet Capulet and Susanna Shakespeare.

25

ℐThe Easter Rising of 1606:
A Little Local Difficulty

usanna added to her father's woes at just the time when he was writing *King Lear*. The day she chose to do so was Easter Sunday, April 20, 1606, after Henry Garnett's trial and before his execution. This was one of the most dangerous moments in English history: not a good time to make a stand. And yet it was precisely when Susanna Shakespeare chose to refuse to receive the Eucharist. She was promptly cited by the local Church Court, popularly known as the Bawdy Court.

Susanna was not alone. When she appeared in Holy Trinity the next month to answer her summons for noncompliance, there stood with her Margaret Reynolds, the mother of Shakespeare's Catholic friend William Reynolds; Wheeler *père et fils* as well as their servant Alice, all three of them from Henley Street; Sibyl Cawdrey; Hamlet and Judith Sadler; one Thomas Stanney and his wife; and two Brooke brothers, one of whom, Robert, also lived in Henley Street, where he now occupied the premises that had previously been the Badgers'. There were others, too. Conspicuously *not* mentioned are Susanna's mother and father, her sister, her aunt, or any of her uncles. Her father had probably already left for London before Easter, to prepare for the new season. Susanna stood her ground alone and apart from her family.

How she came to ally herself with battle-hardened Catholic recusants is a mystery. The Sadlers, close friends of her parents and perhaps the godparents of the Shakespeare twins, held out briefly, pleading that they needed time to "cleanse" their consciences be-fore receiving communion. In response, the court set "a day to re-ceive," which the Sadlers accepted, and that was that. Failure to comply would have resulted in excommunication and a series of crippling exponential fines. Given Susanna's isolation, one wonders whether there was a rift between her and her father over this Easter defiance, and whether it fed into *King Lear*. One of the most terri-fying speeches in all of Shakespeare is Lear's savage curse of his eldest daughter, Goneril. He prays that Nature should render her sterile, but if she must have a baby then it ought to be a bitter creature that will make her weep, ravage her face with premature wrinkles, and thus

> *Turn all her mother's pains and benefits*
> *To laughter and contempt, that she may feel–*
> *That she may feel*
> *How sharper than a serpent's tooth it is*
> *To have a thankless child.*

If Act III dates from after the storm of March 30, 1606, then these lines in the first act were written several weeks before Susanna defied the ecclesiastical authorities. Perhaps she and her father were at odds that spring; if so, the estrangement coincides with the birth of William Davenant. If Susanna found out about his affair with Jane Davenant, she and her father would undoubtedly have become alienated for a time. It is difficult to see what else could account for the sheer vehemence of these lines and why he should so savagely attack the father-daughter relationship here, when it is usually so strong and benign in his work.

Susanna, in whom there was famously "something of Shake-speare," may have been just as headstrong and rebellious as he. On her grave in the chancel of Holy Trinity, she is praised for being "witty above her sex" and "wise to salvation," with the last sentence noting, "Something of Shakespeare was in that." Those who knew her thought that like her father she was bright, funny, witty, and spir-ited. Like him, she may also have been headstrong and defiant. There was a hint of things to come in old Capulet's tirade at Juliet after she begs him not to be marry her off to County Paris. One hears in Capulet's furious rhetoric—in the "Thank me no thankings, nor proud me no prouds...Out, you green-sickness carrion! Out, you baggage, / You tallow-face!"—the voice of an irate and crossed patriarch. In *Romeo and Juliet* we are on Juliet's side, but that does not mean that his own experience of a moody, truculent thirteen-year-old girl may not be reflected there. *Romeo and Juliet* is his most intimate domestic tragedy, and the pain that the father in it unjustly causes his child may bear traces of the author's real life.

Unlike the Sadlers, Susanna Shakespeare did not petition for more time to consult her conscience; she seems to have conformed, having made her point. This may suggest at first that her refusal of communion was only a gesture, but such gestures could be very costly. One is left wondering whether a young unmarried woman would really dare be so defiant, particularly in complete isolation from her family. Maybe Susanna had already met John Hall by Easter 1606 and was now embracing his form of Protestantism, which perhaps saw the Eucharist as too Romanist. She did marry him only a little more than a year later. Perhaps he was not reported for failing to take communion because he had not yet settled in Stratford. The Eucharist was mandatory on major religious holidays, and Susanna had obviously received it the previous Christmas. This suggests that her romance with Hall had moved on to a much more committed stage during the spring of 1606, just when her father's relationship with Jane Davenant may have become all too obvious.

The eighteen months from July 1605 to the end of 1606 rank among the most eventful in Shakespeare's life. This was the time during which he may have been involved with Jane Davenant, who became pregnant in June 1605, just as he was planning the biggest financial investment in his career. His company put on *Othello* in Oxford that October; Shakespeare may have played Iago on that occasion. Then, on November 5, 1605, the Gunpowder Plot was discovered and he started to read Harsnett; meanwhile he once again enjoyed the patronage and friendship of Southampton. And Susanna was being courted by the physician John Hall. Like his famous father-in-law, Hall would become a local legend, but his first encounter with

Shakespeare may have been rather rocky, especially if his blossoming relationship with Susanna led her to break free from the Shakespeares' careful conformism. Perhaps, like Desdemona, Susanna faced "a divided duty," between her father's diplomatic Anglicanism and her future husband's tougher Protestantism; perhaps, like Desdemona, she did not want to be left a mere "moth of peace." Whatever happened, there are reasons for thinking that she and her father had a serious falling-out at this time and that it is echoed in *King Lear*. Between March and December in that same year, 1606, Shakespeare wrote *Lear, Macbeth,* and *Antony and Cleopatra*. This prodigious output must have been owed partly at least to the closure of the theaters from July on, which left Shakespeare free to concentrate on his writing.

These were difficult times for the Catholic Midlands. Like all of London, Shakespeare would have heard of the arrest of Father Garnett at Hindlip Hall. Unlike most Londoners, he would have known about Hindlip's role in the recusant underground. After a daylong sham trial, Garnett was sentenced to death; the execution was carried out a month later, outside the western porch of St. Paul's, less than ten minutes' walk from where Shakespeare lived in Muggle Street. The person who faced the London crowd on the scaffold that Saturday, May 3, 1606, had been publicly "proclaimed" five months earlier along with others, just as Edgar is in *Lear*: "I heard myself proclaimed, / And by the happy hollow of a tree / Escaped the hunt. No port is free, no place / That guard and most unusual vigilance / Does not attend my taking." The proclamation described Garnett, the once slender Wykhamist who had worked as a proofreader for Richard Tottel, the publisher of the celebrated collection of Tudor poems known as *Tottel's Miscellany*, as "a fat man" of medium height aged between fifty and sixty, with a high forehead, thin and graying hair, and with a closely trimmed beard on his cheek and chin.

This is the man whom Shakespeare may have watched die. By the insistence of a sympathetic crowd, he was spared the horror of being disemboweled alive. When his head was cast into the boiling cauldron, "it received no alteration at all; as neither it did after it was placed upon London Bridge, and set up there upon a pole." The head's refusal to turn "black, as usually all heads cut from the bodies do," attracted immense curiosity. It was thought to be a miracle and people flocked to the bridge to see it. The magistrates therefore ordered the head to be reset to face upward, away from the crowds below: so we read in John Gerard's report. Gerard had heard it from Catholics who were present at the execution and desperate to collect a relic. This usually entailed sopping up some blood from the victim with a handkerchief, or retrieving a bloodstained item of his clothing, as happened with Campion's girdle and Debdale's hose, so irritating the pamphleteer Harsnett. According to Gerard, an ear of corn from one of the baskets into which the hangman had flung Garnett's quarters started showing an image of the Jesuit's face after the authorities turned aside the real one on London Bridge. The ear of corn became one of the most famous Catholic relics of the age. It had been retrieved by a devout Catholic who had squeezed in under the scaffold while Garnett was being quartered. Here "he received the blood which streamed down through the chinks of the boards, upon his hat and apparel, and dipped such linen as he had prepared in the same."

Little wonder that *Macbeth* should be so red with blood. When, after the murder of the King and his grooms, Macbeth refers to his bloodstained hands like a hangman's, Shakespeare's audience knew from experience what he meant, as they did when Lady Macbeth exclaims, "Yet who would have thought the old man to have had so much blood in him?" Most of us, thankfully, can only imagine such butchery. Were it not for the searing intensity and imaginative range of *King Lear* above all, we could perhaps dismiss this horror as a facet of a benighted past.

On the very day when his father superior, his mentor, and his friend was killed, John Gerard quietly slipped out of England and crossed to the Continent. He had lasted nearly eight years on the run since his flight from the Tower and believed that the spirit of Henry Garnett guided him to safety that May 3, particularly at the very last moment, when it seemed as if the escape might go terribly wrong. Gerard died peacefully in Rome in 1637, having outlived his contemporary Shakespeare by twenty-one years. His final days in England were probably spent in the very same gatehouse over Ireland Yard that Shakespeare would buy some eight years after the Gunpowder Plot. Sometime around November 1605, Gerard turned up at the gatehouse and asked its then owner to shelter some of the chief conspirators, Catesby, Wintour, Percy, and Digby, "famous and noble men." The lady of the house dared not admit them in the absence of her husband. He was John Fortescue, the nephew of the powerful Master of the Wardrobe across the road, Sir John Fortescue. So the conspirators lodged instead in the house of the recusant Robert Dormer, downhill from the gatehouse. Waiters from a tavern next to the cut of Ireland Yard testified afterward to seeing these men come and go at Dormer's every day. When the Gunpowder Plot was exposed, Gerard was proclaimed throughout the kingdom. Subsequently, and out of the blue, he appeared again at the Blackfriars gatehouse to seek refuge. This time he wore a false beard and a wig. He pleaded with Fortescue to take him in because he knew not where to hide; "the Lord Fortescue looked at him with deep sorrow and said 'You have no-one now to lose other than me and my family.'"*

The crackdown after November 5 marked a turning point in the country's history and the Catholic cause was exhausted. But while the King survived his Catholic enemies, forty-four years later the Puritans would drag his son, King Charles I, to the scaffold. Charles was five years old in 1605. During the early interrogations of Guy Fawkes, King James repeatedly asked him whether he felt no qualms at the thought of killing the innocent royal children. Fawkes had remained defiant.

Given the multiple topical allusions in *Macbeth*, which portrays the murder of a Scottish king by a regicide whose erstwhile compan-

---

*For an account of this, see an odd, but authentic, note from 1631 (Chambers [1930], vol. 2, p. 168). Wilson (pp. 258–59) provides highly suggestive details of Dormer's connections and the ancient underground passages of the precinct. Gerard does not mention any of this in his autobiography, probably to protect the people who had sheltered him. This account is almost certainly true, even though the record of tenancy at the gatehouse suggests that Fortescue may no longer have lived there in November 1605. In 1604, Mathias Bacon sold the gatehouse to Henry Walker, who in turn sold it to Shakespeare in 1613. Walker may, of course, have allowed Fortescue to stay on, even though we know that he issued a lease to one William Ireland. When Shakespeare bought the gatehouse he leased it back to the vendor the next day.

ion Banquo happens to be an ancestor of the Stuarts, the question is whether it contains other encoded references. *Macbeth* came immediately after *King Lear* and was therefore written probably during June, July, and August 1606; perhaps it was even completed in time to premiere before the King in Oxford on August 1.* *Macbeth* is sometimes said to be about the dangers of ambition, and that is certainly a motif in the play; more striking, though, is the obsession with children. No other Shakespeare text features so many children—literal, like little Macduff, Fleance, and even young Siward, but above all metaphoric and symbolic, as in the bloody apparition of "*a child crowned, with a tree in his hand.*" One of the best-known lines in all of Shakespeare is Lady Macbeth's "I have given suck, and know / How tender 'tis to love the babe that milks me," and her vow of killing it to validate her oath. When Macduff learns the dreadful news of the slaughter of his entire family, one of his first baffled reflections is "He has no children."

The portrayal of the Macbeths as a doomed, devoted, and guilt-ridden couple who cannot reproduce is disturbing. Their infertility signals nature's intervention against them. The murder of the King makes Macbeth the most unnatural of men, a deadly traitor to the social concordat that in turn echoes the order of the natural universe. By rendering Macbeth childless, Shakespeare inflicts on him a symbolic version of the ritual punishment of traitors. The official justification for ripping off their "privy members" was that, as freaks of nature, they must never again engender offspring. As a most unnatural man,

---

*There are several indicators of the closeness of these two texts, notably Shakespeare's use of "lily-livered," as in "a lily-livered, action-taking, whoreson" (*King Lear*) and "thou lily-livered boy" (*Macbeth*). Harsnett used "*white*-livered" in "A Declaration" (Bullough, vol. 8, p. 415); this was a phrase that Shakespeare had already used twice before he ever read Harsnett, in *Richard III* and in *Henry V*. He substituted "lily-livered" in *Lear* probably because it was phonetically so much more effective, gliding down the tongue on "l"s, chiming the single vowel sound in the two halves of the compound while alliterating its liquid consonant. Shakespeare clearly enjoyed his new compound, which is why he reused it in *Macbeth*. It was too good to throw away, particularly for the practitioner of an art form that was intrinsically oral.

A masterly account of the enduring links between recusants and the Blackfriars precinct is given by E. K. Chambers in "A Blackfriars House, Shakespeare's Investment, Hiding Holes" (*Times* [London], April 23, 1928).

Macbeth will never have descendants, whereas his wife not only has had a baby but signally fails to turn herself into a monster. Guilt drives her to madness, and her haunting jingle about Lady Macduff, "The Thane of Fife had a wife. Where is she now?," is as famous as her compulsive, futile washing of hands.

The many children in *Macbeth* are all of them male. Indeed, the women in the play, except Lady Macduff, are either half male or try desperately to pervert their feminine nature: the Weird Sisters have beards and Lady Macbeth summons the spirits of darkness to descend on her and turn her milk to gall. Much has been written about Shakespeare's difficult relationship with women, but it is also clear that he associated the feminine with benign nature, with caring for, loving, and protecting the vulnerable, and particularly children, other women, and parents. Few lines in Shakespeare are more revealing in this respect than the jingle about the wife of the thane of Fife; two almost equally telling are spoken by the same character. Lady Macbeth protests that she herself would have killed Duncan if only he had not looked like her father: "Had he not resembled / My father as he slept, I had done't." Here is a glimpse of Lady Macbeth's past, of a time, perhaps, when as a little girl she watched her father asleep. By anchoring her moral nature in this kind of image Shakespeare connects the character to her once gentler self. In the First Folio, the only source text for the play, Shakespeare never actually calls the character Lady Macbeth. She is only ever "lady" and "Macbeth's wife," as if to underline her femininity and her role as a wife rather than the Clytemnestra creature that she has become in the public imagination. Lady Macduff is similarly called "Macduff's wife" and "wife."

In this play gender and nature are intimately connected and in *Macbeth* at least femininity equates with benign nature, the "milk of human kindness" no less. Nature and time are great healers in Shakespeare's plays. For all the Weird Sisters' promises, Macbeth would be perfectly happy not to have to act to become king, and at first he steps back from the prospect of taking power. After all, "If chance will have me king, why chance may crown me / Without my stir." The next line and a half are among the most comforting that Shakespeare ever wrote: "Come what come may / Time and the hour runs through the roughest day." These days we might say "This, too, shall pass." Like the rest of us, Shakespeare needed metaphorical crutches to get through life, and as one of the most perceptive and intelligent people who ever lived he knew full well that there was no such thing as total evil. Macbeth is an almost good man gone bad, rather than a bad man becoming very bad.

The play is steeped in blood, more so than any other Shakespeare text: from the bloody sergeant of the first line of the second scene, to the blood on Macbeth's hands that will "the multitudinous seas incarnadine," to the bloody child, and, finally, to Macduff, the man who kills the killer. Macduff probably killed his mother while being born, for he was delivered by Cesarean section, which was almost invariably fatal before the twentieth century. Newborn babies and the dangers of childbirth may have been on Shakespeare's mind at just this time, if he was the father of Jane Davenant's baby. When Macbeth exhorts his wife to "bring forth men children only," he may be thinking of who was his godson or son. None of Jane Davenant's London pregnancies produced a surviving child; indeed, the Davenants' move to Oxford, which entailed leaving behind a prospering business in the Vintry, has been attributed to just this. In Oxford, Jane bore seven children, including William and Robert, who lived to adulthood. The many children of *Macbeth* may owe their imaginative life partly to Shakespeare's having a son restored to him—not Hamnet, but another William.

One of the metaphorical children in *Macbeth* may conceal a profound and dangerous contemporary gesture of allegiance. This is the "naked new-born babe" evoked by Macbeth. We have reached a point shortly before the murder of the king. Macbeth is pondering the moral implications of his planned assassination. He starts with a number of evasions, circling around the act of murder without naming it: "If it were done when 'tis done, then 'twere well / It were done quickly." Then, and seemingly from nowhere, images of "angels trumpet-tongued" and of heavenly babies surge through the verse:

> *And pity, like a naked new-born babe,*
> *Striding the blast, or heaven's cherubin horsed*

Upon the sightless couriers of the air,
Shall blow the horrid deed in every eye
That tears shall drown the wind.

These images sit incongruously with the King of the "barren sceptre"—unless, that is, the "new-born babe" pays homage to one of the most famous babies in the poetry of the period, the baby Christ in Father Robert Southwell's vision the night before Christmas. The poem is called "The Burning Babe." Here are its opening lines and conclusion:

As I in hoary winter's night stood shivering in the
snow,
Surprised I was with sudden heat, which made my
heart to glow,
And lifting up a fearful eye, to view what fire was
near,
A pretty babe all burning bright did in the air ap-
pear;
Who, scorched with excessive heat, such floods of tears
did shed,
As though his floods should quench his flames, which
with his tears were bred. . . .
With this he vanished out of sight, and swiftly
shrunk away,
And straight I called unto mind that it was Christ-
mas Day.

In their use of the image of a baby and its redemptive reso-nances, Macbeth's soliloquy and the poem chime enough to suggest that Shakespeare was remembering Southwell's poem as he wrote. If the image is a deliberate tribute to the dead Southwell, it might make us think again about the way Shakespeare positions himself with re-gard to the Catholics. It is probably quite characteristic of Shake-speare to pay homage to Southwell's poetic genius while also ridiculing his and Garnett's tactics in the Porter's lines on equivoca-tions.

The plague struck London during the summer of 1606, when Shakespeare was finishing *Macbeth*. The theaters closed and the interdiction that followed lasted all the way into April 1608. After a brief remission, they closed again. Effectively, the moratorium on acting lasted thirty months, two and a half years. It is hard to gauge the extent of the resulting havoc. The actors had to tour to earn a living. Money must have been tight, so that probably the company's footing at court was that much more precious. Fed up, Shakespeare's contemporary the playwright Thomas Dekker printed a work in 1609 in which he laments the closure of the playhouses, which stand like empty taverns "that have cast out their masters, the doors locked up, the flags, like their bushes, taken down; or rather like houses lately infected, from whence the affrighted dwellers are fled, in hope to live better in the country." There is little to do now, Dekker notes, but to stroll idly through the fields or else "to drink up the day and night in a tavern, loathsome, to be ever riding upon that beast with two heads, lechery, most damnable." The bear- and bull-baiting venues continued to operate: "the company of the Bears hold together still; they play their tragicomedies as lively as ever they did; the pied bull here keeps a-tossing and a-roaring when the Red Bull dares not stir."*

In 1606 Shakespeare was forty-two years old, the London theaters had closed, and his daughter Susanna had defied the Church. The thought of retirement must have crossed his mind, though it would have meant something different to him than it does to us. He had surely provided for his old age. He was wealthy now, and as an individual shareholder in the King's Men he must have enjoyed substantial income from the box office receipts of the Globe (and eventually the Blackfriars). There were no pensions or unemployment checks, and no one quite knows how he and the company managed with no income from their London base for a period of two and a half years. We do know that in the teeth of the closure and immediately after *Macbeth*, Shakespeare wrote his rhetorically most spectacular and insouciantly inventive play, *Antony and Cleopatra*. Here Shakespeare just let rip his incomparable command of the language

---

*Barroll, p. 176.

to celebrate the historical adultery between the Roman commander and the Egyptian queen. In *Antony and Cleopatra* the normal boundaries between language and its referents are almost elided and the result is a pure rhetorical theater. Where *Romeo and Juliet* is suffused with tenderness and a lyricism that aims to capture in language the poetry of a teenage relationship, the magic of *Antony and Cleopatra* lies in the sheer inventiveness and cadences of its poetry. When Cleopatra conjures up in her mind's eye her past with Antony, she finds that "Eternity was in our lips and eyes, / Bliss in our brows' bent; none our parts so poor / But was a race of heaven." Her staged appearance in death provokes from Octavius the phrase "strong toil of grace," and Charmian claims that in death there now lies "a lass unparalleled."

The play is cut loose from both conventional morality and apparently also from the physical theater. Every major editor of the play has remarked on the oddity that this undoubted masterpiece of Shakespeare's maturity has not enjoyed a single truly outstanding success in its recorded performance history. This even though such legendary actors as Laurence Olivier and Vivien Leigh have tried their hands. Perhaps Shakespeare grasped the opportunity afforded by the theaters' closure to write a play that is essentially not actable, a drama of utter exuberance and imaginative freedom, a radio play centuries before radio. Maybe, but Shakespeare's plays were the shared property of the entire company and on them depended the welfare of the shareholders. When the plays were great theater, they filled the house; when they were not, the company lost out. That Shakespeare would deliberately write an unstageable play is unlikely.

After the bleakness of *King Lear* and *Macbeth,* the luminous *Antony and Cleopatra* comes as a shock. Something must have happened in the autumn of 1606 to brighten up Shakespeare's mood. Whereas the middle-aged Gloucester suffered dreadfully for his adultery, Antony enjoys his to the full. Shakespeare has, of course, moved away from the essentially Judeo-Christian worlds of *Lear* and *Macbeth*; the classical age had rather different concepts of sexual morality. At the beginning of the play's ten-year action, Antony is forty-three, Cleopatra twenty-eight. The ages are given in Plutarch, whose biography of Antony Shakespeare follows closely. In late

1606, when Shakespeare was writing *Antony and Cleopatra,* he was himself in his forty-third year while Jane Davenant was thirty-eight, Cleopatra's age at the end of the play. The protagonists openly celebrate their "mature" adultery. Cleopatra airily dismisses any comparison of her affair with Antony and her youthful fling with Caesar: during the earlier dalliance she was, as she puts it, in her "salad days." Now she is with "Phoebus' amorous pinches black and wrinkled deep in time" and Antony, her "man of men," is the better for loving the older her.

Cleopatra's darkness as an Egyptian Greek—"a tawny front," in the abusive phrase of the Romans—is an issue in the play and in Shakespeare. At three key points in his career, in the Sonnets, *Othello,* and *Antony and Cleopatra,* Shakespeare explicitly connects sexuality and skin color. I believe that the association can be traced back to Emilia Lanier and that Shakespeare chose to write about Cleopatra at this point because he had connected the affairs with Emilia and Jane, as he may have done earlier in *Othello,* when he called one of his characters Emilia. Less than a year separates the guilt-ridden world of Gloucester and the celebratory sex of *Antony and Cleopatra.* If the works do indeed reflect Shakespeare's moods closely, we would have to conclude that by late 1606 or early 1607 his relationship with Jane Davenant had settled into something more exciting and far more relaxed than is suggested by the earlier works. It is an interesting detail about the play that the children of Antony and Cleopatra are given short shrift although they figure prominently in the source. Shakespeare gets away with it, as he must if he wants us to focus on the lovers. In this way, *Antony and Cleopatra* is antithetical to *Macbeth:* after the child-obsessed play comes one in which children are set aside for the sake of the lovers' full enjoyment. Perhaps Shakespeare was having his fill at almost the same time that his daughter Susanna was preparing to marry John Hall.

What Shakespeare and the company actually did during the closure, we can only guess. There may have been some playing in London after all in late 1607–1608. We know that Shakespeare was back in the capital to play at court, which was extremely lucrative: the company netted as much as £130 in just one Christmas season. If the players toured extensively, it is surprising that no records survive placing them in any given parish at any particular moment. Conversely, if they did not tour, we would want to know how they made ends meet. The year 1606 had started darkly for Shakespeare but the fact that it ended with *Antony and Cleopatra* suggests that he had found peace if not happiness. As Anglican Will Shakespeare, he was guilty of offending against one of the ten commandments; as Antony, he was a free classical spirit. Owing to the long closure of the theaters, he almost certainly spent much more time in the Midlands now and therefore would have had many opportunities to visit Jane Davenant. Perhaps this is what lies behind the guilt-free sexual bliss of *Antony and Cleopatra*. If Southampton, Shakespeare, and Emilia Bassano Lanier were reflected in Bassanio, Antonio, and Portia, Antony and Cleopatra may mirror Will Shakespeare and Jane Davenant.

26.

A Wedding and a Funeral: 1607

usanna married John Hall in Holy Trinity on Friday, June 5, 1607. We can be confident that her father was present to give her away, especially since there was no playing in London. Anne Hathaway presumably stood next to her husband. We know nothing of how she responded to his many absences or whether she knew or suspected anything at all about her husband's life in London and latterly, perhaps, in Oxford. She may have sought comfort in her daughters, who adored her if we may judge by their stirring tribute to Anne after her death. In what might be Shakespeare's coming-home play, *The Winter's Tale* (1611), the mother, Hermione, is rejected by her husband, Leontes, in a temporary fit of insane jealousy. She is a model of virtue and nine months pregnant, while he is a domestic tyrant. At the end of the play, she seems to remain unmoved by his pleas for forgiveness; she does not talk to him but addresses her daughter instead. Perhaps this is the point William and Anne had reached in their marriage by 1611; perhaps Shakespeare had wrongly accused Anne of disloyalty at the time of *Hamlet*. If Leontes and Hermione evoke Will and Anne in middle age, then Shakespeare must have felt desperately sorry for what he had done to her.

A new bride usually moved into the house of the bridegroom and his family, as Anne had done twenty-five years earlier. But there were no Halls in Stratford before John Hall's arrival there, and it is likely therefore that he and Susanna moved into the commodious New Place before eventually settling into the premises that we know as Hall's Croft in Old Stratford. Unlike Will and Anne, John and Susanna seem not to have had sex until they were married. His Puritan backbone may have enabled him to master desire, or perhaps his knowledge of human biology was simply better than his father-in-law's. On that summer wedding night, though, the couple made up for abstinent time: on February 21, 1608, nine months later almost to the day, a daughter was born. The Halls named her Elizabeth after the Queen that was.

At some point during 1607, Shakespeare made his way to London again. He was now a freeholder, a landlord, a tithes collector, a shareholder in both the Globe and Blackfriars, and a land speculator in Welcombe, north of Stratford. Even so, he clearly wanted to stay involved in the theater; he would write another four masterpieces before retiring. He no longer lived alone in London; his youngest brother, Edmund, who was twenty-seven years old in 1607, was there too now. How long Edmund had been in the capital is not possible to determine, but since he had come to play he may have been there since before the closure of July 1606. No one wanting to make a start in theater would have come after that, not until the playhouses opened again. Edmund may have come after his father's death in late 1601, probably hoping to get a helping hand from his big brother.

The most plausible reason for Will and Edmund to be together in London in late autunmn 1607 was to play at court during the Christmas season. A year earlier, the King's Men had performed *King Lear* before James on Boxing Day, December 26. That Shakespeare's villain in *King Lear* is called Edmund may not be unconnected to Edmund's presence, even though the name occurs prominently in Harsnett because Weston assumed it in honor of Campion. Will, the most famous and richest playwright of the age, would surely have wanted to further his kid brother's career. It has already been argued that Shakespeare may have starred in the role of a limping Edgar in *King Lear.* It would perhaps be quite like him to cast Edmund as Edmund, a younger brother wanting to usurp the position of his elder sibling. Having Will play Edgar and Edmund Shakespeare play Edmund Gloucester would have made the part of the Bastard piquantly immediate, at least as far as the Shakespeare brothers were concerned.

It would also have given the younger man a superb dramatic vehicle in one of his brother's masterpieces.

Edmund Shakespeare's triumphs, if any, were brief. He died toward the end of December 1607, having already buried his (probably) illegitimate son shortly before. That year's winter was bitter, even allowing for the fact that in those days the weather was generally harsher in the south of England than it is now. The Elizabethan era saw a small ice age during which the Thames froze over repeatedly. On December 8, 1607, a severe frost set in. By Boxing Day parts of the river were covered in ice and a few days later Londoners were crossing the Thames on foot "at every ebb and half flood ... in divers places." The severe cold continued until the middle of January 1608.* Whenever the Thames froze over, market stalls promptly sprang up on it, London traders then as now being quick off the mark. However, the most imaginative response to the severe frosts came from a woman who lay down on the ice: she wanted, she explained, to be able to say that she had lain with old Father Thames.

Edmund's funeral took place on Thursday, New Year's Eve, in St. Saviour's in Southwark. The relevant entry in the registers for that day reads, "Edmond Shakespeare, a player: in the church." Shakespeare gave his brother a grand send-off—the church's fee book notes "a forenoon knell of the great bell, XXs." As the registry entry makes clear, with that outlay of twenty shillings Shakespeare also ensured that Edmund was buried in the church, not outside in the churchyard. He seems to have been almost as solicitous about his brother's remains as he was about his own.

Shakespeare was of an age when, in common with his contemporaries, he must have expected to lose loved ones. But his parents had lasted well—Mary was still alive—and Edmund was his mother's first child to die since little Anne, twenty-eight years earlier. That he had been the youngest must have been hard on her, one imagines. She did die nine months later.

Shakespeare chose St. Saviour's for the burial probably because it was the Bankside players' church, although the burial of Edmund's baby in St. Giles Cripplegate in the Barbican suggests that he resided

---

*Stow and Howes, p. 891.

in Shoreditch at the time, perhaps even in one of the Burbages' rooms in Holywell.* Shakespeare, on the other hand, may have worshipped in St. Saviour's regularly in the latter half of the 1590s. It was the parish church of Southwark, and nearly half the names listed in the 1623 First Folio under "principal actors" also appear in its registers. Some of the players, for example Heminges and Condell, the future editors of the First Folio, were actively involved in their local parish churches. The funeral service for Edmund was probably held in St. John's Chapel, off the north transept. Three hundred years later this side chapel was renamed the Harvard Chapel in honor of John Harvard, who was baptised there barely a month before Edmund Shakespeare's funeral. Shakespeare knew Harvard's grandfather Thomas Rogers from Stratford; he might even have known about the baptism, since it involved a Stratford family and he had probably spent most of 1607 in New Place.

As Shakespeare sat in the chapel mourning his brother, a monument next to the altar seems to have caught his eye and set off a train of thought in the echo chamber of his imagination. It was the tomb of Chaucer's great contemporary and friend the poet John Gower, the author of, among others, a famous poem called *Confessio Amantis,* which includes tales from Shakespeare's favorite writer, Ovid. The monument migrated to the north side of the main nave long ago, but it is still in the church and it still bears the legend that was on it when Edmund Shakespeare died.

There are no references to the poet Gower in Shakespeare outside of *Pericles.* Since the play came into existence in the spring of 1608, its genesis must be connected with Shakespeare's New Year's Eve visit to St. Saviour's and his seeing Gower's tomb that day. Indeed, it becomes almost impossible not to interpret the visit to the church and the writing of the play as cause and effect. If Shakespeare comforted himself with the Christian promise that the dead would be resurrected, that his brother would live on in eternity, and that all losses would be restored, perhaps those reflections led him to imag-

---

*The entry in the register of St. Giles Cripplegate reads "1607 August 12 B[urial] Edward son of Edward [Edmund] Shakespeare, player: base-born" (Chambers [1930], vol. 2, p. 18).

ine, in the Prologue of *Pericles*, Gower risen from "ashes ancient." He had used Gower's *Confessio Amantis* as a source for one of his earliest plays, *The Comedy of Errors*, and he well knew that as a writer he could wake the dead. He was to use precisely the language of resurrection when writing about his own creative genius, in *The Tempest*.

Edmund probably adored Will and may have moved to London to follow in his footsteps; the loss must have been terrible. Edmund was Shakespeare's mother's child and had been the family's baby brother all his life. Under the circumstances, the fact that the theaters were still closed was probably a blessing, since it meant that Shakespeare could be home to comfort his mother and to take his own solace among his family. Shakespeare had more pleasant reasons, too, for wanting to be home in Stratford in the spring of 1608, for his first grandchild arrived on February 21. It must be this that made him focus so intently in *Pericles* on a mother giving birth. Too, this is a play in which both mother and daughter are lost, then are found again. In *King Lear* a daughter dies in the arms of her despairing father; in *Pericles*, a father rendered mute by grief is reunited with "a beloved daughter and a wife" and learns to speak again.

Pericles was entered on the Stationers' Register on May 20, 1608, which suggests that it had been finished in time for the planned relaunch of playing in April 1608. After a moratorium of nine months the London theaters reopened only to close again three months later, in mid-July. This may have been why George Wilkins, Shakespeare's collaborator on *Pericles*, published a novel closely based on the play that same year. Shakespeare demonstrably did not write the first two acts (they are by Wilkins), but he may have had a hand in revising them, for some of the writing seems unmistakably his. The three acts that are undoubtedly his, III, IV, and V, move the imaginative action to a different plane, away from the stylized plot about incestuous potentates to the birth of a baby girl, the seeming death of her mother at sea, and the restoration of the entire family through good fortune as well as the offices of a brilliant physician.

Gower enters in the prologue to Act III, to alert us to the forthcoming arrival of a baby. She is born during a storm at sea—hence her name, Marina. Her mother, Thaisa, has died during the birth, or so everyone assumes. Before entrusting her body to the sea, Pericles bids farewell to his apparently dead queen with "A terrible childbed hast thou had, my dear, / No light, no fire." The term "childbed" occurs three times in Shakespeare, twice here in *Pericles* and once in *The Winter's Tale,* when Leontes's wronged wife, Hermione, complains bitterly that she was "the childbed privilege denied, which 'longs / To women of all fashion." The term's appearance in *Pericles* cannot really be separated from Susanna's very recent childbirth. It is a bridge between the life and the writing, like "godson" in *King Lear.*

Almost immediately after Thaisa's premature committal to the sea, we encounter Cerimon, the most famous physician in Shakespeare and the only one outside of *All's Well* and *Macbeth* with a significant speaking part. It is hard not to think of Dr. John Hall when Cerimon introduces himself in lines written within weeks of the Halls' becoming parents. Cerimon has always, he claims, preferred "virtue and cunning" to fame and wealth because they are not mutable and instead can make a man a god. What he calls the "secret art" of the physician and the exercise of his craft have granted him understanding of nature's "blessed infusions," and thereby the gift of cures. To be a healer confers true pleasure and peace of mind, whereas honor and money only "please the fool and death." Cerimon sets virtue and skilled knowledge ("cunning") against social standing and wealth, sounding a Calvinist note worthy of John Bunyan. Here, in the middle of *Pericles,* we are probably eavesdropping on Hall talking to Shakespeare about his medical expertise and his idealistic dedication to it. The speaker's contempt for "tottering honour" remarkably anticipates Hall's surprising refusal of a knighthood in 1626. If Cerimon is his alter ego, we would expect no less from him even if he may have had other reasons for the refusal, financial ones above all, because the honors handed out by the new king, Charles I, aimed to raise money for the Crown. Declining a knighthood cost John Hall a fine of ten pounds.

Cerimon restores Thaisa to life from near death. Perhaps Hall did the same for Susanna: perhaps things went badly wrong during Elizabeth's birth, perhaps the reason she remained an only child is that her mother suffered complications that rendered future pregnancies impossible. There is a chance we will know one day, if the first volume of John Hall's medical journal turns up. The extant second volume covers only the years 1617 to 1635, with a handful of cases from before that (not including, unfortunately, Shakespeare's last illness). While Hall records treating his wife and daughter at different times, he never mentions obstetrics; nor would one expect him to, since it was the preserve of midwives. But if the midwife had given Susanna up for lost, her husband may have stepped in. Perhaps that is why Shakespeare makes Cerimon declare that his medical skills make him a god.

Pericles, which boasts the raunchiest brothel scenes in Shakespeare, is one of only two of his plays to use the word "prostitute" (the other is *All's Well*). The brothel scenes are strictly Shakespeare's, although his coauthor, George Wilkins, lived at the corner of Turnmill and Cowcross, the site of today's Farringdon Station, a notoriously louche area of town, and at the very least had inside knowledge of the world and language of London's fleshpots.* Wilkins also knew the Mountjoys and Belotts. He testified in their lawsuit, and the newlywed Belotts ended up boarding in his house. It seems that Wilkins and Shakespeare overlapped at the Mountjoys' for a while and that that is how they met. Whatever dramatic ambitions Wilkins may have harbored in his writing career, his collaboration with Shakespeare did not get him far since after the brief reopening of 1608 the theaters stayed resolutely shut. In any case, Wilkins could not really connect with his collaborator's idiom, which resonates with the most intense lyrical yearning. If ever there was a drama of wish fulfillment, the last three acts of *Pericles* are it. On being reunited with his daughter, Pericles urges Helicanus to give him a gash "Lest this great sea of joys rushing upon me / O'erbear the shores of my mortality / And drown me with their sweetness." This is Shakespeare's rhetoric at its most mature and expressive, in a scene in which a dream does indeed come true, for Pericles is having "the rarest dream that e'er dulled sleep / Did mock sad fools withal." Shakespeare could conjure up harmony and happiness in his plays, but in his own life he could not do so, any more than anyone else could. He could not bring back his son from the dead or save his daughter from

---

*This is the Turnbull of Justice Shallow's lecherous feats "about Turnbull Street."

a dreadful childbed. But perhaps John Hall did just that, and if he coaxed Susanna back from the abyss, that may well account for the emotional charge of *Pericles.*

Shakespeare was probably appearing in the first performances of *Pericles* in London when, back home in Stratford, and on his forty-fourth birthday no less, a murder happened. It was the night of April 22, 1608. In the Swan down on Bridge Street, two men started to row in a downstairs parlor in the tavern part of the inn. They were Richard Waterman *alias* Dixon, the landlord's brother, and a butcher by the name of Lewis Gilbert; there had been bad blood between them for a while. Waterman tried to evict Gilbert, but the latter obstructed the door. Two of Waterman's daughters and their mother witnessed all this and one of them screamed, "He will spoil my father, he will murder my father." Presumably Gilbert had at this point drawn what would later be called his "long knife"; he was, after all, a butcher. At this, Thomas Waterman, the landlord, who was sitting at a fire next door talking to a friend, rushed in to help. He forced open the door and grabbed Gilbert by the collar of his doublet to throw him out. Gilbert there and then stabbed him "in the right side of the navel" and ran off. Waterman died the same evening. The following day, the inquest jury returned a verdict of murder against Gilbert. We do not know what happened to Gilbert, but if he was caught he would have been hanged. Shakespeare undoubtedly knew the dead landlord and his family, because the Watermans had been local glovers before turning publicans. Not only that, but many years earlier John Shakespeare may have been apprenticed to the now dead Waterman's grandfather, whose wife hailed from the wolds south of Snitterfield and knew Will Shakespeare's grandfather Richard.

Shakespeare was now a grandfather and surrounded by women: his mother, his wife, two daughters, and a granddaughter. But he had also gained a son-in-law, who would become a friend and confidant. Happiness over the arrival of the baby and the survival of her mother is very likely reflected in the joyous reunion scenes in *Pericles,* although the recent death of Edmund will have tempered the family's good cheer. What Pericles calls "the shores of my mortality" must now have been in all too plain view.

We have no firm idea where he was in the spring and summer of

1608, but in August the company, remarkably, *expanded* its operating base in London. The King's Men now took possession of the Black-friars theater as a playing space. The seven-strong syndicate consisted of Richard Burbage and his brother Cuthbert, Shakespeare, Heminges, Condell, William Sly, and Thomas Evans. (This latter was presumably the son of the Henry Evans who had led the boy players in the Blackfriars from 1596 until they were dissolved in the spring of 1608, after a performance of a play by Chapman upset the French ambassador.)* Twelve years had passed since James Burbage acquired the premises; the local opposition to playing had died down. Perhaps the company sought to repossess the *frater* now because they needed somewhere more upmarket to perform in, somewhere less public and congested, where plague would not stop play, routinely, contrary to the big house across the river. There could be no other reason for them to move just then when they already had the Globe and that had been lying empty for two years now. The Blackfriars stage was to be very different in concept, not a theater in the round but a much smaller, rectangular indoor space, a precursor to the modern proscenium arch theater. Some tickets cost seven times what the Globe charged. The Blackfriars targeted a very different audience, striking a note halfway between the Globe and the royal court.

Shakespeare must have been involved in the Blackfriars negotiations: he was too important in the company not to be, besides which there was his business flair. So we may safely assume that he was in London during August 1608 and that he had probably been there at least since April, when playing had resumed. Ever since the boy players had been disbanded, repossession of the Blackfriars would have been a priority for the King's Men. The fact that the boys were acting during March suggests that this playing area may have enjoyed certain privileges, perhaps even an exemption from bans. When the main theaters opened again shortly after, the King's Men

---

*The play was George Chapman's *The Conspiracy of Charles, Duke of Byron.* The ambassador complained about its treatment of the queen of France, and because his advice on cutting passages in performance had been ignored he wanted Chapman to be imprisoned.

must have wanted to seize the opportunity. It was now or never. The boys, those pesky little eyasses, had been suspended, the prohibition on playing had just been lifted, and the old *frater* at Blackfriars was theirs again. Big profits could be glimpsed on the horizon. No sooner, though, were the King's Men installed at Blackfriars than the theaters closed again.*

---

*The uncertainty of the times may be what prompted Shakespeare's suit against the son of his former neighbor Richard Hornby. The son, Thomas Hornby, had stood as guarantor for someone who defaulted on a debt to Shakespeare. The amount of money involved was six pounds, a not inconsiderable sum, certainly not an amount that as a businessman Shakespeare was prepared to forfeit. The action lasted from August 1608 to June 1609. It cannot have made the master of the grand *domus* at Chapel Lane very popular in Henley Street, where Joan still lived with her family, but lawsuits of this nature were par for the course in sixteenth- and seventeenth-century Stratford and there was not usually anything personal about them. It was really just a matter of hard-nosed business. By then the Hornbys had diversified, the blacksmith apparently doubling as the owner of a tavern or alehouse called the Bell. In this the Hornbys may have been trendsetters, because in the next century Henley Street acquired several more inns and taverns. As far as Shakespeare was concerned, their expanding interests must have rendered them capable of settling their debt.

27

ℒosing a Mother and
a Daughter: 1609–1611

he move to Blackfriars coincided with Mary Arden's death, nearly seven years to the day after John Shakespeare's. Shakespeare buried his mother on September 9, 1608. The register of Holy Trinity does not tell us whether she rests inside the church or in the churchyard, but if the funeral arrangements for Edmund may be taken as a guide, they suggest that Mary and John were both interred somewhere inside the church. Five weeks later Shakespeare may have been back in Holy Trinity, this time to be present at the baptism of his godson William Walker, whom he would remember in his will. It was "things dying," however, rather than "things living," to borrow Shakespeare's own words from *The Winter's Tale,* that exercised him most now; he wrote a tragedy about a mother and a son. There could be no clearer proof of Shakespeare's obsessive need to write, and to write about his own life above all. The death of his father resulted in *Hamlet,* a vast play in which Shakespeare seems to have worked through obsessions and anxieties about his mother, his brothers, his dead son, and Henry Wriothesley. His mother's death triggered another play, and this time the hero would be a version not of Wriothesley or young Hamnet but, perhaps, of the middle-aged Shakespeare, whose wife, like the chaste Virgilia of the play whom her husband calls "my gracious silence," may have been rendered mute by her husband.

Mary Arden had lived well into her late sixties, if our estimate that she was eighteen or so when she married is roughly correct. She had lived through the early triumphs, trials, and tribulations of John Shakespeare's gloving and wool trading. She must have enjoyed the honor bestowed on the family by her husband's holding office in the town, and particularly by his becoming mayor. The middle years, when John was in disgrace and keeping to home in Henley Street, would have been hard ones, made harder when her eldest son, William, got into trouble. No one could have anticipated his London career, least of all her, but she would have known that it was important: the proof was there in his sheer wealth. He had enough money not only to recover the family fortunes but also to fund a successful application for a coat of arms.

The treatment of mothers in Shakespeare's last plays suggests that his relationship with Mary Arden was never resolved, that all his life Will was closer to his father. Shakespeare's preferred approach to the mothers of his heroes and heroines is to make them disappear. The boy-girl twins in *Twelfth Night* no longer have a mother, nor does Desdemona, nor the daughters in *King Lear,* nor Innogen in *Cymbeline,* nor Miranda in *The Tempest.* When a mother appears in *The Winter's Tale,* she is transformed into a metaphorical statue, her son having died already, and in *Coriolanus* the mother destroys her son.

This last, arguably Shakespeare's most disturbing tragedy, followed in the wake of Mary's death. It features a formidable and destructive mother who is called Volumnia. The play was written after the great frost of 1607–1608 when the Thames was sealed in ice, whence the phrase "the coal of fire upon the ice." If this provides an earliest possible starting date in the winter of 1608, an important clue in the play suggests a much more specific and later date. In Act III, Coriolanus berates the patricians for having allowed "Hydra here to choose an officer" who will turn their "current in a ditch, / And make your channel his." That is, the people, a multiheaded snake, should not be represented by tribunes, because they will eventually push those tribunes to abuse the patricians' privileges. The ditches and channels here evoke Sir Hugh Myddleton's ambitious project for supplying London with spring water from Hertfordshire by cutting a special four-mile-long trench. There may be an even more specific allusion to the profiteering aspect of this new project, which was not a publicly funded venture but a private one that pledged water only to paying customers. Work on the Myddleton project started in February 1609, so Shakespeare probably started writing *Coriolanus* after his mother's death and not before.

The mother-son relationship in *Coriolanus* is suspect and destructive. Volumnia is an overpowering figure who sees her son primarily in martial terms, at the expense of both his humanity and hers. He is rumored to have become an engine of war "to please his mother" and he is lost when she disapproves of his decision to spurn a popular plebiscite. In the end, she famously persuades him not to avenge himself on the treacherous city of Rome by sacking it. He knows that to obey her will mean certain death to him; he obeys anyway. Before parting from Volumnia, he says, "O mother, mother, / What have you done?" This anguished outburst in a mother-son play coming within months of the death of Shakespeare's mother carries a special resonance. There is no maternal warmth in Volumnia. When she asserts that the breasts of Hecuba suckling Hector did not look lovelier than his forehead "when it spit forth blood / At Grecian sword, contemning," we have traveled a long distance from the tenderness of the baby at Lady Macbeth's breast.

While Volumnia is fiercely ambitious for Coriolanus in war and peace, his love for her is unqualified and unquestioning. Everything he has accomplished, we are told, he did only to please her. If Shakespeare's relationship with Mary Arden was anything like this, then perhaps he stood at his mother's graveside in Holy Trinity saying to himself, "O mother, mother! What have you done?" Perhaps Shakespeare had striven ceaselessly to please Mary Arden above all but felt that she never quite reciprocated his devotion. Earlier in the year he had had to break to her the news of her youngest child's death. Shakespeare must have done his utmost by Edmund. After all, only he could pick up a bill like the one he paid in Southwark to send off his mother's son into eternity. What he could not do was to save Edmund. Perhaps his mother blamed him for taking the baby of the family with him to London where Edmund, like his son and perhaps the boy's mother, may have fallen victim to the plague.

Shakespeare's "mother play" is the most austere and masculine in the canon as well as morally the most opaque. Its hostility, its incomprehension and alienation, are unmistakable. As if to connect with just this mind-set, Shakespeare now did something that must have deeply upset his wife, even if it would prove a great boon to posterity. This was to publish his sonnets. It is unlikely that a loving and devoted husband would have published poems that implicated him in at least two extramarital liaisons. Shakespeare clearly did not censor the poems and he was probably responsible for their narrative sequence; after all, only he knew the plot of his own sentimental life. He may have decided to publish the sonnets now partly out of frustration at the theaters' closure. Years earlier, he had similarly put a prolonged prohibition period to good use by writing *Venus and Adonis* and *The Rape of Lucrece*. During the present closure, he had written at least three if not four plays—*Macbeth, Antony and Cleopatra, Pericles,* and *Coriolanus*—with never a chance of putting them on. Nor could he publish them, because to do so would jeopardize his company's future investment in the scripts.

There must have been a commercial reason for releasing the poems for publication in 1609. They were the only pieces of his writing (besides the four plays just listed) that had not been exposed to public view, and Shakespeare was clearly not going to jettison them. The main reason that the poems did not appear earlier in the closure period has to be that Shakespeare did not want his mother to discover the intimate truth of his relationships with Southampton and Emilia Bassano. This scenario conjures up a Shakespeare nervous about a London publication coming to the attention of a forceful mother who probably could read. To the very end he may not have dared to offend or upset her. Now that she was gone he felt no such scruples toward his wife, his children and siblings, or indeed toward the Dark Lady and Southampton.

The fact that the poems were not reprinted after 1609, and the dedication of the First Folio fourteen years later to Pembroke and Montgomery, may point to a temporary cooling between Shakespeare and Southampton over the Sonnets' publication. Or, on the other hand, the poems may have been a peace offering to the Earl. Relations between him and Shakespeare might have been strained anyway at this point, because on January 28, 1609, *Troilus and Cressida* was entered for publication on the Stationers' Register and then printed in quarto. This was most certainly a reopening of old wounds. It is hard to believe that Shakespeare would have been a happy party to the printing, although the long interdiction was bound to cause the company to look elsewhere to generate income. The satirical portrayal of Southampton as Achilles' male whore may well have been a product of political pressure in the first place, but as a slur in a hitherto unpublished play it had long been forgotten. It had no life beyond the spoken word, and the play had probably only ever been seen by a small self-selected elite. Publication was a very different matter. Now everyone could read about the sexual procliv-ities of two of the country's best-known names, with the added innu-endo that the real bond between Southampton and Essex eight years earlier may have been sexual. The history of the publication of *Troilus and Cressida* is notoriously tricky, down to the play's inclusion, at the last minute and anomalously, in the First Folio (it is absent from the Folio contents page). Shakespeare probably had no veto over the printing of the play, but it must have been he who initiated publication of the Sonnets, perhaps in the first instance to counteract the dam-age done by the quarto of the play to his friendship with Wriothes-ley. If so he may have done more harm than good, since the poems augmented suspicions about Southampton's sexual tendencies.

If Shakespeare kept copies of his sonnets, including the early so-called Hathaway poem, it is hard to imagine that he would not also have owned quartos of his plays and poems in what John Hall called his "study of books." The same study probably contained sets of Holinshed and Plutarch. During the long enforced sabbatical from playing, Shakespeare may well have been rewriting plays in his study at home, working from his own printed quartos of them. The fa-mously "revised" Folio text of *King Lear* probably originated with Shakespeare himself annotating one of his own 1608 quartos of the play during the interminable closure.

That the 154 sonnets are in some order is undeniable; the po-ems' story line is immeasurably enhanced by the fact that its narra-tive seems to be chronological. If Shakespeare did offer his copies of the poems to the printer, doing so would have allowed him to revise them and perhaps reshape the story, but this seems not to have happened extensively. The one thing that the middle-aged grandfather of 1609 might have wanted to excise would probably have been the poems' almost confessional gay subtext, but he left it as it was. Perhaps his reluctance to censor himself arose because other copies of the poems had circulated, so that he could not depart from their texts at a whim. In any case, two of the most scandalous sonnets had already been published in the best-selling *The Passionate Pilgrim* in 1599, including Sonnet 144, about the poet's two loves. By 1599 at the latest, therefore, all of literary London must have known about Southampton's sexual past. Part of the sales appeal of the cycle would have been its association with one of England's most prominent and notorious noblemen. To that end, it had to be the real thing. Perhaps this was the price that Shakespeare was prepared to make his wife pay.

Thomas Thorpe published the first quarto of the poems in 1609, under the title *Shakespeare's Sonnets. Never before Imprinted,* and dedicated them, famously and delphically, "To the only begetter of these ensuing sonnets, Mr W. H., all happiness and that eternity promised by our ever-living poet wisheth the well-wishing adventurer in setting forth." He signed this "T[homas].T[horpe]." It is one of the most teasing literary mysteries of all time, for the identity of Master W.H. continues to elude us. It might refer to Shakespeare himself since, as the author, he could be thought of as "the only begetter" of the sonnets. This would at least account for the use of "Master" ("Mr."), which is hardly a suitable form of address for the other obvious candidate, "the Right Honourable Henry Wriothesley, Earl of Southampton, and Baron of Titchfield," to give him his full title as it appears in the dedications of both *Venus and Adonis* and *The Rape of Lucrece.* But if Shakespeare is the "only begetter," then we would have to postulate a serious error, "H" for "S," in this otherwise elaborate and carefully crafted, if maddeningly overpunctuated, dedication, whereas "W. H." can, of course, be read as the inverted initials of Henry Wriothesley.

It has been argued that "W. H." should be read as William Herbert, who shares the dedication of the 1623 Folio with his brother Philip. But the Herberts were Knights of the Garter and in the Folio are properly identified as "William Earl of Pembroke and etc Lord

Chamberlain to the King's most excellent Majesty" and "Philip, Earl of Montgomery, and etc Gentleman of his Majesty's Bedchamber." It is hard to imagine that either would be addressed as simply "Master," besides which Pembroke was only ten years old in 1590 when the first seventeen sonnets were probably written, and Elizabethan records tend to be scrupulously accurate about social rank, almost more than about anything else.* If the Sonnets had been addressed to William Herbert, they would surely have been included in the First Folio. The reason why neither they nor the two long poems were so included is almost certainly that all three were dedicated to Southampton and known to be so. The Pembrokes were understandably not prepared to have someone else's "castoffs" in a volume dedicated to them, while Southampton seems to have been displeased by the entire venture of the Sonnets. However discreet the dedication may seem to us, at the time "W.H." would have been understood, and Southampton would almost certainly have disowned it.

That copies of the printed poems could quite easily reach Stratford is evident. Richard Field was going strong in the capital at just that time and still had plenty of family back in Stratford. It is inconceivable that he did not know about the Sonnets or that he would not have read them. The question ought to be why he himself did not print or publish them. Shakespeare's mention of him in *Cymbeline,* written in 1610, may be more than a coincidence. Even if one does not wish to subscribe wholeheartedly to the view that Shakespeare was a misogynist, the publication of the Sonnets has painful implications for his marriage.

In the autumn of 1609, the theaters at last reopened. The King's Men had several new plays ready to go, and two different venues at which to perform them. As always, they hit the ground running, and playing all-out at Blackfriars at last must have been exciting. The

---

*When Leland visited Charlecote in 1542, however, he referred to Lucy as "Master," demonstrating that the word could be applied to the highest in the land. So the dedication of the Sonnets does not necessarily exclude aristocrats, as is sometimes erroneously assumed.

company had plenty of experience of staging plays at night, thanks to countless evening performances at court, but Blackfriars was different. Shakespeare, characteristically, would try to capitalize on the new stage, its sophisticated audience, and its potential for another kind of theater. He must have been part of the team that regrouped in London, although we have no idea where he lived after 1609.

From just this time, September 9, 1609, a letter has survived by someone who resided at New Place, Shakespeare's "cousin" Thomas Greene, lawyer and Stratford town clerk. Perhaps he and his wife had moved in after Mary Arden's death. Greene planned to buy a large house called St. Mary's House over in Churchway, close to Holy Trinity and directly east of a barn belonging to the Reynoldses. In a memorandum about the impending move, Greene mentions that he cut down the walnut trees with the agreement of the seller, George Brown, and then he notes that Brown in turn had asked Greene's permission to "sow his garden," which Greene readily granted "because I perceived I might stay another year at New Place." Clearly the Greenes and the Shakespeares were close and the fact that the Greenes named two of their children after Will and Anne and another one after the Halls' daughter, Elizabeth, consolidates this sense of ease that comes off Greene's letter to his vendor. We know that the Greenes moved out of New Place over the summer of 1611, because in June that year the Corporation minutes its decision "to repair the churchyard wall at Master Greene's dwelling house." The couple now lived in a large new house with barns and stables, the site of which can still be inspected because a small part of the foundation remains. Quite how substantial this property was is clear from Greene's offering it and his tithes to the Corporation for sale. The year after Shakespeare's death, the whole property fetched a stately £640, considerably more than the total cost of the first Globe in London eighteen years earlier. At the time St. Mary's House was described as "a pretty neat gentlemanlike house with a pretty garden and a little young orchard standing very sweet and quiet; the place and building within this 6 years cost above 400 [four hundred pounds]." A modern real estate agent could hardly do better. Greene was patently rich. His involvement with the Shakespeares was a privileged one: here is a person who not only stayed

with them in the grand family home, but lived there on a semiper-
manent basis at just the time when Shakespeare was writing *Cymbeline* and *The Winter's Tale*. Greene was a man of some gravitas in
Stratford where he held the office of town clerk for fourteen years
from 1603 on.

The Greenes were not long afterward followed to Old Town by
the Halls, and so in 1611 Judith was alone at New Place. She was
now indeed all the daughters of her father's house and all the brothers too, to paraphrase her alter ego, Viola from *Twelfth Night*. It is
from just this year that we have a document showing her "signature,"
twice. It dates from December 4, 1611, and the circumstances and
people involved suggest that Judith was at that very moment moving
away from her father's tutelage. In itself the document is a mere con-
veyance of a house in Wood Street; what renders it remarkable is
that Judith Shakespeare witnessed the transaction, "signing" the deed
of sale with a mark alongside the mark of Lettice Greene, whose
husband was the same Thomas Greene who had until recently lived
at New Place.

The house in Wood Street was sold on behalf of the Quineys,
the family of Judith's future husband. The seller was Elizabeth (Bess)
Phillips Quiney, the widow of a two-time mayor of Stratford,
Richard Quiney. The Quineys were among the richest families in
town, but Bess Quiney had had to provide for a horde of children after her husband's untimely death nine years earlier. In early May
1602, Richard Quiney, who was then mayor of Stratford and making
the rounds in the streets of his town ("at a fair time the bailiff being
late abroad to see the town in order," in the words of the original
document), had walked into a drunken tavern brawl in which some
of Greville's men were threatening the landlord with drawn daggers.
Quiney had tried to quell the riot but "had his head grievously broken" by one of Greville's retainers. A month later he was dead, presumably as a result of that injury.* Gilbert Shakespeare and Quiney
had numbered some of Greville's men among their friends, so perhaps drink was to blame or else the bad blood between Quiney and
Greville himself, who had started to enclose Stratford's common, the

---

*SBTRO ER 1/1/50.

Bancroft, with hedges in spite of strong protests from the Corporation. Several stand-offs ensued between him and the town's people and mayor. The sale of the Wood Street property may have been to benefit one of the dead man's children, Thomas Quiney, by setting him up in business, for two days later he bought a twenty-one-year lease on the so-called Atwood tavern, on the west side of High Street and north of Harvard House. The lease describes it as the house where "Thomas Rutter now dwelleth." Rutter may well have belonged to the Rutter family that eventually purchased the Maidenhead (the east wing of the Birthplace) in Henley Street from the Hiccoxes and whose inventory has survived along with theirs.

The obvious reason for Judith Shakespeare and Lettice Greene to witness the sale must be that the Quiney and Shakespeare families were becoming more closely linked than ever. The two families had long been friends and, before that, neighbors. And Judith's father wrote a play just then about a father surrendering his daughter to a young man. *The Tempest* may be even more deeply "about" Judith than the comedy about twins a decade earlier, though Judith was twenty-six in 1611 whereas Miranda is fourteen, and Judith was not motherless, unlike the princess in the play.

Our first glimpse of the play is a court performance of November 1, 1611, which may have been its premiere. The play and Judith's witnessing of a Quiney deed are too close in time for us not to view them as linked. It may be that Judith was being wooed in the summer or autumn of 1611, and with Shakespeare's blessing, though it meant that he stood to lose his daughter. Perhaps, since the proceeds went to Thomas Quiney, she was witnessing the sale as part of the arrangement between the two families. She may have been betrothed to Thomas Quiney as early as the winter of 1611–12; if so, we will never know why they waited another five years to marry. Maybe she had to look after one of her parents, her mother perhaps. Conversely, it is possible that she held out against marrying Quiney and that in the end her decision to go ahead was prompted by her father's illness. That would account for the couple's failure to observe proper ecclesiastical procedure in 1616: they may have been hurrying to marry so that Shakespeare could give away his daughter as a bride before he died. The daughter behind Miranda, Marina, and Perdita was probably Judith rather than Susanna, who was now the married mother of a three-year old.

If the literary magician from New Place is Prospero on his island, we should also ask who Ariel, Caliban, Ferdinand, and Antonio might be. Clearly Shakespeare did more than just import his own household into this archly self-conscious play, which was almost from the start seen as his most personal work. He is undoubtedly both more and less than Prospero. His friends clearly thought so too when they placed it first in the commemorative 1623 Folio. Not only is it an obvious flagship play for its sheer poetic brilliance and self-advertising artfulness, but it marks his formal leave-taking of the stage.

We may be confident that Shakespeare saw himself as a wizard of language and books who for twenty years had created airy nothings out of his imagination and got rich by it. The thought of Shakespeare, like Prospero, in contemplative retirement with every third thought being of his grave does not quite hold up against the documentary and "anecdotal" records. Broad similarities are nevertheless in evidence. Shakespeare was retiring from the stage; he was a master of words; he was a father with an unmarried daughter; and retiring entailed a physical move from one location to another, from London to Stratford. Whether this real-life Prospero also had his Antonio, a brother who betrayed him and remained resolutely unrepentant, we can't know; if he did, it might have been Richard, for reasons that we have already encountered.

The Tempest hints at a thaw or rapprochement between Shakespeare and Southampton. The only known source for the play's plot is an unpublished account by William Strachey of the Virginia expedition and the shipwreck in 1609 of the Virginia Company's flagship, the *Sea-Adventure,* in the Bermudas, Ariel's famous "still-vexed Bermoothes." It is likely that Shakespeare learned of the wreck from Southampton, who would undoubtedly have known Strachey's account. The wreck's crew reappeared in May 1610 after what seemed like a miraculous drowning and rebirth. Bermuda, which was known at the time as the Isle of Devils, turned out instead to be full of food and timber and everything else that the crew required to build two small pinnaces, in which they sailed safely to Jamestown, where they were headed in the first place. Caliban's genesis probably owes as much to the Virginia colonizers as to Montaigne's seminal essay on cannibals.

At around the time Shakespeare was writing *The Tempest*, the Halls were planning to set up on their own somewhere in Old Stratford. The first rent return that we have for Hall is dated 1612. It does not tell us where he lived, but the returns for the three years after that, each for eight pence, place him in a close by Evesham or "Easome" way, at the southernmost edge of seventeenth-century Stratford. One of his neighbors here was Abraham Sturley, as we know because a 1611 rent return notes that the borough levied eight pence "for a close by Evesham way" of him, too. Another possibility is that Hall took over Sturley's home in 1612; this would account for their paying exactly the same rent in the same close in 1611 and 1612. The question is of some interest, because the Puritan Sturley may have had a hand in bringing Hall to Stratford in the first place. Thirteen years earlier, the same Sturley had corresponded with Quiney about Shakespeare's readiness to invest in the Shottery yardlands. Before that and after Cambridge, he had worked for the Lucys of Charlecote. Another possibility concerning the Halls' house has to do with Susanna's uncle Gilbert, who died on February 3, 1612, in his forty-sixth year. The Holy Trinity register's record of the death calls him "*adolescens,*" "bachelor." He had been William Shakespeare's trusted lieutenant for many years. We cannot rule out the possibility that at some point he had moved out of New Place, if he ever lived there, to set up on his own as a Corporation tenant in Old Town and that it was his residence that the Halls now inherited.

28

"Do Not Go Gentle into That Good Night": 1612–15

n Monday, May 11, 1612, Shakespeare appeared in court in Westminster to testify in the Mountjoy-Belott case. The court records identify him as "William Shakespeare of Stratford-upon-Avon," so he was no longer officially resident in London. He had probably moved out of Muggle Street when the closure of the theaters in 1606 turned into a prolonged interdiction, but when playing resumed he may have returned to his old digs in the autumn of 1609 and stayed until the end of 1611.

The winter of 1612–13 was tepid and wet, with freak gales and severe storms. At Chart near Maidstone, during the Christmas holidays of 1612, some thirty-five people were struck by lightning including the minister in the pulpit. They all recovered, except for a miller who died. The climate during Shakespeare's lifetime was a constant concern in view of its inevitable impact on farming. The strange winter of 1612 recalled the blighted years of the mid-1590s, when the summers were raw and wet and ears of corn rotted on the stalk, and it contrasted with the intense cold of 1607–1608 with its heavy snows and frozen Thames.

Shakespeare's company was busier than ever. In the run-up to the wedding of Princess Elizabeth and Frederick V, the Elector Palatine, on February 14, 1613, the King's Men appeared at court twenty times; on eight of those occasions, they put on plays by Shakespeare.*

---

*The plays were *Much Ado About Nothing* (twice, and also called *Benedict and Beatrice*), *The Tempest*, *The Winter's Tale*, 2 *Henry IV* (*Sir John Falstaff*), *Othello*, *Cardenio*

Ten days before this big event in the Stuart social calendar, Shakespeare buried his brother Richard. Of Mary Arden's eight children, only William and Joan were now alive. Neither Gilbert nor Richard apparently made a will, and the brothers left few traces on their town. Given that Thomas Greene not only held one of the most important offices in the Corporation but also lived at New Place, this is the more surprising. There is something here that eludes us, a reason why one of the richest and most literate men in town and his brothers were not required to serve as burgesses or aldermen on the borough council. That Shakespeare was no longer working actively does not come into it, since other members of the borough served until the bitter end. When he was still writing, Shakespeare would not have been expected to sit on the town council, because he was away from home so much. After 1611, however, he had settled in Stratford more or less permanently, only making occasional forays to London. It is one of the abiding mysteries of the Shakespeare story that this elite family seems to have done so little while all the time broadening its asset base locally. They clearly thought of themselves as a Stratford family, yet only John Shakespeare ever served the town in an official capacity.

By early spring 1613, Shakespeare had probably ceased to be actively involved in the King's Men. At the very least, he was retrenching. His acquisition of a grand London property a few weeks later may also point in that direction, for what better way of making ends meet in retirement than to be a wealthy landlord collecting money from tenants? The Blackfriars gatehouse was Shakespeare's first investment in London real estate. One of several gates into the former monastery, it straddled a passage now called Ireland Yard on the eastern boundary of Blackfriars, opposite the Royal Wardrobe and just up from the church of St. Andrew's. The Cockpit Inn today occupies the southern wing of the property. Shakespeare must have known the precinct well and had probably acted at the new venue when the

---

(twice), and *1 Henry IV* (*The Hotspur*). See *Dramatic Records in the Declared Accounts of the Treasurer of the Chamber 1558–1642*, in Malone Society, *Collections*, vol. 6, ed. David Cook and F. P. Wilson (Oxford: Malone Society, 1961–62), pp. 55–56.

King's Men resumed playing in 1609. He was almost obsessed with English history, far more so than any other dramatist or writer at the time, and would have been acutely conscious of the old *frater*'s spirit of place. It had been one of Henry VIII's favorite venues and had served as a Parliament chamber. It was here that the legatine trial regarding the King's divorce from Catherine of Aragon had taken place, as Shakespeare would have known from Holinshed. In this very place the cardinals had sat, the "great hall" wherein "was preparation made of seats, tables, and other furniture, according to such a solemn session and royal appearance." According to Holinshed, the *frater* had been "platted in tables and benches in manner of a consistory, one seat raised higher for the judges to sit in."* The Blackfriars great hall was one of the most famous chambers in London. If, as seems likely, it boasted a hammerbeam roof similar to the one in Westminster Hall, one can understand why the King's Men could afford to ask seven times more for admission than at the Globe, and why shares in the Blackfriars would in the long run prove so much more lucrative than those at the public venue in Southwark.

Thomas Wolsey as Lord Chancellor and his fellow cardinal Lorenzo Campeggio, the papal envoy, had presided at the divorce hearings. This may well have been what gave Shakespeare the idea for a play about Henry VIII, a play one of whose scenes would be acted out in the exact location where its historical original took place eighty-four years earlier. The disputations of the trial still hung in the air, or so it must have seemed to Shakespeare. He was perhaps angling for the same frisson that the modern tourist experiences in the Jerusalem chamber in Westminster, where the famous deathbed scene in *2 Henry IV* is set. Bolingbroke had tried to dupe his nobles by a distracting crusade to the Holy Land, to take their minds off rebellion at home against an illegitimate king, himself. He had hoped to expiate his usurpation of King Richard by dying in Jerusalem, and in a way he did. But his Jerusalem was in the heart of Westminster, and the usurpation that he so dreaded was undertaken by his son, who took the crown while the old man was still alive. In the

---

*Holinshed, in Bullough, vol. 4, p. 466.

Jerusalem chamber, art and history converge seamlessly. They do so, too, and brilliantly, in *Henry VIII*.

Along with the gatehouse came "all that plot of ground on the west side of the same tenement which was lately enclosed with boards on two sides thereof by Ann Bacon widow...and being on the third side enclosed with an old brick wall."* The land west of Shakespeare's gatehouse had been carved out of the old Prior's Garden, which corresponds to the bulge on Copperplate. Shakespeare's property occupied the northern wing of the gatehouse and rooms across Ireland Yard. The yard cut through to the western range of the monastery and from there connected with Playhouse Yard.† Shakespeare signed the deed of purchase on March 10, 1613; although he had two joint signatories the property was his. The cost was £140, of which he paid £80 cash on that day. The following day he leased the place back to the vendor for the outstanding £60, which was due on September 29. Shakespeare had three trustees: his fellow player John Heminges; William Johnson, who was probably the landlord of the famous Mermaid tavern; and one John Jackson, who has not been positively identified. Why Shakespeare had trustees is a puzzle; some biographers have argued that it cut out Anne Hathaway from enjoying her third of the property in the event that he predeceased her. Perhaps, but there is no other evidence in Shakespeare's will to that effect. We can only guess. The decision to use trustees may have been connected to the fact that this was his first London property; with no brothers to look after his affairs while he was in Warwickshire, as he increasingly was, he may have wished to have friends in an official capacity on the spot. It was not necessarily a sign of a deteriorating relationship with his wife.

---

*Chambers (1930), vol. 2, p. 155.

†On Copperplate, neither Ireland Yard nor either of the two passages from Water Lane is marked, but John Leake's post–Great Fire survey of the City of London (1666) as well as Ogilby's map (1675) show their exact positions. Ogilby also shows New Street, which cut across Prior's Garden as an extension from Creed Lane. It is possible that New Street marked the western boundary of Shakespeare's plot, unless the plot extended all the way west to the old prior's lodging at the end of Ireland Yard.

Shakespeare must have bought the gatehouse to diversify his portfolio of houses, barns, orchards, and tithes. Given his practice of constantly investing, this would seem an obvious explanation. His acting days were almost certainly over and his writing career was drawing to an end. His last solo work, *The Tempest*, lay two years in the past already. If the mansions in the Strand were out of reach of London's rising bourgeoisie, Blackfriars was not. The Burbages had repeatedly invested in the precinct and now Shakespeare followed suit. The man who had bought the largest house in Stratford also desired to dwell among the best people in London, in one of the few parts of the capital where houses enjoyed running fresh water from taps. He was ever conscious of status and rarely shied away from new ways of making money. Perhaps it was through his powerful friends the Combes, local magnates who were second only to the Cloptons in the influence they wielded in Stratford, that Shakespeare heard they were planning to enclose at Welcombe near Stratford and realized that his Warwickshire revenues might be less in the future; or he may have been alarmed at the thought of yet another crop failure and its inevitable domino effect on his revenues. The proximity of the Blackfriars theater evidently did not bother him any more than it did the Burbages; the *frater* was, after all, the shared property of the King's Men. Interestingly, Shakespeare left no shares in either the Globe or Blackfriars. He must have sold them between 1613 and 1616, and perhaps in the wake of what would shortly happen on Bankside, about which we will hear more. Getting rid of his Blackfriars share may, however, have been one of his few bad business decisions.

If Shakespeare had hoped for a quiet summer in 1613, a time to relax among his orchards in Stratford and enjoy a life cushioned by shrewd investments, he was in for a shock. In early June that year, a young man named John Lane alleged that Susanna Hall had contracted gonorrhea from the haberdasher Rafe Smith in the house of one John Palmer. As Susanna's lawsuit, filed on July 15, put it: "about five weeks past the defendant [Lane] reported that the plaintiff [Susanna] had the running of the reins [gonorrhea] and had been caught with Rafe Smith at John Palmer."* It is not clear who John Palmer was; in connection with Shakespeare, the most prominent Palmers are his mother's neighbors in Wilmcote. The house that for over two centuries was thought to be Mary Arden's we now know to have belonged to the Ardens' neighbor Adam Palmer. This might mean that Lane's allegation refers to Susanna being surprised in the proverbial hay with Smith at the Palmers. It all sounds a bit too modern, the thought of a love nest over in Wilmcote in which the thirty-year-old mother of a five-year-old daughter has trysts with a lover while her husband is out healing the sick.

This *is* far-fetched, but it is not impossible. Susanna Hall and Rafe Smith almost certainly had something in common far more important in those days than it usually is now: neighborhood. As a haberdasher, Rafe Smith was probably a scion of the house of Smith & Co., Haberdashers of Henley Street, the first house on the north side's town end. He was five years older than Susanna. If there was an affair it might go all the way back to their days of growing up in Henley Street. Perhaps a youthful neighborhood affair was something else she shared with her father, since he and Anne Hathaway may also have met in Henley Street. John Lane of Alveston near Stratford was in a position to gossip about the Halls probably because his sister Margaret was married to John Greene, the brother of Thomas Greene of New Place. She must have been his source: the Halls had moved to Old Town by now, and Thomas Greene lived not far away, near Holy Trinity. Given the Greenes' closeness to Shakespeare, one wonders whether one of them, probably Thomas, leaked to Manningham details about Shakespeare's sex life in London when Greene and Manningham were at Middle Temple together. But of course Greene may have been unaware that the latter kept a diary (as, indeed, did Greene), even though not knowing about the diary would hardly excuse his spreading gossip about his host and "cousin."

By 1613, the wealthy Lanes lived in the manor of Alveston, which they had bought from the violent Sir Edward Greville, whose

---

*Eccles (1961), p. 113.

men had earlier probably fatally injured the mayor Richard Quiney. To this day the effigies of Nicholas Lane and his son John, who slandered Susanna, can be seen in the local church. John Lane's first cousin was one Thomas Nash, the neighbor of the Shaws and Shakespeares of Chapel Street. In 1626, this same Nash married the Halls' only child, Elizabeth. The Lane-Nash-Hall links that were being forged despite young Lane's defamatory remarks about a leading member of the set have a dynastic logic. New bourgeois money was marrying more money, and we may be sure that Shakespeare would have approved of these unions just as he may at first have warmed to the romance between Judith and Thomas Quiney, and for the same reasons.

The rumor mill was busy in sixteenth-century Stratford, where everybody knew everybody else's business, or thought they did. This may well be why Shakespeare starts his country play *2 Henry IV* with "rumour painted full of tongues." (Rumor and her many tongues start life as a literary motif early in history: with the *Aeneid,* for the image reflects a common experience.) Susanna sued and won; Lane, who did not appear to defend himself, was excommunicated.

The case of Susanna Hall versus John Lane had not yet come to court. In London, the King's Men were putting on a Shakespeare-Fletcher collaboration, *All Is True,* better known to us by its First Folio title, *Henry VIII.* The date was Tuesday, June 29, 1613. The performance would have started at two P.M. and it had reached line 49 of the fourth scene of Act I, where there appears the stage direction "*Drum and trumpet; chambers discharged,*" which provokes from Cardinal Wolsey the question "What's that?" It heralds, of course, the landing of the King's barge and his imminent entry. The actors did not get much further because the firing of the "chambers," or cannon, produced a spark that ignited the thatched roof. Within less than an hour, the Globe had burned to the ground. Miraculously, no one had been injured, and the company's losses were apparently minimal. In the words of an eyewitness, "This was the fatal period of that virtuous fabric wherein yet nothing did perish but wood and straw, and a few forsaken cloaks; only one man had his breeches set on fire that would perhaps have broiled him, if he had not by the benefit of a provident wit put it out with bottle ale."* If the company had lost it costumes and play-books, as happened to the poor players of the Fortune, they would have been "undone."

Within twenty-four hours, the fire at the Globe was the subject of London ballads. Another account, a brilliant antitheatrical satire entitled "A Sonnet upon the Pitiful Burning of the Globe Playhouse in London," was written by someone who had either been there or knew people who had been. He crows about how the "reprobates, though drunk on Monday, / Prayed for the Fool and Henry Condy," and comically evokes the bolting from the burning Globe of "knights," "lords," and Burbage. Shakespeare's friend Heminges gets special mention: "Then, with swollen eye, like drunken Flem-ings, / Distressed stood old stuttering Heminges." The forty-seven-year-old Heminges had plenty of milage left as it turned out, not least in mustering the energy to head up the Folio syndicate that would give the world one of its most precious books. Who can blame him for standing there weeping as one of the company's playhouses burned to the ground? Not even the alehouse next door could save the Globe, the satirist remarks gleefully, although if the fire had "begun below, sans doubt, / Their wives for fear had pissed it out."†

It was left to the shareholders to pick up the bill for rebuilding. They must have thanked the stars for the good fortune of having the Blackfriars *frater* as a second venue. For the next few months they probably shifted their center of gravity entirely north of the river. Since Shakespeare was the coauthor of *All Is True*, he had probably not yet sold his shares in the theaters. There is a temptation to think that he might have done, because the sale of the shares would have financed the earlier purchase of the gatehouse, but the playhouses had been a very safe investment so far. More likely, Shakespeare agreed to collaborate with Fletcher on one or two more plays pre-cisely because he was acquiring more property just then and needed

---

*Letter by Sir Henry Wotton to Edmund Bacon, July 2, 1613 (Evans, p. 1968).
†Evans, pp. 1968–69.

the extra income. For much the same reason, probably, he just then collaborated with Burbage on an *impresa*, an emblematic allegorical device for which Shakespeare wrote the lines while Burbage, a keen draftsman, executed the drawing.

In the end the company stumped up the fourteen hundred pounds required for the new house. When the second Globe rose on the same spot, but now with a tiled roof, it was declared "the fairest that ever was in England."* Shakespeare did not desert his friends and former partners, even if he stopped playing, for his works remained the cornerstone of their repertoire. Burbage, Heminges, and Condell are all remembered in his will. Their loyalty to him in turn extended well beyond the grave, for they produced the First Folio. This Herculean task shows their deep devotion to his memory as well as their natural desire to make money.

Perhaps in the summer of 1614 Shakespeare could at last plant and prune in his orchards. He had always been keenly interested in gardens and now he had the leisure to indulge this passion. But on July 9, 1614, a fire swept through Stratford, with "the wind sitting full upon the town" as the council's petition to the Privy Council put it. The blaze ravaged some fifty-four houses as well as barns and stables; the total damage amounted to an estimated eight thousand pounds. This, the third such disaster in the space of ten years, mercifully spared all the Shakespeare properties, but the money needed to make good the losses would have to come partly out of local coffers and partly from national reserves. This may have been one reason why Shakespeare and John Hall visited London toward the middle of November. Usually, councilors who went to London on Corporation business had their expenses defrayed by the borough (and itemized by the chamberlains); there is no record of payment for the costs of this trip, either because Shakespeare and Hall waived reimbursement, or perhaps because they handled both private and borough business matters. It seems almost inconceivable that the borough council of Stratford would not have sent two of its foremost citizens as delegates to London,

*Chamberlain, vol. 1, p. 544 (June 30, 1614).

and particularly when Shakespeare was known to be well connected to the Privy Council.

Shakespeare and Hall were in London on Wednesday, November 16, 1614. Thomas Greene was there, too, hoping to talk to William Combe about something bad that was brewing in Stratford. He failed to find Combe, but caught up with Shakespeare instead, as his diary records: "At my cousin Shakespeare coming yesterday to town I went to see him how he did." The business that he wanted to raise concerned proposed enclosures in the Welcombe Hills, directly north of Henley Street. This was the first time that the welfare of Stratford's citizens had been threatened in this way since Greville had sought to enclose the Bancroft twelve years earlier. There had long been a pen in the Bancroft for sheep and swine, but full-scale enclosure was another matter; Greville had been implacably opposed by the Corporation and the mayor, Richard Quiney. On that occasion the burghers of Stratford won, although the mayor may have paid a heavy price for his courage and civic leadership. If only he had supplied more detail about his call on Shakespeare and about "how he did." Of course, Greene's primary interest, as opposed to posterity's, was the exact state of affairs over boundaries at Welcombe rather than Shakespeare's health, his appearance, or anything else. The fact that on this visit Shakespeare was accompanied by Hall may suggest that he was no longer in robust enough health to travel alone. Greene's "how he did" could signify more than a greeting.

The Welcombe enclosures have gained considerable prominence in biographies of Shakespeare, because even if the episode's relevance is secondary it is at least well documented, Greene wrote down, probably verbatim, what Shakespeare and Hall said. His account suggests that Shakespeare felt relaxed about the whole business; both he and Hall assumed that no surveying, let alone any active digging of a trench and drawing of hedge mounts, would start before April 1615: "He told me that they assured him they meant to enclose no further than to Gospel Bush . . . and that they mean in April to survey the land and then to give satisfaction and not before and he and Master Hall say they think there will be nothing done at all." They were wrong. William Combe and his enforcer, Mannering, meant all along to dig the moment it thawed, which happened within weeks.

Shakespeare appeared so casual about what was clearly a matter of urgency and importance to his fellow Stratfordians because three weeks earlier he and Greene had struck a deal for compensation with one William Replingham, another possible habitué of New Place, acting on behalf of the enclosers.* Then around December 10 came the precipitate survey of Welcombe, which took everyone by surprise. There could be no doubt now about the imminent enclosing of the land. Greene sought out Replingham in a hurry, noting in his diary that he "came from Wilson to look Master Replingham at the Bear and at New Place [evidently, Replingham was often to be found at one or the other], but missed him."† While not wishing to suggest that Shakespeare and the Combes were in cahoots here, we do know from Combe's will and the Stratford oral tradition that Shakespeare was friendly with the Combes and may have been reluctant to act against them. As a businessman Shakespeare possessed plenty of acumen, even if he was mistaken or misled about the timing of the survey.

The boundaries Combe proposed can still be traced and are marked on the Ordnance Survey maps for the area, as is the track toward the former hamlet of Welcombe and Clopton House. Had the area been successfully enclosed and turned into sheep pastures, it would undoubtedly have been a financial boon for Combe and Mannering. The battle over enclosure intensified that winter of 1614–15 when the women and children of Stratford took up shovels and began filling in the new Welcombe trenches at considerable risk to

---

*The details of the deal are set out in a memorandum dated October 28, 1614: "Articles of agreement indented made between William Shakespeare, of Stratford in the county of Warwick, gent., on the one party, and William Replingham, of Great Harborough, gent., on the other party" whereby the latter covenants to compensate Shakespeare for any loss he or one Thomas Greene should incur "in respect of the increasing of the yearly value of the tithes they ... do jointly or severally hold and enjoy in the said fields or any of them by reason of any enclosure or decay of tillage there meant and intended by the said William Replingham." The witnesses were Thomas Lucas, John Rogers, Anthony Nash, and Michael Olney. Printed by J. O. Halliwell-Phillipps in *Outlines*, 1887 (SBTRO ER1/1/64).

†Chambers (1930), vol. 2, p. 143.

themselves. At the start of 1615 things turned ugly when two Strat-fordians were assaulted by Combe's men, but both sides lost their appetite for a fight when on January 17 there "began a great frost with extreme snow, which continued until the 14 of February." The bitter wintry weather dragged on until March 7, causing huge losses of livestock and endangering travelers.* Everything was paralyzed. Nature, it seems, did not want to see Welcombe enclosed; eventually Combe had to admit defeat when the Lord Chief Justice, Sir Edward Coke, ruled in favor of the Stratford Corporation. Welcombe constituted a real victory for the men, women, and children who had risen against a rapacious local grandee. Shakespeare had not done much to help.

---

*Stow and Howes, p. 1023.

29

Shakespeare Dies: 1616

ohn Shakespeare and Mary Arden were dead, and so were all the siblings except William and Joan. It is hard to imagine that Shakespeare would not call on his sister and her husband whenever he could, since they lived less than ten minutes from New Place. And there was business to conduct in Henley Street, where the bulk of the Shakespeare home had now metamorphosed into Lewis Hiccox's Maidenhead.

In the meantime the Halls were doing well in their splendid house near Holy Trinity. They were rich in their own right, for Susanna's father had conferred on her a dowry of 107 acres. In 1614–15, the Halls are recorded for the last time in Evesham Way. After this they may have started to build their own house, the one we know as Hall's Croft. Dendrochronology—the use of growth rings in trees and wood to establish dates—authoritatively places Hall's Croft in 1614. The house belonged to the Halls according to local tradition recorded even as late as the nineteenth century, and modern science may have confirmed what was at best a plausible rumor. The consonance between the dates for Evesham Way and the timber of Hall's Croft suggests that the Halls probably had this house built for them. They probably moved in sometime in 1615, and they might have spent the rest of their lives in this desirable new residence if Shakespeare had not been taken ill in early 1616 and thus precipitated a return to New Place. Perhaps they kept Hall's Croft on and leased it out; it may have kept their name for that reason, or because it was known as Hall's from the start after its builder and first owner. It is surprising that the house should not feature in either Hall's will or his daughter's; if it was theirs, they must have sold it before Hall died in 1635.

Stratford was too small for people to avoid one another, even if they had wanted to, and their society thrived on talk. For us this is a boon, because it consolidates the view that seventeenth-century Stratford gossip about Shakespeare and his family may contain more than a grain of truth. The town had its share of sexual scandals: we saw one involving Susanna; on another occasion, the play-hating Puritan Daniel Baker was forced to admit to an affair and to his paternity of the woman's offspring. A pity, then, that Judith Shakespeare did not have her ear closer to the ground when she was being courted by Thomas Quiney. He was her junior by four years and was probably named after his grandfather Thomas Phillips of Henley Street, an elder statesman of the borough and the father-in-law of Richard Quiney. The Quineys and Shakespeares lived almost directly across Henley Street from each other; Judith must have known little Tom Quiney from across the road.

One or two houses up west from the Quineys lived Master John Wheeler who, like them, had been expanding in Henley Street. Eventually he consolidated his stake in as many as four properties there through a combination of ownership and leasing; he also had holdings in Windsor and Greenhill Streets. It was his leasehold property at the far corner of Henley Street that caused the council to grumble about its run-down state. The leasehold ran back all the way to the orchard of the White Swan, which by 1598 was owned by Perrott's son-in-law, Master Richard Woodward of Shottery. The Wheelers were recusant and had been so in 1606, when Susanna Shakespeare and they appeared on the same list of those refusing communion. Their children would have played with the Quiney and Shakespeare children. One of the Wheelers, a grandchild of the John Wheeler who had been John Shakespeare's colleague on the borough council years earlier (they left at the same time in 1586), was probably Margaret Wheeler. In the glorious summer of 1615, she and Thomas Quiney started an affair.

Quiney was behaving very badly. If he had indeed been engaged to Judith for several years already, his behavior was even more reprehensible. Judith was certainly a better prospect than her rival. By their recusancy, the Wheelers had put themselves in danger of heavy penalties. The Shakespeares, on the other hand, were rich and now seemingly conformist, Dr. Hall's Puritanism notwithstanding.

One puzzle about Judith's marriage is why she married on Saturday, February 10, 1616, the weekend before Ash Wednesday. This date fell well within the interdicted Lenten period, which began with Septuagesima Sunday on January 28, 1616. In consequence, Judith and Quiney required a special dispensation from the Bishop of Worcester. This recalls the haste with which Judith's parents wed, but unlike them Thomas and Judith did not have the Bishop's permission and ought therefore not to have been allowed to marry at Holy Trinity when they did. Obviously, strings must have been pulled. The brief excommunication that followed would probably not have worried the couple unduly.

The most obvious explanation for their haste would be the imminent arrival of a baby. But no suspiciously premature infant appeared and the baby they did produce came almost exactly nine months after the wedding. It is much more likely that Judith wanted to marry while her father was still alive. Shakespeare had probably been sick in January, when he wrote the first draft of his will; hence probably also the marriage. If Judith and Thomas married in defiance of canon law it was in the hope that Shakespeare could give away his last remaining child. This should have been a happy time for all concerned, but it could hardly be so when the bride's father was dying and the groom's heavily pregnant girlfriend lived in Stratford.

Within six weeks of the wedding, Margaret Wheeler died while giving birth to Thomas Quiney's child. Mother and baby were buried on March 15. This must have been a bombshell. It is almost impossible to believe that Judith was unaware of the affair, and yet that seems to have been the case. Clearly Shakespeare knew nothing about it when he first drafted his will in January 1616; no one else in the family seems to have known, either, even though one would think Stratford was hardly big enough for a successfully clandestine liaison. Maybe the Shakespeare, Hall, and Hart families were all too preoccupied with William's illness to look around them. It is tempting to join the trail of dots left by the documentary record into a narrative that has Shakespeare rewriting his will, just weeks after Judith married, in response to the scandal that had since broken. Shakespeare redrafted his will on Monday, March 25, and the following day his new son-in-law appeared before the consistory court in Holy Trinity. There he "admitted that he had had carnal copulation with Wheeler" and was sentenced to do "public penance in a white sheet on three Sundays in the church of Stratford." He pleaded for a lesser sentence and in the end paid five shillings for the relief of the poor of Stratford and confessed his fault in his own clothes to the minister of the chapel of Bishopton. He got off rather more lightly than he deserved. If Shakespeare had hoped for a serene retirement, Prospero relaxing in his gardens rather than languishing in a monastic cell, he had done so without taking into account the sexual vagaries of youth.

Shakespeare probably had a hand in the lightening of Quiney's penance. It is generally taken for granted that, as Judith's father, he must have been outraged by Quiney's behavior. He probably was, but he could hardly forget his own past; again, Judith may have interceded with him on behalf of her husband, as he now was, and Shakespeare may ever have loved her most, even if the will grants Susanna and her family the bulk of his estate. For the last eighteen years, Judith had been all that was left of the twins. Her father probably saw Hamnet's face in hers every time he looked at her. She may have been Viola and all the daughters of the last plays. Perhaps she should have married sooner, but then again maybe her father could not bear to let her go, or she may have felt that she could not leave him or her mother. Judith Shakespeare may have been her father's muse ever since *Twelfth Night.* Now that he was leaving her behind he must have wanted to do his best by her.

A story was current in Stratford in the middle of the seventeenth century about how Shakespeare met his death. It was first recorded in 1662, which was also the year in which Judith Shakespeare Quiney died, aged seventy-seven. The man who wrote it down lived in Stratford and knew its people well. He was Reverend John Ward, the same who referred to the thousand-pound gift that Southampton allegedly bestowed on Shakespeare. Ward seems to be a pretty reliable witness to what was being said about Shakespeare in Stratford in the late 1650s or the start of the 1660s. His repeated use of the phrase "I have heard" pays tribute to a strong local oral culture. Ward had also "heard" that "Shakespeare, [Michael] Drayton, and Ben Jonson, had a merry meeting, and it seems drank too hard, for Shakespeare died of a fever there contracted." This "merry meeting" might have been Judith's wedding feast on February 10; if so, it would suggest that far from being sick a few weeks earlier, when he first drafted his will, Shakespeare may have been in good and festive form. Drayton was known of in Stratford, of course. He was a Warwickshire lad from Hartshill near Atherstone and John Hall had treated him at some point, calling him "poet laureate" in his case notes. Like Shakespeare, he was a national icon. There is no record that he and Shakespeare ever met in Warwickshire other than Ward's diary entry, but they could have met at New Place every month without leaving a trace. Wining and dining the Earl of Warwick at the Bear or Swan at Corporation expense would need to be recorded but Drayton's would have been private, social calls.

It is also plausible that Jonson called on his friend in the Midlands. Jonson habitually visited friends in the country. By 1616, he was a fêted literary figure, and when he stayed with his friend Drummond of Hawthornden at the latter's castle in the Pentlands south of Edinburgh he was lionized in the Scots capital. If in 1618 he could heave his girth all the way to Scotland, he could certainly get to Stratford-upon-Avon, and where Ben Jonson was, excess of conviviality was never far off.

However, there is reason to be skeptical about this particular social grouping: within two years of his alleged merrymaking with Shakespeare and Drayton, Jonson confided in Drummond that he and Drayton were enemies. "Drayton feared him, and he esteemed not of him," Drummond recorded. Jonson alleged moreover that "Sir W. Alexander was not half kind unto him, and neglected him, because a friend to Drayton."* This makes it rather less likely that they enjoyed a convivial reunion with their mutual friend Shakespeare. It

---

*Sir William Alexander (1577–1640) was a poet and politician and first earl of Stirling. He was a friend of Drummond of Hawthornden's and he was also friends with Drayton, to whose collection *England's Heroical Epistles* (published in 1619) he contributed a complimentary poem.

may be significant that Nicholas Rowe, though he notes that Shakespeare enjoyed the conversation of his friends while in retirement at Stratford, does not repeat the rumor that these three held a drunken literary symposium. Of course, it is not impossible that the animosity between Jonson and Drayton first arose at just this party.

Whatever the truth of this particular occasion, what matters is that friends undoubtedly did visit Shakespeare in Stratford. He may have lived in deepest Warwickshire but not, it would appear, in isolation. We may be quite sure that Burbage, Heminges, and Condell also called in and stayed in New Place from time to time, enjoying the gardens and orchard and walks down by the Avon. As for his other "family," in Oxford, it seems that he saw the Davenants regularly between March 1606 and 1616. According to William Davenant, Shakespeare was a frequent caller, even after his godson was old enough to know the meaning of the word "godfather." Shakespeare probably saw the Davenants in late November 1614 during his last recorded journeys to London, if not right up to the time that he fell ill in late 1615 or January 1616.

Ward may have got it right when he reported that Shakespeare contracted a "fever" during an overdose of drink and good cheer. The wedding of Thomas and Judith, at which family and friends gathered to make merry, would have been fertile breeding ground for infections. One such disease, a particularly virulent one, had just recently hit Warwickshire: typhoid. At the time it was called the "new fever" or the "spotted fever," after the pink spots that appear on the chest and abdomen of the infected person. That typhoid was rampant in south Warwickshire just when Shakespeare died we know from John Hall's diary. In Stratford the year 1616 was a busy one for the Grim Reaper. The higher than usual tally of deaths points to a small local epidemic.

To attribute Shakespeare's death to typhoid has a number of implications, not the least of which concerns the timing of his will. After first contracting the fever he would have been seriously ill within a week and would probably have died within another three weeks. Thanks to antibiotics, typhoid, which is transmitted through water contaminated by raw sewage or by flies and lice from human waste, is almost extinct in the twenty-first century. Those who contracted it in the past did not all necessarily die either. The course of the disease, from infection to death or recovery, is about a month, which is almost exactly how much time elapsed between Shakespeare's final will of March 25 and his death on April 23.

If Shakespeare died of typhoid, then the January draft of the will cannot really have been triggered by the illness that killed him toward the end of April. In that case the draft was probably precautionary, a matter of sorting his affairs and providing for his family in light of his last child's forthcoming marriage. Shakespeare was the last male survivor of the Ardens and Shakespeares of Henley Street. He who had so deeply pondered the meaning of things, who had given such extraordinary expression to suffering and to happiness, who had magically turned the profoundest dilemmas of mankind into life-enhancing public entertainment and great art, now faced his own extinction. As he lay dying, he above all must have known that he had written works that were peerless. Perhaps the knowledge of his achievements was a source of comfort in this extremity. Probably he had been very sick once before, perhaps even with the plague. Then he had been in his thirties. He had survived that time and might do so again. He had often thought about death and one of his least distinguished characters memorably speaks about it as the common lot of all humanity. This is poor Feeble in *2 Henry IV,* a victim of the abuse of the King's levy by Falstaff and Shallow: "A man can die but once," he remarks stoically, and continues with "We owe God a death . . . he that dies this year is quit for the next." Julius Caesar agrees. In a bullish vein he asserts that he will not be cowed by auguries of doom and death, since in life death is a necessary certainty:

> *Cowards die many times before their deaths;*
> *The valiant never taste of death but once.*
> *Of all the wonders that I yet have heard,*
> *It seems to me most strange that men should fear,*
> *Seeing that death, a necessary end,*
> *Will come when it will come.* *

---

*These are the very lines that more than any others of Shakespeare's comforted Nelson Mandela on Robben Island. He wrote his name in the margin of them in

What Caesar glosses over is the chasm between the certain intellectual knowledge of death and its endless psychological deferral in our minds. The truth is that mankind cannot bear too much reality, to paraphrase a later writer, and nothing is more real than the cessation of one's being. Unless, that is, one believes that there is life after death, in which case death becomes a rite of passage. St. Paul first put it like that in 1 Corinthians 55, "O death, where is thy sting? O grave, where is thy victory?," and John Donne borrowed these words for his famous sonnet celebrating the death of death. There is a distinctly religious strain in Shakespeare's last plays—in Prospero's meditations on his grave; in the emphasis on "faith" in *The Winter's Tale,* where a character is named Paulina after, it seems, St. Paul. On the other hand, Shakespeare never served as a churchwarden unlike, for example, his friend Heminges in the City of London, and it may be futile to imagine him seeking comfort in his faith as death approached. Even in the last plays the role of the deity seems merged into the human characters. Prospero may come to regret his usurpation of the Almighty's role, but it is hard to imagine him in a monastic retreat. The end of *The Tempest* almost feels like a gesture, as if this were something Shakespeare thinks Prospero ought to do by way of penance. Prospero's Catholic cell in Milan carries as little imaginative conviction as Chaucer's retraction at the end of his great erotic love poem *Troilus and Criseyde,* when the dead Troilus surveys his past life of love and sex, of eros (romantic love) and of course thanatos (death), from the elevated sphere of agape or divine love. Troilus laughs at the absurdity of human love now that he has achieved a true perspective on it, but readers of the poem rarely laugh with him.

It is to be doubted that during those last few days in his large house opposite the Guild Chapel Shakespeare discovered enough faith in himself to echo St. Paul and deny that death has a sting

---

1979, on p. 980 of the Alexander Shakespeare. A copy of this book circulated clandestinely at the time among the ANC internees and has in it the signatures of a number of them. It is currently (as of May 2006) the centerpiece of the "Complete Works of Shakespeare" exhibition in Nash House, which today guards the entrance to the magnificent gardens of New Place.

because it is the start of life everlasting. Nothing in the plays convincingly points that way. Nor is it clear which faith his would be. Richard Davies's assertion in the seventeenth century that Shakespeare "died a papist" continues to intrigue biographers, particularly because of the ongoing debate about John Shakespeare's famous testament. No letters of Shakespeare's are extant, or at least none of the many that he must have written has come to light so far. Some of his friends and acquaintances kept diaries, notably Thomas Greene, but they forgot to tell us anything of interest about Shakespeare. Similarly with the lawyers in the Mountjoy suit. They never asked their witness the most important question: who he really was. They failed to spot that the vaguely abstracted gentleman from Warwickshire who appeared before them with under-par powers of recall that day was probably the most talented person on earth at that very moment. He would still seem the most talented person ever four hundred years on. How could they be so blind? we wonder, and then we realize that much closer to our time Vincent van Gogh's genius, to cite one example, went unrecognized. At least Shakespeare enjoyed wealth and success in his day.

If we did not have Shakespeare's will, we would want to invent it. One would imagine it to be bursting with information about his family, his friends, perhaps his lovers, and those vast amounts of money that he must have squirreled away; we might learn what provision he might have made for his godson Davenant. We would anticipate finding clues in it to his true faith and we might also wonder whether he would refer lovingly to his wife, or express a longing to be buried near his dead son. (Shakespeare's friend John Heminges asked in 1630 to be buried as close as possible to his adored wife, Rebecca.) At the very least, we would expect the will to convey a strong sense of the man, his family, his circle of acquaintances, in other words to provide a précis of his life toward the end of it. Also, and tantalizingly, the man and the work might come together at last. This legendary dramatist would surely leave behind instructions about his work, perhaps even about a possible publication. His library must have been precious; he would presumably leave it to John and Susanna Hall, since both could read and (probably) write. We know that he must have owned Holinshed, Plutarch, Ovid, and Virgil, as well as many other volumes that we have not identified. At some point in the future we may yet satisfy our curiosity: the inventory that would have been taken of New Place after the master's death in 1616 may yet be found, just as the Hiccox and Rutter inventories of the Birthplace surfaced only very recently. Three volumes from Shakespeare's library may already have been identified and are now in different national collections.

We do, of course, have Shakespeare's last will and testament. It is a long and detailed parceling out of his estate. It is also a singularly dull and elusive piece of writing. Had it been deliberately designed to throw future generations off the scent, it could not have been done more effectively. In spite of extensive unpicking over the years it has yielded little, except for one tantalizing bequest that has exercised generations of writers. We are on the final sheet of the three-sheet will, which Shakespeare is dictating to his solicitor, Francis Collins. There now occurs the famous business of the second-best bed. Here is the passage in question: "Item I give unto my wife my second best bed with the furniture." He does not mention Anne by name, as he does his "niece" (he means his granddaughter) Elizabeth Hall and his daughters, but perhaps that was because there was only one wife, so there could be no confusion about who is meant. Had he called her "my wife, Anne," we would hardly feel more reassured.

The bequest of his "second-best bed" suggests that his best bed had already been disposed of as part of the global bequest of New Place to the Halls, from which were excepted certain items such as his plate (to Elizabeth) and his silver goblet (to Judith). Since John Hall would have looked after Shakespeare in his final illness, he and his wife and daughter had almost certainly removed to New Place by early spring 1616 to help out. Perhaps he and Susanna now occupied the master bedroom and the best bed in it. As in the Birthplace, this might well have been up the stairs, with the dying Shakespeare confined to somewhere on the ground floor. Anne Shakespeare may have wanted "the second-best bed with the furniture" because it was an heirloom that "had come from her old home at Hewlands"; she may have asked for it when the draft will was read out, hence the

interlineating of the bequest.* The beds of Hewland Farm feature almost as intriguingly in her father's will as the second-best bed does
here. Richard Hathaway stipulated that the "two joint-beds in my
parlour shall continue and stand unremoved during the natural life
of...Joan my wife and the natural life of Bartholomew my son and
John my son." At first this would seem to rule out any chance of the
second-best bed in New Place having migrated from Shottery, but
one can never be sure. Perhaps the surviving Hathaways wanted
Anne to have a bed and so she brought one of them with her to Henley Street. This may have been common practice: thus, for example,
the rich brewer Robert Perrott declared in his will that he was leaving
his widow, Elizabeth, "the bed which she brought unto me with all
furniture thereunto belonging." And in 1608 Thomas Combe left his
widow all "tables, bedsteads ... except the best bedsteads which I will
give and bequeathe unto my said son William with the best bed and
best furniture thereunto belonging to have to his own use."†

Perhaps, with Anne's husband's death, the time for returning the
bed to Hewlands had come, and since Shakespeare seemed determined to keep the Hathaways out of his will Anne would hold it in
trust for her family. It is clear from the will that the Shakespeares
owned a "best bed." Perhaps this was the bed that, as the master of
New Place, he had ordered for himself and his wife on his return
home in 1597; it might have had the newly acquired Shakespeare
arms carved on it. This crested bed would have superseded the one
that Will and Anne had shared during the early years of their marriage, in Henley Street. Shakespeare's apparent callousness with respect to Anne is sometimes explained away with reference to
common law, which was supposed to guarantee the widow one
third of her husband's estate as well as continued residence in the
family home. But in that case, there would have been no need for
him to make any additional provision for her and the written will's
sole function would be to dispose of the remaining two thirds of his
estate. How accurately the will declares Shakespeare's total assets is

---

*Chambers (1930), vol. 2, p. 177.
†Chambers (1930), vol. 2, p. 136.

impossible to determine. If there was a way of minimizing his financial liabilities in death he would have known it, as did others among his peers such as the Burbages.

Shakespeare left ten pounds to the poor of Stratford, a reasonable if not overgenerous provision. Other glaring holes in the will hint at other stories. The Hathaways are nowhere to be found, though Shakespeare's brother-in-law Bartholomew of Tysoe and other members of Anne's family were alive at the time. Then there are the missing Globe and Blackfriars shares. We do not know when Shakespeare sold them, but sell them he did, probably sometime in 1613, perhaps in time to pay off the outstanding sixty-pound mortgage on the gatehouse, which fell due in September. Perhaps the sale preceded the fire at the Globe; a sale afterward would have been difficult, since the shareholders would be expected to foot the bill for rebuilding. Any potential buyer would have had to take the long view. As it turned out, this would have been wise: the Globe continued playing successfully for twenty-nine years after the fire.

The Greenes' absence from the will is surprising. Not even a ring for mourning or another symbolic token is left them; it is as though they had never featured in the poet's life. The Greenes were wealthy, of course, and that may be the reason. The friendship between their families endured beyond Shakespeare's death. Greene's brother John of Clement's Inn, for example, acted on Susanna's behalf in 1618 as a trustee of the Blackfriars gatehouse. Thomas Greene left Stratford the year after Shakespeare's death. In a letter written that year he described his time there as "golden days." When he and his beloved wife, Lettice, left the Midlands, it was so that he could pursue a career as a barrister. He had, it seems, kept chambers in London throughout his Stratford years. Eventually he became Reader and Bencher, as befitted a man of his considerable gifts, that is, a lecturer on law and senior member at his inn of court.

Somewhat surprisingly, Thomas Combe, the brother of the Welcombe encloser, features in the will, as does Shakespeare's recusant neighbor from Chapel Street William Reynolds. With regard to Combe, Shakespeare may have been returning a favor, since John Combe had left him five pounds. There is no reference to Shakespeare's friend and boon companion Ben Jonson, but Burbage,

Heminges, and Condell are left the considerable sum of twenty-six shillings and eight pence each to buy themselves mourning rings. Richard Field is missing, and Shakespeare removed "Master Richard Tyler the elder," who had been in the first draft, replacing him with Hamlet Sadler, who was awarded money for a mourning ring. That Tyler was dropped in favor of Sadler, who was probably the godfather of Shakespeare's dead son, may paradoxically consolidate the notion that the Tylers had stood as godparents to one of the Shakespeare children. Some rift with Tyler had occurred in the few weeks that separate the January and March drafts. Indeed, a whiff of corruption had gathered around Tyler after he and others were delegated by the borough to collect money in other counties of England for relief from the conflagration of 1614. In March 1616, he and his companions were censured for "everyone preferring his own private benefits before the general good" and for claiming expenses larger than the donations they gathered. Tyler, it seems, was struck out of the will by his morally indignant friend. This did not prevent the estate from requesting his cooperation shortly afterward in transferring the deeds of the Blackfriars gatehouse.*

The will never alludes to Shakespeare's hidden London past. It is a strikingly Stratford-centric document for someone who spent the best part of his life away. There is no mention of Southampton, the Davenants, Emilia Lanier, or anyone else whose name could cause grief or hurt to his family. Whatever arrangements Shakespeare may have made for Davenant, he would have carried them out privately and well before his illness. The will does feature his "godson William Walker," an eight-year-old Stratford boy who is left twenty shillings in gold. Shakespeare may have set his house in order long before he fell sick; hence, perhaps, the will's bland and unrevealing character.

The idea that the will was revised in late March 1616 to take account of the Quiney debacle adds a certain frisson. It is the case that on the first sheet the word "January" has been deleted and replaced

---

*On February 10, 1618, the Blackfriars gatehouse was conveyed to John Greene of Clement's Inn and Matthew Morris of Stratford "according to the true intent and meaning of the last will and testament of the said William Shakespeare" (Schoenbaum [1975], p. 224). Tyler was one of the signatories on the deed.

with "March." This part of the will treats Judith's inheritance. The phrase "son-in-law," meaning here Thomas Quiney, has been crossed out and replaced with "my daughter Judith," which suggests that this part of the will was indeed rewritten to bypass Quiney so that now Judith's share of the estate devolved directly to her. New Place, the Blackfriars gatehouse, and all his local holdings from the Manor of Rowington passed to Susanna and her family, who thus received the lion's share of her father's possessions. Even eight-year-old Elizabeth Hall was separately and impressively provided for, which suggests that she and her grandfather got on well.

As well as providing for Judith financially, Shakespeare left her his "broad silver gilt bowl," an object that must have been of sentimental value to him. Even if Shakespeare was shaken by Quiney's disgrace, he would not therefore have turned on Judith. Rather, he may rightly have thought that she now needed his help more than ever, hence his careful ring-fencing of her share of his estate. A considerable additional cash reserve of £150 was due to her three years after the drafting of the will, in March 1619; Quiney could access this only by providing land to the same value as collateral. Shakespeare took the long view and this demonstrates just how shrewd he was: he held out the cash as a carrot to encourage Quiney to accumulate landholdings. The money left to Judith was the equivalent roughly of twice Shakespeare's own official outlay for New Place. The £150 left in escrow (that is, as security) to Judith was considerable and sent a clear signal to Quiney that fortune or Shakespeare favored the brave and enterprising in business.

Shakespeare did not forget his sister and her three sons, though he did not recall all three of the boys' names. William and Michael Hart and their anonymous brother Thomas were left five pounds each. Shakespeare left his sister twenty pounds as well as "the house with the appurtenances in Stratford [Henley Street] wherein she dwelleth for her natural life under the yearly rent of 12 pence." She was charged the ground rent for an entire burgage, to be paid to the Shakespeare estate, which was administered after his death by John and Susanna Hall as executors, with his friend Thomas Russell and Francis Collins acting as overseers of the will. By now the house in Henley Street included an annex projecting into the back garden.

This, Joan Hart's cottage, was modest only by comparison with the frontage of the entire Birthplace. The Harts probably moved into the annex after John Shakespeare's death. The levy of twelve pence suggests that either Shakespeare charged his sister a full burgage rate or ground rent for the cottage, as a kind of long-range mortgage, or else that Joan retained ownership of the outer western bay of the Birthplace and the cottage together. This latter is more likely. Shakespeare probably left his sister the outer western bay of the house and the annex, which together probably added up to a burgage, since garden cottages in Stratford were included in the ground rent. Thus in 1555, Thomas Patrick of Henley Street was instructed by the council to pay "2p a year to the chief rent roll for his hovel in the street in the backside of his tenement in Henley Street, or else that he do take down his hovel and pale again." The odds are that Joan Hart and her family lived in the cottage, with access to the gardens at the back, while leasing out the westernmost bay. The entire original three-bay rectangle of the Birthplace therefore constituted the Maidenhead inn; only that way can one account for the number of rooms that made up the Hiccox (1627) and Rutter (1648) inventories. This hypothesis may be underpinned by the fact that in the eighteenth century the Harts *reclaimed* the westernmost bay as living quarters. They could do so only if they had leased them out in the first place, and that may have been as long ago as the time of William Shakespeare.

Shakespeare left five pounds and his ceremonial sword to Thomas Russell, a token of friendship perhaps as well as a vote of confidence in this executor. Russell, who was born in 1570, was a substantial local landowner who lived on the Stour at Alderminster, less than five miles south of Stratford. He was a trusted friend of the poet's, although how long they knew each other is unknown. Russell was connected to the Willoughbys of Wiltshire. The younger son of his friend Henry Willoughby had published *Willobie His Avisa* (1594), which may allude to Shakespeare's involvement with Southampton. Russell's sister-in-law had married the elder brother of *Willobie*'s author. After his first wife's death, Russell married the wealthy widow Anne Digges in 1603; one of her two sons was the Leonard Digges who wrote a prefatory poem for the first Folio. Digges was twelve years *older* than his new stepfather.

There are no hidden clues in the will to Shakespeare's religion. If there ever existed a secret spiritual testament like the one attributed to his father, it has not survived. If it was concealed in New Place then the rebuilding and subsequent demolition of the house would have lost it to posterity anyway. The only clue to Shakespeare's faith is that faith itself emerges in the later plays as an important concept. As it is, Shakespeare's last testament included militant recusants like Reynolds, the Protestant Hall, and others who were, as far as we can ascertain, middle-of-the-road local Anglicans. In that respect he seems evenhanded, guided not by sectarian ideas but by friendship and family.

William Shakespeare died on St. George's Day, April 23, 1616, a Tuesday. He was buried in Holy Trinity two days later, on April 25. We do not know who attended his funeral, but we can safely assume that they comprised—among others—his wife and daughters, his granddaughter, his sister and her family, John Hall and Thomas Quiney, the executors and witnesses of his will, Francis Collins, Thomas Russell, friends and neighbors like July Shaw, the Sadlers, Richard Field, and Robert Whatcott (who may have lived at New Place, since he had testified on Susanna's behalf in 1613). It would have been the grandest funeral since Combe's, two years earlier. Given that Shakespeare's interment involved digging a grave in the very chancel of the church, members of the town council and the mayor were probably present too. Some of his London friends may have attended, if they could arrive in time. As has been mentioned, he left mourning rings for Burbage, Heminges, and Condell. It is hard to imagine that the funeral would have been the occasion of their first visit to Stratford. They probably traveled up at some point to see their friend during his last illness.

The chief mourner among the crowd that processed back from Holy Trinity into Stratford after the funeral would have been Shakespeare's widow, Anne Hathaway. Grief-stricken, heavy-hearted, and solemn they will all have been during this return to New Place for the "funeral-baked meats" waiting there. Perhaps they derived comfort from the thought that their husband, father, and friend was now "with God," as Nurse believed of her daughter, Susan, in *Romeo and Juliet,* or with Hamnet, or both. William Shakespeare was no more. His fifty-two years of life on earth had been fulfilling and busy, and there may have been some comfort in that, as well. Perhaps the prospect of the monument in the chancel provided a lifeline even in this extremity: one of these days they would once again gaze on his features on Sundays in their parish church. Further down the line lay, perhaps, the promise of a large book, the one that would become known as the First Folio. Families then learned to live around funerals much more than most of us do now, but the pain of bereavement would have been the same. It was within the family that Anne and her daughters would have sought comfort. For Judith, their father's death may have been much harder than for her sister: she must still have been aching from the humiliation inflicted on her by the wretched Thomas Quiney. She would have suffered the more if she was her father's favorite.

Since the end of the seventeenth century, it has been rumored that Shakespeare himself wrote the words engraved on his tomb:

> *Good friend for Jesus sake forbear,*
> *To dig the dust enclosed here!*
> *Blessed be the man that spares these stones,*
> *And cursed be he that moves my bones.*

We do not know absolutely that these are his words, but although the grave does not bear a name they almost certainly are. They achieved their purpose. Shakespeare's grave has not been opened and his bones were never moved into the charnel house. No one has ever been interred with him, only next to him; there the Shakespeares still rest. While most of the town's citizens were buried in its churchyard, William Shakespeare was placed in the chancel: a rare honor. It is hard to imagine that this would have been done without a special dispensation, perhaps by the Bishop of Worcester. By the time he died Shakespeare had become a senior tithe collector, with particular responsibilities for looking after Holy Trinity; these tithes had been levied by the College before the Reformation. That position may have entitled him to burial in the chancel. If so, his £440 of 1605 was an investment in eternity as well as material business.

London may have had a hand in his tomb's location, too. Shakespeare inspired loyalty and affection. As Rowe remarked, "[E]veryone who had a true taste of merit, and could distinguish men, had generally a just value and esteem for him." Rowe was echoing Hamlet's famous avowal of friendship to Horatio, that once his "dear soul was mistress of her choice" and "could of men distinguish her election," she chose Horatio. These words, among the most powerful Shakespeare ever wrote about friendship and loyalty, further testify to the importance in his imagination of bonds between men. It is not impossible that some of the most powerful people in the land, arty aristocrats like Southampton, for example, would have helped the players out if they had solicited their assistance in securing a place for Shakespeare in the chancel. The capricious Earl survived Shakespeare by eight years. And it is clear from Pembroke's heartfelt response to Burbage's death in 1619 that other influential patrons were also devoted to the players. Pembroke felt that he could not attend an after-dinner play laid on for the French ambassador because it was too "soon after the loss of my old acquaintance Burbage." Shakespeare demonstrably enjoyed the two Herberts' patronage later in his life, although he never addressed anything to them.

A poem from the period may throw interesting light on the grave in the chancel. It was written by one William Basse from neighboring Oxfordshire at some point, we know, between Shakespeare's death and 1623, because Jonson echoed it in his elegy to Shakespeare in the First Folio. It urges Spenser, Chaucer, and also Beaumont, who died the month before Shakespeare did, to make room for Shakespeare in Westminster Abbey. If they cannot do so, the poem says, then he may have to sleep serenely alone "under this carved marble of thine own" and rest in "unmolested peace," like a lord in his "unshared cave." Since the bust is not of marble, Basse's poem probably refers to the tombstone in the chancel rather than the monument up on the wall. Marble was used for the tombstone of Judith Combe in the chancel of Holy Trinity. Its inscription is framed by white marble and constitutes a perfectly preserved example of "carved marble," meaning marble with an inscription on it. That the original slab on the Shakespeare tomb was moved in the middle of the eighteenth century has been repeatedly asserted by leading scholars in the field, all of them following the great Shakespeare antiquarian Halliwell-Phillipps, although the evidence is more tenuous than is sometimes suggested. The Basse poem may support a move, though, to the extent that the original stone may have been framed with marble like the Combe one. Shakespeare's current tombstone reproduces the legend on the original faithfully, as we know because several seventeenth-century visitors recorded the curse. As has been mentioned, the stone does not bear Shakespeare's name and the grave looks foreshortened and recessed into the communion table. It can hardly have been so in April 1616. The likelihood is that the name on the tombstone was covered by the communion table when that was drawn across the top of it. This had happened by 1737, when Vertue sketched the chancel, because Shakespeare's tomb was shorter than Anne's even then.

The arrangements for Shakespeare's funeral and for his place of burial must have been made before he died, probably around the same time as the drafting of the verses that now feature on his tombstone. Since he set aside no money in his will for either the grave or the bust, we must assume that he made the arrangements himself, probably during the last four months of his life when it became clear to him that he might not recover. Shakespeare obviously knew John Combe's monument, which nestles in an alcove in the northern corner of the east wall of the church. This was none other than his "ten in the hundred" friend John Combe who predeceased Shakespeare by two years.* The monument was the work of a Southwark stonemason by the name of Gerard Johnson or, to give him his real name, Gheerhart Janssen. He had earlier worked on a

---

* In 1618 an epitaph on John Combe was printed by one Richard Braithwaite in a book called *Remains After Death*. It was attributed, for the first time, to Shakespeare some sixteen years later by the same Lieutenant Hammond who left an account of a visit to Holy Trinity in 1634. Aubrey and later Rowe both attribute it to Shakespeare. Rowe writes that the epitaph arose during a convivial get-together in Stratford, with Combe challenging Shakespeare to pen his epitaph: "and since he could not know what might he said of him when he was dead, he desired it might be done immediately. Upon which Shakespeare gave him these four verses:

Ten in the hundred lies here engraved,
'Tis a hundred to ten, his soul is not saved;
If any man ask who lies in this tomb,
'O ho,' quoth the devil, 'tis my John-a-Combe'"

(Chambers [1930], vol. 2, pp. 268–69).

Lucy grave at Charlecote. How he came to be active in the Midlands is not clear.

The elaborate Combe grave was in all likelihood completed between July 10, 1614, when Combe died, and 1616. Shakespeare must have seen it and may have been prompted to commission Janssen to do his memorial, too. He may also have been familiar with Janssen's workshop from his days in Southwark. Combe's will had earmarked a princely £60 to pay for his remembrance, and although Shakespeare's is on a smaller scale it would not have been cheap. The bust is a highly professional piece of work and shows Shakespeare as he appeared toward the end of his life, a solid middle-aged pillar of the community. There is no question of its being generic, any more than Combe's is. The poet's upper body and head are perfectly proportioned, and the expression of the face seems so vivid that it probably derives from a life mask. This would seem to suggest that the idea for a bust in the chancel originated before Shakespeare's death and that he himself was consulted about it. It further strengthens the hypothesis that the verses on the slab are indeed his, that he wanted to rest inside the church in full view of his monument on the north wall. The face that looks out at us from its niche is that of William Shakespeare as he was in the last few weeks of his life. It is what his family saw as they sat with him during the winter and early spring of 1616.

Someone who knew Shakespeare late in life was the already mentioned Leonard Digges, who may have met him following his mother's marriage to Russell in 1603. As well as being the stepson of one of the poet's executors, he was a great aficionado of Shakespeare; on a flyleaf in a copy of Lope de Vega's poems, published in 1613, Digges compared them to those of "our Will Shakespeare."* Digges knew the monument in the chancel of Holy Trinity. His and Jonson's testimonies in the First Folio establish beyond a doubt that the bust in Holy Trinity and the portrait in the Folio are authentic. In his 1623 paean to the memory of Shakespeare, Digges apostrophizes the poet and vows that through the Folio his works will live

---

*Digges's reference to Shakespeare in the context of his visit to Spain and Lope de Vega is quoted by Jonathan Bate in Nolen, p. 117.

on forever: "When that stone is rent, / And Time dissolves thy Stratford monument, / Here we alive shall view thee still."

The monument to Shakespeare was in place by the time the First Folio appeared. Since the head is almost certainly based on a plaster cast made during the last weeks of Shakespeare's life, the intention must have been to execute the memorial more or less immediately. According to the Reverend Greene, writing in 1749, the bust and the cushion on which the poet's hands rest were all "one entire lime-stone, naturally of a blueish or ash-coloured cast, yet of a texture and solidity almost equal to common marble, which could be had from no quarry in our neighbourhood except from a village called Wilmcote." Greene was writing in the year of the monument's one and only major restoration. He was scrupulous and honest and stresses that nothing about it was changed, except that marble was substituted for the original alabaster of the architraves. That the limestone came from Wilmcote, Shakespeare's mother's home village, tells us that Shakespeare had a say over how his bust should look and also where Janssen procured his materials. The masons may have come from Southwark but the stone would be Warwickshire limestone.

We know that the bust was constructed between 1616 and 1623, but no one has so far convincingly narrowed the range any further. While there are good reasons for thinking that Shakespeare had invested much in it personally, not least a sum of money, and that therefore the stonemasons would have started at once, other factors point in the opposite direction. The chancel was in a parlous state at this time; by 1618, it was decayed, ruinous, and damp and it required urgent attention. In March 1619, the council decided that it would fund the necessary work by cutting down and selling "all the trees in the churchyard" of Holy Trinity. The chancel repairs were carried out during 1621–22. This was the only major overhaul of the church between the year in which Shakespeare was born and 1763, when its wooden steeple was replaced with the current stone spire. By a miracle almost, the ferocious flood of 1588 did not invade the chancel. The church builders had wisely erected it on a gravel terrace some seventeen feet above the Avon, both to enhance its visibility and to safeguard it from the river. The twenty-six misericords in the chancel date from the fifteenth century; their exquisitely carved vivid motifs include one of a scold grabbing her husband by the beard with one hand while thumping him with a ladle or pot with the other. They remain perfectly preserved, as they could not be had the church ever been flooded for any length of time.

In light of the impending works in the chancel, it would have been sensible for Shakespeare's executors and John Hall to delay the monument, and that may be exactly what happened. The bust was almost certainly completed by the summer of 1622, when Shakespeare's troupe, the King's Men, paid their first ever visit to Stratford. To their amazement, one imagines, they were paid a fee of six shillings "for *not* playing in the [gild] hall." For the locals this was their first sight ever of the London source of Master Shakespeare's wealth. The players must have seemed like the circus come to town. An obvious explanation for their first visit to Stratford as a company is that they had come to see the recently completed memorial to their friend in Holy Trinity. Since a Southwark firm of stonemasons was carrying out the commission, the players on Bankside were probably apprised of its progress as much as the locals in Stratford. They would have had to plan a break from the lucrative Globe and Blackfriars performance schedules, and may have combined the journey to the Midlands with performances in Oxford or Banbury.

The journey would have been a melancholy one, for the players' friends Jane and John Davenant had both died that spring. Jane was buried at St. Martin Carfax in Oxford on April 5, 1622, and her husband followed on April 23, exactly six years after Shakespeare's death. John Heminges must have met them two years earlier, when he contributed ten shillings toward "the clock and chimes" of St. Martin Carfax. He was the only nonparishioner to do so and his name is added on at the end of the churchwardens' accounts, which suggests that he became involved in the Davenants' church while visiting, since otherwise his name would have featured alongside the others in the main body of the list. So the links between the Davenants and Shakespeare's circle clearly extended beyond his death. It is not at all clear, though, why Heminges should take an interest in St. Martin Carfax. He was, of course, a Midlander like Shakespeare, but he had put down roots in London. Probably he was in Oxford and at the Davenants' to inform them that he and Condell were collecting the scripts and securing publication rights in readiness for the First Folio. There were pressing reasons for Shakespeare's friends to get on with the Folio at this point, because in 1619 a less than scrupulous London printer by the name of Thomas Pavier had attempted to publish an unauthorized collection of Shakespeare's works.

When the King's Men entered the chancel of Holy Trinity in 1622, work on the Folio was well under way. The injunction not to play might suggest that the men were not made particularly welcome, even though the six-shilling fee they were paid compared well with the usual payment for performance. One might similarly be tempted to expect that the Puritan rector Thomas Wilson would give the Shakespeares a wide berth, since Puritans execrated the theater. Instead Wilson and John Hall were close friends. Indeed, with Wilson's arrival in 1619, Daniel Baker's ascendancy on the council, and Hall's undisputed status as the chief physician of the county, Protestants ruled Stratford; yet it was probably at the height of their dominance that Shakespeare's elaborate bust was erected in Holy Trinity and Anne Hathaway was interred in the chancel under it. This may have been thanks to Hall's long reach. He had been Shakespeare's de facto lieutenant since his marriage to Susanna, and on business matters, for example the Welcombe enclosures, he and his father-in-law spoke with one voice. The size of Shakespeare's legacy to him and Susanna leaves one in no doubt that he had been anointed as the new head of the family.

If financially the London players could afford to take a relaxed view of the council's impromptu prohibition, the Shakespeare family may not have done. Anne and her daughters would surely have wanted to see the King's Men perform one of Shakespeare's great works in Stratford. That may well have been the men's intention: to celebrate the unveiling of the monument with a performance of a Shakespeare play, to let his literary voice resound for the first time in his own backyard. That performance never happened. One might venture a guess that they would have played *The Tempest,* which for Heminges and Condell seems the quintessence of their friend's work. By the time the King's Men left, presumably with fanfare, tabor drums, and the customary festive mayhem, they would all have gotten to know Shakespeare's family, including the teenage Miss Hall. Anyway, many of them—Heminges, Condell, the now dead Burbage—must have known the Shakespeares from previous visits.

Dating the monument in Holy Trinity to the summer of 1622 may help solve the puzzle of the odd position of Anne Shakespeare's grave in the chancel. Alone among the tombs around Shakespeare's hers sits to his left and directly underneath the bust. If the sculpture and Shakespeare's grave had been contemporary, they would undoubtedly have been situated close to each other. However, they may be separated by as much as six years, whereas Anne's tomb and the bust are separated by little over a year. She died on August 6, 1623, three months before the First Folio appeared. The proximity of her grave to her famous husband's bust of 1622 suggests that she wanted to rest in full sight of him. Anne Hathaway may have felt that she and William Shakespeare did, after all, belong together in eternity. She had been his wife for nearly thirty-four years and his widow for seven. Since early August 1623 Anne and William Shakespeare have lain side by side and surrounded by their loved ones in adjacent plots of earth in Holy Trinity.

Anne's two daughters, speaking as one, bade her farewell in one of the most poignant tributes from the period. It is a Latin intercessory prayer, just the kind of thing that the Anglican church had tried to eradicate. Nothing much has ever been made of the apparent Catholicism of Anne Hathaway's funerary inscription, and yet few educated contemporaries could have missed it. Here is an English translation:

> Oh Mother, you fed me with the milk from your breasts and you gave me life. Woe is me then that I have to return a tombstone for such gifts! How dearly I yearn for a good angel to remove this stone and release into the light your soul, the image of the body of Christ. But my prayers are to no avail. Come quickly, oh Christ; set free my mother from her prison tomb and let her rise to the stars.

One wonders what John Hall made of his wife and sister-in-law thus apparently praying openly for their mother in Catholic ways,

and in the chancel of Holy Trinity no less, which had a zealous
Protestant vicar just then. Anne Hathaway's daughters perhaps offered this prayer for their dead mother because she had never shed
her Catholic faith. They obviously adored her and probably understood how much she had suffered from their father's prolonged absences and his infidelities. The bond between mother and daughters
would have been all the deeper because she had brought them up
mostly on her own.

Neither Susanna nor Judith can have produced the Latin text.
They may have asked the brilliant but doomed George Quiney, Judith Shakespeare's young brother-in-law. He had returned to Stratford from Balliol College Oxford in 1621. At the time of Anne's
death, he was helping out both at the grammar school and as curate
at Holy Trinity, where he was a "reading-minister"—that is, he read
the lessons and sermons but did not preach.* Quiney died at the age
of twenty-four, probably of tuberculosis. He was attended by John
Hall, who wrote in his case notes that Quiney "was a man of a good
wit, expert in tongues, and very learned."

---

*Fripp (1928), p. 73.

30

ℒife After Death: 1623 –

nne had survived her husband long enough to witness the love and loyalty that his friends in the royal company of players bore him. She would undoubtedly have known about the plans for the First Folio; she and her family may even have seen an advance copy. That the Halls owned a copy we can hardly doubt, and there may have been a handful of others in Stratford. The most famous book in English literature was first noted mundanely in a 1622 Frankfurt book fair catalogue, which advertised it among the books printed during April and October that year. Certainly the printing, at Isaac Jaggard's press in London, seems to have started early in 1622, but it went on for the best part of two years: the Folio appeared in November 1623. The impact must have been considerable in London, and even more so in Stratford. Such was the status of the book and its commercial success that it was reissued within nine years. This Second Folio, of 1632, was sumptuously printed on the best available paper and provoked from the Puritan William Prynne the complaint that "Shakespeare's plays are printed in the best crown paper, far better than most Bibles." Indeed.

In their prefatory exhortation "to the great variety of readers," the volume's editors, who spell their names "John Heminges" and "Henrie Condell," remind us that the fate of all books depends "not of your heads alone, but of your purses ... and you will stand for your privileges, we know: to read and censure. Do so, but buy it first." An elite public seems to have done just that. It has been estimated that up to a thousand copies of the First Folio were printed, of which 228 are currently known to exist.* Only the wealthy could afford this huge volume. It cost around about one pound, at a time when the head teacher of the Stratford grammar school earned twenty pounds a year.† By law, the Bodleian library received a copy, which was eagerly consulted by Oxford students. During the Folio's first four decades in the Bodleian, the tragedies were the most widely read, while the histories were least popular. The favorite was *Romeo and Juliet,* followed by *Julius Caesar, 1 Henry IV,* and *Macbeth.*‡ Other owners must have been Jonson, the Burbages, the dedicatees, Southampton, and of course the editors and heads of the syndicate, Heminges and Condell. The closest link with the original story of the Folio is provided by Elizabeth Condell, Henry's widow. They married in 1596, so she must have known Shakespeare for at least twenty years. When she died she left "all her books" to one of her executors, Thomas Seaman. It is inconceivable that her library did not include a First Folio. One imagines that the Lord Chamberlain, the Master of the Revels, and various panjandrums associated with the theater would have bought copies. Certainly there must have been a ready market, even if we find it hard to gauge the spread of copies across the nation. Jaggard had spent nearly two years printing it, and the cost of wages alone necessitated a substantial return. The reprint of

---

*About seventy surfaced in the twentieth century alone, so there are bound to be others that have so far not been traced. A number would have been lost, one imagines, during the Great Fire of London, and others again perhaps in subsequent fires. As far as we know, though, none of the ones that Sidney Lee identified in 1902 were lost during World War II, although, of course, others that were held privately in London may have been.

†If his equivalent in 2007 earned a pretax salary in the region of £55,000, a First Folio would cost £2,750. The latest First Folio to be auctioned, at Sotheby's on July 12, 2006, sold for £2.8 million.

‡After an absence of two and a half centuries, this volume finally returned home to the Bodleian in 1906. It had probably been sold in 1664 as part of a consignment of "superfluous library books," the First Folio being deemed superfluous because of the Third Folio of 1663–64. In the end, after a fierce fund-raising campaign that became national news, Oxford retrieved her treasure on March 31, 1906, for the then enormous sum of £3,000, beating out the Folger Library. The volume is badly damaged, but it survives in its original University of Oxford calf binding of 1624 (West [2003], pp. 20, 111–14; Duncan-Jones, pp. 283–84).

1632, with a new prefatory poem by a young writer who was just hitting his stride, John Milton, proves that it had sold well.

Shakespeare's plays now became a truly national treasure for the first time. In book form, they reached out to the whole country as they could not do while they existed only as performances in London. The First Folio includes a famous frontispiece engraving of Shakespeare. This portrait, by Martin Droeshout (the Elder or the Younger), and the bust in Holy Trinity were seen by contributors to the First Folio who had known Shakespeare for many years and clearly approved of it as a true likeness. Martin Droeshout the Younger was only twenty-two when Shakespeare died and could therefore not have drawn him from life at the age depicted in the engraving. But he could easily have copied an earlier depiction of Shakespeare, such as the one that was available to "Gullio" in Cambridge around the time of *Hamlet*. If, as is now widely thought, the picture was done by the elder Martin Droeshout, his uncle, who was only a year younger than Shakespeare, then it could be a true portrait from life. Droeshout the Elder could easily have met Shakespeare; in 1604, he lived in Crutched Friars in Aldgate ward, not very far from Shakespeare in Muggle Street.

The man in the Folio picture is in his late thirties. The reference in *Parnassus* to a picture of Shakespeare may be to the version that underlies this portrait. Multiple copies of the underlying picture were probably available, not least perhaps in the Shakespeare household. If that picture was sketched from life, then Shakespeare obviously saw it and, presumably, approved it. It is undoubtedly a true likeness, even if it is not a great picture. It is tempting to think that the original might have been drawn by Burbage because of his skill at sketching. In a celebrated essay on the Shakespeare portrait, M. H. Spielmann argued from the play of light and shadow on the face that "the artist worked not from an oil painting, but from an existing 'limning' of the poet—a portrait consisting of an outline drawing, with perhaps delicate flat washes of colour—as in a Hilliard miniature."* There are, it seems, technical as well as practical reasons for believing that behind the Folio portrait there lies a sketch or limning

---

*Spielmann, p. 33.

of Shakespeare. If the artist was not Burbage, there is an outside chance that it was someone like Hilliard acting on behalf of Shakespeare's friend Southampton, who had been the subject of one of Hilliard's most famous miniatures. But Hilliard would probably have produced a more accomplished matrix. Perhaps we ought to look no further than Richard Burbage for the source of the picture. The editors would have had easy access to any sketches or drawings by their friend, not least through his widow and surviving family. This would have been his posthumous contribution to the Folio.

A copy of the original picture may yet turn up, particularly if prints were widely distributed at the time. It would look like the one in the First Folio, but probably with a different ruff and clothing. In the Folio engraving, the head looks superimposed on a rather too opulent costume, one more fitting for the Earl of Essex. Since the time of the original drawing, which would have been made around 1602, Shakespeare's status had changed. True, he was armiger by 1597, but he was not yet the man eulogized by Jonson as the paragon of dramatists and he did not have a monument in the chancel of his parish church. Renaissance England was acutely conscious of status and it is therefore quite likely that the editors prevailed on Droeshout to impose Shakespeare's head on a ruff and aristocratic costume, for all to *see*, as well as read, that William Shakespeare was indeed a gentleman. The result is an unfortunate head-on-platter effect, with head and torso neither fully joined nor in proportion, either. Some sixteen years or so separate the likeness in the First Folio from the one in the chancel of Holy Trinity. Even if we knew nothing at all about them, we would probably still guess that they showed the same man at different stages of his life.

Another work has long been proposed as a true likeness of Shakespeare, and that is the so-called Chandos portrait. This picture, in which the subject provocatively establishes eye contact with his audience, dates from the first decade of the seventeenth century; the publisher Jacob Tonson put a version of it on the cover of Rowe's 1709 edition of Shakespeare. The actor Thomas Betterton, who had been Rowe's most important source for his early biography of Shakespeare, was rumored to have acquired the picture from Davenant, but we know that he purchased it at a sale and not from Davenant, who died intestate. In the eighteenth century, it was alleged that the picture had once been owned by one John Taylor, but Shakespeare had no known associate by that name. "John" may be a mistake for *Joseph* Taylor (c.1586–1652), who was among the twenty-six "principal actors" listed in the First Folio. Malone credited him with painting the picture, but his evidence for this claim is no longer extant and Joseph Taylor seems to have been too young: he joined the company only after Shakespeare's death. He may eventually have come to own the portrait, however; indeed, his track record in the company and his contacts with people from the time of Shakespeare to the Restoration both seem to point in just that direction. Joseph Taylor succeeded Richard Burbage in the King's Men after the latter's death in 1619 and eventually he and John Lowin headed the company for seventeen years, until the closure of the theaters in 1642. The long-lived Lowin apparently shared his knowledge of Shakespeare's directions for *Henry VIII* with Davenant, while Taylor did the same for the much bigger part of Hamlet: "*Hamlet* being performed by Master Betterton, Sir William Davenant, having seen Master Taylor [Joseph Taylor] of the Blackfriars Company act it, who being instructed by the author Master Shakespeare, taught Master Bettterton every particle of it."* Taylor and Lowin died in 1652 and 1659 (sometimes given as 1653) respectively. We know that Lowin acted with Davenant and it is inconceivable that Taylor would not have known Davenant.

If Taylor, who died without leaving a will, owned the Chandos portrait, he could easily have passed it on to Davenant as its obvious heir. The eighteenth-century source that attributes the Chandos picture to John Taylor also reports the rumor that the artist might have been Richard Burbage.† In other words, the Chandos could have passed from Richard Burbage, who painted it, to his successor in the company, Joseph Taylor, hence to Davenant and, indirectly, to Betterton, who let Rowe reproduce it in 1709. If the Chandos were a Burbage picture, it would, of course, be authentic (though not

---

*According to John Downes, who was a professional prompter in the London theaters between 1662 and 1706 (Chambers [1930], vol. 2, p. 263).

†William Oldys, quoted in Schoenbaum (1970), p. 281.

necessarily of Shakespeare) and might then show Shakespeare in a particular dramatic role, maybe one that he had famously rendered his and that required an earring—perhaps a part like Iago. There are superficial similarities between the Chandos, the Folio engraving, and the bust, but their craniums seem too different to belong to the same person. Also, the man in the Chandos portrait is older than the one in the First Folio. Burbage could easily have painted and drawn Shakespeare more than once, but it is unlikely that the oblong egg-like head in the First Folio evolved into the rounded, broader, receding face in the Chandos.

A further twist concerning the Chandos picture involves the artist and engraver George Vertue, our source for the appearance of New Place. When Tonson commissioned Vertue in 1723 to engrave the famous bust, Vertue produced what he affirmed to be a true copy. And so it appears to be when one compares it to the bust—except for the most important detail of all. As the foremost authority on the Shakespeare portraits put it, "The deadly thing is that this engraving . . . presents that monument to us pretty well *exactly as it is to-day*—all except the head."* In executing the Tonson commission, Vertue followed someone else's drawing of the memorial. Since this drawing was demonstrably most accurate, it must also have featured the head that graces the bust today, because that head is an integral part of the single limestone block. What probably happened is that Tonson wanted to reuse the Chandos plate, which he still had from printing Rowe's Shakespeare in 1709, in conjunction with the drawing. He must have been certain that the Chandos showed the real Shakespeare, since its provenance reached back all the way to Davenant, and beyond him to Shakespeare's company. Vertue himself had jotted down just this point in his notebooks in 1719, remarking that the Chandos portrait had been "bought for forty guineas of Master Betterton, who bought it of Sir William Davenant, to whom it was left by will of John Taylor, who had it of Shakespeare; it was painted by one *Taylor,* a player and painter contemporary with Shakespeare and his intimate friend." In the left-hand margin the name "Richard Burbage" has been crossed out. Clearly Vertue had heard about Burbage's draftsmanship and had

---

*Spielmann, p. 22.

considered that he might be the painter. Vertue and Tonson agreed that the real Shakespeare was the face of the Chandos portrait. By superimposing the Chandos head on the Holy Trinity bust, Tonson and Vertue wanted to confect for their readers the authentic look of the poet and of the monument, although they had before them a highly accurate drawing of the real bust.

We are left to account for the representation of the monument that lies behind the 1723 Tonson frontispiece. Perhaps Vertue drew on sketches made by Betterton during the latter's visit to Stratford. Betterton was a keen collector of drawings, paintings, and prints, but he would have needed to be a superb draftsman himself to capture the detail of the picture behind Vertue's 1723 engraving. In any event, whoever drew the monument at the time would also undoubtedly have drawn the correct head. Vertue finally went up to Stratford in 1737, but even as he sketched the bust in its evocative setting in the chancel of Holy Trinity he could not resist the temptation to conflate the head in front of him with the Chandos portrait, and his drawing presents a wispy hybrid of the two. Vertue must have known exactly what to expect in the chancel, since his 1723 engraving derived from an almost photographically exact drawing of the bust. Yet his attempt at a compromise now was almost painfully evasive. The surmised pedigree of the Chandos had led him and Tonson to override the evidence in front of them. In the chancel, Vertue seems to have been less sure. Perhaps as a professional artist who took pride in his work, he could not bring himself to repeat the fraud of 1723, benignly intended though it was. After all, he was sketching the chancel of Holy Trinity not to fulfill a commission for a book, but to convey a sense of its atmosphere. So he decided, it seems, to err on the side of truth, but only up to a point.

It is impossible to establish whether it was Betterton who drew the original behind the 1723 Tonson plate. Whoever did was meticulous and had connections to London publishing circles. If it was Betterton, that would have important implications, namely that this actor turned investigator returned to London from Stratford equipped with skillfully executed drawings as well as a wealth of information that he imparted to Rowe. If he was as scrupulous about his gathering of oral history as he may have been about representing Stratford's visual heritage, then his credibility is enhanced immeasurably. In this story of three pictures it may be interesting to note that as early as 1723 the Chandos was made to usurp a validated representation of Shakespeare. With its trendy actor's earring and intriguing looks, it remains the most popular of the Shakespeare pictures. But we have no witnesses, as we do with the other two, to state categorically that this was William Shakespeare.

The monument in Holy Trinity was touched up twice, once in 1748 and then again in 1793, when Malone had it whitewashed. In 1861 the paint was stripped off and the colors underneath it were restored. The quirks of history allow us to travel back in time, to see the thirty-eight-year-old author of *Hamlet* in the First Folio and the fifty-two-year-old Stratford burgher in Holy Trinity. Here we gaze on William Shakespeare, husband, lover, father, and friend. This is what his contemporaries saw four hundred years ago, the human face of that extraordinary imagination.

At the end of March 1625, King James I died; shortly afterward, Shakespeare's granddaughter left for the capital. Perhaps she wanted to be in the nation's epicenter for this great rite of passage, the departure of one king and the accession of another, the second Stuart monarch. She was seventeen at the time. She can hardly have gone to London on her own, even though that seems to be implied in her father's notes on an illness she suffered around this time. An older woman must have accompanied her, and perhaps male members of the family, too, or others from Stratford. We have no idea where she stayed during her fortnight in London; perhaps a room had been set aside for her in the Blackfriars gatehouse, or she lodged with friends of the family.

John Hall's record of Elizabeth's illness counts her as a success story and also rings a bell for us. He notes that "in the beginning of April she went to London, . . . returning homewards the 22d of the said month," after which she suffered fierce pains on the right side of her face. Three months earlier, her left side had been similarly afflicted, her mouth had convulsed, and she did not menstruate. Her father repeatedly purged her and eventually she recovered fully, as she did this time too. With relief he notes that by his skill and "by the blessing of God she was cured in sixteen days."

It is striking that Elizabeth Hall returned to Stratford in time for April 22, 1625, and that her father deemed this date important enough to highlight it in his diary. April 22 is also the day on which she was married a year later. Elizabeth clearly wanted to be home for that day, the most important in her calendar and one that meant something to her father as well. April 22 was the red-letter day in the family's year, and it can only have been so because it was Shakespeare's birthday. Elizabeth and her grandfather seem to have been close. She was the only daughter of his beloved Susanna and she may nearly have lost her mother at birth. Shakespeare prominently remembered her in his will. She was eight when he died; for the rest of her life she lived with the memory of her grandfather, the famous "London" writer whose bust graced the chancel of Holy Trinity and whose very large book, the First Folio, she may well have read. She was undoubtedly literate, as we noted when discussing her exquisite italic signature.

On April 22, 1626, Elizabeth Hall married Thomas Nash, her parents' neighbor from Chapel Street. She was eighteen like her grandfather at his wedding forty-four years earlier. A suspicion that the wedding was deliberately timed for Shakespeare's birthday was first articulated by Thomas de Quincey. Unlike us, Elizabeth would, of course, have known exactly the day that Shakespeare was born. It was easy to remember, as it could only be a very few days before or after St. George's Day, April 23. Indeed, it has to have fallen before. As Halliwell-Phillipps astutely points out with reference to the monument in Holy Trinity, "Whatever opinions may be formed respecting the precise interpretation of the record of the age under the monumental effigy, the latter is a certain evidence that Shakespeare was not born after the 23rd of April."* The inscription reads, "OBIT ANO DOI 1616 AETATIS 53 DIE 23 April." That is, Shakespeare, who was baptised on April 26, must have been born *on or before* April 23, 1564, because otherwise he would have been fifty-two at the time of his death, not fifty-three. Had the birthday been St. George's Day itself, Elizabeth Hall would, one imagines, have rushed at the chance to marry then. The force of this point is weakened, however, because

---

*Halliwell-Phillipps (1887), vol. 2, p. 332.

April 23, 1626, fell on a Sunday, when one could not marry. Both April 22, 1564, and April 22, 1626, were Saturdays. If Elizabeth Hall shadowed her grandfather's life by marrying on his birthday in 1626, she may have done something similar when she married again in 1649, barely a month before her mother died. Perhaps she did not feel that she could replicate the time of her first wedding, twenty-three years earlier, or perhaps she just wanted to do things differently. In any case, this time she chose Billesley chapel, with which neither she nor her new husband had any connection as far as we can determine but which, as we saw, may have some claim to being the chapel in which William Shakespeare married.

By the time John Hall died, in 1635, Shakespeare's fame had spread throughout the land, among ordinary people as well as the rich. Only the year before, a visitor who had no known connection to Stratford had called in, with two fellow travelers, to Holy Trinity. There they saw, among other things, "a neat monument of that famous English poet, Master William Shakespeare, who was born here." The traveler also noticed the Combe memorial and spotted Shakespeare's "witty and facetious verses" on Combe. The name of this visitor was Lieutenant Hammond. Nothing is known about him. He matters because he was an ordinary person whose knowledge of Shakespeare would have come exclusively from the dramatist's spreading fame.

It seems that there were unsettled debts after Hall's death because New Place and its study were raided in 1637 by some ruffians at the behest of one Baldwin Brooks, who claimed that the estate owed him money. Brooks's men forced their entry into New Place, breaking down doors, and carried off "divers books" and "other goods of great value." So Susanna and her son-in-law, Thomas Nash, alleged in the suit that they brought against Brooks in chancery. Whether or not Brooks was right to claim that the Halls were trying to renege on their debt to him, he would hardly get away with breaking and entering. That Brooks went on to enjoy a civic career at Stratford and indeed to become mayor suggests that he and the Hall-Nash families eventually came to an accommodation. By the time we next hear of the study at New Place, the books appear to have been returned.

In his will, John Hall had casually referred to his books as items of no particular value, which could be disposed of by burning. This may have been a ruse to duck creditors like Baldwin Brooks. Like the Burbages and, perhaps, Shakespeare, Hall had drafted a will that deliberately underplayed the value of his estate. Or perhaps by "books" he meant his own handwritten manuscripts. One of these may hold the key to the mystery of Shakespeare's last illness. The first volume of Hall's medical diary has not been found; it may languish unrecognized in a collection somewhere, because we know that it left New Place at the same time as its mate, which is in the manuscripts section of the British Library. This Latin text, unusually for early-seventeenth-century England, is written in a clear italic hand. Its reference number is BL Egerton MS 2065. The italic script supports the notion that Hall had studied medicine in France after attending Cambridge, for European writers predominantly used italic. In the seventeenth century, the first volume looked identical to the second: James Cooke (1614–88), its English translator and a surgeon himself, tells us so. When Shakespeare's daughter, who was sixty-one at the time, expressed doubt that some of her husband's papers were indeed his own manuscripts, Cooke responded that he knew Hall's handwriting. He must have recognized it by the distinctive italic longhand, which helped to identify it at once as European.

Cooke had been brought to New Place by a friend of John Hall's. Whoever he was, he knew the family well enough to invite a stranger into their home to inspect Hall's books. He may have been another doctor or surgeon, perhaps even one of the two physicians who treated Hall when he was seriously ill in 1632. Here is how Cooke remembered his encounter with Susanna fourteen years later:

> Being in my art an attendant to parts of some regiments to keep the pass at the bridge of Stratford-upon-Avon, there being then with me a mate allied to the gentleman that writ the following observations in Latin, he invited me to the house of Mrs Hall, wife of the deceased, to see the books left by Master Hall. After a view of them, she told me she had some books left, by one that professed physic with her husband, for some money. I told her, if I liked them, I would give her the money again; she brought them forth, amongst which there

was this with another of the author's, both intended for the press. I being acquainted with Master Hall's hand, told her that one or two of them were her husband's and showed them her; she denied, I affirmed, till I perceived she begun to be offended. At last I returned her the money.*

What happened on this day at New Place was that Cooke and his companion were shown John Hall's study, which must formerly have been Shakespeare's. The study contained a library, and it was these books that Susanna exhibited proudly. It was quite possibly the only such library in Stratford. Here among "the books left by Master Hall" would have been Shakespeare's Ovid, Plutarch, Holinshed, and other works, including, perhaps, quartos of his plays, a 1623 Folio, and even first draft manuscripts. The library of New Place probably enjoyed a certain celebrity in the town, where everyone by now knew that William Shakespeare was famous. Susanna's proprietary attitude suggests that these were big books with leather bindings, items that she was proud to show off to a stranger. After Cooke and his friend had finished admiring the books in the study, Susanna remarked that she had more books left. It is fairly clear from what followed that she meant a separate cache and that these were medical manuscripts or treatises. Had Cooke not been a doctor, she would never have thought of producing them. They had been written, she said, by someone who worked alongside her husband as a doctor; who this was we do not know. She showed her visitors several manuscripts, some of which the Halls had paid for. Or so she claimed. The point about money changing hands is made three times.

Among these new papers were "one or two" in Hall's handwriting. Cooke was of course right, as MS 2065 proves. But Susanna was adamant that all the papers belonged to her husband's colleague and that the Halls had paid for them. It beggars belief that she would not know her husband's handwriting, especially since she was literate, as her two signatures of 1639 and 1647 demonstrate. She probably knew full well that they were Hall's, but she wanted or needed cash

---

*From the first English edition of Hall's casebook, quoted in Schoenbaum (1975), p. 291.

and saw a chance of making some from Cooke; hence, perhaps, the afterthought in "by one that professed physic with her husband, for some money." Perhaps her fortunes were at a low ebb because the civil war had hurt the local economy. When she realized that Cooke had recognized Hall's distinctive italic longhand, she must have felt acutely put on the spot. In the end Cooke bought the two manuscripts, John Hall's complete medical case studies. The mistress of the house had gotten some money, of course, but it had been a bruising encounter. It is worth noting that she did not part with any of the printed books from her father's library. Clearly the "real" books were out of bounds, but medical manuscripts were a different matter. When Susanna sold Hall's manuscripts to a physician she probably knew exactly what she was doing. The case histories could not possibly be of any interest to her in the future. Her father's books, on the other hand, were the family's heritage. The bulk of Shakespeare's papers remained in New Place at the time of Cooke's visit. Their subsequent fate is harder to trace, but it may not be as unknowable as is sometimes assumed.

A volume from Shakespeare's library eventually found its way into the possession of Colonel Richard Grace, who was with Queen Henrietta Maria when in July 1643 she stayed over at New Place for two nights. This was the *Marvellous Discourse upon the Life of Katherine de Medicis* by Henri Estienne; the inscription on the title page reads "Liber R: Graeci ex dono amicae D. Susanne Hall," "the book of Richard Grace, as a gift from his friend D. Susanne Hall." The handwriting dates from the seventeenth century, but it is not hers. The "D." may serve to identify Susanna as the wife of Dr. John Hall ("D." for "Doctor"), a bit perhaps like calling her Mrs. John Hall; or, if "D" stands for *domina*, that is lady, the inscription could mean "from his friend the lady [of the house] Susanna Hall." We don't know why she gave Grace this book. Perhaps he was billeted at New Place as Henrietta Maria's bodyguard on that visit, or maybe, like Cooke, he visited the library there because it was famous and ended up walking away with the gift of a book. More likely, the Queen herself browsed through the books in Hall's study and stumbled across the Estienne volume. The French-born queen of Charles I may have been drawn to a book about Catherine de' Medici because she herself was the daughter of Maria de' Medici, who had died the year before. Anything to do with the Medicis might have been of interest, particularly now that her life in England seemed very unstable. That the inscription recalls Susanna rather than Shakespeare may be worth noting. It suggests that the recipient cherished the book as a gift from her rather than as a trophy from William Shakespeare's library. The *Marvellous Discourse* left New Place more than 350 years ago, but since its purchase by the Shakespeare Birthplace Trust at Sotheby's in 1973 it has been home again in Stratford. Why the Queen stayed over in New Place has never been satisfactorily explained, unless she remembered that her protégé William Davenant, who had been drawing a royal pension since 1638, had links to this house. There is no record of his spending time with Susanna and Judith during any of his periodic visits to Oxford, where his parents were buried. Stratford was only a day's ride away and it is hard to believe that Davenant would not have visited Holy Trinity and the Shakespeare graves, while calling in on the surviving Shakespeares. If, though, he and the Shakespeare daughters did not meet, at the very least Susanna and Judith would have heard about Davenant now from the Queen.

Susanna died on July 11, 1649, just over a month after her daughter Elizabeth's second marriage, which took place on June 5. Perhaps Elizabeth wanted her dying mother to witness the wedding. Elizabeth's aunt Judith seems to have had similar reasons for marrying Quiney two months before Shakespeare's death.

Judith outlived her father by forty-six years. Barely a year after her father's death her firstborn, a baby boy called Shakespeare Quiney, had died. That was in May 1617. The ghost of poor Margaret Wheeler and her dead baby may have haunted her marriage in the years that followed. Judith's other two children with Quiney died at the ages of nineteen and twenty-one, long before either of their parents. There must have been times when Judith felt that they were all paying for the sins of her husband, whose various attempts at business in Stratford only further exposed his fecklessness. Over the years, the space before the altar became crowded with her relatives. Eventually, in her late seventies, she joined them. The year was 1662. She was the last of the Shakespeares of Stratford. Her niece had left the town years earlier and her aunt, Joan Hart from Henley Street, had died in 1646. In her twenties, Judith may have been her father's Miranda; in her seventies, she was a childless old lady surrounded by memories and the ghosts of her father, her mother, her sister, and above all, perhaps, of the twin brother who died sixty-six years before she did. When her time came, she may still have been saddled with her husband Thomas Quiney and may still have lived in the house known as the Cage opposite Market Cross. We know that Quiney enjoyed a long life, but his death is not recorded. Quite apart from his early betrayal of Judith, his civic record in Stratford is unimpressive. It seems that neither the Corporation nor Judith's family trusted him.

Unlike other graves in the chancel, Judith's is not marked, but in the Shakespeare row and to the right of Susanna are two further graves. The pattern of the tombs before the communion table suggests that these graves all belong to Shakespeares or those who married into the family: Anne Hathaway, John Hall, and Thomas Nash, spouses of William, Susanna, and Elizabeth respectively. Judith and Thomas should be here, and the two additional graves next to Susanna's probably belonged to them, though they bear the names of a couple who were buried here within thirty and forty years of Judith's death. The Quiney graves may have suffered the same fate as Susanna's, which was opened in the early years of the eighteenth century to receive another tenant.

If only we could be sure that John Ward spoke to Judith. On a list of tasks that he jotted down in his diary in 1662, the very year of her death, appears this item: "to see Mrs Quiney." It may well relate to another memo to himself: "Remember to peruse Shakespeare's plays and be versed in them, that I may not be ignorant in the matter." Mrs. Quiney lived about five minutes' walk from Ward. She was then seventy-seven years old and may have been ailing. His visit to her may have been pastoral rather than literary. If he did see her, he left no record of what she said.

Susanna, Joan in Henley Street, and Elizabeth Hall Nash all experienced some privations during the billeting of troops in the town in the 1640s. But whereas the Harts had to give up some of their silverware, for which their lawyers sought compensation, Thomas

Nash demanded to be indemnified for Elizabeth's "scarlet petticoat and lacework." Nash's request seems almost frivolous, since this was a somewhat unusual luxury item that his wife could surely afford to lose. In a way it is heartening to know that the daughter of the Puritan John Hall affected beautiful undergarments. As long as the children of Puritans wore scarlet petticoats, there would be no need for scarlet letters. Stratford was, it seems, keeping steadfastly to its history of sensible religious compromise.

Perhaps Elizabeth had a particular reason for getting her husband to complain about her petticoat. Many years earlier her grandfather had been issued with scarlet cloth for the coronation of King James. Shakespeare would have worn his outfit on the day and then never again, like an expensive wedding dress. It is likely that his wife or daughter would have recycled this wonderful fabric, and what better use for it than to turn it into a luxury petticoat? Elizabeth's wearing of it might even have been a way to commemorate her grandfather. And using the cloth for a petticoat, an intensely private if not secret garment, may have been prudent. Royal fabrics were to be treated with the utmost respect; they could hardly be reworked for public attire. This prestigious petticoat may have passed from Anne Hathaway to her daughter and then to Elizabeth, like a royal talisman.

Along with her mother and her aunt, Elizabeth carried the glorious burden of direct descent from William Shakespeare. Since her early teens, she had seen her grandfather's effigy in the chancel of her parish church and she can have had no doubt about his standing in the community and the scale and nature of her heritage. Hence the importance of Sir Hugh Clopton's claim, made to the actor Charles Macklin in 1742 and recorded by Malone, that, by "an old tradition," when Elizabeth left New Place after her second marriage to live on her husband John Barnard's estate in Abington in Northampton, "she had carried away with her from Stratford many of her grandfather's papers." This is the same Hugh Clopton who spoke to Joseph Greene about the Shakespeare daughters' graffiti in the leaded glass of New Place.

That Elizabeth Barnard should have taken with her the family papers, including Shakespeare's and her father's, is perfectly plausible.

Not only books and manuscripts would have gone with her, but also other hugely important family papers such as the grant of the coat of arms to John Shakespeare. Although the copy at the College of Arms survives in London, the Shakespeares' own has not come to light. It was probably done on parchment so its chances of surviving must be excellent. The papers that were moved out of New Place would almost certainly have been stored in Abington. Malone and Halliwell-Phillipps first proposed searching behind the paneling at Abington, but there is no reason why Elizabeth Barnard should have hidden anything of Shakespeare's or Hall's, and her grandfather's library and coat of arms must have been among her most prized possessions. Common sense suggests that they would have been willed on down among Barnard's descendants. It is hard to believe that among them there was not a First Folio.

In 1670 Elizabeth Hall died in Abington as Lady Barnard: in 1661 John Barnard had been knighted for doing the Crown good service during the civil war. How that sat with the daughter of the famous Puritan doctor is impossible to know. Among the most significant features of Elizabeth's will are her bequests to descendants of the Hathaways of Shottery and Stratford. (Shakespeare, as we saw, had left them nothing.) Earlier, Elizabeth and her mother had made two of the Hathaways trustees of their estate. Toward the end of her life, Susanna Hall may have been making her peace ever more deeply with her mother's family; her daughter evidently followed suit. Four years after his wife, Barnard himself died and New Place was sold to Sir Edward Walker, who left it to his daughter, who in turn married John Clopton. And so after a century and a half the house was back in Clopton hands. It is as if they had only ever loaned it out.

The inventory taken after Barnard's death included, in the "study" of the house, "desks, chests, cabinet, trunks, and boxes" to the value of over £5, the family "plate" at around £29, "rings, jewels and a watch" for £30, and finally "all the books, £29.11.0."* This is a thumping high value: the books weigh in as the equivalent of the

---

*1674 Abington inventory (Fripp [1928], p. 79). The Barnard inventory was published by the *New Shakespeare Society Transactions* (1880–85), pt. 2.

Barnard "plate" and of all their jewels. One of these books may survive in the Bodleian. It is an Aldine edition of Ovid's *Metamorphoses* from 1502. Ovid was Shakespeare's favorite author. On the flyleaf opposite the title page someone has written, "This little book of Ovid was given to me by W. Hall who said it was once Will Shakespeare's." The writer of the note signs himself TN and dates the inscription 1682.* The initials TN may invert those of the noted antiquary and Anglo-Saxon scholar Edward (known as Neddy) Thwaites of Queen's College Oxford; his correspondent was William Hall of Lichfield, with whom he shared a passion for Shakespeare. If the copy of Ovid was given to Thwaites, that would explain how it came to be preserved in the Bodleian: his entire estate, including his books, was claimed by his college after his death. The question is whether the book did indeed come from Shakespeare's library in New Place.

In 1682, Thwaites and William Hall, Jr., were both still at school. Eventually they would become contemporaries at Queen's College Oxford, from where they both graduated in 1694. The fact that Hall was called Junior means that his father was probably also William Hall. Chambers deciphered Hall's father's first name as "G<ul?>," which may stand for "Guillaume." By an odd coincidence William Hall, Jr., of Lichfield fetched up as rector in Acton, the very place where the father of Shakespeare's son-in-law John Hall had lived; and John Hall's father, a physician like himself, was yet another William Hall. In his will in November 1635 John Hall left his father's house in Acton to his daughter, Elizabeth. John Hall himself came

---

*Just above Aldus's *impresa* of a dolphin wrapped around an anchor is the signature "W.^{m} Sh.^{e}." It resembles those in the will but has been suspected of being a forgery, a copy of an eighteenth-century reproduction of one of the signatures. The 1682 date was queried in 1917, along with just about everything else about the inscription, by the distinguished paleographer E. M. Thompson. But he was mistaken, as Falconer Madan, a painstakingly scrupulous librarian at the Bodleian, demonstrated conclusively the year after. Madan matched every detail of the handwriting queried by Thompson with Bodleian manuscripts from the same year. He even made a strong case for the authenticity of the Shakespeare signature above the emblem while acknowledging that this would fly in the face of expectation (*The Library* [1917–18]). As Fripp remarks in his discussion of the pedigree of the Aldine Ovid, "Foolish legends but not forgeries had begun in 1682" (*MA,* vol. 3, p. xxvi).

from Carlton in Bedfordshire. It seems that the Halls of Lichfield, Acton, and Carlton were all somehow related and the name William may have been a Hall family name. That at least one of these Halls was apparently called Guillaume may suggest that the Halls were of Huguenot descent; hence, perhaps, their Protestantism. They may have been immigrants.

A French family connection might account for John Hall's odd educational progress after Cambridge, when he disappears from view to train as a doctor somewhere on the Continent and probably France. If the various Halls are all related, then the William Hall on the flyleaf of the Aldine Ovid probably inherited the book after Lady Barnard's death in 1670, or her husband's in 1674. We know that Elizabeth was deeply family-minded; in her will, she even remembered Hathaways descended from her grandmother's brother. She may have extended the same kindness to her father's extended family. That someone called Hall should possess a book from Shakespeare's home makes perfect sense.

Thwaites and Hall move the story forward to the end of the seventeenth century. William Hall of Lichfield may be one of the last clear links with the Halls of New Place. In 1735, the Reverend Joseph Greene became master at the grammar school. From then on and until the middle of the next century, the Shakespearian treasures of Stratford were ably guarded locally by the Reverends Greene (1712–90) and Davenport (1787–1841) and by Robert B. Wheler (1785–1857). This is well, because Stratford's Shakespeare heritage might have been most at risk during these decades from forgers and rumors, not least because of the publicity generated by Garrick's Jubilee in 1769. With the arrival of Halliwell-Phillipps (1820–89), the founding of the Shakespeare Society in 1840, and the creation of the Shakespeare Birthplace Trust in 1847, legal guardianship of the Shakespeare heritage was officially assumed by the nation.

The days are long gone when Greene could discover Shakespeare's will to please a wealthy patron, or when Wheler was able to trace the bond for the Shakespeare marriage because it was there waiting to be found. Stratford may have yielded all its major secrets, but significant local discoveries are still being made. It is only since 2000 that we have known the real Mary Arden house, unlike anyone before us since the late seventeenth century. For hundreds of years, the house on the green in Wilmcote was right before our eyes, and yet invisible, until Nathaniel Alcock's brilliant archival detective work identified it. Similarly, Catharine Page and Ronald Page discovered the exact site of Shakespeare's grandfather's home in Snitterfield in 1982, while Jeanne Jones recently unearthed two important seventeenth-century inventories for the Birthplace. They add depth of field to our discussions of the building by offering incontrovertible evidence about the interior of the house in 1627 and 1648. (These arrangements cannot easily be mapped on to the current interior.) In an age of digitization, we are arguably better placed for new finds than any generation since 1836, the year when Wheler turned up the Shakespeare marriage bond. As more and more manuscripts and other documents become readily accessible through electronic archival databases, serendipitous finds of materials relevant to Shakespeare should not be ruled out.

Henry James wisely cautioned, "Never say you know the last word about any human heart." We can only guess at the infinite complexity of Shakespeare's mind and personality; in these pages, I have tried to convey my sense of who he was. His life and writings may well be intimately linked. Keats thought so, and he is arguably Shakespeare's finest reader to date. Shakespeare emerges from these pages as a restless character, a contrary, turbulent, and impetuous youth who had sex before he was married. Boys and girls have, of course, always found ways around the mores and sexual sanctions of their societies, and Shakespeare celebrates the power of sexuality in his works. It is one of his enduring themes. His plays are touchingly ingenuous about the romantic convergence toward marriage of young men and women, and this makes us wonder about him and Anne and about how they might have felt about the baby girl who arrived in 1583. If the literary and documentary records prove anything, it is that Shakespeare adored his children and that he and his daughters always enjoyed an affectionate and close relationship. It is true that with respect to his wife things are more complicated.

What Shakespeare may not have known himself until he fetched up in London was that there existed another kind of sexual love, one that dared not speak its name any more then than it did in later centuries. If Shakespeare had sex with men, it was probably among the acting community in Shoreditch. He was a country boy with a past when he arrived in the metropolis. A convicted felon from Charlecote might be more likely to experiment with forbidden sex than a sober glover from Henley Street. Not only had Will Shakespeare poached, it seems, but he had retaliated against the lord of the manor by satirizing him in verse. It was this above all that caused his disgrace. Here was someone to match Kit Marlowe, the daredevil author of the most famous play in the land, *Tamburlaine*.

There can be little doubt about the homosexual strain that runs through Shakespeare's plays and poems. It resonates particularly in the Sonnets, and not surprisingly since these are addressed to a beautiful young man. This young nobleman was so androgynous in appearance that one early picture of him was long assumed to be of a young woman with delicate and refined features. Although he and Shakespeare were not involved sexually, the bond between them was deep. All along, Shakespeare had a family to support back home in Warwickshire: every gesture of love and every tenderness granted to the young man was a betrayal of them. Then Shakespeare trespassed further by taking a mistress. He could not be contained by social conventions any more than Marlowe could.

But he hardly ever ventured into the dark forbidden place of sectarian politics, and this is where he and Marlowe parted company. Whatever temperamental bonds existed between them, Shakespeare was politically always more guarded. That which may have propelled him toward Marlowe, a run-in with the authorities, may also have made him more careful. He probably came close to losing everything in Charlecote. He would not run the same risk again once he was making it big in London, especially not when it fell to him to fend for his entire family. His love of his father may have been the overwhelming emotion in his early life. Having compounded the family's disgrace through felony, young William may have felt doubly implicated in the misfortunes of the Shakespeares of Henley Street.

Where Shakespeare stood on the greatest national issue of the day, the Catholic question, is one of the mysteries of his life. There are plenty of clues, but they pull in opposite directions. The Borromeo will in the rafters of Henley Street would appear to be a gift to the Catholics, and so might Shakespeare's purchase of the Blackfriars gatehouse, which had associations with the core of the recusant underground. His apparent abuse of the revered proto-Protestant Oldcastle in the *Henry IV* plays comports with this view: lampooning a Wycliffite hero would seem to be the act of a Catholic sympathizer. The rousingly anti-Popish *King John,* however, points in the other direction, as does Shakespeare's use in *King Lear* of a cruel anti-Catholic tract. Though his sympathies appear on balance to lean toward the Catholics, not surprisingly perhaps given his mother's links with the ancient and grand Catholic Ardens of Warwickshire, we cannot be sure.

If he deemed it prudent not to commit himself politically, writing was a different matter. He could not help writing. He wrote because he had to. While he sometimes composed with source texts demonstrably propped up on his desk, as in *Romeo and Juliet, Henry V,* and *Antony and Cleopatra,* his highly wrought metaphors and similes flowed from the heart and soul. The bookishness of the writing process in no way affects that. *Romeo and Juliet* is a case in point. If this play commemorates Shakespeare's dead son, then no work in the canon can have been more painfully personal to him. Yet its literary source is a dour poem that Shakespeare follows closely, dramatizing it sometimes almost line by line. The scholar and the creative artist go together in Shakespeare in a way that they rarely do in the period. Beneath Shakespeare's iambic pentameters the private self beats its drum with percussive ardor.

We know what Shakespeare looked like and we can safely assume that in conversation he was witty, charming, and deep. Here was someone who had thought profoundly about the human condition. One is tempted to say that he must have been irresistible to women, this man who loved women and who never lost his sense of wonder over female beauty and sheer feminine otherness. His view of women, Tamora, Goneril, and Regan notwithstanding, is that they are kind and gentle, "tender-hefted," and endlessly desirable. Such is his imaginative gift for creating women in his plays that we tend to forget that they were played by boys and young men, that Juliet, Rosalind, Viola, Desdemona, Cleopatra, and all the young women of the last plays were transvestites on stage. But they were inspired by his knowledge of real-life women, his own daughters above all, as well as his wife and his two mistresses, the Dark Lady and the English Lady. Emilia Lanier had been the lover of a powerful nobleman for several years and probably knew about contraception; certainly she seems not to have become pregnant by either Shakespeare or Southampton. Jane Davenant, though, may have conceived her son William with Shakespeare. The fact that Shakespeare probably wrote his affairs with Emilia and Jane into the Sonnets, *The Merchant of Venice, Othello,* and *King Lear* is food for thought.

His writing life and daily routines are rarely separable. Far from being impersonal, he is almost compulsively subjective. One should expect no less from the author of the Sonnets. Shakespeare must have been high-strung and the sheer intensity of the plays and poems arises out of his personal investment in them. The reason they revert to limping time and again is that this issue lies close to his heart. Similarly with Hamnet and *Hamlet.* In calling his most ambitious tragedy after his own dead son Shakespeare reveals how deeply affected he was by the loss. In the comedy before *Hamlet, Twelfth Night,* a play about twins who are miraculously reunited, he is pursuing the same agenda, trying to create a counterreality in which he is king of all he surveys. Shakespeare's art was ever an extension of his life. *The Tempest* makes just this point, with William Shakespeare as Prospero, creator of heaven and earth, lording it over life and death. The fact that his people are puppets, mere characters in a play, is almost forgotten. There is a supreme confidence, and perhaps even arrogance, about the Shakespeare of that last great play of death and resurrection. Shakespeare knew it, of course, which is why he has Prospero return to Milan to seek forgiveness in prayer and retreat. While in *The Tempest* Prospero claims that we are ourselves the stuff of dreams, the author of the play knew full well that no amount of make-believe and playing can alter the facts of life and death.

Shakespeare communicates not through the international medium of music and sound but through the English language. His appeal has nevertheless stretched well beyond the bounds of English to become as universal as writing can be. The reason must be partly at least the sheer scale and intelligence of the moral and philosophical questions that are posed in his works. Shakespeare looked deeply into the seeds of things. He tried to understand life, to see whether it had a meaning or not, and he refused the consolations afforded by traditional religion. His is the most articulate voice from a time when humankind in the western world first unthroned the deity, when the certainties of the godhead became the doubts of ordinary men and women.

Shakespeare was steeped in the Bible and in the classics, and they gave him a rhetorical and imaginative platform. Neither, though, had as deep an impact on him as the death of his son, his love for his father and his daughters, his homoerotic involvement with a feckless young man, or indeed his triumphalist womanizing (in spite, perhaps, of not being blessed with good looks). He was a man of prodigious energy, always writing, acting, and transacting. He never stopped, and he always remained a Warwickshire man at heart. He commuted regularly and increasingly between London and Stratford, and he probably wrote to his loved ones at home just as other actors did. There is something peculiarly modern about Shakespeare the successful London playwright cultivating his gardens and orchards in Stratford, but then there is no reason why he should be any different from the rest of us. As a son, husband, and father he had the same concerns as everyone else, and in wanting to make good he was no different from others among his contemporaries. The timeless voice in his plays and poems is precisely the reason why we want to know ever more about the man who wrote them.

Main Characters

Edward Alleyn (1566–1626) starred in Marlowe's plays, notably *Tamburlaine*; he made a fortune and married the stepdaughter of the wealthy entrepreneur Henslowe and, after her death, John Donne's daughter.

Edward Arden (1533–1583) was the head of the ancient Arden family of Park Hall with whom the Shakespeares claimed kinship. The Arden family were broken by the alleged Somervile plot.

Alexander Aspinall taught at the King's New School in Stratford for many years and resided close to New Place; he may have received gloves from Shakespeare along with a posy of verses.

John Aubrey (1626–1697) was a seventeenth-century biographer and antiquary who left us tantalizing glimpses of Shakespeare's life.

Anthony Babington (1561–1586) was a young Catholic nobleman and follower of Mary Stuart; he and others were found guilty of conspiring to overthrow Queen Elizabeth I.

The Badgers were recusant neighbors of the Shakespeares in Henley Street; they were arrested in the aftermath of the Gunpowder Plot.

Daniel Baker was a play-hating Puritan relative of the Quineys.

John Barnard (d. 1674) married Shakespeare's granddaughter Elizabeth Hall in Billesley in 1649.

Stephen Belott was apprenticed to a family of Huguenots with whom Shakespeare lodged; he seems to have successfully interceded on their behalf with Belott.

Thomas Betterton (1635–1710), a famous Restoration actor, was the main source for Nicholas Rowe's biography.

Richard Burbage (1568–1619), of the Lord Chamberlain's Men and King's Men, played a number of the most important Shakespearian roles, including Hamlet, Othello, and King Lear.

Edmund Campion (1540–1581), a charismatic Jesuit who had been a renowned student at Oxford, led the 1580 mission to England, which culminated in his martyrdom.

Henry Carey, first Baron Hunsdon (1526–1596), acted as patron of the Lord Chamberlain's Men, Shakespeare's company, until his death; Emilia Bassano had been his mistress.

The Cawdreys were Stratford recusants and George Cawdrey, a near contemporary of William Shakespeare's at school, trained as a Jesuit at Rheims.

William Cecil, Lord Burghley (father: 1521–1598), and Robert Cecil, Lord Salisbury (son: 1563–1612), were courtiers par excellence and the most skillful and powerful members of the Privy Council for most of Shakespeare's life.

Henry Chettle (c. 1560–c. 1607), playwright and printer of Robert Greene's polemic against Shakespeare and Marlowe; he subsequently apologized for libeling Shakespeare.

The Cloptons were one of the grandest Warwickshire Catholic families and were the chief benefactors of Stratford-upon-Avon for several centuries.

Lord Cobham (Sir William Brooke) (1527–1597) was the father-in-law of Robert Cecil; he was briefly Lord Chamberlain at just the time when Shakespeare called his fat knight Oldcastle, a historical character who had been an illustrious ancestor of Cobham.

William Combe of the powerful Combe family was the son of Shakespeare's friend John Combe; William tried to push through enclosures in Welcombe in the teeth of fierce local opposition and a ruling by the Lord Chief Justice.

Henry Condell (1576–1627) was a member of the King's Men and joined forces with John Heminges to produce the 1623 commemorative Folio of Shakespeare's plays.

James Cooke was an army surgeon who bought John Hall's medical diaries from Susanna.

The Cottoms were a recusant family from Lancashire; one of their sons, John, became a teacher at Shakespeare's school while the other one, Thomas, joined Campion as a Catholic priest.

Jane Davenant (1568–1622) was the wife of a play-loving, wealthy London merchant; she may have become Shakespeare's lover after she moved to Oxford.

William Davenant (1606–1668) was reputedly Shakespeare's son or godson.

The Debdales were an "obstinate" Catholic family from Shottery who must have known Anne Hathaway's family well. Their son Robert was a Jesuit and a friend of Campion's.

Robert Devereux, second earl of Essex (1565–1601), was a powerful courtier and the Queen's favorite until his disastrous Irish campaign; in the end he rose up against her, dragging the young Southampton down with him.

Leonard Digges (1588–1635) was the stepson of one of Shakespeare's executors and wrote a prefatory poem for the First Folio in which he refers to the monument at Holy Trinity.

Martin Droeshout the Younger (1601–1650) is usually credited with the frontispiece of the First Folio, which he may have copied from an earlier drawing of Shakespeare.

Guy Fawkes (1570–1606) was a major participant in the Gunpowder Plot.

Richard Field (1561–1624), a London printer and publisher, came from Bridge Street in Stratford; he probably knew Shakespeare at school and the two men seem to have remained friends all their lives.

John Florio (1553–1625) was Southampton's Italian tutor and a translator of Montaigne.

Simon Forman (1552–1611), astrologer and alchemist, was a quack who was consulted by, among others, Emilia Lanier, Jane Davenant, Winifred Burbage, and Marie Mountjoy, Shakespeare's landlady in the early seventeenth century.

Henry Garnett (1555–1606) was a former printer turned Jesuit; he succeeded William Weston as the movement's Father Superior in England and remained so until his arrest in 1606.

John Gerard (1564–1637) was a tall and aristocratic Jesuit who pursued his apostolate even after his capture, torture, and escape from the Tower.

Robert Greene (1558–1592) was a Cambridge-educated dramatist and author of a notorious pamphlet in which he warns his fellow players against Shakespeare.

Thomas Greene and his brother John seem to have been cousins of the Shakespeares. Thomas trained as a lawyer at Middle Temple and lived in New Place for a while; he served on the Stratford borough council for a long time.

William Greenway was a Stratford carrier with business premises in Henley Street; he operated some kind of shuttle between London and the Midlands.

Elizabeth Hall (1607–1670) was Shakespeare's granddaughter by Susanna.

John Hall (c. 1575–1635) married Susanna Shakespeare and went on to become the most renowned physician in Warwickshire.

Samuel Harsnett (1561–1631) was the author of a virulent anti-Catholic tract called *Popish Impostures,* which Shakespeare, surprisingly perhaps, used in *King Lear.*

John Heminges (1566–1630) played in Shakespeare's troupe and, together with Henry Condell, headed up the syndicate that oversaw the publication of the First Folio.

Philip Henslowe (c. 1555–1616) was a London businessman who owned theaters, brothels, and bear-baiting venues.

William Herbert, third earl of Pembroke (1580–1630), godson of Queen Elizabeth I and nephew of Sir Philip Sidney, has sometimes been thought to be the W.H. of the dedication of the Sonnets. Heminges and Condell dedicated the 1623 Folio to him and his younger brother Philip.

Lewis Hiccox became Shakespeare's tenant in the house in Henley Street after John Shakespeare's death.

Richard Hornby was the Henley Street blacksmith whose forge stood just up from the Shakespeares' home.

Simon Hunt would have taught Shakespeare between the ages of seven and eleven; Hunt may have left the grammar school to become a Jesuit.

Thomas Jenkins probably taught Shakespeare at school in his early teens and seems to have provided the model for Sir Hugh Evans in *Merry Wives.*

Davy Jones was a Stratford impresario who staged the town's Whitsun play in 1583; he was the brother-in-law of Shakespeare's friend and correspondent Richard Quiney.

Ben Jonson (1572–1637), playwright and poet, knew Shakespeare well.

Edmund Lambert was married to one of Shakespeare's mother's sisters; after his death the Shakespeares litigated against his son over property.

John Lane of the Lanes of Alveston spread unsubstantiated rumors about Susanna Hall's sexual behavior.

Francis Langley (1548–1602) was a shady London businessman who owned the Swan theater on Bankside and was implicated in the unsavory affair of the Madre de Dios diamond.

Emilia Lanier (née Bassano) (1569–1645), the daughter of talented musicians of Venetian Jewish extraction, married Alfonso Lanier in 1592 after becoming pregnant by her aristocratic lover Henry Carey Hunsdon. At some point she may have become Shakespeare's mistress and therefore the so-called Dark Lady of the Sonnets.

Sir Thomas Lucy (1532–1600) of Charlecote welcomed Queen Elizabeth to his home when Shakespeare was a little boy and may have been the justice of the peace before whom the young Shakespeare was arraigned for poaching.

John Manningham (c. 1575–1622) was training as a lawyer when he saw *Twelfth Night* performed at Middle Temple.

Christopher Marlowe (1564–1593) was the author of *Tamburlaine* and *Dr. Faustus* and may have been the rival poet of the Sonnets.

John Marston (1576–1634) was a playwright and, like his father, a member of Middle Temple.

Francis Meres (1565–1647) wrote *Palladis Tamia* in which he acclaims Shakespeare as the heir to Ovid and refers to his "sugared sonnets among his private friends."

The Mountjoys were a Huguenot family with whom Shakespeare boarded and whose domestic dispute about a dowry he helped resolve.

Thomas Nash (1593–1647) was Shakespeare's neighbor at New Place and the first husband of the poet's granddaughter Elizabeth Hall.

Thomas Nashe (1567–c. 1601), poet, playwright, and pamphleteer, overlapped with Marlowe at Cambridge; he dedicated his novel *The Unfortunate Traveller* to the young Southampton.

Edmund Neville was related to the great Warwickshire family of Edward Arden and staged several spectacular, if futile, attempts to escape from the Tower.

Nicholas Owen (d. 1606) built the Catholics' hiding places and was himself an aspiring Jesuit; he died under torture in the Tower of London.

Robert Perrott, a wealthy Puritan landowner and brewer at Luscombe near Stratford, was the grandfather of Susanna Woodward of Shottery.

Augustine Phillips (d. 1605) was an actor in the Lord Chamberlain's Men; he was summoned before the Privy Council to explain the company's putting on *Richard II* the Saturday before the Essex rebellion.

Thomas Platter (1574–1628), a Swiss visitor to London and a diarist, recorded seeing a production of *Julius Caesar* at the newly opened Globe in the autumn of 1599.

Richard Quiney (d. 1602) was a friend and neighbor of the Shakespeares from Stratford and wrote the only surviving letter addressed to the dramatist; his son Thomas married Judith Shakespeare.

William Replingham was one of the Combes' lieutenants and an occasional guest in Shakespeare's New Place during the proposed Welcombe enclosures.

The Reynolds family lived up from the Shakespeares in Chapel Street and were deeply recusant.

John Rigby had been converted to Catholicism by John Gerard and was cruelly executed in the Old Kent Road.

Walter Roche from Lancashire may have been the infant William Shakespeare's first teacher at the King's New School in Stratford.

Nicholas Rowe (1674–1718), Shakespeare's first biographer, had access to information from seventeenth-century Stratford and is the main source for the Charlecote poaching story.

The Sadlers were a rich Stratford family with close links to the Shakespeares, who may have named their twins Judith and Hamnet after the Sadlers.

Rafe Smith was a haberdasher with whom, it was alleged, Susanna Hall had an affair that left her with a venereal infection.

William Smith from Henley Street served alongside Shakespeare's father, John, on the town council; he may have stood as godfather to William.

John Somervile (1560–1583) was Edward Arden's son-in-law. On his way to London from Warwickshire he publicly proclaimed his intention to kill the Queen, thus bringing about the perdition of himself and of the Ardens.

Robert Southwell (1561–1595) was a Jesuit and poet who perished at Tyburn; his best-loved poem is recalled in *Macbeth*.

Abraham Sturley was a Puritan businessman and bailiff in Stratford who urged Richard Quiney to get Shakespeare to invest in the Stratford area.

Thomas Thorpe (c. 1572–c. 1625) published Shakespeare's Sonnets in 1609, perhaps in close collaboration with their author.

Richard Topcliffe (1531–1604) was the regime's cruel and loathed inquisitor-in-chief.

Richard Tyler, husband of Susanna Woodward, may have acted as godparent to the Shakespeares' firstborn; he was crossed out in the final draft of Shakespeare's will.

William Tyler was a butcher in Sheep Street and served with John Shakespeare on the borough council.

George Vertue (1684–1756), an engraver, sketched Shakespeare's New Place, the chancel of Holy Trinity, and the Shakespeare bust in the eighteenth century.

John Ward reported rumors about Southampton's munificence toward Shakespeare and about the dramatist's earnings that were circulating in Stratford in the middle of the seventeenth century.

William Wedgewood was a bad-tempered and bigamist tailor in Henley Street.

William Weston (c. 1549–1615) spent many years in prison in Wisbech and London after a brief spell as Father Superior of the Jesuits in England.

The Whateleys were a rich family of glovers from Henley Street with roots in Henley-in-Arden; their allegiances were suspect as they had "unsound" Catholic priests in the family.

Margaret Wheeler was probably related to the Wheelers of Henley Street; she conceived an illegitimate child from Thomas Quiney, who was engaged to be married to Judith Shakespeare.

George Wilkins (d. 1618) was Shakespeare's collaborator on *Pericles*.

Robert Willis, a Puritan, recorded how his father took him to see a play in Gloucester Town Hall.

Thomas Wilson became the Puritan rector of Holy Trinity in 1619; he was a friend of John Hall.

The Woodwards, who resided at Shottery Manor, had a daughter called Susanna. She married Richard Tyler and may have been a lifelong friend of Anne Hathaway's to whose firstborn she may have stood as godmother.

Henry Wriothesley, third earl of Southampton (1573–1624), was the young man to whom the Sonnets may have been addressed. He had been a ward of Lord Burghley but became a close friend of the Earl of Essex with whom he stood trial for treason.

Richard Young was chief justice of Middlesex and a close collaborator of Topcliffe.

Appendix

Stratford in Shakespeare's Time. After Samuel Winter (1768) and Fripp, and showing the population and housing density of Stratford in the middle of the eighteenth century. This was not very different from Shakespeare's time.

Shakespeare's Henley Street. The detailed information for the Henley Street map is provided by a combination of borough and Corporation levies and by an important list of manorial tenants from October 6, 1590. The list contains all the freeholders or *liberi tenentes,* notably the borough, the College, and the Crown, and a number of named individuals, who answered directly to the Lord of the Manor. For the borough and Corporation tenants the rent rolls help determine who lived where, although they are not an entirely reliable guide. Also properties changed hands repeatedly during Shakespeare's lifetime, a process that may have been accelerated by the various fires that affected Henley Street.

Using the 12 pence per burgage ground rent as a guide (one burgage = 57.75 feet frontage and 198 feet depth) I have drawn the fronts of the houses proportionately. Thus a 4-pence house like Combe's, for example, on the north side near the town end of Henley Street, is one third as wide as the 12-pence property of George Whateley next door. Things are, however, rarely clear-cut, since not all the ground rents are levied for houses. Gardens and barns are also counted and they probably did not attract the same levy. There may have been as many as five gardens on the north side, including one between John Shakespeare and his neighbor Badger.

Again, several freeholders are also borough tenants. John Wheler leased two properties from the Corporation while also owning two. The ever expanding Robert Johnson, vintner and innkeeper, was in a similar situation. In 1591, he acquired the large Ichiver property, which eventually became the White Lion and is now the site of the Birthplace archives. Johnson also leased a large barn from John Shakespeare, and in 1599 he successfully bid to the borough to redevelop the fire-damaged site of the Cawdrey house a few yards across from the Birthplace. His empire was spreading at the same rate as the Hiccoxes', who were becoming his neighbors on both sides of the street.

In order to match borough tenants, who paid rent, to unidentified borough property addresses in the 1590 survey, the frontages of the houses and the rents recorded in the various rent rolls need to be correlated. It appears to be the case that one burgage at 12 pence may entail a rent of 18 shillings, so that 1s=0.66d, 6s=4d, and so on. The resulting matches can then be cross-referenced to the borough rent rolls. Since the rent collectors did not follow a standard topographical template when recording their levy, it is not always clear whether their ledger entries start at the east end or west end of Henley Street, or indeed on the north or south side. Also their entries sometimes crisscross the road without signaling that they are doing so. They did not need to, since unlike us they knew exactly who was who and whereabouts they lived in sixteenth-century Stratford.

The anomaly of the Hart and Hiccox rates at the Birthplace is discussed in the main text. The 1590s levy of 19 pence ground rent suggests that the western wing of the Birthplace attracted over twice the ground rent of the east house. But the two smaller bays are not twice the size or width of the substantial east house. The reason the separate levy for the west wing of this unified structure is so high must be either that the cottage at the back was, after all, already there in 1590 and was included in the estimate for the west wing, or else that the levy was for the west wing without the back extension, but with a garden between John Shakespeare and George Badger.

Bibliographical Note

SBTRO=Shakespeare Birthplace Trust Record Office, Henley Street, Stratford-upon-Avon

MA=Fripp, Edgar Innes, and Richard Savage. *Minutes and Accounts of the Corporation of Stratford-upon-Avon, and Other Records, 1553–1592.* Transcribed by Richard Savage. With introduction and notes by Edgar Innes Fripp. 4 vols. The Dugdale Society, 1921–1929. Volume 5, covering 1593–98. Ed. Levi Fox. The Dugdale Society, 1990.

The most influential biography of the twentieth century was undoubtedly Samuel Schoenbaum's *William Shakespeare: A Documentary Life,* which first appeared in 1975 and has since been issued in various revised versions. It was preceded by *Shakespeare's Lives* (1970), in which Schoenbaum surveyed the whole field of writing biographies about Shakespeare. He did so with consummate brilliance, bringing a razor-sharp intelligence to the project. *Shakespeare's Lives* is a lucid and stylish exposition of the problems encountered by generations of Shakespearian biographers. In the folio-size first edition of the documentary life, Schoenbaum also made a vast amount of primary material available to the wider public for the first time. At the same time, he erected barriers where there had been none before and need not be now. When he could not absolutely prove his information, he queried its validity altogether or disposed of it in a manner that impressed by its urbane wit and acuity if not invariably by its accuracy. Thus Schoenbaum won his verbal fencing match with A. L. Rowse from All Souls College Oxford over the mistress of the Sonnets, but as a historian Rowse was more sure-footed when it came to archives and coal-face research, even if his paleography was not always as good as it ought to have been. Schoenbaum's cool positivism carried the day during their public spat, but Schoenbaum also relied on Rowse's piece from the *Times* on Madame Mountjoy and her affair with another shopkeeper. Moreover, Rowse may well have been right about the Dark Lady.

Schoenbaum stood on the shoulders of E. K. Chambers and J. O. Halliwell-Phillipps. Chambers's two volumes dealing with the facts and problems of Shakespeare's life (1930) are the bible of all biographers of Shakespeare. They accumulate a vast quantity of the materials essential for a biography, and Chambers's notes are informative and reliable. His was one of the most acute and discriminating minds ever to survey this field. Behind Chambers lies Halliwell-Phillipps, and not just Halliwell-Phillipps's own attempt at a biography but also the two indispensable volumes called *Outlines* (1887). These offer fascinating and still unparalleled insights into the physical places associated with Shakespeare in Stratford, in addition to a wealth of other information. And there is more. One of Halliwell-Phillipps's most brilliant contributions, and for the researcher arguably the most important of all, is his 1863 *A Calendar of Stratford Records* or, to give it its full title, *A Descriptive Calendar of the Ancient Manuscripts and Records in the Possession of the Corporation of Stratford-upon-Avon*. For anyone researching Shakespeare's Stratford and the wealth of documents at the Shakespeare Birthplace Trust, this is an indispensable volume. Chambers and Halliwell-Phillipps are usefully supplemented by R. B. Lewis's magnificent two volumes, *The Shakespeare Documents* (Stanford University Press, 1940); its copious notes are endlessly suggestive of new directions.

There has been a remarkable surge of activity in recent years in the field of Shakespearian biography. This includes a brand-new entry in the *Oxford Dictionary of National Biography*, the first new national essay on the poet since Sidney Lee's in 1897. One of the reasons for this renewed confidence that the project is once more worth undertaking is the gradual receding of the long shadow cast by Schoenbaum, even if his biographical studies retain their freshness and validity. Furthermore, national and international digitization projects of local archives, including the collections of the Shakespeare Birthplace Trust, have opened up new resources that have barely been tapped. The more documents become available online the more likely that sooner or later a major new Shakespeare find will emerge. Another rich seam has been the questions about Shakespeare's spiritual allegiances that are being asked with increasing urgency; the works as well as the broader environment of the period are being scoured for traces of a hidden trail that might, or might not, end up in the rafters of the house in Henley Street where a workman found a handwritten Catholic testament.

My most pressing debts in this book are to the archives of the Shakespeare Birthplace Trust in Stratford-upon-Avon, which are readily available to the general reader thanks to the superb work of Richard Savage, Edgar Innes Fripp, and latterly Levi Fox and the present team of archivists. Fripp wrote with unmatched expertise about Shakespeare's Stratford, its streets and houses, and its surrounding villages. He was the author also of a major study of the way in which Shakespeare's life and plays converge. This was published posthumously and, however flawed, remains a treasure trove of information. Fripp's studies provide the basis for Mark Eccles's sound but austere survey of Shakespeare's Warwickshire connections, which in turn becomes the source for Schoenbaum's pages on Shakespeare's home county. I have learned much from Robert Bearman's articles on the Shakespeare homes, on John Shakespeare, and on the testament in the rafters of Henley Street, as well as a number of other publications on Stratford. These include, among others, an edited collection of benchmark essays by different hands, *The History of an English Borough: Stratford-upon-Avon 1196–1996*. In addition to this, my main sources for information on matters relating to Stratford-upon-Avon are above all *The Minutes and Accounts* of the borough, edited by Fripp and Savage, Halliwell-Phillipps's *Descriptive Calendar* (1863), and Philip Styles's classic account of Warwickshire and Holy Trinity in the third volume of the *Victoria County History*, published separately by Oxford University Press in 1946 as *The Borough of Stratford-upon-Avon and the Parish of Alveston*.

I have been inspired by a number of recent biographies of Shakespeare, notably those by Katherine Duncan-Jones, Stephen Greenblatt, Anthony Holden, and Park Honan, as well as by James Shapiro's *1599: A Year in the Life of William Shakespeare*, Stanley Wells's wide-ranging *Shakespeare for All Time*, and Michael Wood's impressive *In Search of Shakespeare*, written to accompany his evocative and moving BBC series on Shakespeare's life. The *Oxford English Dictionary*, the *Oxford Dictionary of National Biography*, and the masterly *Oxford Companion to Shakespeare*, edited by Michael Dobson and Stanley Wells, were constantly to hand, as were Weinreb's and Hibbert's *The London Encyclopaedia*, John Stow's *Survey of London*, and latterly Andrew Dickson's inspired *Rough Guide to Shakespeare*.

For information on the personnel of Shakespeare's company and the theater of his time, I am indebted above all to Chambers's four volumes on the Elizabethan stage and to the work of Andrew Gurr. One of the most productive lines of inquiry since Schoenbaum has been into the Catholic background of Elizabethan England and how that affected the Shakespeare family. Among the many who have enhanced our understanding of this important topic are, most recently, Richard Wilson on the Catholic ghosts at Blackfriars, Gerard Kilroy on the enduring literary presence of Edmund Campion, and Clare Asquith on how the Catholic underground negotiated literary symbols. Greenblatt's superb meditation on what made Shakespeare Shakespeare fully acknowledges the enormous burden that the sectarian divide in the country placed on its citizens, as does Wood's book. The autobiographies of two Jesuits, John Gerard and William Weston, brilliantly translated and annotated by Philip Caraman, S.J., provide indispensable information about Elizabethan culture, and particularly its grim underbelly of prisons and torture.

The list that follows contains a selection of the books and articles that I found particularly useful during the writing of this book. It is not meant to be exhaustive.

Akrigg, George Philip Vernon. *Shakespeare and the Earl of Southampton.* Hamish Hamilton, 1968.

Alcock, Nathaniel, and Robert Bearman. "Discovering Mary Arden's House: Property and Society in Wilmcote, Warwickshire." *Shakespeare Quarterly* 53 (2002), pp. 53–82.

Asquith, Clare. *Shadowplay.* Public Affairs, 2005.

Baker, Oliver. *In Shakespeare's Warwickshire and the Unknown Years.* Simpkin Marshall, 1937.

Baldwin, T. W. *William Shakespeare's Small Latine and Lesse Greeke.* University of Illinois Press, 1944.

Barroll, J. Leeds. *Politics, Plague, and Shakespeare's Theater.* Cornell University Press, 1991.

Bate, Jonathan. *The Genius of Shakespeare.* Picador, 1997.

Bearman, Robert. *Stratford-upon-Avon: A History of Its Streets and Buildings.* Nelson, 1988.

————. "'Was William Shakespeare William Shakeshafte?' Revisited." *Shakespeare Quarterly* 53 (2002), pp. 83–94.

————. "John Shakespeare, a Papist or Just Penniless?" *Shakespeare Quarterly* (2006), pp. 411–33.

————, ed. *The History of an English Borough: Stratford-upon-Avon 1196–1996.* Sutton, 1997.

Bevington, David, ed. *Troilus and Cressida.* Arden 3, 1998.

Bloom, Harold. *Shakespeare: The Invention of the Human.* Fourth Estate, 1998.

Braines, W. W. *The Site of the Globe Playhouse.* Hodder & Stoughton, 1924.

Brinkworth, E. R. C. *Shakespeare and the Bawdy Court of Stratford.* Phillimore, 1972.

Brock, Susan, and E. A. J. Honigmann, eds. *Playhouse Wills, 1558–1642.* Manchester University Press, 1993.

Bullough, Geoffrey. *Narrative and Dramatic Sources of Shakespeare.* 9 vols. Routledge, 1966–75.

Caraman, Philip. *Henry Garnet 1555–1606.* Longmans, 1964.

————, ed. *John Gerard: The Autobiography of an Elizabethan.* Trans. Philip Caraman, with an introduction by Graham Greene. 2nd ed. Longmans, 1956.

————, ed. William Weston. *The Autobiography of an Elizabethan.* Trans. Philip Caraman, with a foreword by Evelyn Waugh. Longmans, 1955.

Carlin, Martha. *Medieval Southwark*. Hambledon, 1996.

Challoner, Richard. *Memoirs of Missionary Priests*. 1741.

Chamberlain, John. *John Chamberlain: Letters*. 2 vols. ed. Norman E. McClure (American Philosophical Society, 1939).

Chambers, E. K. *The Elizabethan Stage*. 4 vols. Oxford University Press, 1923.

————. "A Blackfriars House, Shakespeare's Investment, Hiding Holes." *The Times* (London), April 23, 1928.

————. *William Shakespeare: A Study of Facts and Problems*. 2 vols. Oxford University Press, 1930.

Cressy, David. *Birth, Marriage, and Death: Ritual, Religion, and the Life-cycle in Tudor and Stuart England*. Oxford University Press, 1997.

Crystal, David, and Ben Crystal. *Shakespeare's Words: A Glossary and Language Companion*. Preface by Stanley Wells. Penguin, 2002.

Davidson, Clifford. *The Guild Chapel Wall Paintings at Stratford-upon-Avon*. AMS Press, 1988.

Dickson, Andrew. *The Rough Guide to Shakespeare*. Penguin, 2005.

Dobson, Michael, and Stanley Wells. *The Oxford Companion to Shakespeare*. Oxford University Press, 2001.

Duncan-Jones, Katherine. *Ungentle Shakespeare*. Arden, 2001.

Dutton, Richard. *Mastering the Revels*. Macmillan, 1991.

Eccles, Mark. *Christopher Marlowe in London*. Harvard University Press, 1934.

————. *Shakespeare in Warwickshire*. University of Wisconsin Press, 1961.

Edmond, Mary. *Rare Sir William Davenant*. Manchester University Press, 1987.

Edmondson, Paul. *Twelfth Night: A Guide to the Text and Its Theatrical Life*. Palgrave, 2005.

————and Stanley Wells. *Shakespeare's Sonnets*. Oxford University Press, 2004.

Elton, Charles Isaac, *William Shakespeare: His Family and Friends*. John Murray, 1904.

Evans, G. Blakemore. *The Riverside Shakespeare*. 2nd ed. 2 vols. Houghton Mifflin, 1997.

Foakes, R. A., ed. *Henslowe's Diary*. 2nd ed. Cambridge University Press, 2002.

Fox, Levi. *The Correspondence of the Reverend Greene*. The Dugdale Society, 1956.

————.*The Shakespeare Birthplace Trust: A Personal Memoir*. The Shakespeare Birthplace Trust, 1997.

Fraser, Antonia. *The Gunpowder Plot*. Phoenix, 2002.

Fripp, Edgar Innes. *Master Richard Quyny*. Oxford University Press, 1924.

————. *Shakespeare's Stratford*. Oxford University Press, 1928.

————. *Shakespeare's Haunts Near Stratford*. Oxford University Press, 1929.

————. *Shakespeare, Man and Artist*. 2 vols. Oxford University Press, 1938.

Gray, J. W. *Shakespeare's Marriage*. Chapman & Hall, 1905.

Greenblatt, Stephen. *Hamlet in Purgatory*. Princeton University Press, 2001.

————. *Will in the World*. Jonathan Cape, 2004.

Gurr, Andrew. "Shakespeare's First Poem: Sonnet 145." *Essays in Criticism* 21 (1971), pp. 221–26.

————. *The Shakespearian Playing Companies.* Oxford University Press, 1996.

Halliwell-Phillipps, J. O. *The Life of William Shakespeare.* Smith, Warwick, Cooke, 1848.

————. *A Descriptive Calendar of the Ancient Manuscripts and Records in the Possession of the Corporation of Stratford-upon-Avon.* J. E. Adlard, 1863.

————. *Outlines of the Life of Shakespeare.* 2 vols. Longmans, Green, 1887.

Harrison, William. *The Description of England.* Ed. Georges Edelen. Cornell University Press, 1968.

Harsnett, Samuel. "A Declaration of Egregious Popish Impostures." 1603.

Holden, Anthony. *William Shakespeare: His Life and Work.* Little, Brown, 1999.

Holinshed, Raphael. *The Chronicles of England, Scotland, and Ireland.* 2nd ed. 1587.

Honan, Park. *Shakespeare: A Life.* Oxford University Press, 1998.

Hotson, Leslie. *The First Night of Twelfth Night.* Hart-Davis, 1954.

Hyde, Ralph. *The A to Z of Restoration London.* With an index compiled by John Fisher and Roger Cline. London Topographical Society, 1992.

Ingleby, C. M., ed. *Shakespeare and the Enclosure of Common Fields at Welcombe. Being a Fragment of the Private Diary of Thomas Greene, Town Clerk of Stratford-upon-Avon.* 1885.

Ingram, William. *A London Life in the Brazen Age: Francis Langley, 1548–1602.* Harvard University Press, 1978.

Jackson, Peter. *London Bridge.* Cassell, 1971.

Jones, Jeanne. *Stratford-upon-Avon Inventories 1538–1699.* 2 vols. The Dugdale Society, 2002, 2003.

Kastan, David Scott. *Shakespeare and the Book.* Cambridge University Press, 2001.

Keay, Anna. *The Elizabethan Tower of London.* London Topographical Society, 2001.

Kemp, Thomas. *The Black Book of Warwick.* 1898.

Kermode, Frank. *Shakespeare's Language.* Allen Lane, 2000.

————. *The Age of Shakespeare.* Weidenfeld & Nicolson, 2004.

Kilroy, Gerard. *Edmund Campion: Memory and Transcription.* Ashgate, 2005.

Kirkwood, A. E. M. "Richard Field, Printer, 1589–1624," *The Library* (1931), pp. 1–35.

Kuriyama, Constance Brown. *Christopher Marlowe: A Renaissance Life.* Cornell University Press, 2002.

Lane, Joan. *John Hall and His Patients.* The Shakespeare Birthplace Trust, 1996.

Lasocki, David, and Roger Prior. *The Bassanos.* Scolar Press, 1995.

Leland, John. *The Itinerary of John Leland in or about the Years 1535–1543.* Ed. Lucy Toulmin Smith. Vol. 2. George Bell & Sons, 1908.

Leishman, J. B., ed. *The Three Parnassus Plays (1598–1601).* Nicholson & Watson, 1949.

Le Roy Ladurie, Emmanuel. *Histoire humaine et comparée du climat.* Fayard, 2004.

Levenson, Jill L. *Romeo and Juliet.* Oxford University Press, 2000.

Lewis, B. Roland. *The Shakespeare Documents.* 2 vols. Stanford University Press, 1940.

McClure, Norman E. *John Chamberlain: Letters.* 2 vols. American Philosophical Society, 1939.

Macdonald, Màiri. "Not a Memorial to Shakespeare, but a Place for Divine Worship: The Vicars of Stratford and the Shakespeare Phenomenon, 1616–1964." *Warwickshire History* 9 (2001–2002).

Madan, Falconer W. "Two Lost Causes and What May Be Said in Defence of Them." *The Library* (1918), pp. 97–105.

Meres, Francis. *Palladis Tamia, Wit's Treasury.* 1598. With an introduction by Don Cameron Allen. Scholars' Facsimiles and Reprints, 1938.

Nicholl, Charles. *The Reckoning: The Murder of Christopher Marlowe.* Jonathan Cape, 1992.

Nolen, Stephanie. *Shakespeare's Face.* Knopf, 2002.

Ogilby, John. *Britannia: Or an Illustration of the Kingdom of England . . . by a Geographical and Historical Description of the Principal Roads Thereof . . .* 1675.

Orrell, John. *The Quest for Shakespeare's Globe.* Cambridge University Press, 1983.

Page, Catharine, and Ronald Page. "The Location of Richard Shakespeare's Farm in Snitterfield." *Warwickshire History* 3 (1982).

Platter, Thomas. *Thomas Platter's Travels in England.* Trans. Clare Williams. Jonathan Cape, 1937.

Prockter, Adrian, and Robert Taylor. *The A to Z of Elizabethan London.* London Topographical Society, 1979.

Riggs, David. *The World of Christopher Marlowe.* Faber & Faber, 2004.

Rowe, Nicholas. "Some Account of the Life, etc of Mr. William Shakespeare," in *The Works of Mr. William Shakespeare.* Jacob Tonson, 1709.

Rowse, A. L. "Secrets of Shakespeare's Landlady." *The Times* (London), April 23, 1973.
————. *Simon Forman: Sex and Society in Shakespeare's Age.* Weidenfeld & Nicolson, 1974.

Rutter, Carol Chillington, ed. *Documents of the Rose Playhouse.* Manchester University Press, 1984.

Schoenbaum, Samuel. *Shakespeare's Lives.* Oxford University Press, 1970.
————. *William Shakespeare: A Documentary Life.* Oxford University Press, 1975.
————. *William Shakespeare: A Compact Documentary Life.* 1977.

Schofield, John. *The London Surveys of Ralph Treswell.* London Topographical Society, 1987.
———— and Ann Saunders. *Tudor London: A Map and a View.* London Topographical Society, 2001.

Shapiro, James. *Shakespeare and the Jews.* Columbia University Press, 1996.
————. *1599: A Year in the Life of William Shakespeare.* Faber & Faber, 2005.

Shell, Alison. *Catholicism, Controversy, and the English Literary Imagination, 1558–1660.* Cambridge University Press, 1999.

Sisson, C. J. "Shakespeare's Friends: Hathaways and Burmans of Shottery." *Shakespeare Survey* 12 (1959), pp. 95–106.

Slater, T. R. "Domesday Village to Medieval Town: The Topography of Medieval Stratford-upon-Avon." In Robert Bearman, ed. *The History of an English Borough: Stratford-upon-Avon 1196–1996.* Sutton, 1997.

Smith, Bruce. *Homosexual Desire in Shakespeare's England: A Cultural Poetics.* University of Chicago Press, 1991.

Smith, Irwin. *Shakespeare's Blackfriar's Playhouse.* Owen, 1966.

Sorlien, R. P., ed. *The Diary of John Manningham of the Middle Temple.* University Press of New England, 1976.

Spielmann, M. H. *The Title-page of the First Folio of Shakespeare's Plays.* Humphrey Milford, 1924.

Stopes, Charlotte M. *Shakespeare's Warwickshire Contemporaries.* Shakespeare Head Press, 1907.

Stow, John. *A Survey of London.* 1603. Ed. C. L. Kingsford. 2 vols. Oxford University Press, 1908.

————— and Edmond Howes. *Annals, or a General Chronicle of England; Begun by J. Stow . . . Continued and Augmented . . . Unto the End of . . . 1631, by E. Howes. . . .* 1631.

Styles, Philip. *The Borough of Stratford-upon-Avon and the Parish of Alveston.* Oxford University Press, 1946.

Sugden, Edward H. *A Topographical Dictionary to the Works of Shakespeare and His Fellow Dramatists.* Manchester University Press, 1925.

Thomas, David. *Shakespeare in the Public Records.* Her Majesty's Stationery Office, 1985.

Traister, Barbara Howard. *The Notorious Astrological Physician of London.* University of Chicago Press, 2000.

Vickers, Brian. *Shakespeare, Co-author: A Historical Study of Five Collaborative Plays.* Oxford University Press, 2002.

Wallace, C. W. *The First London Theatre: Materials for a History.* University of Nebraska, 1913.

Ward, John. *Diary of the Rev. John Ward, A.M., Vicar of Stratford-upon-Avon, Extending from 1648 to 1679.* Arranged by Charles Severn. 1839.

Weinreb, Ben, and Christopher Hibbert. *The London Encyclopaedia.* Macmillan, 1983.

Wells, Stanley. *Shakespeare for All Time.* Macmillan, 2002.

West, Anthony James. *The Shakespeare First Folio: The History of the Book.* 2 vols. Oxford University Press, 2001, 2003.

Wheler, R. B. *A Guide to Stratford-upon-Avon.* 1814.

Wilson, Richard. *Secret Shakespeare.* Manchester University Press, 2004.

Wood, Michael. *In Search of Shakespeare.* BBC Books, 2003.

—————. *In Search of Shakespeare.* BBC television series, aired 2003; PBS DVD, 2004.

Woudhuysen, H. R., ed. *Love's Labour's Lost.* Arden 3, 1998.

Acknowledgments

During the writing of this book I have incurred a number of debts, which it is a pleasure to acknowledge. I am grateful to Robert Bearman and his staff at the Shakespeare Birthplace Trust Record Office in Henley Street whose expertise in the collections held in trust there made all the difference. The pioneering work on the Stratford records by archivists at the Birthplace Trust is as groundbreaking today as it was eighty years ago. I must thank the chief guides at Hall's Croft, Nash house, the Birthplace, Anne Hathaway's cottage, and Mary Arden's house for their erudition and enthusiasm. Their ability to conjure up Shakespeare for visitors is impressive, as Jim Shapiro and I discovered late one cold autumn afternoon in Wilmcote. I must thank him for his encouragement and for instructing me, somewhere on the road between Snitterfield and Norton Lindsey, to trust my instincts on topography and not to be unduly intimidated by Schoenbaum. His own recent book on the year 1599 has already established itself as a classic, a master lesson in how to write about moments in Shakespeare's life.

In Stratford I was privileged on many occasions to enjoy the company of Stanley Wells and Paul Edmondson of the Education Department of the Shakespeare Birthplace Trust. They were generous to a fault with their time and expertise. I particularly remember spending time with them one summer's evening in the chancel of Holy Trinity, pondering the layout of the Shakespeare graves, inspecting the misericords, and taking instruction from Nigel Penn about Shakespeare's church. Paul kindly invited me to a conference in Charlecote in the great hall of that same country house where the young Shakespeare may have been arraigned by Sir Thomas Lucy, while Russell Jackson asked me to chair a seminar on biography at the Shakespeare Institute. At the Bath Literary Festival I appeared alongside a number of distinguished writers and scholars who impressed on me the importance of the sectarian divide in the England of Shakespeare's time. It was my good fortune to share my interest in John Gerard of the Society of Jesus with Gerard Kilroy, whose devotion to the memory of Edmund Campion made me realize that the first Elizabethan age endures not just because of Shakespeare.

Anthony West patiently answered queries about the history of the Shakespeare folios after 1623. His two Oxford volumes on the First Folio offer a fascinating survey of the kind of detective work on Folio trails that may yet lead us back one day to Shakespeare's friends in the King's Men or even to Lady Elizabeth Barnard, the poet's granddaughter. Gabriel Egan responded to my queries about Shakespeare's theaters with the exemplary thoroughness of his entries in *The Oxford Companion to Shakespeare*. Michael Wood has been an inspiration ever since his riveting programs about the Trojan War set new standards for understanding the past as a real place that echoes in timeless landscapes. In his recent quest for Shakespeare he transports us back into the poet's world with flair, enthusiasm, and intellectual rigor.

My students at UCL have been a constant source of pleasure and friendship. Alison Thorne and Marinella Salari made possible a visit to the *università degli studi di Perugia* to lecture on Shakespeare's life and work. My greatest intellectual debt is to my friend and colleague Henry Woudhuysen, who was once more the most giving of men with his peerless erudition, time, and library. When I was a graduate student Ross Woodman of the University of Western Ontario in Canada gave me his copy of the original Scolar Press edition of Samuel Schoenbaum's *William Shakespeare: A Documentary Life*. Ever since then I have wanted to write on Shakespeare's life. On retiring from UCL Keith Walker left me his set of Geoffrey Bullough's nine-volume *Narrative and Dramatic Sources of Shakespeare*. Bullough's work was my constant companion during the research for this book as were my fond memories of Keith. Peter Swaab urged me to consider that Shakespeare's works could not possibly be divorced from his life, while Nathalie Jacoby caused me to hone my views on Shakespeare's London. In Foster Court in the 1970s David Daniell, the Arden Shakespeare editor of *Julius Caesar* and the world's leading authority on William Tyndale, father of the English Bible, offered some of the most cutting-edge teaching of Shakespeare in the country. For this and for much else I want to thank him. Over the years I have accumulated broader intellectual debts to a number of colleagues at UCL, particularly to Rosemary Ashton, Mark Ford, Helen Hackett, Philip Horne, Dan Jacobson, Danny Karlin, Tim Langley, Kathy Metzenthin, Karl Miller, Charlotte Mitchell, Neil Rennie, John Sutherland, David Trotter, and Sarah Wintle. I am grateful to David Scott Kastan of Columbia for his friendship and guidance, to George Walton Williams for the most scintillating table talk on Shakespeare since Coleridge, and to David Bevington for his inspirational writing on Shakespeare.

While writing this book I worked with two singularly benign deans. It is a pleasure to thank Gerard O'Daly and Jane Fenoulhet of UCL for all their help and goodwill, and also Michael Worton for his selfless hard work and friendship. UCL once again backed me and granted me extra leave toward completing this book. John Allen of the UCL library readily tendered sound advice and John Spiers was a mine of information. It is a pleasure again to record a debt to Emmanuel Le Roy Ladurie for responding so instructively to my queries about the weather during Shakespeare's lifetime. His recently published *Histoire humaine et comparée du climat* appeared in time for me to consult it on the crops and wet summers of the 1590s and on the frosts of the early seventeenth century. There can never have been a more opportune moment for writing on *le climat;* it is hard to imagine anyone doing it nearly as well as Le Roy Ladurie.

Sarah Lee took photographs for me in Shakespeare's home county, which also happens to be hers. I want to thank her for the pleasure of her company during our visits to Warwickshire and for her outstanding work. James Hutchinson alerted me to ways in which beggars in *King Lear* may connect back into Shakespeare's real world. I must thank two outstanding former research students, Tom Rutter and Chris Laoutaris, from both of whom I learned more than I could ever teach them. Kate Mossman came to my rescue over the King's Men and on many occasions shared with me her incomparable literary gifts.

On February 2, 2002, Emmanuel Bock treated me to *Twelfth Night* in the glorious Middle Temple hall on the four hundredth anniversary of the play's performance there, while the stellar Josepha Jacobson made possible dinner with her lawyer peers in the same. Here Shakespeare's cousin Greene once sat as did John Marston and his father. So did John Manningham, whose racy anecdote about Shakespeare's sex life may have had its origin in after-dinner table talk right here. Shakespeare almost certainly performed in Middle Temple and was probably gossiped about in it. In 2006 Geoffrey Gower-Kerslake entertained me in another great hall, that of Gray's Inn. There, staring down at us from the wall behind the dais of benchers and judges, were portraits of Robert Cecil and Henry Wriothesley, third earl of Southampton, as he looked in later life. The picture records the date 1587 when the young Southampton first joined Gray's Inn. In this very hall, which, unlike the one at Middle Temple, escaped the Blitz unharmed, Shakespeare's *Comedy of Errors* was performed on December 28, 1594. The title turned out to be peculiarly fitting since that night's proceedings descended into anarchy. A note of wry humor echoes beneath the chronicler's remark that with the play "that night was begun, and continued to the end, in nothing but confusion and errors, whereupon it was ever afterwards called *The Night of Errors*."

Philippe and Pascale Delarche afforded me the chance to work quietly on the book in Pernand-Vergelesses and John Snelson of the Royal Opera House Covent Garden caused me to think again about *Macbeth, Romeo and Juliet,* and *The Tempest* when I needed to do so most.

It gives me special pleasure to thank Matthew Roberts and Emma Page-Roberts for their friendship, encouragement, and generosity.

I wish to thank everyone involved in the publication of the book at Henry Holt and Company, particularly Jack Macrae, Supurna Banerjee, Christopher O'Connell, Meryl Levavi, Thomas Nau, and Dana Trombley. Thanks also to Jolanta Benal, the copy editor; Don Kennison and Kathleen King, the proofreaders; and Lisa Kleinholz, the indexer.

I am grateful to Emma Parry, George Lucas, and the Carlisle Agency in New York. Bill Hamilton of A. M. Heath & Co. once again gave me much of his precious time and was always calm, steady, and kind.

Index

About the Author

RENÉ WEIS is a professor of English at University College London. He is the author of *The Yellow Cross* and *Criminal Justice*.